Waris Dirie is an internationally renowned model and was a face of Revlon skin-care products. In 1997 she was appointed by the United Nations as special ambassador for women's rights in Africa, in its effort to eliminate the practice of female genital mutilation.

Desert Dawn

Waris Dirie's foundation, is a non-profit organisation with a simple and yet profound mission to empower the children of Somalia with better health, education and opportunity. Desert Dawn will work at grassroots level to assist others who share Waris' vision of a new Somalia where famine, disease and violence no longer threaten to destroy the lives, hopes and dreams of childhood.

Desert Dawn Inc
320 East 65th Street
Suite 116
New York
NY 10021

www.desertdawn.org

Join the Fight Against FGM

If you would like to help us fight the mutilation of millions of girls, you can send contributions to a special trust that has been set aside to eliminate female genital mutilation. These funds will be used to promote educational and outreach programmes in twenty-three countries. To learn more about this programme write to:

The Campaign to Eliminate FGM
UNFPA (United Nations Population Fund)
220 E. 42nd Street
New York, NY 10017
USA

www.unfpa.org

DESERT FLOWER

waris dirie

and Cathleen Miller

DESERT DAWN

waris dirie

and Jeanne D'Haem

Virago

VIRAGO

First published in this omnibus edition in 2004
by Virago Press
Reprinted 2006

A CIP catalogue record for this book
is available from the British Library.

ISBN 978 1 84408 105 9

Printed and bound in Australia by
Griffin Press

Virago Press
An imprint of
Time Warner Book Group UK
Brettenham House
Lancaster Place
London WC2E 7EN

www.virago.co.uk

FOR MAMA

I realize that when one travels the road of life, weathering storms, enjoying the sunshine, standing in the eye of many hurricanes, survival is determined only by the strength of one's will. Therefore I dedicate this book to the woman upon whose shoulders I stand, whose strength is unyielding: my mother, Fattuma Ahmed Aden.

She has shown her children evidence of faith while staring into the face of unthinkable adversity. She has balanced an equal devotion to twelve children (an amazing feat on its own) and shown wisdom that would humble the most insightful sage.

Her sacrifices have been many; her complaints, few. And all along we, her children, knew that she gave what she had, no matter how meager – without reservation. she has known the agony of losing a child more than once, and still she maintains her strength and courage to continue struggling for her remaining children. Her generosity of spirit and inner and outer beauty are legendary.

Mama, I love , respect, and cherish you, and thank Almighty Allah for giving me you as my mother. My prayer is to honor your legacy by parenting my son as you have tirelessly nurtured your children.

Oh, you are a kilt which a young dandy set out to choose
Oh, you are like a costly rug for which thousands were
    paid
Will I ever find you like – you who have been shown to me
    only once?
An umbrella comes apart; you are as strong as looped
    iron;
Oh, you who are as the gold of Nairobi, finely molded,
You are the risen sun, and the early rays of dawn,
Will I ever find you like, you who have been shown to me
    only once?

—Traditional Somali poem

AUTHOR'S NOTE

Desert Flower is the true story of Waris Dirie's life, and all the events presented are factual, based on Waris's recollection. While all the people portrayed in *Desert Flower* are real, we have used pseudonyms for most of them to protect their privacy.

ACKNOWLEDGEMENTS

I would like to thank the following people who helped make this book possible, not only in its actual production, but also for simply being a part of my life.

To my Leeki-Leek, what a deep joy to have you in my life. I'm so grateful to God that He brought you to me. You fulfill me more than words can say.

To my darling Dana, thank you for shining your light around me. It was destiny that our paths crossed. I love you.

To Dana's parents, thank you for taking me in and making me one of your own. It's nice to have a family close to me again. Especially to my granny, who was there every inch of the way. I love you more than you can know.

To Christy Fletcher and her associates at the Carol Mann Agency, for being the most trustworthy, loyal, and dedicated agents I've ever had.

To everyone at William Morrow, and especially Betty Kelly, who really understood and believed in my vision and made this book her baby, too.

To Cathy Miller, who while trying to get into my mind almost lost her own. Thank you for all your hard work and effort.

To Tyrone Barrington, for always taking care of me and supporting me through all this.

To my right hand, Sabrina Cervoni, I can't function with our you. Thank you for coming into my life.

To my dearest friend, George Speros, what can I say, but I have nothing but love for you, baby.

To Barbara Walters, Ethel Bass, and everyone at *20/20*, thank you for giving me the opportunity to tell my story on your show and for always supporting me.

To Laura Ziv, who wrote that unforgettable article that touched more people than I expected.

To everyone at the United Nations, for being on my side and fighting for my beliefs. You've given me and millions of others hope that there will be an end to this practice.

To all my family and everyone who has crossed my path and might not understand my reasons for writing this book. This book isn't intended to hurt anyone, and I don't hold any bad feelings, especially not toward my family. Thank you for being who you are. I love you so.

And finally, most important, to God, the creator of the earth. Thank you for giving me the gift of life, and for giving me the strength and courage to travel through all these rivers, whether they are calm or stormy. You've created a world full of beauty and love. I truly hope everyone will learn to love and appreciate this paradise planet we have.

DESERT
FLOWER

1.

RUNNING AWAY

A slight sound woke me, and when I opened my eyes, I was staring into the face of a lion. Riveted awake, my eyes stretched wide—very wide—as if to expand enough to contain the animal in front of me. I tried to stand up, but I hadn't eaten for several days, so my weak legs wobbled and folded beneath me. Collapsing, I slumped back against the tree where I had been resting, sheltered from the African desert sun that becomes so merciless at noon. I quietly leaned my head back and closed my eyes, and felt the rough bark of the tree pressing into my skull. The lion was so near I could smell his musty scent in the hot air. I spoke to Allah: "It's the end for me, my God. Please take me now."

My long journey across the desert had come to an end. I had no protection, no weapon. Nor the strength to run. Even under the best of circumstances, I knew I couldn't beat the lion up the tree, because like all cats, lions with their strong claws are excellent climbers. By the time I got halfway up—BOOM— one swipe and I'd be gone. Without any fear I opened my eyes again and said to the lion, "Come and get me. I'm ready for you."

He was a beautiful male with a golden mane and a long tail switching back and forth to flick away flies. He was five or six years old, young and healthy. I knew he could crush me instantly; he was the king. All my life I'd watched those paws take down wildebeest and zebras weighing hundreds of pounds more than me.

The lion stared at me and slowly blinked his honey-colored eyes. My brown eyes stared back, locked on his. He looked away. "Go on. Take me now." He looked at me again, then looked away. He licked his lips and sat down on his haunches. Then the lion rose and paced back and forth in front of me, sexily, elegantly. Finally, he turned and walked away, no doubt deciding that I had so little flesh on my bones, I wasn't worth eating. He strode across the desert until his tawny-colored fur was lost against the sand.

When I realized he was not going to kill me, I gave no sigh of relief, because I hadn't been afraid. I'd been ready to die. But evidently God, who has always been my best friend, had something else planned, some reason to keep me alive. I said, "What is it? Take me—direct me," and struggled to my feet.

This nightmare journey began because I was running away from my father. I was about thirteen at the time, and living with my family, a tribe of nomads in the Somalian desert, when my father announced he had arranged my marriage to an old man. Knowing I had to act fast or suddenly one day my new husband would come to get me, I told my mother I wanted to run away. My plan was to find my aunt, my mother's sister, who lived in Mogadishu, the capital of Somalia. Of course I had never been to Mogadishu—or any other city for that matter. Nor had I ever met my aunt. But with the optimism of a child, I felt somehow things would magically work out.

While my father and the rest of the family were still sleeping, my mother woke me and said, "Go now." I looked around for something to grab, something to take, but there was nothing, no bottle of water, no jar of milk, no basket of food. So, barefoot, and wearing only a scarf draped around me, I ran off into the black desert night.

I didn't know which direction led to Mogadishu, so I just ran. Slowly at first, because I couldn't see; I stumbled along, tripping over roots. Finally, I decided to just sit down because snakes are everywhere in Africa, and I was terrified of snakes. Each root I stepped on I imagined to be the back of a spitting cobra. I sat watching the sky gradually lighten. Even before the sun came up—*whoosh*—I was off like a gazelle. I ran and I ran and I ran for hours.

By midday I'd traveled deep into the red sand, and deep into my own thoughts. Where in the hell was I going? I wondered. I didn't even know what direction I was heading in. The landscape stretched on to eternity, the sand broken only occasionally by an acacia or thorn tree; I could see for miles and miles. Hungry, thirsty, and tired, I slowed down and walked. Strolling along in a bored daze, I wondered where my new life would take me. What was going to happen next?

As I pondered these questions, I thought I heard a voice: "W-A-R-I-S . . . W-A-R-I-S. . . ." My father was calling me! Whipping around in circles, I looked for him, but saw no one. Maybe I was imagining things, I thought. "W-A-R-I-S . . . W-A-R-I-S . . ." the voice echoed all around me. The tone was pleading, but I was frightened all the same. If he caught me, he would surely take me back and make me marry that man, and probably beat me besides. I was not hearing things; it was my father, and he was getting closer. In earnest now, I started to run as fast as I could. Even though I had gotten a head start of several hours, Papa had caught up with me. As I later realized, he'd tracked me down by following my footprints through the sand.

My father was too old to catch me—so I had thought—because I was young and fast. To my childish thinking, he was an old man. Now I recall with a laugh that at the time, he was only in his thirties. We were all incredibly fit, because we ran everywhere; we had no car, no public transportation of any kind. And always I was fast, chasing the animals, heading after water, racing the oncoming darkness to reach home safely before the light was lost.

After a while I didn't hear my father calling my name anymore, so I slowed down to a jog. If I kept moving, Papa would get tired and go back home, I reasoned. Suddenly I looked back toward the horizon and saw him coming over the hill behind me. He'd spotted me, too. Terrified, I ran faster. And faster. It was as if we were surfing waves of sand; I flew up one hill, and he glided down the one behind me. On and on we continued for hours, until eventually I realized I hadn't seen him for some time. He no longer called out to me.

My heart pounding, finally I stopped, hiding behind a bush, and looked around. Nothing. I listened closely. No sound. When I came across a flat rock outcropping, I stopped to rest. But I'd learned from my mistake the night before, and when I began to run again, I went along the rocks where the ground was hard, then changed my direction so my father couldn't follow my footprints.

Papa, I reasoned, had turned around to try to make it back home, because now the sun was setting. Still, he would never make it back before the light faded. He'd have to run back through the darkness, listening for the night-time sounds of our family, tracing his path by the voices of children screaming, laughing, the animal noises of the herds mooing, bleating. The wind carries sounds great distances across the desert, so these noises acted as a lighthouse when we were lost in the night.

After walking along the rocks, I changed my direction. It didn't really matter what direction I chose, since I had no idea which was the right one to lead me to Mogadishu. I kept running until the sun set, the light was gone, and the night was so black I couldn't see. By this time I was starving, and food was all I could think about. My feet were bleeding. I sat down to rest under a tree and fell asleep.

In the morning, the sun burning my face woke me. I opened my eyes and looked up at the leaves of a beautiful eucalyptus tree stretching to the sky. Slowly the reality of my circumstances came to me. *My God, I'm all alone. What am I going to do?*

I got up and continued to run; for days I managed to keep it up. How many days, I'm not sure. All I know is that for me, there was no time; there was only hunger, thirst, fear, pain. When the evening grew too dark to see, I would stop and rest. At midday, when the sun was at its hottest, I would sit under a tree and take a siesta.

It was during one of these siestas that I fell asleep and the lion woke me. By this point I no longer cared about my freedom; I simply wanted to go back home to Mama. What I wanted more than food or water was my mother. And even though it was common for us to go for a day or two without food or water, I knew I couldn't survive much longer. I was so weak that I could barely move, and my feet were so cracked and sore that each step was agony. By the time the lion sat in front of me licking his lips in hunger, I had given up. I welcomed his quick kill as a way out of my misery.

But the lion looked at the bones jutting out of my skin, my sunken cheeks and bulging eyes, and walked away. I don't know if he took pity on such a miserable soul, or if it was simply a pragmatic decision that I wouldn't even make a worthy snack. Or if God had interceded on my behalf. But I decided God wouldn't be so heartless as to spare me, simply to let me die in some other, crueler way, like starving to death. He had another plan in store for me, so I called out for his guidance: "Take me—direct me." Holding on to the tree to steady myself, I rose to my feet and called out for his help.

I began to walk again, and within a few minutes came to a grazing area with camels everywhere. I spotted the animal carrying the most fresh milk, and ran to it. I nursed, sucking the milk like a baby. The herdsman spotted me and yelled out, "Get out of there, you little bitch!" and I heard a bullwhip crack. But I was desperate, and kept right on sucking, draining the milk as fast as my mouth could take it.

The herdsman ran at me, yelling, loud and mean. He knew that if he didn't scare me away, by the time he reached me, it would be too late. The milk would all be gone. But I'd had plenty, so I started to run. He chased after me, and managed to lash me with the whip a couple of times before I outran him. But I was faster than he was, and left him behind me, standing in the sand, cursing in the afternoon sun.

Now I had fuel in me; I was energized. So I kept running and running until I came to a village. I had never been in a place like this before; it had buildings, and streets made from hard-packed dirt. I walked down the middle of the street, just assuming this was the spot for me to walk. As I strolled through town, gawking at the strange setting, my head swiveled in every direction. A woman passed by me, looked me up and down, then called out: "You are so stupid. Where do you think you are?" To some of the other villagers walking down the street, she cried, "Oh, my goodness. Look at her feet!" She pointed at my feet, cracked and caked with bloody scabs. "Eh! Oh, my God. She must be a stupid little country girl." She knew. This woman yelled out to me, "Little girl, if you want to live, get off the street. Get off the road!" She waved me to the side, then laughed.

I knew everybody heard, and I was so embarrassed. I just hung my head down, but continued to walk in the middle of the road, because I didn't understand what she was talking about. Pretty soon, along came a truck. BEEP! BEEP! And I had to jump out of the way. I turned around to face the traffic, and as the cars and trucks headed toward me, I stuck out my hand. I can't say I was hitchhiking, because I didn't even know what hitchhiking was. So I just stood in the road with my hand stuck out to try and get someone to stop. A car careened past and nearly chopped my hand off, so I jerked it in. I thrust my hand out again, but this time not quite as far, moved a little farther to the side of the road, and kept walking. I looked into the faces of the people driving past me in their cars, silently praying for one of them to stop and help me.

Eventually a truck stopped. I am not proud of what happened next—but it happened, so what can I say, but to tell the truth? To this day, whenever I think of that truck stopping, I wish I had trusted my instincts and not gotten in.

The truck was hauling a load of stones for construction; they were jagged and the size of softballs. In front were two men; the driver opened the door and said in Somali, "Hop on, darling." I felt helpless, sick with fear.

"I'm headed to Mogadishu," I explained.

"I'll take you wherever you want to go," he said, grinning. When he smiled, his teeth showed red, tobacco red. But I knew that what made them that color wasn't tobacco, because I'd seen my father chew it once. It was khat, a narcotic plant the men in Africa chew that's similar to cocaine. Women are not allowed to touch it, and it's just as well; it makes the men crazy, overexcited, aggressive, and has destroyed many lives.

I knew I was in trouble, but I also didn't know what else to do, so I nodded. The driver told me to climb in the back. This brought me some relief, the thought of being away from the two men. I climbed into the truck bed and sat down in one corner, trying to make myself comfortable on the pile of rocks. It was dark now, and cool in the desert; as the truck started moving I was cold and lay down out of the wind.

The next thing I knew, the man riding with the driver was

next to me, kneeling on the stones. He was in his forties, and ugly, ugly. He was so ugly, his hair was leaving him; he was going bald. But he'd tried to make up for this fact by growing a little mustache. His teeth were chipped and some were missing; the remaining ones were stained a nasty red with the khat, but still he grinned at me, proudly displaying them. No matter how long I live, I will never forget his face leering at me.

He was also fat, as I learned when he took his pants down. His erect penis bobbed at me as he grabbed my legs and tried to force them apart.

"Oh, please, please, no," I begged. I wrapped my skinny legs around each other like pretzels and locked them shut. He grappled with me and tried to force them apart. Then, as he wasn't successful with this attempt, he drew back his hand and slapped me hard across the face. I let out a shrill scream that the air carried away as the truck sped into the night.

"OPEN YOUR FUCKING LEGS!" We struggled, with all his weight on top of me, the rough stones cutting into my back. He hauled back his hand and slapped me again, this time harder. With the second slap I knew I had to think of some other tactic; he was too strong for me to fight. This man obviously knew what he was doing. Unlike me, he was experienced, no doubt raping many women; I was simply about to become the next one. I deeply, deeply wanted to kill him, but I had no weapon.

So I pretended to want him. I said sweetly, "*Okay, okay.* But first let me pee-pee." I could see he was growing even more excited now—hey, this little girl wanted him!—and he let me up. I went to the opposite corner of the truck and pretended to squat and pee in the darkness. This bought me a few minutes to think of what to do next. By the time I finished my little charade, I had formed my plan. I picked up the largest stone I could find and, holding it in my hand, went back and lay down beside him.

He climbed on top of me and I squeezed the stone in my hand. With all my strength I brought it up to the side of his head and hit him squarely in the temple. I hit him once and saw him go dizzy. I hit him again and saw him go down. Like a warrior, I suddenly had tremendous strength. I didn't know that I had it, but when someone is trying to attack you, kill you, you become powerful. You don't know how strong you can be until that moment. As he lay there I hit him again and saw the blood flowing out of his ear.

His friend who was driving the truck saw all this happening from inside the cab. He started yelling, "What the fuck is going on back there?" and looked for a place to pull the truck into the bushes. I knew it was over for me if he caught me. As the truck slowed down, I crawled to the back of the bed, and poised on the rocks, I jumped to the ground like a cat. Then I ran for my life.

The truck driver was an old man; he jumped out of the cab and screamed in a raspy voice, "You killed my friend! Come back! You killed him!" He chased me through the scrubby bushes for a short distance, then gave up. Or so I thought.

The driver went back, crawled inside his truck, fired it up, and started driving through the desert after me. The twin headlight beams illuminated the ground around me; I heard the roar of the truck behind me. I was running as fast as I could, but of course the truck was gaining on me. I zigzagged and circled back through the darkness. He couldn't keep me in sight, so finally he gave up and headed back to the road.

I ran through the desert like a hunted animal; I ran through desert, then jungle, then desert again, with no idea of where I was. The sun came up and I continued to run. Finally I came upon another road. Even though I was sick with fear at the thought of what might happen, I decided to hitchhike again, because I knew I needed to get as far away as possible from the truck driver and his friend. What happened to my attacker after I hit him with the stone, I've never known, but the last thing I wanted was to meet up with those two men again.

Standing on the side of the road in the morning sun, I must have been a pretty sight. The scarf I was wearing was now a filthy rag; I had been running through the sand for days and my skin and hair were coated with dust; my arms and legs looked like twigs that might snap in a hard wind and my feet were covered with sores that would rival a leper's. Holding my hand out, I flagged down a Mercedes. An elegantly dressed man pulled the car to the side of the road. I crawled onto the leather seat and gaped at the luxury of it. "Where are you going?" the man asked.

"That way," I said, and pointed straight ahead, in the direction the Mercedes was already traveling. The man opened his mouth, showing his beautiful white teeth, and started to laugh.

2.

GROWING UP
WITH ANIMALS

Before I ran away from home, my life had been built around nature, family, and our strong bond with the animals that kept us alive. Stretching back to my earliest days, I shared a common trait with children the world over: my love of animals. In fact, my earliest memory is of my pet goat, Billy. Billy was my special treasure, my everything, and maybe I loved him most because he was a baby, like me. I used to sneak him all the food I could find, until he was the plumpest, happiest little goat in the herd. My mother constantly questioned, "Why is this goat so fat, when all the rest are so skinny?" I took perfect care of him, grooming him, petting him, talking to him for hours.

My relationship with Billy was representative of our lives in Somalia. My family's fate intertwined with that of the herds we tended daily. Dependence on the animals created our great respect for them, and those feelings were present in everything we did. All the children in my family tended our animals, a task we began helping with as soon as we were able to walk.

We grew up with the animals, prospered when they prospered, suffered when they suffered, died when they died. We raised cattle, sheep, and goats, but while I dearly loved my little Billy, there was no doubt that our camels were the most important animals we owned.

The camel is legendary in Somalia; Somalia boasts more camels than any country in the world; there are more camels in Somalia than people. In my country we have a long tradition of oral poetry, and much of it is devoted to passing along the lessons of the camel from one generation to the next, telling of its essential value to our culture. I remember my mother used to sing us a song, which basically said, "My camel has gone away to the bad man, who will either kill it or steal it from me. So I'm begging, I'm praying, please bring back my camel." From the time I was a baby, I knew of the great importance of these animals, because they're absolutely gold in our society. You simply cannot live in the desert without them. As one Somali poet put it:

A she-camel is a mother
To him who owns it
Whereas a he-camel is the artery
Onto which hangs life itself . . .

And it's true. A man's life is measured by camels, with one hundred camels being the price for a man who has been killed. A hundred camels must be paid by the killer's clan to the surviving family of the victim, or the dead man's clan will attack the killer in retribution. The traditional price for a bride is paid in camels. But on a daily level, the camels kept us alive. No other domestic animal is so well suited for life in the desert. A camel wants to drink once a week, but can go as long as a month without water. In the meantime, however, the female camel gives milk to nourish us and quench our thirst, an enormous asset when you're far from water. Even in the hottest temperatures, camels retain liquid and survive. They graze on the scrubby bushes found in our arid landscape, leaving the grasses for the other livestock.

We raised them to carry us across the desert, haul our meager belongings, and pay our debts. In other countries, you might hop in your car and go, but our only transportation, other than walking, was our camels.

The animal's personality is very similar to that of a horse; a camel will develop a close relationship with his master, and do things for him that he wouldn't do for anybody else. Men break the young camels—a dangerous practice—and train them to be ridden and follow a lead. It's important to be firm with them, because otherwise, when they sense a weak rider, they'll buck him off, or kick him.

Like most Somalis, we lived the pastoral lifestyle of herdsmen. Even though we struggled constantly for survival, our large herds of camels, cattle, sheep, and goats marked us as wealthy by the standards in my country. Following tradition, my brothers usually tended the large animals, the cattle and camels, and the girls watched over the smaller ones.

As nomads we traveled constantly, never staying in one place for more than three or four weeks. This constant movement was driven by the need to care for our animals. We were seeking food and water to keep them alive, and in the dry Somalian climate these necessities were seldom easy to find.

Our home was a hut woven from grass; being portable, it served the same purpose as a tent. We built a framework from sticks, then my mother wove grass mats that we laid over the bent twigs to form a dome about six feet in diameter. When it came time to move on, we dismantled the hut and tied the sticks and mats, along with our few possessions, to the backs of our camels. They're incredibly strong animals, and the babies and small children would ride on top, while the rest of us walked alongside, herding the animals to our next home. When we found a spot with water and foliage for grazing, we'd set up our camp again.

The hut provided shelter for the babies, shade from the midday sun, and storage space for fresh milk. At night, the rest of us slept outside under the stars, with the children cuddled together on a mat. After the sun went down, the desert was cold; we didn't have enough blankets for each child to have his own, and since we had very little clothing, we used the heat from our bodies to keep us warm. My father slept off to one side, as our guardian, the protector of the family.

In the morning we got up with the sun. Our first chore was to head out to the pens where we kept the herds, and milk them. Wherever we went we cut saplings to make pens for the animals, to keep them from straying at night. The baby animals were kept in a pen separate from the mothers so they wouldn't take all the milk. One of my tasks was to milk the cows, taking some of the fresh milk to make butter, but leaving enough for the calves. After the milking, we'd let the babies come in and nurse.

Then we had our breakfast of camel's milk, which is more nutritious than other animals' milk as it contains vitamin C. Our region was very dry, without enough water to grow crops, so we had no vegetables or bread. Sometimes we followed warthogs, large wild African pigs, tracking them to plants. They sniffed out edible roots, digging down with their hooves and snouts to feast on them. Our family shared in their bounty by taking some home to add to our diet.

We looked at slaughtering animals for meat as wasteful, and only resorted to this in case of emergency, or for special occasions, such as a wedding. Our animals were too valuable for us to kill and eat, as we raised them for their milk and to trade for the other goods we needed. For everyday sustenance, we had only camel's milk for breakfast, and again in the evening for supper. Sometimes there wasn't enough for everybody, so we fed the smallest children first, then the older ones, and so on. My mother never took a bite of food until everyone else had eaten; in fact, I don't remember ever seeing my mother eat, although I realize she must have. But if we didn't have anything for supper at night, it was no big deal, nothing to panic about. No need to cry or complain. The little babies might cry, but the older children knew the rules, so we just went to sleep. We tried to remain cheerful, kept calm and quiet, and tomorrow, God willing, we'd find a way. *In'shallah*, which means it will happen "if God is willing," was our philosophy. We knew our lives were dependent on the forces of nature, and God controlled those forces, not us.

A big treat for us—as people in other parts of the world might regard a holiday feast—was when my father brought home a sack of rice. Then we'd use the butter we made by shaking cow's milk in a basket that my mother had woven. Occasionally we'd trade a goat for corn grown in the wetter regions of Somalia, and grind the corn into meal and make porridge, or pop it in a pan over the fire. Or, when other families were around, we always shared whatever we had. If one of us had some food—dates or roots—or maybe killed an animal for meat, we'd cook it and divide the meal among us. We shared our good fortune, because even though we were isolated most of the time, traveling with one or two other families, we were still part of a larger community. On the practical side, since there were no refrigerators, meat or anything fresh needed to be consumed right away.

Each morning after breakfast, it was time to take the animals from their pen. By the age of six, I was responsible for taking herds of about sixty or seventy sheep and goats into the desert to graze. I got my long stick and headed off alone with my herd, singing my little song to guide them. If one strayed from the group, I used my staff to guide it back. They were eager to go, because they realized coming out of the pen meant that it was time to eat. Getting an early head start was important, to find the best spot with fresh water and lots of grass. Each day I quickly searched for water, in order to beat the other herders; otherwise their animals would drink what little there was. In any case, as the sun grew hotter, the ground became so thirsty that it would suck it all up. I made sure the animals drank as much water as they could, because it might be another week before we found more. Or two. Or three—who knows? Sometimes during the drought the saddest thing was to watch all the animals die. We traveled further and further each day looking for water; the herd tried to make it, but eventually they couldn't go anymore. When they collapsed, you had the most helpless feeling in the world, because you knew that was the end and there was nothing you could do.

No one owns the grazing land in Somalia, so it was up to me to be cunning, and discover areas with lots of plants for my goats and sheep. My survival instincts were honed to look for signs of rain, and I scanned the sky for clouds. My other senses also came into play, because a particular smell or a certain feeling in the air predicted rain.

While the animals grazed, I watched for predators, which are everywhere in Africa. The hyenas would sneak up and snatch a lamb or kid that had wandered off from the herd. There were lions to worry about and wild dogs; they all traveled in packs, but there was only one of me.

Watching the sky, I carefully calculated how far I had to travel to return home before night fell. But many times I miscalculated, and that's when trouble began. As I was stumbling along in the dark, trying to get home, the hyenas would attack, because they knew I couldn't see them. I'd swat one here, and another would sneak up behind me. As I chased that one away, another would run up while I wasn't looking. The hyenas are the worst, because they're relentless; they never quit until they get something. When I got home each evening and put the animals in the pen, I counted several times to see if any were missing. One night I returned home with my herd, and as I counted my goats, I noticed I was one short. I counted again. And again. Suddenly I realized I hadn't seen Billy, and hurried through the goats checking for him. I ran to my mother screaming, "Mama, Billy's missing—what should I do?" But of course it was too late, so she simply stroked my head as I cried when I realized that the hyenas had eaten my fat little pet.

Whatever else happened to us, the responsibility of taking care of our livestock went on and was always our first priority, even in times of drought, sickness, or war. Somalia's constant political turmoil caused enormous problems in the cities, but we were so isolated that for the most part no one bothered us. Then, when I was about nine years old, a large army came and camped close by. We'd heard stories about soldiers raping girls they caught out alone, and I knew a girl this had happened to. It didn't matter if they were the Somalian army or the Martian army, they were not part of our people; they were not nomads, and we avoided them at all costs.

One morning my father had given me the chore of watering the camels, so I headed off with the herd. Evidently, during the night, the army had arrived, and now sat encamped all around the road, their tents and trucks stretching as far as I could see. I hid behind a tree and watched them milling about in their uniforms. I was frightened, remembering the other girl's story; certainly I had no one around to protect me, so the men were free to do whatever they pleased. At first sight I hated them. I hated their uniforms, I hated their trucks, I hated their guns. I didn't even know what they were doing; for all I knew they could have been saving Somalia, but I didn't want any part of them all the same. Yet my camels needed water. The only route I knew that would avoid the army camp was too long and circuitous for me to travel with my herd, so I decided to turn the camels loose, and let them walk through the camp without me. They marched right through the middle of the soldiers, making straight for the water, as I had hoped they would. I scurried around the camp, ducking behind bushes and trees, until I joined the camels on the other side at the watering hole.

Then, as the sky grew dark, we repeated the procedure and headed home safely.

Each evening, when I returned home at sunset and secured my herd back in the pen, it was time to start the milking again. Around the camels' necks we hung wooden bells. The sound of these bells is indeed music to the nomad, who listens to their hollow clunk at twilight as the milking begins. The bells always act as a beacon to the traveler searching for home as the light fades. During the ritual of our evening chores, the great curve of the desert sky darkens, and a bright planet appears, a signal that it's time to herd the sheep into their pen. In other nations this planet is known as Venus, the planet of love, but in my country we call it *maqal hidhid*, meaning "hiding the lambs."

Frequently, it was around this time I would get into trouble, because after working since sunup, I couldn't hold my eyes open any longer. Walking through the dusk, I'd fall asleep and the goats would bump into me, or as I squatted milking, my head would begin to nod. If my father caught me dozing off, watch out! I love my father, but he could be a son of a gun; when he caught me sleeping on the job he'd beat me, to make sure I took my work seriously and paid attention to my business. After we finished our chores, we'd have our supper of camel's milk. Then we'd gather wood for a big fire and sit around its warmth talking and laughing until we went to sleep.

Those evenings are my favorite memories of Somalia: sitting around with my mother and father, sisters and brothers, when everybody was full, everybody was laughing. We always tried to be upbeat, optimistic. Nobody sat around complaining or whining or saying, "Hey, let's have a conversation about death." Life there was very hard; we needed all our strength just to survive and being negative sapped our vital energy.

Even though we were far from any village, I was never lonely, because I played with my sisters and brothers. I was a middle child, with an older brother and two older sisters and several younger siblings. We chased each other endlessly, climbed trees like monkeys, played tic-tac-toe in the sand by drawing lines with our fingers, collected pebbles, and dug holes in the ground to play an African game called mancala. We even had our own version of jacks, but instead of a rubber ball and metal pieces, we threw up one rock and grabbed other rocks in place of the jacks. This was my favorite because I was very good at it, and I always tried to get my little brother, Ali, to play it with me.

Our greatest pleasure, though, was pure joy at being a child in the wilderness, the freedom to be part of nature and experience its sights, sounds, and smells. We watched packs of lions lie around all day, baking in the sun, rolling onto their backs, sticking their feet up in the air and snoring. The cubs chased each other and played just as we did. We ran with the giraffes, the zebras, the foxes. The hyrax, an African animal that's the size of a rabbit but is actually a descendant of the elephant, was a particular favorite. We waited patiently outside their burrows for their little faces to appear, then chased them through the sand.

Once, on an excursion, I discovered an ostrich egg. I decided to take it home with me because I wanted to watch the baby ostrich hatch, then keep it as a pet. The egg is about the size of a bowling ball, and I hoisted it up from its hole in the sand and was carrying it away when Mama Ostrich came after me. She chased me—and believe me, ostriches are fast; they can run forty miles an hour. She quickly caught me and started pecking my head with her beak, ka-ka-ka. I thought she was going to crack my skull like an egg, so I put down her baby and ran for my life.

Seldom were we close to forested areas, but when we were, we loved to see the elephants. From a great distance we'd hear their thundering roar and climb a tree to spot them. Like lions, monkeys, and humans, elephants live in communities. If they had a baby in their midst, every adult elephant, the cousin, the uncle, the auntie, the sister, the mother, the grand—all of them would watch after that baby, to make sure nobody touched it. All of us children would stand high in the top of a tree and laugh, watching the elephant world for hours.

But gradually all those happy times with my family disappeared. My sister ran away; my brother went to school in the city. I learned sad facts about our family, about life. The rain stopped coming, and taking care of our animals was more and more difficult. Life became harder. And I became harder with it.

Part of that hardness formed watching my brothers and sisters die. Originally there were twelve children in my family, but now there are only six of us left. My mother had a set of twins who died right after they were born. She had another beautiful baby girl who was about six months old. One day the baby was strong and healthy, the next my mother called to me, "Waris!!!" I ran to her and saw her kneeling over the baby. I was just a little girl, but I could tell something was terribly wrong, the baby didn't look right. "Waris, run get me some camel's milk!" my mother commanded. But I couldn't move. "Run, hurry!" I stood staring at my sister in a trance—in terror. "What's wrong with you?" Mama screamed at me.

Finally, I tore myself away, but I knew what would be waiting for me when I got back. I returned with the milk, but the baby was totally still, and I knew she was dead. When I looked at my sister again, Mama slapped me hard. For a long time she blamed me for the baby's death, feeling that I had some sort of sorcerer's powers, and when in my trance I stared at the baby, I caused its death.

I had no such powers, but my little brother did have supernatural gifts. Everyone agreed he was no ordinary child. We called him Old Man, because when he was roughly six, his hair turned completely gray. He was extremely intelligent, and every man around us came to ask for his advice. They would walk up and say: "Where's the Old Man?" Then, by turns, they would sit this little gray-haired boy on their laps. "What do you think about the rain this year?" they would ask. And honest to God, even though in years he was a child, never did he act like a child. He thought, talked, sat, and behaved like a very wise elderly man. While everyone respected him, they were frightened of him, too, because he was so obviously not one of us. While he was still technically a young boy, Old Man died, as if in a few short years he'd crammed in an entire lifetime. No one knew the cause, but everyone felt his passing made sense, because: "There's no way he belonged to this world."

As in any large family, each of us developed a role. Mine became the role of rebel, a reputation I earned in a series of actions that to me seemed perfectly logical and justified, but to my elders— particularly my father—seemed outrageous. One day my younger brother, Ali, and I sat under a tree eating white rice with camel's milk. Ali wolfed his down greedily, but because this was a rare treat for us, I took each bite slowly. Having food was not something we took for granted; I always appreciated mine, savoring each bite with pleasure. Only a small amount of rice and milk remained in my bowl, and I anticipated it eagerly. Suddenly Ali stuck his spoon in my dish and scooped out my last bite, taking every last grain of rice. Without thinking, I retaliated by grabbing up a knife lying next to me and burying the blade in Ali's thigh. He shrieked, but took it out and sunk the knife in exactly the same spot in my leg. Now both of us sat with wounded legs, but because I was the one who had struck first, the blame went to me. Today, we carry matching scars from this meal.

One of the earliest outbursts of my rebel behavior centered on my longing for a pair of shoes. All my life I've been obsessed by shoes. Today even though I'm a model, I don't own many clothes—a pair of jeans, a couple of T-shirts—but I have a cupboard stacked full of high heels, sandals, tennis shoes, loafers, and boots, even though ironically I have nothing to wear them with. As a child I desperately wanted shoes, but not all the children in my family had clothes, and certainly there was no money to buy shoes. Yet it was my dream to wear beautiful leather sandals like my mother wore. How I wished to put on a pair of comfortable shoes and look after my animals, walk without worrying about rocks and thorns, snakes and scorpions. My feet were always bruised and marked, and I still carry the black scars today. Once a thorn came all the way through my foot; sometimes they would break off in my feet. We had no doctors in the desert, or medicine to treat the wound. But still we had to walk, because we had to look after the animals. No one said, "I can't." We just did it, went out each morning and limped along as best we could.

One of my father's brothers was a very wealthy man. Uncle Ahmed lived in the city, in Galcaio, but we looked after his camels and the rest of his animals. I was the favorite to care for his goats, because I always did a thorough job, making sure they were well fed and watered, and I did my best to keep them safe from predators. One day, when I was about seven years old, Uncle Ahmed visited us and I said, "Look, I want you to buy me some shoes."

He looked at me and laughed. "Yeah, yeah, all right. I'll get you shoes." I knew he was surprised, because it was very unusual for a girl to ask for anything, let alone anything as extravagant as shoes.

The next time my father took me to see him, I was excited, because today would be the day I got my first pair of shoes. At my earliest opportunity I said eagerly, "Well, did you bring them?"

He said, "Yeah, I have them right here," and handed me a parcel. I took the shoes in my hand and examined them; they were rubber sandals, flip-flops. Not beautiful leather sandals like Mama's, but cheap, yellow flip-flops. I couldn't believe it.

"These are my shoes?!" I cried, and threw them at him. When the flip-flops bounced off his brother's face, my father tried to be upset, but this time he couldn't help himself—he doubled over laughing.

My uncle said to him, "I don't believe it. How are you raising this child?"

I started fighting with my uncle, swinging at him, because I was so disappointed, I was furious. "I worked so hard for this shit!" I screamed. "I did all this work for you, and this is it? I get a pair of cheap rubber sandals? Fah!! I'd rather go barefoot— I'll go barefoot till my feet bleed before I wear this garbage!" and I motioned toward his gift.

Uncle Ahmed just looked at me, then raised his eyes to heaven and moaned, "Oh, Allah." He stooped with a sigh, picked up his flip-flops, and took them back home.

I was not content to give up so easily, however. After that day I kept sending my uncle messages by every relative, friend, or stranger heading to Galcaio: "Waris wants shoes!" But I had to wait many years until I realized my dream of owning a pair. In the meantime, however, I continued to raise Uncle Ahmed's goats, and help my family care for our herds, walking thousands of miles barefoot.

Several years before the shoes episode with Uncle Ahmed, when I was a tiny girl, around four years old, we had a visitor one day. The man, Guban, was a good friend of my father's and frequently came to see us. At twilight he stood talking with my parents, until finally my mother, staring at the sky, watching the bright planet *maqal hidhid* emerge, said it was time to bring in the lambs. Guban said, "Oh, why don't you let me do that for you? Waris can help me."

I felt important at being chosen over the boys to help Papa's friend with the animals. He took my hand and we walked away from the hut and began to round up the herd. Normally I would have been running everywhere like a wild animal myself, but it was getting dark now, and since I was frightened, I stayed close to Guban. Suddenly he took off his jacket and laid it on the sand and sat down on top of it. I stared at him, confused, and protested: "Why are you sitting down? It's getting dark— we have to get the animals."

"We have time. We'll do that in a minute." He rested on one side of his jacket and patted the empty space next to him. "Come sit down."

Reluctantly I came to him. Since I always loved stories as a kid, I realized this might be a good opportunity to hear one. "Will you tell me a story?"

Guban patted his coat again. "If you sit down, I'll tell you one." As soon as I sat next to him, he started trying to push me back onto his coat. "I don't want to lie down. I want you to tell me a story," I insisted stubbornly and squirmed upright.

"Come, come." His hand pushed my shoulder firmly. "Lie down and look at the stars and I'll tell you a story." Stretching out with my head on his jacket, I stuck my toes in the cold sand and stared at the phosphorescent Milky Way. As the sky deepened from indigo to black, the lambs ran in circles around us, crying in the dark, and I waited anxiously for the story to begin. Abruptly, Guban's face came between me and the Milky Way; he squatted between my legs and yanked up the little scarf wrapped around my waist. Next I felt something hard and wet pressing against my vagina. I froze at first, not understanding what was happening, but I knew it was something very bad. The pressure intensified until it became a sharp pain.

"I want my Mama!" Suddenly I was flooded with a warm liquid and a sickening acrid odor permeated the night air. "You pee-peed on me!" I screamed, horrified. I jumped up and rubbed my scarf against my legs, mopping off the foul-smelling liquid.

"No, no, it's okay," he whispered soothingly and grabbed my arm. "I was just trying to tell you a story." Jerking free, I ran back to my mother, with Guban chasing after me, trying to catch me. When I saw Mama standing next to the fire, the orange light glowing off her face, I ran up and threw my arms around her legs.

"What's wrong, Waris?" Mama said in alarm. Guban ran up behind me panting, and my mother looked at him. "What happened to her?"

He laughed casually and waved his arm at me. "Oh, I was trying to tell her a story and she got scared." I held on to my mother with a grip of iron. I wanted to tell her what Papa's friend had done to me, but I didn't have the words—I didn't *know* what he'd done. I looked at his smiling face in the firelight, a face I would have to see again and again over the years, and knew I'd hate him forever.

She stroked my head as I pressed my face into her thigh. "Waris, it's okay. There, there, it was only a story, baby. It's not *real*." To Guban, she said, "Where are the lambs?"

3.

A NOMAD'S LIFE

Growing up in Africa I did not have the sense of history that seems so important in other parts of the world. Our language, Somali, did not have a written script until 1973, so we did not learn to read or write. Knowledge was passed down by word of mouth—poetry or folktales—or, more important, by our parents teaching us the skills we needed to survive. For example, my mother taught me how to weave from dried grass containers tight enough to hold milk; my father taught me how to care for our animals and make sure they were healthy. We didn't spend much time talking about the past—nobody had time for that. Everything was today, what are we going to do *today*? Are all the children in? Are all the animals safe? How are we going to eat? Where can we find water?

In Somalia, we lived the way our ancestors had for thousands of years; nothing had changed dramatically for us. As nomads we did not live with electricity, telephones, or automobiles, much less computers, television, or space travel. These facts, combined with our emphasis on living in the present, gave us a much different perspective on time than the one that dominates the Western world.

Like the rest of my family, I have no idea how old I am; I can only guess. A baby who is born in my country has little guarantee of being alive one year later, so the concept of tracking birthdays does not retain the same importance. When I was a child, we lived without artificial time constructions of schedules, clocks, and calendars. Instead, we lived by the seasons and the sun, planning our moves around our need for rain, planning our day around the span of daylight available. We told time by using the sun. If my shadow was on the west side, it was morning; when it moved directly underneath me, it was noon. When my shadow crossed to the other side, it was afternoon. As the day grew longer, so did my shadow—my cue to start heading home before dark.

When we got up in the morning, we decided what we'd do that day, then did that task the best we could until we finished or the sky grew too dark for us to see. There was no such notion of getting up and having your day all planned out for you. In New York, people frequently whip out their datebooks and ask, "Are you free for lunch on the fourteenth—or what about the fifteenth?" I respond with "Why don't you call me the day before you want to meet up?" No matter how many times I write down appointments, I can't get used to the idea. When I first came to London, I was mystified by the connection between people staring at their wrist, then crying, "I've got to dash!" I felt like everyone was rushing everywhere, every action was timed. In Africa there was no hurry, no stress. African time is very, very slow, very calm. If you say, "I'll see you tomorrow around noon," that means about four or five o'clock. And today I still refuse to wear a watch.

During my childhood years in Somalia, it never occurred to me to fast-forward into the future, or delve into the past enough to ask, "Mama, how did you grow up?" As a consequence I know little of my family history, especially since I left home at such an early age. I constantly wish I could go back and ask those questions now—ask my mother what her life was like when she was a little girl, or ask where her mother came from, or how her father died. It disturbs me that I may never know these facts.

However, one thing I do know about my mother is that she was very beautiful. I know I sound like the typical adoring daughter, but she was. Her face was like a Modigliani sculpture, and her skin so dark and smooth, that she looked as if she'd been perfectly chiseled from black marble. Since Mama's skin was jet black and her teeth dazzlingly white, at night when she smiled all you could see were her teeth glowing, as if they floated all by themselves in the night. Her hair was long and straight, very soft, and she'd smooth it with her fingers, since she never owned a comb. My mother is tall and slender— traits that all her daughters inherited.

Her demeanor is very calm, very quiet. But when she starts talking, she's hysterically funny and she laughs a lot. She tells jokes, and some of them are funny, some are really dirty, and some are just stupid little things she'd say to crack us up. She'd look at me and say, "Waris, why are your eyes disappearing into your face?" But her favorite silly joke was calling me Avdohol, which means "small mouth." Mama would look at me for no reason and say, "Hey, Avdohol, why is your mouth so small?"

My father was very handsome, and believe me, he knew it. He was about six feet tall, slim, and lighter than Mama; his hair was brown, and his eyes were light brown. Papa was cocky because he knew he was good-looking. He always teased Mama, "I can go and get another woman if you don't—" and then he'd fill in the blank with whatever he was after. Or, "Look, I'm getting bored around here. I'm getting me another woman. . . ." My mother would tease back, "Go ahead. See what you can do." They really loved each other, but unfortunately one day these taunts came true.

My mother grew up in Mogadishu, the capital city of Somalia. My father, on the other hand, was a nomad and had always lived roaming the desert. When she met him, my mother thought Papa was so handsome that a life wandering with him as nomads sounded like a romantic idea; they quickly decided to get married. Papa went to my grandmother, since my grandfather was dead, and asked permission to marry my mother. My grandmother said, "No, no, *no*, absolutely not." To my mother she added, "He's just a playboy!" Grandmother was not about to allow her beautiful daughter to throw her life away raising camels in the wilderness with *this man*, this desert man! However, when my mother was about sixteen, she ran away and married Papa anyhow.

They went to the other side of the country and lived with his family in the desert, which created a whole series of problems for my mother. Her family had money and power, and she had never known this type of harsh nomadic life. Greater than that dilemma, however, was the fact that my father was from the Daarood tribe, and my mother was from the Hawiye tribe. Like Native Americans, the citizens of Somalia are divided into individual tribes, and each has a fanatical loyalty to its own group. This tribal pride has been the source of wars throughout our history.

A great rivalry exists between the Daaroods and Hawiyes, and my father's family always treated my mother badly, assuming she was a lesser mortal by virtue of being from a different tribe than their own. Mama was lonely for a very long time, but she had to adapt. After I ran away from home and was separated from my family, I realized what life must have been like for her, living all alone among the Daaroods.

My mother started having babies, and raising her children gave her the love she missed being away from her own people. But again, now that I'm grown, I look back and realize what she went through having twelve children. I remember when Mama was pregnant, she would suddenly disappear, and we wouldn't see her for days. Then she would show up—carrying a tiny baby. She went off into the desert alone and gave birth, taking along something sharp to cut the umbilical cord. Once after she disappeared we had to move our camp in the endless search for water. It took her four days to find us; she walked across the desert carrying the newborn baby while she looked for her husband.

Of all her children, though, I always felt I was my mother's special favorite. We had a strong bond of understanding between us, and I still think about her every day of my life, praying to God to take care of her until I'm able to do the job. As a child I always wanted to be near her, and all day I would look forward to coming home in the evening when I would sit next to Mama and she would stroke my head.

My mother wove beautiful baskets, a skill that takes years of practice to achieve. We spent many hours together as she taught me how to make a small cup that I could drink milk from, but my attempts at larger projects were never like hers. My baskets were raggedy and full of holes.

One day my desire to be with Mama and my natural childish curiosity drove me to secretly follow her. Once a month she left our camp and went away by herself for the afternoon. I said to her, "I'm so determined to know what you do, Mom—what is this thing you do every month?" She told me to mind my own business; a child in Africa has no right meddling in parents' affairs. And, as usual, she told me to stay home and watch after the younger children. But when she walked away, I hurried behind her at a distance, hiding behind bushes to stay out of sight. She met with five other women, who had traveled long distances also. Together they sat under a huge, beautiful tree for several hours during our siesta, when the sun was too hot to do much else. During that time the animals and family were all resting, so they could spare a little time for themselves. Their black heads gathered close in the distance like ants, and I watched as they ate popcorn and drank tea. What they talked about, I still don't know, as I was too far away to hear. Eventually I decided to risk revealing myself, mainly because I wanted some of their food. I walked up meekly and stood next to my mother.

"Where did you come from?" she cried.

"I followed you."

"Bad, naughty girl," she scolded.

But all the other women laughed, and cooed, "Oh, look at the cute little girl. Come here, darling . . ." So my mother relented and let me have some popcorn.

When I was this young age, I had no conception of another world different from the one we lived in with our goats and camels. Without travel to different countries, books, TV, or movies, my universe simply consisted of the sights I saw around me each day. I certainly had no conception that my mother had come from a different life. Before Somalia's independence in 1960, Italy had colonized the southern region. As a result, Mogadishu's culture, architecture, and society were full of Italian influences, so my mother spoke Italian. Occasionally, when she was angry, she'd spew a string of Italian cusswords. "Mama!" I'd look at her in alarm. "What are you saying?"

"Oh, that's Italian."

"What's Italian? What does it mean?"

"Nothing—mind your own business," and she'd wave me aside.

Later I discovered for myself—like I discovered cars and buildings—that Italian was part of a broader world outside our hut. Many times we children questioned Mama about her decision to marry our father. "Why did you ever follow this man? Look where you're living, while your brothers and sisters are living all over the world—they're ambas- sadors and what have you! Why did you run away with this loser?" She replied that she'd fallen in love with Papa, and made her decision to run away with him so they could be together. Yet my mother is a strong, strong woman. In spite of everything I watched her go through, I never heard her complain. I never heard her say, "I'm fed up with this," or "I'm not doing this anymore." Mama was simply silent and hard as iron. Then without warning, she'd crack us up with one of her silly jokes. My goal is to someday be as strong as she is, then I can say my life has been a success.

Our family was typical in our choice of occupations, since over 60 percent of Somalis are pastoral nomads, earning a living by raising animals. My father periodically ventured into a village and sold an animal in order to buy a sack of rice, fabric for clothes, or blankets. Occasionally, he sent along his goods for sale with anybody traveling into town, and a shopping list of items he wanted purchased in return.

Another way we made money was by harvesting frankincense, the incense mentioned in the Bible as one of the gifts the Magi brought the baby Jesus. Its scent is still a valued commodity today, as it has been since ancient times. Frankincense comes from the Boswellia tree, which grows in the highlands of northeastern Somalia. It's a beautiful little tree, about five feet tall, and the limbs hang in a curve like an open umbrella. I would take an ax and strike the tree lightly— not enough to damage it—just enough to slash the bark. Then the tree would bleed a milky fluid. I waited a day for the white juice to harden into gum; in fact, sometimes we would chew it like gum for its bitter taste. We gathered the clumps into baskets, then my father sold them. My family also burned frankincense at night in our campfires, and whenever I smell it today I'm transported back to those evenings. Sometimes, in Manhattan, I'll find incense advertised as frankincense. Desperate for a little reminder of home, I buy it, but its smell is such a weak imitation that it can never match the rich exotic perfume of our fires burning in the desert night.

Our large family was also typical in Somalia, where the average woman has seven children. Children are looked at as the future old-age pension for the elders, as they will take care of their parents when they grow old. Somali children regard their parents and grandparents with great respect, never daring to question their authority. All your elders, even your older brothers and sisters, must be treated with respect, and you must follow their wishes. This fact was one of the reasons my rebellious acts were considered so incredibly scandalous.

Part of the reason for large families, other than lack of birth control, is that the more people who share the work, the easier life is. Even basic functions such as having water—not plenty of water, or enough water, but any water at all—required back-breaking work. When the area around us dried up, my father went in search of water. He strapped huge bags onto our camels, bags my mother had woven from grass. Then he left home and was gone for days until he found water, filled the bags, and traveled back to us. We tried to stay in one spot waiting for him, but each day would become increasingly challenging, as we traveled miles and miles to water the herds. Sometimes we had to move on without him, yet he always found us, even without the aid of roads, street signs, or maps. Or, if my father was away, if he'd gone to the village in search of food, one of the children had to do this job, because Mama had to stay home and keep everything running.

Sometimes the job fell to me. I'd walk and walk for days, however long it took to find water, because there was no point in coming back without it. We knew never to come home empty- handed, because then there was no hope. We had to keep going until we found something. No one accepted the excuse "I can't." My mother told me to find water, so I had to find water. When I came to the Western world, I was amazed to find people complaining, "I can't work because I have a headache." I wanted to say to them, "Let me give you hard work. You'll never complain about your job again."

One of the techniques for providing more hands to ease the workload was increasing the number of women and children, which means that having multiple wives is a common practice in Africa. My parents were unusual in that only the two of them were together as a couple for years and years. Finally, one day, after having twelve children, my mother said, "I'm too old . . . why don't you get yourself another wife and give me a break? Leave me alone now." I don't know if she meant it or not—she probably never thought my father would take her up on it.

But one day, Papa disappeared. At first we thought he'd gone in search of water, or food, and my mother looked after everything by herself. After he'd been gone for two months, we thought he was dead. Then one evening, as suddenly as he'd left, my father reappeared. All the children were sitting around in front of our hut. He strolled up and said, "Where's your mother?" We told him she was still out with the animals. "Well, hey-hey, everyone," he said, grinning, "I want you to meet my wife." He pulled forward this little girl, about seventeen years old—not much older than I was. We all just stared at her, because we weren't allowed to say anything; besides, we didn't know *what* to say.

When my mother came home, it was a horrible moment. All the children waited tensely to see what would happen. Mama glared at my father, not noticing the other woman in the darkness, and said, "Oh, you decided to show up, did you?"

Papa shifted his weight from one foot to the other, and looked around. "Yeah, well, yeah. By the way, meet my wife," and he put his arm around his new bride. I can never forget my mother's face in the firelight. It just fell to the ground. Then she realized, "Damn, I lost him now to this little, little girl!" Mama was dying from jealousy, although, bless her heart, she tried so hard not to show it.

We had no idea where my father's new wife was from, nor did

we know anything about her. But that didn't stop her from immediately bossing all his children around. Next this seventeen-year-old girl started bossing my mother around— telling Mama to do this, get me that, cook me this. Things were already growing very tense when one day she made a fatal mistake: she slapped my brother Old Man.

The day this happened all we kids were in our hangout (each time we moved, we found a tree close to the hut that was the children's "room"). One day I was sitting under this tree with my brothers and sisters when I heard Old Man crying. I stood up and spotted my little brother walking toward me. "What's wrong with you? What happened?" I said, bending over to wipe his face.

"She slapped me—she slapped me so hard." I didn't even have to ask who, because no one in our family had ever hit Old Man. Not my mother, not any of his older siblings, not even my father, who beat the rest of us on a regular basis. There was no need to hit Old Man, since he was the wisest one among us and always did the right thing. Slapping my brother was the breaking point; this was more than I could stand, and I went looking for this foolish girl.

"Why did you slap my brother?" I demanded.

"He drank my milk," she said in her haughty way, as if she were the queen and owned all our milk from our herds.

"*Your* milk? I put that milk in the hut, and if he wants it, if he's thirsty, he can have it. You don't need to hit him!"

"Oh, shut the hell up and get away from me!" she yelled, dismissing me with a wave of her hand. I stared at her and shook my head, because even though I was only about thirteen, I knew she'd made a big mistake.

My brothers and sisters sat waiting under the tree, straining to hear the conversation between Papa's wife and me. As I approached them, I pointed at their questioning faces and said, "Tomorrow." They nodded.

The next day luck was with us, because my father said he was leaving for a couple of days. When it was time for siesta I brought my animals home and found my sister and two brothers. "Papa's new little wife is taking over," I began, stating the obvious. "We've got to do something to teach her a lesson, because this has to stop."

"Yeah, but what are we going to do?" asked Ali.

"You'll see. Just come with me, and help me out." I got a thick, tough rope, the rope we used to tie our belongings onto the camels when we were traveling. We led Papa's scared wife away from our camp, took her into the bushes, and forced her to take off all her clothes. Then I threw one end of the rope around the limb of a huge tree and tied it around Little Wife's ankles. She alternated between cussing us, screaming, and sobbing while we pulled the rope and hauled her up off the ground. My brothers and I played the rope back and forth to position her head dangling about eight feet from the dirt, ensuring no wild animals could eat her. Then we tied the rope off and returned home, leaving her there—twisting and screaming in the desert.

The next afternoon, my father showed up a day early. He asked us where his little woman was. We all shrugged and said we hadn't seen her. Fortunately, we'd taken her far enough away so no one could hear her screaming. "Hmmm," he said, and looked at us suspiciously. By dark he still hadn't found any trace of her. Papa knew something was very, very wrong, and began questioning us: "When did you see her last? Have you seen her today? Did you see her yesterday?" We told him she hadn't come home the night before, which was, of course, true.

My father panicked and began frantically searching for her everywhere. But he didn't find her until the next morning. Father's bride had been hanging upside down for nearly two days by the time he cut her down, and she was in bad shape. By the time he came home he was furious. "Who's responsible for this?" he demanded. We all went quiet and looked at each other. Of course she told him. She said, "Waris was the leader. She attacked me first!" Papa came after me and started beating me, but all the kids jumped on him. We knew it was wrong to hit our own father, but we simply couldn't take it anymore.

After that day, Papa's new little wife was a changed person. We had set out to teach her a lesson, and she learned it well. After having the blood rush to her head for two days, I guess her brain was refreshed and she turned sweet and polite. From that point on, she kissed my mother's feet and waited on her like a slave. "What can I get you? What can I do for you? No, no—I'll do that. You sit down and relax."

And I thought, "There you go. You should have acted like this from the beginning, you little bitch, and saved us all that unnecessary grief." But the nomad's life is a harsh one, and even though she was twenty years younger than my mother, father's new wife wasn't as strong. In the end Mama learned she had nothing to fear from this little girl.

The nomad's life is a harsh one, but it is also full of beauty—a life so connected to nature that the two are inseparable. My mother named me after a miracle of nature: Waris means desert flower. The desert flower blooms in a barren environment where few living things can survive. Sometimes it doesn't rain in my country for over a year. But finally the water pours down, cleansing the dusty landscape, and then like a miracle the blooms appear. The flowers are a brilliant yellowish orange, and for this reason, yellow has always been my favorite color.

When a girl marries, the women from her tribe go out into the desert and collect these flowers. They dry them, then add water to them and make a paste to spread on the bride's face that gives her a golden glow. They decorate her hands and feet with henna, drawing ornate designs. They rim her eyes with kohl, so they look deep and sexy. All these cosmetics are made from plants and herbs, so they're completely natural. Next the women drape her in brightly colored scarves—reds and pinks and oranges and yellows—the more the better. Maybe they don't own much; many families are incredibly poor, but there is no shame over this fact. She'll simply wear the best she or her mother or sisters or friends can find, and carry herself with fierce pride—a trait all Somalis bear. By the time her wedding day comes, she walks out to greet her groom as a stunning beauty. The man doesn't deserve it!

For their wedding, the people in the tribe bring gifts; again, there's no need to feel pressured to buy certain things, or worry that you can't afford something better. You give whatever you have: weave a mat for them to sleep on, or give them a bowl, or if you have none of these, bring some food for the celebration after the ceremony. There's no such thing in my culture as a honeymoon, so the day after the wedding is a workday for the newlyweds, and they will need all their gifts to start their married life together.

Other than weddings, we have few celebrations. There are no holidays arbitrarily marked by a calendar. Instead, the other major cause for rejoicing is the long-awaited rain. In my country water is so scarce, yet it is the very essence of life. Nomads living in the desert have a deep, deep respect for water, regarding every drop as a precious commodity, and to this day I love water. Simply looking at it gives me great joy.

After months and months of drought, sometimes we would grow desperate. When this happened, the people would gather together and pray to God for rain. Sometimes it worked and sometimes it didn't. One year we had passed into what was supposed to be the rainy season, but still not a drop had fallen. Half our animals were dead and the other half were weak from thirst. My mother told me that we were all going to gather to pray for rain. The people converged, seemingly from out of nowhere. We were all praying and singing and dancing, trying to be happy and lift our spirits.

The next morning the clouds gathered, and the rain began to pour. Then, as always when it rains, the true rejoicing began. We would strip off our clothes and run into the water, splashing, and washing for the first time in months. The people celebrate with our traditional dancing: the women clapping their hands and chanting, their low sweet voices humming across the desert night, and the men leaping high into the air. Everyone contributes food, and we eat like kings to praise the gift of life.

In the days after the rains, the savannahs blossom with golden flowers, and the grasslands turn green. The animals are able to eat and drink their fill, offering us a chance to relax and enjoy life. We can go to the lakes newly created by the rain and bathe and swim. In the fresh air, the birds begin to sing and the nomads' desert becomes paradise.

4.

BECOMING A
WOMAN

The time had come for my oldest sister, Aman, to be circumcised. Like all younger siblings, I was envious, jealous that she was entering this grown-up world that was still closed to me. Aman was a teenager, much older than the normal age for circumcision, but so far the timing had never been right. As my family traveled Africa in our endless cycle, we had somehow missed the gypsy woman who performed this ancient ritual. When my father finally found her, he brought her to circumcise my two oldest sisters, Aman and Halemo. But when the woman came to our camp, Aman happened to be off searching for water, so the gypsy circumcised only Halemo. My father was growing concerned, because Aman was reaching marriageable age, but no marriage could take place unless she had been properly "fixed." The prevailing wisdom in Somalia is that there are bad things between a girl's legs, parts of our bodies that we're born with, yet are unclean. These things need to be removed—the clitoris, labia minora, and most of the labia majora are cut off, then the wound is stitched shut, leaving only a scar where our genitals had been. But the actual details of the ritual cutting are left a mystery—it's never explained to the girls. You just know that something special is going to happen to you when your time comes.

As a result, all young girls in Somalia anxiously await the ceremony that will mark their transformation from being a little girl to becoming a woman. Originally the process occurred when the girls reached puberty, and the ritual had some meaning, as the girl became fertile and capable of bearing her own children. But through time, female circumcision has been performed on younger and younger girls, partially due to pressure from the girls themselves, since they eagerly await their "special time" as a child in the West might await her birthday party, or Santa Claus's arrival on Christmas Eve.

When I heard the old gypsy was coming to circumcise Aman, I wanted to be circumcised, too. Aman was my beautiful older sister, my idol, and anything she wanted or had, I wanted, too. The day before the big event, I begged my mother, tugging at her arm, "Mama, do both of us at the same time. Come on, Mama, do both of us tomorrow!"

Mother pushed me away. "Just hush, little girl." However, Aman was not so eager. I remember her muttering, "I just hope I don't wind up like Halemo." But at the time I was too young to know what that meant, and when I asked Aman to explain she just changed the subject.

Very early the next morning my mother and her friend took Aman to meet the woman who would perform the circumcision. As usual, I pleaded to go, too, but Mama told me to stay home with the younger children. But using the same sneaky techniques I used the day I followed my mother to meet her friends, I followed along, hiding behind bushes and trees, staying a safe distance behind the group of women.

The gypsy woman arrived. She is considered an important person in our community, not only because she has specialized knowledge, but because she earns a great deal of money from performing circumcisions. Paying for this procedure is one of the greatest expenses a household will undergo, but is still considered a good investment, since without it, the daughters will not make it onto the marriage market. With their genitals intact, they are considered unfit for marriage, unclean sluts whom no man would consider taking as a wife. So the gypsy woman, as some call her, is an important member of our society, but I call her the Killer Woman because of all the little girls who have died at her hand.

Peering from behind a tree, I watched my sister sit on the ground. Then my mother and her friend both grabbed Aman's shoulders and held her down. The gypsy started doing something between my sister's legs, and I saw a look of pain flash across Aman's face. My sister was a big girl, and very powerful, and suddenly—*phoom!* She raised her foot and shoved against the gypsy's chest, knocking her over on her back. Then my sister struggled free from the women holding her down, and leaped to her feet. To my horror, I saw blood pouring down her legs and onto the sand, leaving a trail as she ran. They all ran after her, but Aman was far ahead of them until she collapsed and fell to the ground. The women rolled her over on the spot where she had fallen, and continued their work. I felt sick and couldn't watch anymore, so I ran home.

Now I knew something I really wished I didn't know. I didn't understand what had happened, but was terrified at the thought of going through it myself. I couldn't very well ask my mother about it, because I wasn't supposed to have witnessed it. They kept Aman separated from the rest of the children while she healed, and two days later I took her some water. I knelt beside her and asked quietly, "What was it like?"

"Oh, it was horrible . . ." she began. But I guess she thought better of telling me the truth, knowing that I would have to be circumcised, and then I'd be frightened, instead of looking forward to it. "Anyway, you're not far from it; they will do it to you soon enough." And that's all she would say.

From then on, I dreaded the ritual that I would pass through on the way to womanhood. I tried to put the horror of it out of my mind, and as time passed, so did my memory of the agony I had witnessed on my sister's face. Finally, I foolishly convinced myself that I wanted to become a woman, too, and join my older sisters.

A friend of my father's and his family always traveled with us. He was a grouchy old man, and anytime my younger sister or I pestered him, he would wave us away as if shooing flies, and tease us by saying, "Get away from me, you two unsanitary little girls—you dirty little girls. You haven't even been circumcised yet!" He always spat the words out as if the fact we weren't circumcised made us so disgusting that he could barely stand to look at us. These insults agitated me until I vowed to find a way to make him shut his stupid mouth.

This man had a teenage son named Jamah, and I developed a crush on this boy, even though he always ignored me. Instead of me, Jamah was interested in Aman. Through time I got the idea that his preference for my older sister revolved around the fact she was superior to me since she'd been circumcised. Like his father, Jamah probably didn't want to associate with dirty, uncircumcised little girls. When I was about five years old, I went to my mother and nagged, "Mama, just find me this woman. Come on, when are you going to do it?" I thought, *I have to get it over with—get this mysterious thing done.* As my luck would have it, only a few days passed until the gypsy woman showed up again.

One evening my mother said to me, "By the way, your father ran into the gypsy woman. We're waiting for her; she should be here any day now."

The night before my circumcision, Mama told me not to drink too much water or milk, so I wouldn't have to pee-pee much. I didn't know what that meant, but didn't question her, only nodded my head. I was nervous but resolved to get it over with. That evening the family made a special fuss over me and I got extra food at dinner. This was the tradition I'd witnessed through the years that made me envious of my older sisters. Just before I went to sleep, my mother said, "I'll wake you up in the morning when the time comes." How she knew when the woman was coming I have no idea, but Mama always knew these things. She simply sensed intuitively when someone was coming, or the time was right for something to happen.

I lay awake with excitement that night until suddenly Mama was standing over me. The sky was still dark, that time before dawn when the black has lightened imperceptibly to gray. She motioned for me to be silent and took my hand. I grabbed my little blanket, and still half asleep stumbled along after her. Now I know the reason they take the girls so early in the morning. They want to cut them before anybody wakes up, so nobody else will hear them scream. But at the time, even though I was confused, I simply did as I was told. We walked away from our hut, out into the brush. "We'll wait here," Mama said, and we sat down on the cold ground. The day was growing faintly lighter; I could barely distinguish shapes, and soon I heard the click-click of the gypsy woman's sandals. My mother called out the woman's name, then added, "Is that you?"

"Yes, over here," came a voice, although I still could see no one. Then, without my seeing her approach, she was right beside me. "Sit over there." She motioned toward a flat rock. There was no conversation, no hello. No "How are you?" No "What's going to happen today is going to be very painful, so you must be a brave girl." No. The Killer Woman was strictly business.

Mama grabbed a piece of root from an old tree, then positioned me on the rock. She sat behind me, and pulled my head back against her chest, her legs straddling my body. I circled my arms around her thighs. My mother placed the root between my teeth. "Bite on this."

44

I was frozen with fear as the memory of Aman's tortured face suddenly flooded back before me. "This is going to hurt!" I mumbled over the root.

Mama leaned over and whispered to me, "You know I can't hold you. I'm on my own here. So try to be a good girl, baby. Be brave for Mama, and it'll go fast." I peered between my legs and saw the gypsy woman getting ready. She looked like any other old Somali woman—with a colorful scarf wrapped around her head and a bright cotton dress—except there was no smile on her face. She looked at me sternly, a dead look in her eyes, then foraged through an old carpet bag. My eyes were fixed on her, because I wanted to know what she was going to cut me with. I expected a big knife, but instead, out of the bag she pulled a tiny cotton sack. She reached inside with her long fingers, and fished out a broken razor blade. Turning it from side to side, she examined it. The sun was barely up now; it was light enough to see colors but no details. However, I saw dried blood on the jagged edge of the blade. She spat on it and wiped it against her dress. While she was scrubbing, my world went dark as my mother tied a scarf around my eyes as a blindfold.

The next thing I felt was my flesh, my genitals, being cut away. I heard the sound of the dull blade sawing back and forth through my skin. When I think back, I honestly can't believe that this happened to me. I feel as if I were talking about somebody else. There's no way in the world I can explain what it feels like. It's like somebody is slicing through the meat of your thigh, or cutting off your arm, except this is the most sensitive part of your body. However, I didn't move an inch, because I remembered Aman and knew there was no escape. And I wanted Mama to be proud of me. I just sat there as if I were made of stone, telling myself the more I moved around, the longer the torture would take. Unfortunately, my legs began to quiver of their own accord, and shake uncontrollably, and I prayed, Please, God, let it be over quickly. Soon it was, because I passed out.

When I woke up, I thought we were finished, but now the worst of it had just begun. My blindfold was off and I saw the Killer Woman had piled next to her a stack of thorns from an acacia tree. She used these to puncture holes in my skin, then poked a strong white thread through the holes to sew me up. My legs were completely numb, but the pain between them was so intense that I wished I would die. I felt myself floating up, away from the ground, leaving my pain behind, and I hovered some feet above the scene looking down, watching this woman sew my body back together while my poor mother held me in her arms. At this moment I felt complete peace; I was no longer worried or afraid.

My memory ends at that instant, until I opened my eyes and the woman was gone. They had moved me, and I was lying on the ground close to the rock. My legs had been tied together with strips of cloth binding me from my ankles to my hips so I couldn't move. I looked around for my mother, but she was gone, too, so I lay there alone, wondering what would happen next. I turned my head toward the rock; it was drenched with blood as if an animal had been slaughtered there. Pieces of my meat, my sex, lay on top, drying undisturbed in the sun.

I lay there, watching the sun climb directly overhead. There was no shade around me and the waves of heat beat down on my face, until my mother and sister returned. They dragged me into the shade of a bush while they finished preparing my tree. This was the tradition; a special little hut was prepared under a tree, where I would rest and recuperate alone for the next few weeks until I was well. When Mama and Aman had finished working, they carried me inside.

I thought the agony was over until I had to pee, then I understood my mother's advice not to drink too much milk or water. After hours of waiting, I was dying to go, but with my legs tied together I couldn't move. Mama had warned me not to walk, so that I wouldn't rip myself open, because if the wound is ripped open, then the sewing has to be done again. Believe me, that was the last thing I wanted.

"I have to pee-pee," I called to my sister. The look on her face told me this was not good news. She came and rolled me over on my side and scooped out a little hole in the sand.

"Go ahead."

The first drop came out and stung as if my skin were being eaten by acid. After the gypsy sewed me up, the only opening left for urine and menstrual blood was a minuscule hole the diameter of a matchstick. This brilliant strategy ensured that I could never have sex until I was married, and my husband would be guaranteed he was getting a virgin. As the urine collected in my bloody wound and slowly trickled down my legs onto the sand—one drop at a time—I began to sob. Even when the Killer Woman was cutting me to pieces I had never cried, but now it burned so badly I couldn't take any more.

In the evening, as it grew dark, my mother and Aman returned home to the family and I stayed in the hut by myself. But this time, I wasn't scared of the dark, or the lions or the snakes, even though I was lying there helpless, unable to run. Since the moment when I floated out of my body and watched that old woman sewing my sex together, nothing could frighten me. I simply lay on the hard ground like a log, oblivious to fear, numb with pain, unconcerned whether I would live or die. I couldn't care less that everyone else was at home laughing by the fire while I lay alone in the dark.

As the days dragged on and I lay in my hut, my genitals became infected and I ran a high fever. I faded in and out of consciousness. Dreading the pain of urination, I had held back the urge to pee until my mother said, "Baby, if you don't pee, then you're going to die," so I tried to force myself. If I had to go, and no one was around, then I scooted over an inch or so, rolled myself onto my side and prepared myself for the searing pain I knew was coming. But my wound became so infected for a time that I was unable to urinate at all. Mama brought me food and water for the next two weeks; other than that I lay there alone with my legs still tied together. And waited for the wound to heal. Feverish, bored, and listless, I could do nothing but wonder: Why? What was it all for? At that age I didn't understand anything about sex. All I knew was that I had been butchered with my mother's permission, and I couldn't understand why.

Finally, Mama came for me and I shuffled home, my legs still bound together. The first night back at my family's hut, my father asked, "How does it feel?" I assume he was referring to my new state of womanhood, but all I could think about was the pain between my legs. Since I was all of five years old, I simply smiled and didn't say anything. What did I know about being a woman? Although I didn't realize it at the time, I knew a lot about being an African woman: I knew how to live quietly with suffering in the passive, helpless manner of a child.

For over a month my legs were tied together so my wound would heal. My mother constantly admonished me not to run or jump, so I shuffled along gingerly. Considering I had always been energetic and active, running like a cheetah, climbing trees, jumping over rocks, this was another kind of agony for a young girl—sitting around while all my siblings were playing. But I was so terrified of having to go through the whole process again that I barely moved an inch. Each week Mama checked me to see if I was healing properly. When the ties that bound me were removed from my legs, I was able to look at myself for the first time. I discovered a patch of skin completely smooth except for a scar down the middle like a zipper. And that zipper was definitely closed. My genitals were sealed up like a brick wall that no man would be able to penetrate until my wedding night, when my husband would either cut me open with a knife or force his way in.

As soon as I could walk again, I had a mission. I'd been thinking about it every day as I lay there, for all those weeks, ever since the day that old woman butchered me. My mission was to go back to the rock where I'd been sacrificed and search to see if my genitals were still lying there. But they were gone—no doubt eaten by a vulture or hyena, scavengers who are part of the life cycle of Africa. Their role is to clear away carrion, the morbid evidence of our harsh desert existence.

Even though I suffered as a result of my circumcision, I was lucky. Things could have been much worse, as they frequently were for other girls. As we traveled throughout Somalia, we met families and I played with their daughters. When we visited them again, the girls were missing. No one spoke the truth about their absence, or even spoke of them at all. They had died as a result of their mutilation—from bleeding to death, shock, infection, or tetanus. Considering the conditions in which the procedure is performed, that isn't surprising. What's surprising is that any of us survived.

I barely remember my sister Halemo. I was around three, and I remember her being there, then she wasn't there anymore, but I didn't understand what had happened to her. Later I learned that when her "special time" came, and the old gypsy woman circumcised her, she bled to death.

When I was around ten, I heard the story of my younger cousin's experience. At the age of six she was circumcised, and afterward one of her brothers came to stay with our family and told us what had happened. A woman came and cut his sister, then she was placed in her hut to recuperate. But her "thingy," as he called it, began to swell, and the stench coming from her hut was unbearable. At the time he told this story, I didn't believe him. Why should she smell bad, as this had never happened to me or Aman? Now I realize he was telling the truth: as a result of the filthy conditions the practice is performed in, hacking girls up in the bush, her wound became infected. The awful smell is a symptom of gangrene. One morning, their mother came in to check on her daughter who, as usual, had spent the night alone in her hut. She found the little girl lying dead, her body cold and blue. But before the scavengers could clear away the morbid evidence, her family buried her.

5.

THE MARRIAGE CONTRACT

One morning I woke to the sound of people talking. I stood up from my mat and saw no one, so I decided to investigate. Through the early stillness I tracked the voices, jogging about half a mile to where my mother and father were waving good-bye to a group of people walking away. "Who is that, Mama?" I asked, pointing at the back of a slight woman with a scarf wrapped around her head.

"Oh, that's your friend, Shukrin."

"Is her family moving from here?"

"No, she's getting married," came my mother's reply.

Stunned, I stared at the figures disappearing. I was around thirteen, and Shukrin was only slightly older than me, about fourteen, and I couldn't believe she was getting married. "To whom?" No one answered me, as such a question was considered none of my business. "To whom?" I repeated my question, which was again met by silence. "Will she be leaving here—with the man she marries?" This was common practice and my greatest fear was that I would never see my friend again.

My father said gruffly, "Don't worry about it. You're next." My parents turned and walked back to our hut, while I stood there grappling with the news. Shukrin was getting married! Married! It was a term I'd heard over and over, but until that morning I'd never really questioned what it meant.

As a girl in Somalia, I never thought about marriage or sex. In my family—in our whole culture—nobody ever talked about any of that. It never, ever, came to mind. My only thoughts on boys were competing with them to see who could be best at caring for the animals, racing with them, and beating them up. The only thing anyone ever said on the topic of sex was "Be sure you don't mess with anybody. You're supposed to be a virgin when you marry." Girls know they will marry as a virgin, and will marry only one man, and that's it. That's your life.

My father used to say to my sisters and me, "You girls are my queens," because he was considered very lucky to have some of the best-looking daughters around. "You are my queens, and no man will mess with you. If he tries, just let me know. I'm here to protect you—I'll die for you."

More than one opportunity came for him to guard his "queens." My oldest sister, Aman, was out one day taking care of her animals, when a man approached her. This guy kept pestering her, and she kept repeating, "Leave me alone. I'm not interested in you." Finally, when his charm didn't work, he grabbed Aman and tried to force himself on her. This was a big mistake, because she was an amazon, well over six feet tall, and strong as any man. She beat him up, then came home and told my father the story. My father went looking for this poor fool, then *Papa* beat him up. No man would mess with his daughters.

One night I awoke when another sister, Fauziya, let out a piercing scream. As usual we were sleeping outside under the stars, but she was separated from the rest of us, and lay off to one side. I sat up and dimly saw the shape of a man running away from our camp. Fauziya continued to scream as my father jumped up and chased the intruder. We went to her and she reached down to touch her legs, which were covered with white, sticky semen. The man escaped from my father, but in the morning, we saw the prints of the pervert's sandals next to where my sister had slept. Papa had an idea who the culprit was, but couldn't be sure.

Sometime later, during an intense dry spell, my father had traveled to a local well to gather water. As he stood in the damp earth at the bottom, a man approached. This man grew restless waiting his turn for the water and yelled out to Papa, "Hey, come on! I got to get some water, too!" In Somalia, wells are open areas where someone has dug down deep enough to reach groundwater, sometimes one hundred feet deep. As water becomes scarcer, everyone becomes very competitive, trying to get enough water for the livestock. My father replied that the gentleman should come ahead and get what he needed.

"Yeah, I will." This man wasted no time and climbed down into the hole. He went about his business, filling his bags with water, and as he walked about, my father noticed the prints of his sandals in the mud.

"It was you, wasn't it?!" Papa said, grabbing the man by the shoulders and shaking him. "You sick bastard, you're the one who was messing with my girl!" My father hit him, beating him like the cur that he was. But the cur took out a knife, a big African killer knife, carved with an ornate pattern like a ceremonial dagger. He stabbed my father four or five times in the ribs, before Papa managed to wrestle the weapon away from him and stab the man with his own knife. Now they were both seriously wounded. My father barely managed to climb out of the well, and make it back to our hut; he returned home bloody and weak. After a long illness, Papa recovered, but I realized later he had told the truth: he'd been prepared to die for my sister's honor.

My father always joked with us girls, "You are my queens, my treasures, and I keep you under lock and key. And I've got the key!"

I would say, "But Papa, where's the key?"

He would laugh like a madman and say, "I threw it away!"

"Well, how are we going to come out?" I would cry, and we'd all laugh.

"You're not, my darling. Not till I say you're ready."

These jokes were handed down from my oldest sister, Aman, all the way to the youngest baby girl. But they were not really jokes. Without my father's permission, there would be no access to his daughters. But more was at stake here than Papa protecting us from unwanted advances. Virgins are a hot commodity in the African marriage market, one of the largest unspoken reasons for the practice of female circumcision. My father could expect a high price for beautiful virgin daughters but had little hope of unloading one who had been soiled by having sex with another man. When I was a girl, however, none of these facts concerned me, because I was a child and never thought about the subjects of sex or marriage.

That is, until I learned of my friend Shukrin's wedding. A few days later, my father came home one evening and I heard him call out, "Hey, where's Waris?"

"Over here, Papa," I yelled.

"Come here," he called in a soft voice. Normally he was very stern and aggressive, so I knew something was up. I assumed he wanted me to do him a favor, do something with the animals tomorrow, look for water, hunt for food, or some similar chore. So I stayed where I was, staring at my father cautiously, trying to imagine what he had planned for me. "Come, come, come, come," he said impatiently.

I walked a couple of steps toward him, eyeing him suspiciously, but didn't say anything. Papa grabbed me and sat me down on his knee. "You know," he began, "you been really good." Now I *knew* something serious was up. "You been really good, more like a boy, more like a son to me." I knew this was his highest praise.

"Hmmm," I responded, wondering why I was receiving such accolades.

"You've been just like a son to me, working hard as any man, taking good care of the animals. And I just want to let you know that I'm going to miss you very much." When he said this, I thought my father was afraid that I was going to run away like my sister Aman had. When Papa had tried to arrange her marriage, she ran away. He was afraid I was going to run away, too, and leave him and Mama with all the hard work.

A flood of tenderness came over me, and I hugged him, feeling guilty for being so suspicious. "Oh, Papa, I'm not going anywhere!"

He pulled back from me, and stared at my face. In a soft voice he said, "Yes, you are, my darling."

"Where am I going? I'm not going anywhere—I'm not leaving you and Mommy."

"Yes, you are, Waris. I found you a husband."

"No, Papa, no!" I jumped up and he tried to grab me back, tried to grab my arms and hold on to me. "I don't want to leave, I don't want to leave home, I want to stay with you and Mama!"

"Sh, sh, sh, it's going to be fine. I found you a good husband."

"Who?" I said, curious now.

"You will meet him."

My eyes filled with tears, even though I tried hard to be tough. I started swinging at him, and screaming, "I don't want to get married!"

"Okay, Waris, look . . ." Papa reached down and grabbed a rock, pulled his hands behind his back, and swapped the rock back and forth. Then he held his hands out in front of him, with both fists clenched, so I couldn't see which one held the prize. "Choose the right hand or the left hand. Choose the one that holds the rock. If you guess right, you're going to do what I say and have good luck for the rest of your life. If you choose wrong, your days will be full of sorrow, because you'll be banned from the family."

I stared at him, wondering what was going to happen if I chose the wrong hand. Was I going to die? I touched his left hand. He turned up an empty palm toward the sky. "I guess I'm not going to do what you tell me," I murmured sadly.

"We can do it again."

"No." I shook my head slowly. "No, Papa. I'm not going to marry."

"He's a good man!" my father cried. "You've got to trust me—I know a good man when I see one. And you're going to do what I say!"

I stood there with my shoulders slumped, feeling sick and scared, and shook my head.

He tossed the rock hiding in his right hand into the darkness and shouted, "Then you'll have bad luck all your life!"

"Well, I guess I'm the one who'll have to live with it, won't I?" He slapped me hard across the face, because no one talked back to my father. I realize now that he had to marry me off quickly, as much for this type of behavior as for any traditional reasons. I had grown into a rebel, a tomboy, sassy and fearless, and was getting a reputation as such. Papa had to find me a husband while I was still a valuable commodity, because no African man wanted to be challenged by his wife.

The next morning I got up and took my animals out to graze as usual. While I watched them I thought about this new notion of marriage. I tried to think of a plan to persuade my father to let me remain at home, but knew in my heart this would never happen. I wondered who my new husband would be. To date, my only childish romantic inkling had been an interest in Jamah the son of my father's friend. I had seen him many times, because our families often traveled together. Jamah was considerably older than me, and I thought him very good-looking, but he wasn't married yet. My father loved him like a son, and thought Jamah was a good son to his own father. But probably my biggest attraction to Jamah was that he'd once had a serious crush on my sister Aman and didn't know I was alive. I was just a little girl to him, where Aman had been a desirable woman. When I whispered that Jamah liked her, Aman waved her hand and said, "Pshhh." She never gave him a second look, because she'd seen enough of the nomadic life and had no desire to marry a man like our father. She always talked about going to the city and marrying a man with lots of money. And when Papa tried to marry her off to one of his fellow nomads, she ran away in search of her big city dreams. We never heard from her again.

All that day, as I sat watching my animals, I tried to convince myself that marriage might not be so bad, and envisioned myself living with Jamah, the way my mother and father lived together. As the sun was going down, I walked back to our camp with my herd. My little sister ran to meet me and announced, "Papa has somebody with him and I think they're waiting for you." My sister was suspicious of this sudden interest in Waris, thinking perhaps she was being left out of some worthwhile treat. But I shuddered, knowing my father was continuing with his plan—just as if I'd never objected.

"Where are they?" My sister pointed in one direction, and I turned and headed in the other.

"Waris, they're waiting for you!" she cried.

"Oh, shut up! Get away from me!" I put my goats in their pen and began to milk them. When I was about halfway through the job, I heard my father calling my name. "Yes, Papa. I'm coming." I stood up with dread but knew there was no point in putting off the inevitable. A small hope flickered that maybe my father would be waiting with Jamah, and I envisioned his smooth handsome face. I walked toward them with my eyes closed. "Please let it be Jamah . . ." I muttered as I stumbled along. Jamah had become my salvation from this unsavory notion of leaving home to live with a strange man.

Finally, I opened my eyes and stared into the blood-red sky; the sun melted into the horizon, and I saw two men in front of me in silhouette. My father said, "Oh, there you are. Come here, my darling. This is Mr.—"; I didn't hear another word he said. My eyes fastened onto a man sitting down, holding on to a cane. He was at least sixty years old, with a long white beard.

"Waris!" I finally realized my father was talking to me. "Say hello to Mr. Galool."

"Hello," I said, in the iciest voice I could muster. I had to be respectful, but I did not have to be enthusiastic. The old fool just sat there grinning at me, leaning on his stick with all his might, but did not reply. He probably didn't know what to say, looking at this girl he was about to marry, who only stared at him in horror. To hide the look in my eyes, I hung my head down and stared at the ground.

"Now, Waris, dear, don't be shy," Papa said. I looked at my father, and when he saw my face, he realized that his best tactic was to shoo me away, so I didn't scare off my prospective husband. "Well, okay, you go ahead and finish your chores." He turned to Mr. Galool and explained, "She's just a shy, quiet young girl." I didn't linger another second but ran back to my goats.

All that evening I thought about what my life would be like married to Mr. Galool. Never having been away from my parents, I tried to imagine living not with them, but instead with a person who I didn't even know. At least it was fortunate that I didn't add to my misery by including the thought of having sex with a disgusting old man. But at the tender age of thirteen, I was naive about that part of the bargain. As a distraction to take my mind off my marriage dilemma, I beat up my little brother.

Early the next morning my father called me. "You know who that was last night?"

"I can guess."

"That's your future husband."

"But Papa, he's so old!" I still couldn't believe my father thought so little of me that he'd send me to live with an old man like that.

"That's the best kind, darling! He's too old to run around, chasing after other women, bringing home other wives. He's not going to leave you—he'll look after you. And besides"—Papa grinned proudly—"do you know how much he's paying for you?"

"How much?"

"FIVE camels! He's giving me FIVE camels." Papa patted my arm. "I'm so proud of you."

I looked away from my father, watching the golden rays of morning sun bring the desert landscape to life. Closing my eyes, I felt its warmth on my face. My thoughts returned to the previous night when I couldn't sleep. Instead, I lay there sheltered in the midst of my family, watching the stars spin overhead, and made my decision. I knew if I protested against marrying the old man, that wouldn't be the end of the situation. My father would just find another man, then another one, then another one, because he was determined to get rid of me . . . and get his camels. I nodded my head. "Well, Father, I got to take my animals out now." Papa looked at me with satisfaction, and I could read his mind: "Hey, that was much easier than I thought it would be."

As I sat watching the goats playing that day, I knew it would be the last time I looked after my father's herd. I pictured my life with the old man, the two of us in some completely isolated desert place. Me doing all the work, while he limped around with his cane. Me living alone after he had a heart attack, or better yet, me raising four or five babies alone after he died, because in Somalia, widows do not remarry. I made up my mind—this was not the life for me. That night when I came home, my mother asked me what was wrong. "Have you met that man?" I snapped.

She didn't need to ask me which man. "Yes, I saw him the other day."

In a frantic whisper, so my father couldn't hear, I said, "Mama, I don't want to marry that man!"

She shrugged. "Well, my darling, it's out of my hands. What can I do? It's your father's decision." I knew that maybe tomorrow or the next day, my new husband would come for me, bringing his five camels in exchange. I formed my plan to run away before it was too late.

That evening after everyone went to sleep, I listened for Papa's familiar snoring. Then I got up and went to my mother, who still sat next to the fire. "Mama," I whispered, "I can't marry that man—I'm going to run away."

"Shhh, quiet! Where, child? Where are you going to go?"

"I'll find Auntie in Mogadishu."

"Do you know where she is? I don't!"

"Don't worry, I'll find her."

"Well, it's dark now," she rationalized, as if this could stop destiny.

"Not now, in the morning," I whispered. "Wake me up before the sun comes up." I knew I needed her help, because it wasn't as if I could just set the alarm clock. I needed to get some rest before I set off on my long journey, but I also needed to get a head start before my father woke up.

"No." She shook her head. "It's too dangerous."

"Oh, *please*! Mama, I cannot marry this man—go and be his wife! Please, please. I'll come back for you. You know I will."

"Go to bed." She had that stern look, her look that told me the subject was closed. I left my tired mother looking into the fire and I pushed into the tangle of arms and legs, between my brothers and sisters, to get warm.

While I was sleeping, I felt my mother lightly tap my arm. She knelt on the ground beside me. "Go now." Immediately I was jolted awake, then flooded with the sick sensation of what I had to do. I wriggled carefully from the warm bodies and checked to make sure my father was in his usual position guarding the family. He still lay snoring.

I shivered and walked away from our hut with my mother. "Mama, thank you for waking me." In the gloomy light I struggled to see her face, trying to memorize its features, because I wouldn't see that face again for a long time. I had planned to be strong, but instead choked on my tears and hugged her hard.

"Go—go before he wakes up," she said softly into my ear. I felt her arms tighten around me. "You're going to be all right—don't you worry about that. You just be very careful. Careful!" She turned me loose. "And Waris . . . please, one thing. Don't forget me."

"I won't, Mama . . ." I spun away from her and ran into the darkness.

6.

ON THE ROAD

We'd driven only a few kilometers when the elegantly dressed man pulled his Mercedes over. "I'm afraid this is as far as I'm going. I'll let you out here so you can get another ride."

"Oh . . ." This was disappointing news indeed, since after running away from my father, walking across the desert, starving for days, being stalked by a lion, whipped by a herdsman, and attacked by a truck driver, this gentleman in the Mercedes had been the best thing that had happened to me since I left home.

"Good luck on your journey," he called from the open window and, waving, displayed his white teeth again. I stood in the sun on the side of the dusty road and waved back without much enthusiasm. I watched his car speed away into the shimmering waves of heat and started walking again, wondering if I'd ever make it to Mogadishu.

That day I got a few more rides, but they were for short distances; in between I kept walking. As the sun was going down, another big truck pulled over to the side of the road.

Frozen with fear, I stared at the red brake lights, remembering my last experience with a trucker. While I stood there thinking, the driver turned around inside the cab to look at me. If I didn't act soon, I knew he'd pull away without me, so I hurried up to the cab. The truck was a huge semi; when the driver opened the door from inside, I struggled to climb in. "Where are you headed?" he said. "I'm only going as far as Galcaio."

When the driver said "Galcaio," a great idea flashed into my mind. I hadn't realized I was close to the city, but my rich uncle lived in Galcaio. Instead of wandering all over Somalia looking for Mogadishu, I could stay with Uncle Ahmed. In my mind we still had some unfinished business anyway, because I'd never received my shoes in exchange for taking care of his animals. I imagined eating a big meal at his fine home that night and sleeping there instead of under a tree. "Yeah, that's where I'm going." I smiled, liking the idea. "I'm headed to Galcaio, too." In the back, the truck was loaded with food: heaps of yellow corn, sacks of rice and sugar. Looking at them reminded me of how hungry I was.

The truck driver was about forty, and a big flirt. He kept trying to strike up a conversation; I wanted to be friendly, but I was disgustingly scared. The last thing I wanted was for him to think I was interested in messing around with him. Looking out the window, I tried to imagine the best way to find my uncle's house, since I had no idea where he lived. But then one of the driver's comments caught my attention: "You're running away, aren't you?"

"Why do you say that?" I said in surprise.

"I can just tell—I know you are. I'm turning you in."

"What—NO! Please, please . . . I'm going. I've got to go. I just want you to take me . . . take me to Galcaio. I've got to go visit my uncle there. He's expecting me." The look on his face told me he didn't believe me, but all the same he kept driving. My mind raced ahead—where should I tell the driver to let me out? After this story, that my uncle was expecting me, I couldn't admit I didn't know where to go. As we entered the city I looked around at the streets crowded with buildings, cars, and people; this was much bigger than the village I'd encountered earlier, and for the first time I realized what I was up against trying to find Uncle.

From high up in the cab of the semi, I nervously looked down on the confusion of Galcaio. To my eyes, the city was mass chaos, and I was torn between not wanting to get out of the truck, and feeling I'd better get out damn quick before this guy decided to turn me in as a runaway. When he pulled up next to an outdoor market, and I saw the stalls full of food, I decided to go. "Hey, um, friend, I'll get out here. My uncle lives down there," I said, pointing toward a side street and jumping out the door before he could stop me. "Thanks for the lift," I called as I slammed the door.

I walked through the market in astonishment. Never, ever in my life had I seen so much food. I remember thinking how beautiful it was! Piles of potatoes, mountains of corn, racks of dried pasta. And my God, all the colors! Bins piled high with bright yellow bananas, green and golden melons, and thousands and thousands of red tomatoes. I had never seen these foods before, and I stood in front of a display of tomatoes. This moment was the beginning of my love of luscious, ripe tomatoes, and to this day I've never gotten enough of them. I stared at the food, and all the people walking through the market stared at me. The woman who owned the stand headed toward me, frowning. She was a complete mama. (In Africa, "mama" is a term of respect for women. It means you're mature, you've come of age, and in order to deserve this title you must actually be a mother.) All her colors and scarves were flashing. "What do you want?" this mama demanded.

"Please, can I have some of this?" I said, pointing to the tomatoes.

"Do you have money?"

"No, but I'm so hungry—"

"Get out of here—GO!" she cried, shooing me away from her stall with one hand.

I went to another vendor and started in again. This woman said, "I don't need any beggars hanging around in front of my place. I'm trying to run a business here. Go on, go away."

I told her my story, that I needed to find Uncle Ahmed, and asked if she knew where he lived. I assumed since my uncle was a wealthy businessman, the people of Galcaio would know him. "Look, shut up. You can't come here from out in the bush and start shouting like that. Sh-h-h-h. Have some respect, girl. You have to be quiet. *Quiet.* Don't be yelling out your family names here in public." Staring at her, I thought, *Oh, Lord, what is this woman talking about, and how am I ever going to communicate with these people?*

Off to one side of us, a man leaned against a wall. He called out, "Girl, come here." I went to him excitedly and tried to explain my predicament. The man was about thirty, a very ordinary-looking African man—nothing special—but he had a friendly face. He said patiently, "Just hush. I can help you, but you've got to be careful. You can't go around yelling out the name of your tribe like that. Now what tribe are you?" I told him all I knew about my family and Uncle Ahmed. "Okay, I think I know where he lives. Let's go and I'll help you find him."

"Oh, please—please. Can you take me there?"

"Yeah, come on. Don't worry, we'll find your man." We walked away from the busy market area, heading down one of the shady side streets. The man paused in front of a house. "Are you hungry?" This, of course, was pitifully obvious to anyone with eyes.

"Yes."

"Well, this is my house. Why don't you come in and I'll give you something to eat, then we can find your uncle?" I gratefully accepted his offer.

When we went inside, I was struck by a very peculiar smell, some strange odor that I'd never smelled before. He sat me down and brought me food. As soon as I'd taken the last bite, he said, "Why don't you come lie down with me and have a nap?"

"A nap?"

"Yeah, take a rest."

"No, please, I just want to find my uncle."

"I know, I know. But first let's have a nap. It's siesta time. Then don't worry, we'll go find him."

"No, please. You go ahead—I'll wait for you here. I don't mind." Even though it was siesta time, I had no intention of lying down with this strange man. I knew at this point that something was very, very wrong. But ignorant little girl, I didn't know what to do about it.

"Look, little girl," he said in an angry tone, "if you want me to take you to find your uncle, you better lie down and have a nap." I knew I needed this man's help to find Uncle Ahmed. And as he grew increasingly belligerent and insistent, I became frightened, so I finally did the worst possible thing I could have done. I gave in to his suggestion. Of course, the minute we lay on his bed, a nap was the last thing on his mind. In two seconds this fucking ass was trying to get on top of me. When I struggled and turned away from him, he slapped the back of my head. Don't say a word, I thought; but seizing my opportunity, I leaped from his arms and tore out of the room. As I ran, I heard him calling from his bed, "Hey, little girl, come back here . . ." Then I heard a low laugh.

I bounded onto the dark street crying hysterically and fled back to the market seeking the safety of other people. An old mama came to me, a woman about sixty years old. "Child, what's the matter?" She took my arm firmly and made me sit down. "Come, come. Talk to me—tell me what's wrong." I couldn't bring myself to admit what had just happened. I was too embarrassed and ashamed to ever tell anyone. I felt like such a fool, such a stupid little fool because I had let the whole episode happen by going into his house. Between sobs I explained to her that I was looking for my uncle, and I couldn't find him.

"Who is your uncle? What's his name?"

"Ahmed Dirie."

The old mama lifted her bony finger and pointed toward a bright blue house diagonally across the corner. "It's right there," she said. "You see that? That's your house." It was right there. All along, it was right there, across the street from where I had stood begging that bastard to help me find my uncle. Later I realized that when I was telling him my story, he knew exactly who I was, and exactly who my uncle was. The old woman asked me if I wanted her to take me there. I looked at her hard, because now I didn't trust anyone. But in her face I could see that she was a real mother.

"Yes, please," I answered faintly.

We walked across the corner and I knocked on the door of the blue house. My aunt opened the door and stared at me in shock. "What are you doing here?" The old woman turned and walked away.

"Auntie, I'm here!" I replied stupidly.

"What in Allah's name are you doing here? You ran away, didn't you!?"

"Well . . ."

"I'm taking you back," she said firmly.

Uncle Ahmed, my father's brother, was amazed to see me as well, but particularly amazed that I was able to find his house. My explanation skipped the details of clobbering a truck driver with a boulder and nearly being raped by his neighbor. However, even though he was impressed with my ability to make my way across the desert and track him down, he had no intention of letting me stay. Uncle worried about who was

going to look after his animals—a task that had been my job for
years, and for all my trouble he'd bought me a pair of flip-flops.
All my father's older children were gone from home now. I was
the oldest one left—the tough one—who was more dependable
than the younger children. "No, you have to go back home.
Who's going to help your mother and father with all the work?
What are you going to do if you come here? Sit on your ass?"
Unfortunately, I didn't have good answers for any of these
questions. I knew there was no point telling him I ran away
because Papa was making me marry a white-bearded old man.
Uncle would look at me like I was crazy and say, "So? So?
Waris, you have to get married. Your father needs the camels
. . ." There was no point trying to explain that I was different
from my family; I loved my parents, but what they wanted for
me wasn't enough. I knew there had to be more to life,
although I wasn't sure what. After a few days I learned Uncle
had sent a messenger to look for my father, and Papa was on
his way.

I knew Uncle Ahmed's two sons well because they used to
come and stay with my family during holidays when they
weren't in school. They helped us care for their animals, and
taught us some Somali words. At the time, this was the
tradition: the kids who went to school in town came out into
the desert over break to teach the nomadic children. While I
was staying with them in Galcaio, my cousins mentioned
they knew where my oldest sister, Aman, was: when she ran
away from home, she went to Mogadishu and got married. I
was overjoyed at this news, because when she left I never
heard from her again; she might as well have been dead. I
realized talking to them that my parents had known where
Aman was, but she'd been banned from the family, so they
never spoke of her.

When I found out my father was coming to take me home,
we hatched a plan. The boys gave me directions on how to find
my sister once I arrived in the capital. And one morning they

led me to the road out of town, then gave me what little money they had. "There you go, Waris," they said, pointing. "That's the way to Mogadishu."

"Promise me you won't tell anyone where I've gone. Remember—when my father gets here, you don't know what happened to me. The last time you saw me was this morning at the house, okay?" They nodded and waved good-bye as I started walking.

The journey to Mogadishu was excruciatingly slow. It took days, but at least now that I had a little money, I was able to buy something to eat along the way. My rides were sporadic and I walked many miles in between. Frustrated with my slow progress, I finally paid for a ride aboard an African bush taxi, a big truck with about forty people aboard. These trucks are common in Africa. After dumping their load of grain or sugarcane, they'll take passengers back in the empty trailer. Around the bed of the truck is a wooden frame like a fence; sitting or standing beside it, the people on board look like children in a gigantic playpen. The bush taxi is also crowded with babies, luggage, household goods, furniture, live goats, and crates of chickens, and the driver will pack on as many paying passengers as he can get. But after my recent experiences, I was willing to be crowded in with a large group, rather than going alone with strange men. When we got to the outskirts of Mogadishu, the truck stopped and let us off at a well where people had gathered to water their animals. I cupped some water in my hands and scooped up a drink, then splashed some on my face. I'd noticed that by this time there were many roads, since Mogadishu is the largest city in Somalia, with a population of seven hundred thousand. I approached two nomads standing with their camels and asked, "Do you know which of these roads goes to the capital?"

"Yeah, over there," the man said, pointing. I headed off in the direction he'd shown me, walking toward the interior of the city. Mogadishu is a port city on the Indian Ocean, and it was beautiful then. Walking along, I craned my neck to look at the stunning white buildings surrounded by palm trees and brightly colored flowers. Much of the architecture was built by the Italians while Somalia was an Italian colony, giving the city a Mediterranean feel. The women walking past me wore gorgeous scarves in yellow, red, and blue prints. The long scarves circled their faces, and they'd hold them under their chins as the sea breezes lifted the ends. The filmy fabric floated gracefully behind the women as they undulated down the street. I saw many Moslem women with scarves draped over their heads, the dark veils covering their faces altogether. I stared at them, wondering how they could find their way. The city sparkled in the bright sun and all the colors seemed electrified.

As I walked, I stopped people and asked directions to my sister's neighborhood. I had no street address but planned to repeat my system of finding Uncle Ahmed in Galcaio; once I got to her area, I'd go to the market and ask if anyone knew her. However, I would not be so gullible this time about letting strange men "help me."

When I arrived in the neighborhood, I quickly found a market and strolled through examining the food, deciding what I would buy with the last of my precious Somali shillings. Finally, I bought some milk at a stall run by two women; I chose them because their milk was the best price. But when I took the first sip of it, I knew something was fishy—it didn't taste right. "What's wrong with this milk?" I asked.

"Nothing! Nothing is wrong with our milk!"

"Ah, come on. One thing I know about is *milk*. It doesn't taste right. Did you put water in it or something?" Finally they admitted they mixed the milk with water so they could sell it cheaper. Their customers didn't mind. Our conversation continued and I told them I'd come to the capital to find my sister, asking if they knew Aman.

"Yeah, I thought you looked familiar!" one of the women cried. I laughed, because when we were little, I was the spitting image of my sister. They knew her because she came to that market every day. The milk lady called to her young son and told him to show me where my sister lived. "Take her to Aman's house, then come straight back here!" she commanded the boy.

We walked along the quiet streets; by now it was siesta time and people were resting from the heat of midday. The boy pointed out a tiny shack. I walked inside the house and found my sister asleep. Shaking her arm, I woke her up. "What are you doing here . . ." she said groggily, looking at me as if I were a dream. I sat down on the bed and told her my story, that I had run away just as she did many years ago. At last I had someone to talk to who I knew would understand. She would understand that at thirteen, I just couldn't bring myself to marry this stupid old man for Papa's sake.

Aman told me how she had come to Mogadishu and found her own husband. He was a good, quiet man who worked hard. She was expecting their first child, which was due in about a month. But when she stood up, she certainly didn't appear to be a woman about to give birth. At six foot two, she merely seemed tall and elegant, and in her loose African dress, she didn't even look pregnant. I remember thinking how beautiful she was, and hoped I carried my baby so well when I was expecting.

After we talked for a while, I finally worked up the courage to ask the question I'd been dying to ask: "Aman, please. I don't want to go back—can I stay here with you?"

"So you ran away and left Mama with all the work," she said sadly. But she agreed I could stay as long as I needed. Her cramped place had two rooms: a tiny one where I slept and another room she shared with her husband. We seldom saw him, however; he left in the morning and went to work, came home for lunch, took a nap, then went back to work, returning late in the evening. When he was in the house he had so little to say that I can barely remember anything about him—his name even, or what he did for a living.

Aman gave birth to a beautiful little girl and I helped take care of the baby. I also cleaned the house and carried our clothes outside and scrubbed them, hanging them on the line to dry.

I went to the market and did the shopping, learning the fine art of haggling with the vendors over prices. Mimicking the locals, I walked up to a stand and immediately demanded, "How much?" The ritual might as well have been scripted, because every day it was the same: a mama places in front of me three tomatoes, one big one and two smaller ones, and quotes me the price I'd expect to pay for three camels.

"Ah, too much," I'd respond with a bored look and a wave of my hand.

"Well, come, come, come, how much you wanna pay?"

"Two fifty."

"Oh, no, no, no! Now come *on* . . ." At this point I'd make a great show of walking away and talking to the other vendors with keen interest, always in direct view of my target. And then I'd go back and pick up where I left off, arguing until one of us got tired and gave in.

My sister constantly mentioned her concern for our mother; she worried that since I'd run away, Mama was stuck doing all the work alone. Whenever she brought up this subject, it was as if the sole blame for the situation rested on me. I shared her worry over Mama, but Aman never mentioned that *she'd* run away, also. Forgotten memories of our childhood years together came back to me now. Much had changed in the five or so years since I'd last seen her, but to Aman I was still the same goofy little sister she'd left behind; meanwhile, she would always, *always* be the oldest and the wisest. It became clear to me that even though we looked alike, our personalities were nothing alike. I grew resentful of her constant bossiness. When Papa tried to marry me off to the old man, I ran away because I thought there had to be more to life. And cooking, washing, and taking care of babies—something I'd already had plenty of with my little brothers and sisters—was not what I had in mind.

One day I left Aman's to find out what else fate had in store for me. I didn't discuss it with her; I didn't tell her I was leaving—I simply walked out one morning and never came back. It seemed like a good idea at the time, but I didn't know then that I'd never see her again.

7.

MOGADISHU

While I was living with Aman, she took me to visit some of our other relatives who were living in Mogadishu. For the first time in my life, I was able to meet some of my mother's family. She grew up in the capital with her mother, four brothers, and four sisters.

I'm grateful I got to know my grandmother while I was in Mogadishu. Today, she's around ninety years old, but when I first met her, she was in her seventies. Granny is a complete mama. Her face is light-skinned, and shows that she's a tough cookie, a woman of character and strong will. Her hands look like she's been digging in the earth so long that they've developed crocodile hide.

My grandmother grew up in one of the Arab countries, but I don't know which one. She's a devout Moslem, prays five times a day facing Mecca, and always wears a dark veil over her face when she leaves the house; she's covered up from head to toe. I used to tease her: "Granny, are you okay? You sure you know where you're going? Can you see through that thing?"

"Oh, come, come, come," she'd bark. "This thing is completely see-through."

"Good—so you can breathe and everything?" I'd laugh.

Staying at my grandmother's house, I realized where Mama got her strength. My grandfather had been dead many years, and Granny lived alone, taking care of everything by herself. And when I went to visit her, she'd wear me out. As soon as we got up in the morning she was ready to go. She'd start in on me right away: "Get going. Come on, Waris. Let's go."

Granny lived in a neighborhood of Mogadishu that was a good distance from the market. Each day we'd shop for food, and I'd say, "Come on, Granny—let's take it easy and ride the bus. It's hot and the market's too far from here to walk."

"What!? *Bus!* Now, come, come, come. Let's go. Young girl like you, wanting to take the bus. What are you complaining about? You're getting lazy these days, Waris. All you children today—I don't know what's wrong with you. When I was your age, oh, I'd walk for miles and miles . . . girl, are you coming with me or not?" So off we went together, because if I dawdled, she was obviously going to go without me. On the way home, I'd come trudging along behind her, carrying the bags.

After I left Mogadishu, one of my mother's sisters died, leaving nine children. My grandmother took care of these kids, raising them just as she did her own. She's a mama and she did what had to be done.

I met another one of her sons, Mama's brother Wolde'ab. I had gone to the market one day, and when I returned, he was sitting at my grandmother's with one of my cousins on his lap. Even though I'd never seen him before, I ran to him, because suddenly here was this man who looked exactly like my mother—and I was desperate for anything that reminded me of Mama. I ran to him, and since I also look very much like my mother, it was a wonderful but strange moment, like looking in some sort of crazy, distorted mirror. He had heard that I'd run away and was staying in Mogadishu. As I came closer to him, he said, "Is this who I think it is?" That afternoon I laughed more than I had since I left home, because not only did Uncle Wolde'ab look like my mother, he had her silly sense of humor. The brother and sister must have been quite a team growing up, cracking everyone in the family up till they cried, and I wish I could have seen them together.

But it was to Aunt L'uul's home that I went the morning I ran away from my sister's. Shortly after I arrived in Mogadishu, we had gone there together for a visit. The day I left Aman's, I decided that I would go to Aunt L'uul's house and ask if I could stay with her. She was my aunt by marriage, since she was married to my mother's brother, Uncle Sayyid. However, she spent her days raising their three children alone, as he was living in Saudi Arabia. Because the economy in Somalia was so poor, Uncle worked in Saudi and sent money back home to support his family. Unfortunately, he was away the whole time I lived in Mogadishu, so I never got to meet him.

When I arrived, Aunt L'uul was surprised, but she seemed genuinely glad to see me. "Auntie, things aren't working out very well between Aman and me, and I wondered if I could stay here with you for a while."

"Well, yes, you know I'm here by myself with the children. Sayyid is gone most of the time and I could use a hand. That would be nice." Immediately I felt relieved; Aman had grudgingly let me stay with her, but I knew she didn't like the situation. Her place was too tiny, and she was still a relative newlywed. Besides, what she really wanted was for me to go back home, to ease her conscience about running away from Mama all those years ago.

Staying first at Aman's, then Auntie L'uul's, I got accustomed to life indoors. At first, the confinement of living in a house seemed strange to me—having my view of the sky blocked by a ceiling, the space I could move around in limited by walls, the brush and animal smells of the desert replaced by the sewage and carbon monoxide smells of a crowded city. Auntie's place was somewhat bigger than Aman's, but still not spacious by any means. And even though the facilities offered me new luxuries—keeping warm at night and dry when it rained— they were primitive by contemporary Western standards. My respect for water continued, as it remained a precious com- modity. We purchased it from a vendor who transported his wares through the neighborhood by donkey, then we stored the water outside in a barrel. The family dipped it out sparingly for bathing, cleaning, making tea, cooking. In the small kitchen, Auntie prepared meals on a camp stove using bottled gas. In the evening, we sat around the house and talked by kerosene lamps, as there was no electricity. The toilet was typical of this part of the world: a hole in the floor where the waste fell and remained stinking in the heat. Bathing meant carrying a bucket of water in from the barrel outside, and sponging off, letting the excess run down the hole into the toilet.

Soon after I arrived at Auntie L'uul's, I realized I was getting more than I'd bargained for when I asked for a place to stay. I was also getting a full-time job as baby-sitter for her three rotten children. Well, I guess I couldn't really categorize the little baby as rotten, but its behavior distressed me all the same.

Each morning Auntie got up around nine, and right after breakfast she gleefully left the house to visit her friends. Then she spent the entire day with these women, gossiping endlessly about their friends, enemies, acquaintances, and neighbors. Eventually she meandered back home in the evening. While she was gone, the three-month-old baby cried constantly, wanting to be fed. When I held it, it started sucking me. Every day I would say, "Look, Auntie—for God's sake—you've got to do something. The baby's trying to suck me every time I pick it up, and I don't have any milk. I don't even have any breasts!"

"Well, don't worry. Just give him some milk," she said pleasantly.

Besides cleaning the house, and taking care of the baby, there was a nine-year-old and a six-year-old to look after. And these two were like wild animals. They had no idea how to behave, because obviously their mother never taught them anything. I tried to rectify this situation immediately by whipping their ass every chance I got. But after years of running around like hyenas, they were not going to become little angels over night.

As the days passed, I got more and more frustrated. I wondered how many more of these hopeless situations I was going to have to go through before something positive happened. I was always looking for a way to make things better, push myself forward, and find whatever that mysterious opportunity was that I knew was waiting for me. Every day I wondered, "When is it going to happen? Is it today? Tomorrow? Where am I going to go? What am I going to do?" Why I thought this, I've never known. I guess at that time I thought everyone had these voices inside them. But as far back as I can remember, I always knew my life was going to be different from those around me; I just had no idea how different.

My stay with Aunt L'uul reached a crisis after I'd been there about a month. Late one afternoon, as Auntie was off making her rounds of the gossip mill, the oldest child, her nine-year-old daughter, disappeared. First I went outside and called her. When she didn't reply, I started walking through the neighborhood looking for her. Finally, I found her in a tunnel with a young boy. She was a strong-minded, inquisitive child, and by the time I caught up to her, she had become very inquisitive about this little boy's anatomy. I marched into the tunnel, grabbed her arm, and jerked her to her feet; the boy took off running like a frightened animal. All the way back to the house I whipped my cousin with a switch, as I had never been so disgusted with a child in my life.

That evening when her mother came home, the daughter cried about the spanking I had given her. Aunt L'uul was furious. "Why are you spanking this child?" she demanded. "You keep your hands off my baby or I'm going to beat you up and see how you like it!" she shouted, and came toward me menacingly.

"Believe me, you don't want to know the reason I spanked her, because you don't want to know what I know! If you had seen what she did today, you would say she's no daughter of yours. This child is out of control—she's like an animal." My explanation did not make matters any better between the two of us. Suddenly after leaving me—a thirteen-year-old girl—to cope with three children under the age of ten, her daughter's welfare was of major importance to her. My aunt came at me shaking her fist, threatening to beat me for what I'd done to her little angel. But I'd had enough—not only from her, but from the whole world. "Look, you're not going to touch me!" I screamed. "If you do, you're going to wind up bald-headed." This ended any discussion of anyone beating me, but I knew at this point I had to go. But where would I run to this time?

Raising my fist to knock on Aunt Sahru's door, I thought, *Here we go again, Waris.* Sheepishly, I said hello when she answered the door. Auntie Sahru was Mama's sister. And she had five children. This fact, I felt, did not bode well for my happiness in her household, but what choice did I have? Become a pickpocket or beg for food on the street? Without going into details about my departure from Auntie L'uul's, I asked if I could stay with her family for a while.

"You have a friend here," she said to my surprise. "If you want to stay with us, you can. If you want to talk about anything, I'm here." Things were off to a better start than I'd imagined. As expected, I began helping around the house. But Auntie Sahru's oldest daughter, Fatima, was nineteen years old. The majority of the responsibility for running the house fell to her.

My poor cousin Fatima worked like a slave. She got up early each day and went to college, then came home at twelve-thirty to cook lunch, returned to school and came back again around six in the evening to make dinner. After dinner she would clean up, then study late into the night. For some reason her mother treated her differently, demanding much more from her than she did from any of the other children. But Fatima was good to me; she treated me like a friend, and at that time in my life I certainly needed one. However, the way she was treated by her mom seemed unfair to me, so I tried to help my cousin in the kitchen at night. I didn't know how to cook, but I tried to learn by watching her. The first time I ever tasted pasta was when Fatima made it, and I thought I was in heaven.

My responsibilities were largely cleaning, and to this day Auntie Sahru says I'm the best cleaner she ever had. I scrubbed and polished the house, which was hard work. But I definitely preferred cleaning to baby-sitting, especially after my adventures of the past few months.

Like Aman, Auntie Sahru continued to worry about my mother, and the fact that Mama was left without any older girls to help her with the work. My father might help with the animals, but he wouldn't lift a finger to help with the cooking, or clothing, or making baskets, or taking care of the children. This was woman's work, and Mama's problem. After all, hadn't he done his part by bringing home another wife to help? Yes, he certainly had. But I, too, had been worried about this issue since the dark morning when I last saw my mother. Whenever I thought of her, I remembered her face in the firelight the night before I left, and how tired she'd looked. While I was running across the desert looking for Mogadishu, I couldn't get these thoughts out of my mind. The journey had seemed as endless as my dilemma: Which would I chose—my desire to take care of my mother or my desire to be rid of the old man? I remember collapsing under a tree at dusk and thinking, *Who's going to look after Mama now? She's going to look after everyone else, but who's going to look after her?*

There was no point in turning back now, however; it would simply mean I had gone through all the hardships of the past few months for nothing. If I went back home, a month wouldn't pass before my father started dragging around every lame, decrepit fool in the desert who owned a camel, trying to marry me off. Then not only would I be stuck with a husband, I still wouldn't be there to take care of my mother. But one day I decided that a partial remedy for this problem was to earn some money and send it to her. Then she could buy some of the things my family needed and wouldn't have to work so hard.

I set out to find a job, and began looking all over the city. One day my aunt sent me to the market to do her shopping, and on the way home I passed a construction site. I stopped and watched the men carrying bricks, mixing pits of mortar by tossing in shovels of sand and stirring in water with a hoe. "Hey," I yelled out, "do you have any jobs?"

The guy laying bricks stopped and started laughing at me. "Who wants to know?"

"I do. I need a job."

"Nope. We don't have any work for a skinny girl like you. Somehow I don't think you're a bricklayer." He laughed again.

"Hey, you're wrong," I assured him. "I can do it—I'm very strong. Really." I pointed at the guys mixing the mortar; they stood there with their pants hanging down to their buttocks. "I can help them. I can bring all the sand, and mix as good as they can."

"Okay, okay. When can you start?"

"Tomorrow morning."

"Be here at six and we'll see what you can do." I floated back to Auntie Sahru's without touching the ground. I had a job! I would be earning money—real cash! And I would save every penny and send it to Mama. She'd be so surprised.

When I got to the house, I told Auntie my news. She couldn't believe it. "You got a job *where?*" First of all, she couldn't believe any girl would want to do this kind of work. "And exactly what are you going to do for these men?" she asked. Second, she couldn't believe the boss would hire a female, especially me, as I still looked half-starved. But when I insisted it was true, she had no choice but to believe me.

Once she believed me, she was angry that I planned to live with her, yet instead of helping out with the household chores, I'd be working for someone else. "Look," I said tiredly. "I need to send Mama money, and in order to do that, I have to get a job. Either it's this one, or a different one, but all the same, I have to do it. Okay?"

"All right."

The next morning my career as a construction worker began. And it was horrible. I struggled carrying back-breaking loads of sand all day; I didn't have any gloves, the bucket handle cut into my hands. Then, along my palms, I developed enormous blisters. By the end of the day the blisters had burst and my hands were bleeding. Everyone thought that was the end of me, but I was determined to come back the next morning.

I stuck it out for a month, before my hands were so torn up and sore that I could barely bend them. But by the time I quit, I had saved the equivalent of sixty dollars. I told my auntie proudly that I had saved some money to send home to Mama. Recently a man she knew had visited us; he was soon heading out into the desert with his family and offered to take the money to my mother. Auntie Sahru said, "Yeah, I know his people; they're all right. You can trust them to take the money." Needless to say, that was the end of my sixty dollars. After all that, I found out later that my mother never saw a penny of it.

When I retired from construction work, I started cleaning house for my aunt again. Not long after this, I was working one day as usual, when a distinguished guest arrived: the Somalian ambassador to London. The ambassador, Mohammed Chama

Farah, happened to be married to yet another aunt, my mother's sister Maruim. As I dusted my way around the next room, I overheard the ambassador talking to Auntie Sahru. He had come to Mogadishu to find a servant before he began his four-year diplomatic appointment in London. Instantly, I knew this was it. This was the opportunity I had been waiting for.

Bursting into the room, I called to Aunt Sahru, "Auntie, I need a conversation."

She looked at me in exasperation. "What is it, Waris?"

"Please—in here." When she walked through the door and out of his sight, I grabbed hold of her arm fiercely. "Please. Please tell him to take me. I can be his maid." She looked at me and I could see the hurt on her face. But I was a strong-willed kid only thinking about what I wanted, instead of what she'd done for me.

"You! You don't know nothing about nothing. What are you going to do in London?"

"I can clean! Tell him to take me to London, Auntie! I want to GO!"

"I don't think so. Now, stop bothering me and get to work." She walked back into the other room and sat beside her brother-in-law. I heard her say quietly, "Why don't you take her? You know—she really is good. She's a good cleaner."

Auntie called me into the room and I leaped through the door. I stood there with my feather duster in my hand, smacking my gum. "I'm Waris. You're married to Auntie, aren't you?"

The ambassador frowned at me. "Would you mind taking that chewing gum out of your mouth?" I spat the wad into the corner. He looked at Auntie Sahru. "This is the girl? Oh, no, no, no."

"I'm excellent. I can clean, I can cook—and I'm good with children, too!"

"Oh, I'm sure you are."

I turned to Auntie. "Tell him—"

"Waris, that's enough. Get back to work."

"Tell him I'm the best!"

"Waris! Shush!" To my uncle she said, "She's young still, but she really is a hard worker. Believe me, she'll be okay . . ."

Uncle Mohammed sat still for a moment looking at me with disgust. "Okay, listen. I'm taking you tomorrow. Okay? I'll be here in the afternoon with your passport, then we'll go to London."

8.

GOING TO LONDON

London! I didn't know anything about it, but I liked the sound of it. I didn't know where it was, but I knew it was very far away. And far away was where I wanted to be. It seemed like the answer to my prayers, and yet too good to be true. I wailed, "Auntie, am I really going?"

She wagged her finger at me sternly. "You shut up. Don't start." When she saw the look of panic on my face, she smiled. "All right. Yes, you're really going."

On fire with excitement, I ran to tell my cousin Fatima, who was just starting dinner. "I'm going to London! I'm going to London!" I shouted and began to dance in circles around the kitchen.

"What? London!" She grabbed my arm in midspin and made me explain. "You're going to be white," Fatima announced matter-of-factly.

"What did you say?"

"You're going to be white, you know . . . *white.*"

I did not know. I had no idea what she was talking about,

since I had never seen a white person, and in fact didn't know such a thing existed. However, her comment didn't trouble me in the slightest. "Shut up, please," I said in my most superior fashion. "You're just jealous that I'm going to London and you're not." I resumed my dancing, swaying and clapping my hands as if I were celebrating the rain, then chanted, "I'm going to London! Ohhh-aiyeee—I'm going to London!"

"WARIS!" Aunt Sahru called in a threatening tone.

That evening Auntie outfitted me for my journey; I received my first pair of shoes—fine leather sandals. On the plane I wore a long, brightly colored dress she'd given me, covered by a loose African robe. I had no luggage, but it didn't matter because I had nothing to take, except the outfit I'd be wearing when Uncle Mohammed picked me up the next day.

As we left for the airport, I hugged and kissed Auntie Sahru, dear Fatima, and all my little cousins good-bye. Fatima had been so kind to me that I wanted to take her with me. But I knew there was only a job for one person, and since that was the case, I was glad it was me. Uncle Mohammed gave me my passport and I looked at it in wonder—my first official document—since I had never owned a birth certificate, or any paper with my name on it. Getting into the car, I felt very important and waved farewell to the family.

Before this day I had seen airplanes from the ground; occasionally I would even see them fly overhead in the desert when I was out tending my goats, so I knew such things existed. But I certainly had never seen one up close until the afternoon I left Mogadishu. Uncle Mohammed walked me through the airport, and we paused at the door leading outside to the plane. On the tarmac, I saw a gigantic British jet gleaming in the African sun. It was at this point I heard my uncle jabbering something about ". . . and your Aunt Maruim is expecting you in London; I'll join you in a few days. I've got some business to finish up here before I can leave."

My mouth gaped as I turned around to stare at him. He thrust the plane ticket into my hand. "Now, don't lose your ticket—or your passport—Waris. These are very important documents, so hang on to them."

"You're not coming with me?" It was all I could do to choke out these words.

"No," he said impatiently, "I have to stay here for a few more days." I immediately started to cry, scared of going alone, and now that leaving Somalia was imminent, I wasn't sure it was such a good idea after all. For all its problems, it was the only home I'd ever known, and what waited ahead of me was a complete mystery.

"Go on—you'll be fine. Somebody's going to meet you in London; they'll tell you what to do when you get there." I snuffled and let out a little whimper. Uncle pushed me gently toward the door. "Go on now, the plane is leaving. Just get on . . . GET ON THE PLANE, WARIS."

Stiff with dread I walked across the sizzling tarmac. I studied the ground crew scurrying around the jet, preparing for takeoff. My eyes followed men loading luggage, the crew checking the plane, then I looked up the stairs, wondering how I was supposed to get inside this thing. Deciding on the stairs, I started up. But unused to walking in shoes, I had to struggle to make it up the slick aluminum steps without tripping over my long dress. Once on board, I had no idea where to go, and must have looked like a perfect idiot. All the other passengers were already seated, and as they sat looking at me inquiringly, I could read their faces: "Who on earth is this dumb country girl who doesn't even know how to travel on an airplane?" I spun around just inside the door and sat in an empty seat.

This was the first time I ever saw a white person. A white man sitting next to me said, "This is not your seat." At least I assume that's what he said, since I spoke not one word of English. Staring at him in panic, I thought, *Oh, Lord. What is this man saying to me? And why does he look like that?* He repeated his statement, and I repeated my panic. But then, thank God, the flight attendant came and took the ticket from my hand. Obviously, this woman knew that I was completely clueless. She took my arm and led me down the aisle to my seat—which was certainly not in first class, where I'd originally deposited myself. As I passed, each face turned to stare at me. The attendant smiled and pointed to my seat. I flopped down, grateful to be out of view; with a goofy grin, I jerked my head at her by way of saying thanks.

Shortly after takeoff, the same flight attendant returned with a basket of sweets, which she held out to me with a smile. I took one hand and picked up the fold of my dress to make a pouch, as if I were gathering fruit, and with the other, grabbed a huge handful of candy. I was famished, so I planned to load up. Who knew when I'd see any more food? As my hand came back for a second swipe, the attendant tried to move the candy out of my reach. I stretched, grabbing at the basket as she moved it farther and farther away. Her face said, "Oh, my. What am I going to do with this one?"

While I unwrapped and devoured my candy, I examined the white people around me. They looked cold and sickly to me. "You need sun," I would have said to them if I had known English; I assumed this problem was a temporary condition. They couldn't always look like that, could they? These people must have turned white because they'd been out of the sun too long. Then I decided I wanted to touch one of them the first chance I got, because maybe the white would rub off. Perhaps underneath they were really black.

After about nine or ten hours on the plane, I was desperate to pee. I was absolutely bursting, but I had no idea where to go. I thought, come on, Waris, you can figure this out. So I watched closely how all the people sitting around me got up and went to this one door. This must be it, I reasoned. I got up, and went to the door just as someone else was coming out. Once inside, I closed the door, and looked around. This has to be the right place, but where's the right spot? I looked at the sink, but disregarded it. I examined the seat, sniffed, and decided this was the right spot for my business. Happily, I sat down and—phew!

I was greatly relieved until I stood up and realized that my pee-pee was just sitting there. Now what do I do? I didn't want to leave it there for the next person to come in and see it. But how do I get it out of there? I couldn't speak English—or read—so the word *Flush* printed over the button meant nothing to me. And even if I'd understood the word, I'd never seen a flush toilet in my life. Studying every lever, knob, and screw in the room, I wondered if *this one* was the right one to make my urine disappear. Time after time, I returned to the flush button, as it seemed the obvious choice. But I was afraid if I pushed it, the plane would blow up. In Mogadishu, I'd heard of such things happening. With the constant political fighting there, people talked of bombs and explosions, blowing up this and blowing up that. Maybe if I pressed this button, the whole plane would explode and we'd all die. Maybe that's what this button said; it warned: DO NOT PRESS! WILL BLOW UP PLANE. Best not to chance it over a little pee-pee, I decided. Still, I didn't want to leave the traces of my business for others to find. And I knew they'd know exactly who left it, because by now, they were all outside pounding on the door.

In a flash of inspiration I grabbed up a used paper cup and filled it from the drizzling faucet. I poured this into the toilet, reasoning if I diluted the urine enough, the next person in would think this bowl was simply full of water. Steadily I set to work, filling the cup and pouring, filling the cup and pouring. By now, people were not only pounding on the door, they were shouting, too. And I couldn't even answer them with "Just a minute . . ." So, in silence, I kept working at my plan, filling up the soggy cup from the dripping faucet, and pouring it into the toilet bowl. I stopped when the water level was right under the rim of the seat; I knew if I added another drop, it was going to pour out onto the floor. But at least the contents looked like ordinary water, so I stood up, smoothed down my dress, and opened the door. Looking down, I pushed past the throng gathered outside, grateful that at least I hadn't poo-pooed.

When we landed at Heathrow, my fear at coping with the strange country was outweighed by my relief to get off that plane. At least Auntie would be there to greet me, and I was thankful for that. As the plane descended, the sky outside the window changed from foamy white clouds to a gray blur. When the other passengers stood up, I stood up, and let myself be swept along in the tide of bodies exiting the plane, with no idea of where to go, what to do. The crowd pushed forward until we reached a set of stairs. There was only one problem: the stairs were moving. I stopped cold, watching them. The sea of people parted around me, and I watched them smoothly step on the moving stairs and rise to the top. Mimicking them, I stepped forward too, and boarded the escalator. But one of my new sandals slipped off and stayed on the floor. "My shoe! My shoe!" I cried in Somali and rushed back to retrieve it. But the mob packed on behind me wouldn't let me pass.

When we got off the escalator, I limped along with the crowd, wearing only one sandal. Next we reached customs. I looked at the white men in their very proper British uniforms—only I had no idea who these people were. A customs official spoke to me in English, and seizing my chance for assistance, I gestured back toward the escalator, shouting in Somali, "My shoe! My shoe!"

He glared at me steadily with a bored, long-suffering expression, and repeated his question. I giggled nervously, temporarily forgetting my shoe. The official pointed at my passport, and I handed it to him. After examining it closely, he stamped it and waved me through.

Outside customs, a man in a chauffeur's uniform walked up to me and asked in Somali, "Are you here to work for Mr. Farah?"

I was so relieved to find someone who could speak my language, I cried ecstatically, "Yes! Yes! That's me, I'm Waris." The driver started to lead me away, but I stopped him. "My shoe, we have to go downstairs and get my shoe."

"Your shoe?"

"Yes, yes, it's back there."

"Where is it?"

"It's at the bottom of those moving stairs." I pointed in the opposite direction. "I lost it when I got on." He looked down at my one sandaled foot and one bare foot.

Luckily, the driver also spoke English, so he got permission for us to reenter the gate and fetch my missing sandal. But when we reached the point where I'd left my shoe, there was no sign of it. I couldn't believe my bad luck. I took off my other sandal and carried it in my hand, scanning the floor as we came back upstairs. But now I had to go through customs all over again. This time the same official got to ask me the questions he'd wanted to ask the first time around, by using the chauffeur to translate.

"How long are you staying?" the customs man asked me. I shrugged. "Where are you going?"

"To live with my uncle, the ambassador," I said proudly.

"Your passport says you're eighteen; is that correct?"

"Huh? I am not eighteen!" I protested to the driver. He translated to the customs man.

"Do you have anything to declare?" This question I didn't understand.

The driver explained, "What are you bringing with you into the country?" I held up my one sandal. The customs official stared at my shoe for a minute, then shaking his head slightly, returned my passport and flagged us through.

As the driver led me out of the crowded airport, he

explained, "Look, your passport says you're eighteen, so that's what I told the man. If anyone asks you, you should say you're eighteen."

"I am NOT eighteen," I said angrily. "That's old!"

"Well, how old are you?"

"I don't know—maybe fourteen—but I'm not *that* old!"

"Look, that's what your passport says, so that's how old you are now."

"What are you talking about? I don't care what my passport says—why does it say that, when I'm telling you it's not true?"

"Because that's what Mr. Farah told them."

"Well, he's crazy! He doesn't know anything!" By the time we reached the exit we were shouting and Uncle Mohammed's chauffeur and I had developed a hearty dislike for each other.

As I walked out to the car barefoot, snow was falling on London. I put my one sandal back on and shivered, pulling my thin cotton robe around me. I had never experienced weather like this before, and had certainly never seen snow. "Oh, my God—it's so cold here!"

"Get used to it."

As the driver eased the car out of the airport and into the London morning traffic, I was overcome by such a sad, lonely feeling, in this completely foreign place, with nothing but white sickly faces around me. Allah! Heaven! Mama! Where am I? At that moment I desperately wanted my mother. Even though he had the only other black face around, Uncle Mohammed's chauffeur was no comfort to me; obviously he considered me beneath him.

While driving, he filled me in on the household I was joining: I'd be living there with my uncle and aunt, Uncle Mohammed's mother, another uncle I hadn't met—one of my mother and Aunt Maruim's brothers, and the seven children, my cousins. After he told me who lived in the house, he informed me when I would get up, when I would go to bed, what I would be doing, what I would be cooking, where I would sleep, when I would go to bed, and how I'd fall into that bed exhausted at the end of each day.

"You know, your aunt, the mistress, runs this household with an iron fist," he confided matter-of-factly. "I warn you, she gives everybody a hard time."

"Well, she may give *you* a hard time, but she's *my* aunt." After all, she's a woman and my mother's sister, I reasoned. I thought of how much I missed Mama, and how good Auntie Sahru and Fatima had been to me. Even Aman had meant well, but we just couldn't get along. The women in the family cared, and looked after each other. I leaned back against the seat, suddenly very tired after my long journey.

I squinted out the car window, trying to see where the white flakes came from. The snow was gradually turning the sidewalks white as we glided through the posh residential section of Harley Street. When we stopped in front of my uncle's home, I stared at the house in astonishment, realizing that I was going to live in this grand place. In my limited experience in Africa, I'd never seen anything like it. The ambassador's residence was a four-story mansion, and it was yellow, my favorite color. We walked to the front door, an impressive entrance with a fanlight above. Inside the door, a large gilt-framed mirror reflected a solid wall of books from the library opposite.

Auntie Maruim walked into the foyer to greet me. "Auntie!" I cried.

A woman slightly younger than my mother, wearing stylish Western clothes, stood in the hall. "Come in," she said coolly. "Close the door." I had planned to rush to her and hug her, but something about the way she stood there with her hands pressed together made me freeze in the doorway. "First I'd like to show you around and explain what your duties are."

"Oh," I said quietly, feeling the last spark of energy leave my body. "Auntie, I'm very tired. I just want to lie down. Can I please go to sleep now?"

"Well, yes. Come with me." She walked into the living room, and as we climbed the stairs, I saw the elegant furnishings: the chandelier, white sofa covered with dozens of pillows, abstract oils hanging over the mantel, the logs crackling in the fireplace. Aunt Maruim took me into her room and told me I could sleep in her bed. The four-poster was the size of my family's entire hut and was covered with a beautiful down comforter. I ran my hand across the silky fabric, enjoying its feel. "When you wake up, I'll show you the house."

"Are you going to wake me up?"

"No. You wake up when you wake up. Sleep as long as you like." I climbed under the covers and thought I had never felt anything so soft and heavenly in my life. Auntie closed the door quietly, and I fell asleep as if I were falling down a tunnel—a long black tunnel.

9.

THE MAID

When I opened my eyes, I thought I was still dreaming—
and it was a beautiful dream. Waking up in the huge bed in
the lovely room, at first I couldn't believe it was real. Aunt
Maruim must have slept with one of the children that night,
because I lay unconscious in her room until the following
morning. But as soon as I got out of bed, my fantasy life
crashed back to real life.

I came out of Auntie's room, and was wandering through the
house when she found me. "Good. You're up. Let's go to the
kitchen and I can show you what you'll be doing." In a daze, I
followed her into the room she called the kitchen; however, it
did not look like the kitchen in my auntie's house in
Mogadishu. The room was surrounded by creamy-white
cabinets, gleamed with blue ceramic tiles, and was dominated
in the center by a monstrous six-burner stove. Auntie opened
and slammed drawers, calling out, ". . . and here are the
utensils, the cutlery, the linens . . ." I had no idea what this
woman was talking about—no idea what these things were she

was showing me, let alone what I was supposed to do with them. "At six-thirty each morning you'll serve your uncle's breakfast, because he goes to the embassy early. He's a diabetic, so we must watch his diet carefully. He always has the same thing: herbal tea and two poached eggs. I'd like my coffee in my room at seven; then you'll make pancakes for the children; they eat at eight sharp, because they have to be at school by nine. After breakfast—"

"Auntie, how am I supposed to know how to do all these things? Who's going to teach me? I don't know how to make— how you call it—pancakes. What's pancakes?"

Aunt Maruim had just inhaled a big breath before I interrupted her, and she'd extended her arm pointing at a door. She held the breath for a moment with her arm still out-stretched, while she stared at me with sort of a panicky look on her face. Then she exhaled slowly and brought her arm down to her side, pressing her hands together the way she had when I first saw her. "I'll do these things the first time, Waris. But you must watch me closely. Watch me very closely, listen, and learn." I nodded, and she inhaled again, picking up where she'd left off.

After the first week, and a few minor disasters, I had the routine down to a science and followed it every day, 365 days a year, for the next four years. For a girl who had never been aware of time, I learned to watch the clock closely—and live by it. Up at six, Uncle's breakfast at six-thirty, Auntie's coffee at seven, children's breakfast at eight. Then I cleaned the kitchen. The chauffeur brought the car back from taking my uncle to the embassy, and took the children to school. Then I cleaned my aunt's room, then her bathroom, then worked through each room of the house, dusting, mopping, scrubbing, and polishing my way up all four floors. And believe me, if I didn't clean the house to someone's satisfaction, I heard about it. "I don't like the way you cleaned the bathroom. Make sure it's clean, next time. This white tile should be spotless—shining."

Other than the chauffeur and the chef, I was the only servant for the entire household; my aunt explained there was no need to hire more help for a small place like ours. Chef made dinner only six nights a week, and on Sunday, his day off, I cooked. In four years I never had a day off. The few times I asked, my aunt threw such a fit that I gave up trying.

I didn't eat with the family. I grabbed something when I had a chance, and kept working until I fell into bed around midnight. But I didn't feel that missing dinner with the family was any great loss, because in my opinion, the chef's cooking was garbage. He was a Somali, but from a different tribe than mine. I thought he was a pompous, wicked, lazy man, who loved to torment me. Whenever my aunt would walk into the kitchen, he would start in out of the blue: "Waris, when I came back in on Monday morning, you had left the kitchen in a disgusting mess. It took me hours to clean it." Of course this was a total lie. All he ever studied were ways to make himself look good in front of my aunt and uncle, and he knew it wasn't going to be with his food. I told my aunt I didn't want to eat her chef's cooking, and so she said, "Well, make whatever you want, then." At this point I was really glad I had watched my cousin Fatima cook back in Mogadishu. But intuitively I had a talent for cooking and began making pasta dishes and creating all sorts of things strictly out of my imagination. When the family saw what I was eating, they wanted some too. Soon they were asking me what I'd like to make, what ingredients I needed from the market, and so on. This did nothing to increase my popularity with Chef.

By the end of my first week in London, I realized that I and my aunt and uncle held two vastly different notions of the role I'd play in their lives. Throughout most of Africa it's common for more affluent family members to take in the children of their poor relations, and those children work in return for their upkeep. Sometimes the relatives educate the children and treat them like one of their own. Sometimes they don't. Obviously I was hoping my situation would fall into the former category, but soon I learned that my aunt and uncle had more important issues on their minds than cultivating this ignorant child they'd received from the desert who was supposed to perform as a maid. Uncle was so busy with his work that he paid little attention to what went on at home. But my auntie, who I had fantasized would be like a second mother to me, apparently had no such fantasies about making me a third daughter. I was simply a servant. As this fact became brutally clear, along with the drudgery of my long workdays, my joy at coming to London withered. I discovered that my aunt was obsessed with rules and regulations; everything must always be done exactly the way she said, at exactly the time she said, every day. No exceptions. Perhaps she felt she needed to be rigid in order to succeed in this foreign culture so different from our homeland. However, fortunately, I found a friend in the house in my cousin Basma.

Basma was my uncle and aunt's oldest daughter, and we were the same age. She was stunning, and all the boys were after her, but she paid no attention. She went to school, and at night the only thing she was interested in was reading. My cousin would go to her room and lie across the bed reading for hours. Frequently she would be so engrossed in a book that she would miss meals, sometimes for the whole day until someone dragged her out of her room.

Bored and lonely, I would go into Basma's room to visit, and sit down on a corner of her bed. "What are you reading?" I'd ask.

Without looking up she'd mumble, "Leave me alone. I'm reading. . . ."

"Well, can't I talk to you?"

Still staring at the book, she'd respond in a flat voice, slurring her words, as if she were talking in her sleep, "What do you want to talk about?"

"What are you reading?"

"Hmmm?"

"What are you reading? What's it about?" Finally, once I got her attention, she'd stop and tell me what the whole book was about. More often than not, they were romantic novels, and the climax came when, after several interruptions and misunderstandings, the man and woman finally kissed. Since I've had a lifelong love of stories, I enjoyed these times enormously, and I'd sit spellbound while she went through the entire plot in great detail, her eyes flashing and arms waving. Listening to her stories made me want to learn to read, because then, I figured, I could enjoy stories whenever I wanted.

Mama's brother who lived with us, Uncle Abdullah, had come to London with his sister, so he could attend the university. He asked me if I wanted to go to school. "You know, Waris, you need to learn how to read. If you're interested, I can help you." He told me where the school was located, what times it met— and most important—that it was free. The notion that I could go to school would have never occurred to me on my own. The ambassador paid me a tiny sum each month for pocket money, but certainly not enough to pay for school. Excited about learning to read, I went to Auntie Maruim and told her I wanted to go to school. I wanted to learn how to read, write, and speak English.

Even though I lived in London, we spoke Somali at home, and since I had no contact with the outside world, I knew only a few words of English. Auntie said, "Well, let me think about it." But when she discussed it with my uncle, he said no. I kept pressing her to let me go, but she didn't want to go against my uncle. Finally, I decided to go without their permission. School met three nights a week, from nine to eleven. Uncle Abdullah agreed to take me the first time and show me where to go. By now I was about fifteen, and this was my first time in a classroom ever. The room was full of people of all ages from all over the world. After the first night, an old Italian man would pick me up when I sneaked out of my uncle's house, then bring me home again when we were finished. I was so eager to learn that the teacher would say to me, "You're good, Waris, but slow down." I learned the alphabet, and was beginning on the fundamentals of English, when my uncle discovered I was sneaking out at night. He was furious that I'd disobeyed him and put an end to my attending school after only a couple of weeks.

Even though I was no longer permitted to go to school, I borrowed my cousin's books and tried to teach myself to read. I wasn't allowed to watch TV with the family, but sometimes I'd linger at the door and listen to the English, trying to develop an ear for the language. Everything continued as usual until one day Auntie Maruim called to me as I was cleaning. "Waris, come down here when you've finished upstairs. I have something to tell you." I was making the beds, and when I'd done them all I walked into the living room, where my aunt stood by the fireplace.

"Yes?"

"I got a phone call today from home. Ah . . . what's your little brother's name?"

"Ali?"

"No, the youngest one, the little one with gray hair."

"Old Man? You're talking about Old Man?"

"Yeah. Old Man and your big sister, Aman. Well, I'm sorry. They both died." I couldn't believe what I was hearing. My eyes fixed on Auntie's face, thinking she must be joking—or maybe she was mad at me about something, and she was trying to punish me by telling me that awful story. But she had no expression of any kind to give me a clue; her face was completely blank. *She must be serious, or why would she say this? But how can it be true?* I froze in that spot and couldn't move, until I felt my legs giving way, and sat down on the white sofa for a minute. I didn't even think to ask what had happened. My aunt might have been talking, she might have explained the horrible events to me, but all I could hear was a roaring in my ears. Numbly, walking stiffly like a zombie, I went up to my room on the fourth floor.

I lay there in shock for the rest of the day, stretched out on my bed under the eaves in the tiny room that I shared with my young cousin. Old Man and Aman both dead! How could it be? I had left home, missing my opportunity to spend time with my brother and sister, and now I would never see either one of them again. Aman, always the strong one; Old Man, always the wise one. It didn't seem possible that they could die—and if *they* could, what did that mean for the rest of the family—those of us with lesser abilities?

By that evening, I decided I didn't want to suffer anymore. Nothing in my life had gone the way I'd hoped since that morning I ran away from my father. Now, two years later, I missed the closeness of my family terribly, and knowing two of them were gone forever was more than I could bear. I walked downstairs to the kitchen, opened a drawer, and removed a butcher knife. With the knife in my hand I returned upstairs to my room. But as I lay there trying to get the courage to cut myself, I kept thinking of my mother. Poor Mama. I lost two this week, she'd lose three. It hardly seemed fair to her, so I laid the knife on the table next to the bed and stared at the ceiling. I'd forgotten about the knife, when later my cousin Basma came in to check on me. She looked at it in shock. "What the hell is that! What are you doing with a knife?" I didn't try to answer, just went back to looking at the ceiling. Basma took the knife and went away.

After a few days my aunt called me again: "Waris! Come down." I lay there pretending not to hear. "WARIS! COME DOWN!" I went downstairs and found her waiting at the foot. "Hurry up! Telephone!" This news astonished me, as I never got phone calls. In fact, I'd never spoken on the telephone.

"For me?" I said quietly.

"Yes, yes." She pointed to the receiver lying on the table. "Here, pick it up—pick up the phone!"

I held the receiver in my hand, looking at the contraption as if it were going to bite me. From about a foot away, I whispered, "Yes?"

Aunt Maruim rolled her eyes. "Speak! Speak—talk into the phone!" She turned the receiver right side up and pushed it next to my ear.

"Hello?" Then I heard an amazing sound: my mother's voice. "Mama! Mama! Oh, my God, is it really you?" A grin spread across my face for the first time in days. "Mama, are you okay?"

"No, I've been living under the tree." She told me that after Aman and Old Man died, she went crazy. At this point in Mama's story, I was so thankful I had given up the notion of adding to her grief by killing myself. My mother had run into the desert; she didn't want to be with anyone, look at anyone, talk to anyone. Then she went on to Mogadishu alone and visited her family. She was still there with them now, calling from Auntie Sahru's house.

Mama tried to explain how it happened, but still nothing made sense. Old Man had fallen ill. As was so typical of our lives as nomads in Africa, there was no medical help; nobody knew what was wrong, or what to do about it. In that society there were only two alternatives: live or die. There was no in between. As long as someone lived, everything was okay. We didn't worry much about illness, since without doctors or medicine, there was nothing we could do to fix it. When someone died, well, that was okay, too, because the survivors would continue. Life went on. Always, the philosophy of in'shallah ruled our lives: "If God is willing." There was an acceptance of life as a gift, and death as the unarguable decision of God.

But when Old Man fell sick, my parents were frightened, because he was a special child. Mama—not knowing what else to do—had sent a messenger to Aman in Mogadishu, asking for help. Aman was always the strong one; she would know what to do. And she did. Aman set off on foot from Mogadishu to come and get Old Man and take him to a doctor. Exactly where my family was camped at the time, or how far they were from the capital, I have no idea. But what Mama couldn't have known when she sent for her was that Aman was eight months pregnant. As my sister carried Old Man to the hospital, he died in her arms. Aman went into shock, and she also died a few days later, and the baby with her. I was never even sure where they were when they died, but after learning this, Mama, who had always been so quietly steadfast, fell apart. And since she was the center that held our family together, it sickened me to think what life was like for the rest of them. More than ever, I felt terrible about being stuck in London and unable to help Mama when she needed me most.

However, life went on for all of us, and in London I tried to enjoy it as much as I could. I did my duties in the house, and joked with my cousins and their friends who visited.

One night I recruited Basma to help me with my first modeling job. Since arriving in London, I had grown to love clothes, but I didn't particularly want to own them—there was just something fun about trying them on. It was like playacting; I could pretend to be someone else. While the family was in the den watching television, I went into Uncle Mohammed's room and closed the door. I opened his armoire and took out one of his best suits, a navy wool pinstripe. I laid it on the bed with a white shirt, silk tie, dark socks, elegant black English shoes, and felt hat. I put everything on, struggling to knot the tie as I'd seen Uncle do. Then I pulled the hat down low. When my ensemble was complete, I went to find Basma. She doubled over laughing.

"Go tell your dad there's a man here to see him."

"Those are his clothes? Oh, my God, he's going to kill—"

"Just go do it."

I stood out in the hallway and listened to my cousin, waiting for the right moment to make my big entrance. "Father," I heard Basma say, "there's a man here to see you."

"A man at this time of night?" Uncle Mohammed didn't sound too happy. "Who is it? What does he want? Have you ever seen him before?"

Basma stammered, "I, uh, I don't know. I think, yeah, I think you know him."

"Well, tell him . . ."

"Why don't you see him," she said quickly. "He's right outside the door."

"Okay," my uncle agreed tiredly. That was my cue. I pulled the hat all the way down over my eyes till I could barely see, stuck my hands in the pockets of his jacket, and swaggered into the room.

"Hi, don't you remember me?" I said in a baritone voice. Uncle's eyes bugged out, and he ducked down trying to get a look under the hat. When he realized who it was, he cracked up laughing. Auntie and all the rest of the family roared.

Uncle Mohammed wagged his finger at me. "Now, did I give you permission to . . ."

"I just had to try, Uncle. Don't you think it's fun?"

"Oh, Allah."

I did this stunt a few more times, each time waiting long enough till I figured my uncle wasn't expecting it. Then he would say to me, "That's enough, now, Waris. Don't try on my clothes anymore, all right? Leave them alone." And I knew he was serious, but still he thought it was funny. Later I'd hear him laughing and telling his friends, "This girl will go in my room and try on my clothes. Then Basma will come in and say, 'Dad, there's a man here to see you.' Then she strolls in wearing my things from head to toe. You should see it. . . ."

My auntie said her friends had mentioned that I should try modeling. But Auntie's response was "Um-hmmm. But we don't do that sort of thing, being from Somalia and being Moslem, you know." However, my aunt never seemed to object to the modeling career of her old friend's daughter, Iman. Auntie had known Iman's mother for years and years, so whenever either of them were in London, Aunt Maruim insisted they stay with us. Listening to discussions of Iman was how I first became acquainted with the idea of modeling. I had cut many of her pictures from my cousin's magazines and taped them to the wall in my little room. If she's a Somali woman and she can do this, I reasoned, why can't I?

When Iman came to our house, I always wanted to find the right opportunity to talk to her. I wanted to ask, "How do I become a model?" I barely even knew that such a thing existed; I certainly had no idea how to become one. But each time she'd visit, she would spend the evening talking with the elders; I knew my aunt and uncle would never approve of my interrupting their conversation for such nonsense as my desire to be a model. Finally, one night I found the right moment. Iman was in her room reading, and I knocked on the door. "Can I get you something before you go to sleep?"

"Yes, I'd like a cup of herbal tea." I went down to the kitchen and brought back a tray.

As I set it down on the nightstand, I began. "You know, I have so many of your pictures in my room." I listened to the clock ticking on the nightstand, feeling like a perfect idiot. "I'd really like to do modeling, too. Do you think it's hard . . . how did you do it . . . how did you start, anyway?"

I don't know what I expected her to say; maybe I hoped she'd wave a magic wand over me and turn me into Cinderella. But my dream of modeling was an abstract one; the whole idea seemed so far-fetched that I didn't spend much time thinking about it. Instead, after that night, I went on with my daily chores, focusing on the day-to-day business of breakfast, lunch, dishes, and dusting.

By this point I was about sixteen, and had lived in London

for two years. I had actually become acclimated enough that I knew what date the Western world attributed to this span of time: 1983.

During the summer of that year, Uncle Mohammed's sister died in Germany, leaving behind a young daughter. Her daughter, little Sophie, came to live with us, and my uncle enrolled her in All Souls Church School. My morning routine now also included walking Sophie several blocks to her school.

On one of those first mornings, as Sophie and I strolled toward the old brick building, I saw a strange man staring at me. He was a white man around forty with a ponytail. He didn't try to hide the fact he was staring at me and, in fact, he was quite bold. After I left Sophie at the door, the man walked toward me and started speaking to me. But of course I didn't speak English, so I had no idea what he was saying. Frightened, I wouldn't look at him and ran back home. This routine continued: I'd drop off Sophie, the white man would be waiting, he'd try to talk to me, and I'd run.

On the walk home after I met Sophie in the afternoons, she'd frequently mention a new friend—a little girl she'd met in her class. "Yeah, um-hmmm," I'd say, completely uninterested. One day I was a little bit late arriving to pick up Sophie. When I got there, she was waiting outside the school, playing with another little girl. "Oh, Waris, this is my friend," Sophie said proudly. Standing next to the two girls was the man with the ponytail, the guy who had been bothering me for nearly a year.

"Yeah, let's go," I said nervously, eyeing my man. But he bent over and said something to Sophie, who spoke English, German, and Somali. "Come on, Sophie. Get away from that man," I warned, and snatched her hand.

She turned to me and said brightly, "He wants to know if you speak English." Sophie shook her head at the man. He said something else and Sophie translated, "He wants to ask you something."

"Tell him I'm not talking to him," I replied haughtily and

looked in the other direction. "He can just go away. He can just . . ." But I decided not to finish my sentence, because his daughter was listening, and Sophie would immediately translate. "Forget it. Let's just go," and I grabbed at her hand and pulled her away.

Shortly after this encounter, I dropped Sophie off one morning as usual. Then I walked back home and was upstairs cleaning when the doorbell rang. I headed downstairs, but before I could reach the door, Aunt Maruim was opening it. Peering through the railing from the stair landing I couldn't believe what I saw; there stood Mr. Ponytail. He must have followed me. My first thought was that he was going to make up some stories to tell my aunt—say that I was doing something wrong. Some lies, like I was flirting with him, slept with him, or he'd caught me stealing something. Auntie said in her fluent English, "Who are you?"

"My name is Malcolm Fairchild. I'm sorry to bother you—but can I talk to you?"

"What do you want to talk to me about?" I could see Auntie was shocked.

Walking back upstairs, I felt ill, wondering what he was going to say, but within two seconds I heard the door slam shut. I rushed into the living room as Aunt Maruim was storming toward the kitchen.

"Auntie, who was that?"

"I don't know—some man who said he's been following you, wanted to talk to you, some nonsense about wanting to take your picture." She glared at me.

"Auntie, I didn't tell him to do it. I didn't say anything to him."

"I KNOW THAT! That's why he's here!" She marched past me. "Go do your work—don't worry about it. I took care of *him*." But Auntie refused to go into details about their conversation, and the fact that she'd been so angry and disgusted led me to believe he wanted to take some sort of porno pictures. I was horrified and never brought up the incident after that morning.

From then on, each time I saw him at All Souls Church School, he never talked to me. He simply smiled politely and went on about his business. Until one day when I was picking up Sophie, he startled me by walking up and handing me a card. My eyes never left his face as I took it and stowed it in my pocket. I watched him steadily as he turned around to walk away, then started cussing him in Somali: "Get away from me, you dirty man—you fucking pig!"

When I got home, I ran upstairs; the kids all slept on the top floors, so this part of the house was our sanctuary from the adults. I went into my cousin's room and, as usual, interrupted her reading. "Basma, look at this," I said, fishing the card from my pocket. "This is from that man, remember that man I told you about, the one who's always bothering me, and who followed me here? He gave me this card today. What does it say?"

"It says he's a photographer."

"But what kind of photographer?"

"He takes pictures."

"Yeah, but what kind of pictures?"

"It says, 'fashion photographer.' "

"Fashion photographer," I said, sounding out each word slowly. "You mean, he takes pictures of clothes? He'd take pictures of me wearing clothes?"

"I don't know, Waris," she sighed. "I really don't know." I knew I was bothering her, that she wanted to get back to her book. Standing up from the bed, I took the card and left. But I hid the fashion photographer's card in my room. Some little voice told me to hang on to it.

My cousin Basma was my only adviser; this girl was always there for me. And never was I more grateful for her guidance than when I sought advice concerning her brother Haji.

Haji was twenty-four years old, my uncle's second-oldest son. He was considered very bright and, like Uncle Abdullah, was attending university in London. Haji had always been friendly to me from the time I arrived in London. When I'd be upstairs cleaning, he'd say, "Hey, Waris, are you finished with the bathroom?"

"No," I'd reply, "but if you want it, go ahead and I'll clean it afterward."

"Oh, no . . . I just wondered if you needed some help." Or he'd say, "I'm going to get something to drink. Would you like something?" I was pleased that my cousin cared for me. We frequently talked and joked around.

Sometimes, when I opened the door to walk out of the bathroom, he was standing right outside, and wouldn't let me pass. When I tried to duck around him, he moved too. When I tried to push him, yelling, "Get out of my way, you slob," he'd laugh. These little games went on, and although I tried to shrug them off as corny jokes, I was confused. There was something underneath his behavior that made me nervous. He'd look at me in a funny, moony-eyed way, or he'd stand a bit too close. When I'd get that queasy feeling, I tried to stop and remind myself, *No, come on, Waris, Haji is like your brother. What you're thinking is sick.*

Then one day I was walking out of the bathroom carrying my cleaning bucket and rags and when I opened the door he was standing there. He grabbed my arm and pushed himself against me, his face a hair's width from mine. "What's going on here?" I started laughing nervously.

"Oh—nothing, nothing." He turned me loose instantly. I took my bucket and went to the next room, very casually, as if nothing had happened. But my mind was racing, and after that moment, I didn't wonder anymore if something was going on. I knew. I knew something wasn't healthy here.

The next night I was in my room asleep, and my cousin Shukree, Basma's little sister, was asleep in her bed. But I'm a very light sleeper, and around three in the morning, I heard someone coming up the stairs; I figured it must be Haji, since his room was across the hall from mine. He'd just gotten home, and from the way he was stumbling in the hallway, I could tell he was drunk. This sort of behavior was not tolerated in my uncle's household—coming in at this hour, and certainly nobody drank. They were strict Moslems, and drinking alcohol of any kind was forbidden. But I guess Haji thought he was old enough to be his own man and he'd give it a try.

The door to my room opened quietly and my body went rigid. Both the beds in this room were on a raised platform, up a couple of steps from the door. I could see Haji tiptoeing up the stairs, trying hard not to wake my little cousin, who was in the bed closest to the door. But he missed a step and tripped, then crawled the rest of the way over to my bed. In the light from the windows behind him, I watched him craning his neck to see my face in the shadows. "Hey, Waris," he whispered. "Waris . . ." His breath reeked of liquor, confirming my suspicion that he must be drunk. But I lay completely still in the darkness, pretending to be asleep. He reached out his hand and started feeling around the pillow to find my face. I thought, *Oh, my God, please don't let this happen.* Snorting, "HAYYUH," I flopped over on my side as if I were dreaming, trying to make enough noise to wake up Shukree. At this point he lost his nerve and ran quietly back to his room.

The next day I went to Basma's room. "Look, I need to talk to you." I guess the look of panic on my face told her this wasn't one of my ordinary visits just to kill time.

"Come in, close the door."

"This is about your brother," I said, taking a deep breath. I didn't know how to tell her this, and I just prayed she'd believe me.

"What about him?" Now she looked alarmed.

"Last night he came into my room. It was three o'clock in the morning and pitch-black."

"What did he do?"

"He was trying to touch my face. He whispered my name."

"Oh, no. Are you sure? You weren't dreaming?"

"Come on. I see the way he looks at me, the way he looks at me when I'm alone with him. I don't know what to do."

"Shit—SHIT! Get a fucking cricket bat and put it under your bed. Or a broom. No—take the rolling pin from the kitchen. Put that under your bed, and when he comes into your room at night, mash him in the head! And you know what else to do?" she added. "Scream. Scream your head off so everybody can hear." Thank God, this girl was definitely on my side.

All day I kept praying, "Please don't make me do this horrible thing; please just make him stop." I didn't want to make trouble. I worried about what lies he might offer his parents as an explanation, or that they might throw me out. I just wanted him to stop—no more games, no more late-night visits, no more groping—because I had a sick feeling where it was all headed. But my instincts told me to prepare for battle in case prayer didn't work.

That night I went to the kitchen, smuggled the rolling pin up to my room, and hid it under the bed. Later, when my cousin was asleep, I brought it out and laid it next to me, never releasing my grip on the handle. And in a repeat performance of the previous night, Haji came in around three in the morning. He paused in the doorway and I saw the light from the hallway glinting off his glasses. I lay there with one eye open, watching him. He crept over to my pillow and started tapping me on the arm. His breath stank of Scotch so bad that I wanted to gag, but I didn't move an inch. Then, kneeling next to the bed, Haji groped around until he found the bottom hem of the covers, and pushed his hand underneath and across the mattress to my leg. Sliding his palm up my thigh, he was going all the way to my knickers, my underwear.

I have to break his glasses, I thought, *so at least there's proof he was in the room*. I tightened my hand around the rolling-pin handle and brought the wood down across his face with all my might. First there was a sickening thud, then I screamed, "GET OUT OF MY FUCKIN' ROOM, YOU FUCKIN'—"

Shukree sat up in her bed, crying, "What's happening?" Within seconds I heard footsteps running from all corners of the house. But because I had broken Haji's glasses, he couldn't see, so he resorted to crawling back to his room on hands and knees. He got into his bed with all his clothes on, pretending to be asleep.

Basma came in and threw on the lights. Of course she was in on the whole plan but pretended total ignorance. "What's going on here?"

Shukree explained: "Haji was in here, crawling around on the floor!"

When Aunt Maruim walked in with her robe pulled around her, I yelled, "Auntie, he was in my room! He was in my room, and he did it yesterday too! And I hit him!" I pointed at Haji's shattered glasses next to my bed.

"Shhh," she said sternly. "I don't want to hear this—not now. Everybody, get back to your rooms. Go to bed."

10.

FREE AT LAST

After the night I mashed Haji's face with the rolling pin, no one in the house ever mentioned the incident again. I might have thought his late-night visits were merely a bad dream, except for one big difference. Whenever I saw Haji in the hallway, he no longer gazed at me with longing. That expression had been replaced by one of naked hatred. I was thankful that as I'd prayed, this unpleasant chapter in my life had come to an end. However, it was soon replaced by a new concern.

Uncle Mohammed announced that in a few weeks the family would be returning to Somalia. His four-year term as Somalian ambassador was up, and we were going home. Four years had sounded like a lifetime to me when I'd first arrived, but now I couldn't believe the time was over. Unfortunately, I wasn't excited about going back to Somalia. I wanted to go home wealthy and successful, as every African dreams of returning home from a rich nation like England. In a poor country like my homeland, people are constantly searching for a way out, clawing to make it to Saudi or Europe or the States, so they can make some money to help their destitute families.

Now here I was about to return home after four years abroad—with nothing. What could I say I'd accomplished when I went back? Would I tell my mother I'd learned how to cook pasta? Back traveling with my camels, I'd probably never see pasta again. Would I tell my father I'd learned how to scrub toilets? "Huh? What's a toilet?" he'd say. Ah, but money, *cash*, there was something he could understand—the universal language. There was something my family had never had much of.

By the time my aunt and uncle were ready to return to Somalia, I had saved a pittance from my maid's wages, which was difficult enough considering my pathetic salary. My dream, however, was to make enough money to buy my mother a house—a place where Mama could live without having to travel constantly and work so hard to survive. This isn't as far-fetched as it might sound, since with the exchange rate, I could buy a house in Somalia for a couple of thousand dollars. To accomplish this goal, I felt since I was already in England, I wanted to stay and make some money, because once I left, I certainly couldn't come back. How I would manage this, I didn't know. But I had faith that somehow things would work out, once I was free from working like a slave for my aunt and uncle. However, they didn't agree. "What on earth are you going to do here?" my aunt exclaimed. "An eighteen-year-old girl, with no place to stay, no money, no job, no work permit, and no English? It's ridiculous! You're coming home with us."

Long before the scheduled departure, Uncle Mohammed advised us all of two things: the date we were leaving, and the need to make sure our passports were in order. I did. I promptly took mine into the kitchen, sealed it in a plastic bag, then buried it in the garden.

Waiting till the day before our flight to Mogadishu, I announced that I couldn't find my passport. My plan was simple enough: if I didn't have a passport, they couldn't take me back. Uncle smelled something rotten and kept asking, "Well, Waris, where could your passport be? Where have you been that you could possibly have left it?" Obviously he knew the answer to that question, since in four years I had barely been out of the house.

"I don't know—maybe I accidentally threw it away while I was cleaning," I answered with a straight face. He was still the ambassador and he could help me if he wanted. I kept hoping that if my uncle realized how desperately I wanted to stay, he wouldn't make me go home, but instead would help me get a visa.

"Well, *now* what are we going to do, Waris? We can't just leave you here!" He was livid that I'd put him in this position. For the next twenty-four hours we played a game of nerves, to see who would give in. I kept insisting my passport was lost; Uncle Mohammed kept insisting there was nothing he could do to help me.

Aunt Maruim had her own ideas. "We'll just tie you up, put you in a bag, and smuggle you on board the plane! People do it all the time."

This threat got my attention. "If you do that," I said slowly, "I'll never, ever, forgive you. Look, Auntie, just leave me here. I'll be fine."

"Yeah, yeah, you'll be fine," she answered sarcastically. "NO, you are NOT going to be fine." I could see in her face that she was very worried, but was she worried enough to help me? She had plenty of friends in London; my uncle had all his contacts at the embassy. A simple phone call was all it would take to provide me with a link to survival, but I knew if they believed for an instant they could bluff me into coming back to Somalia, they wouldn't make that call.

The next morning the entire four-story mansion was in complete chaos with everyone packing, the phone ringing, and swarms of people running in and out of the house. Upstairs, I prepared to leave my little room under the eaves, packing my cheap bag with what few belongings I'd accumulated during my stay in England. In the end, I threw most of the hand-me-down clothes in the trash, deciding they were too ugly and old-womanish for me. Why haul around a bunch of garbage? Still a nomad, I'd travel light.

At eleven o'clock, everyone gathered in the living room as the chauffeur loaded the bags into the car. I paused for a second to remember this was the way I had come so many years ago—the chauffeur, the car, walking into this room, seeing the white sofa, the fireplace, meeting my aunt for the first time. That gray morning was also the first time I'd seen snow. Everything about this country had seemed so bizarre to me then. I walked outside to the car with my distressed Aunt Maruim, who said, "What am I going to tell your mother?"

"Tell her I'm fine, and she'll hear from me soon." She shook her head and got into the car. I stood on the sidewalk and waved good-bye to everyone, then walked into the street, watching the car until it was out of sight.

I'm not going to lie—I was scared. Up until that moment I hadn't really believed that they would leave me there all alone. But as I stood in the middle of Harley Street, I was exactly that—all alone. I have no hard feelings toward my aunt and uncle, though; they're still my family. They gave me an opportunity by bringing me to London, and for that I will forever be grateful. When they left, I guess they thought, "Well, you wanted to stay—here's your chance. Go ahead then—do what you want. But we're not going to make it easy for you, because we think you should come home with us." I'm sure they felt it was a disgrace for a young woman to remain in England alone, unchaperoned. However, in the end the decision had been mine, and since I had chosen to remain, I would have to take charge of my own destiny now.

Fighting an overwhelming feeling of panic, I went back

inside the house. I closed the front door and walked into the kitchen to talk to the only other person left—my old friend the chef. He greeted me with "Well, you know, you've got to go today. I'm the only one who's staying on—not you. You've got to leave." He pointed toward the front door. Oh, yes, the minute my uncle was gone, he just couldn't wait to give it to me. The smug look on his unfriendly face showed that ordering me around gave him great pleasure. I stood there leaning against the door frame, thinking how quiet the house seemed now that everybody was gone. "Waris, you've got to go now. I want you to get out . . ."

"Oh, *shut up*." The man was like an obnoxious barking dog. "I'm going, okay? I just came in to get my bag."

"Grab it now—quickly. Quickly. Hurry up, because I have to—" By this time I was climbing the stairs, paying no attention to his noise. The master was gone, and in the brief interim before the new ambassador arrived, Chef would be master. I walked through the empty rooms, thinking of all the good and bad times here, wondering where my next home would be.

I picked up my little duffel from the bed, slung it over my shoulder, walked down the four flights of stairs, and out the front door. Unlike the day I had arrived, today was a gorgeous, sunny day with a blue sky and fresh air like springtime. In the tiny garden, I used a stone to unearth my passport, slipping it out of its plastic bag and stowing it in my duffel. I brushed the soil from my hands and headed down the street. I couldn't help smiling as I walked along the sidewalk—free at last. My whole life stretched before me with nowhere to go, and no one to answer to. And somehow I knew things would work out.

Close to my uncle's house was my first stop: the Somalian embassy. I knocked on the door. The doorman who answered knew my family well, since sometimes he also drove for my uncle. "Hello, miss. What are you doing here? Is Mr. Farah still in town?"

"No, he's gone. I wanted to see Anna, to find out if I can get a job at the embassy." He laughed, returned to his chair, and sat down. He put his hands behind his head and leaned back against the wall. As I stood there in the middle of the lobby, he made no attempt to move. His attitude puzzled me, as this man had always been polite to me. Then I realized that—like Chef's—his attitude had changed with the departures that occurred that morning. My uncle was gone, and without my uncle, I was nobody. I was less than nobody, and these oafs were thrilled to have the upper hand.

"Oh! Anna's far too busy to see you." The doorman grinned.

"Look," I said firmly, "*I need to see her.*" Anna had been my uncle's secretary, and she'd always been kind to me. Luckily, she heard my voice in the lobby and walked out of her office to see what was happening.

"Waris! What are you doing here?"

"You know, I really didn't want to go back to Somalia with my uncle," I explained. "I just didn't want to go back. So I— I'm not staying at the house anymore, you know. And I was wondering if you know anybody who maybe—anybody I can work for—anything—I don't care what it is. I'll do anything."

"Well, my darling"—she raised her eyebrows—"it's a bit too short notice. Where are you staying?"

"Oh, I don't know. Don't worry about that."

"Well, can you give me a number where I can find you?"

"No, because I don't know where I'm staying. I'll find some cheap hotel tonight." I knew she would invite me to stay at her place if she hadn't had a tiny little flat. "But I can come back and give you a number later, so you can let me know if you hear of anything."

"Okay, Waris. Listen, take care of yourself—are you sure you're going to be all right?"

"Yeah, I'll be fine." From the corner of my eye I saw the doorman constantly grinning like a fool. "Well, thanks—look, I'll see you later."

With relief I headed out into the sunlight again, and decided to go shopping. All I had to live on until I landed a job was the small sum of money I'd squirreled away from my maid's wages. But now that I was a woman about town, I needed to buy something decent to wear, a new dress to lift my spirits. I walked from the embassy to the big department stores at Oxford Circus. I'd been there before with my cousin Basma when I'd first come to London. Aunt Maruim had sent us down to buy me a few things, since when I arrived I had no winter clothes. Actually I'd had no clothes at all, except the outfit I'd worn on the plane and one fine leather sandal.

Strolling through the racks at Selfridges, I found the enormous variety of choices mesmerizing. The thought that I could stay here as long as I wanted and try on all these clothes—all these colors, styles, sizes—was intoxicating. The thought that for the first time in my history, I was in charge of my own life was intoxicating—nobody yelling at me to milk the goats, feed the babies, make the tea, scrub the floors, scour the toilets.

For the next several hours, I set to work trying on outfits in the dressing room with the help of two sales clerks. Using my limited English and sign language, I communicated that I wanted something longer, shorter, tighter, brighter. At the end of my marathon session, when dozens of discarded garments lay in stacks outside my fitting room, one of the clerks smiled at me and said, "Well, love, what did you decide to have?"

The sheer volume of choices overwhelmed me, but by this point I was getting nervous that down the street, in the next store, there might be something even better. Before I parted with any of my precious pounds, I'd better find out. "I'm not having anything today," I said pleasantly, "but thank you." The poor clerks, standing with their arms full of dresses, looked at me in disbelief, then at each other in disgust. I sailed past them and continued on my mission: to examine every inch of Oxford Street.

After several places, I still hadn't bought anything; but as always, the true joy for me was simply to try on things. As I left one building and entered another, I realized the spring-like day was fading, the winter evening coming on, and I still had no place to spend the night. With this thought in mind, I entered the next store and saw a tall, attractive African woman examining a sale table of sweaters. She looked like a Somalian, and I studied her, trying to decide how to talk to her. Picking up a sweater, I smiled at her and said in Somali, "I'm trying to buy something, but I can't decide what I want. And believe me, girl, I've seen a lot of clothes today."

We began talking and the woman said her name was Halwu. She was quite friendly and laughed a lot. "Where do you live, Waris? What do you do?"

"Oh, you're going to laugh. I'm sure you'll think I'm crazy, but I live nowhere. I don't have any place to live, because my family left me today. They went back to Somalia." I saw the look of empathy in her eyes; as I later learned this woman had been through a lot herself.

"You didn't want to go back to Somalia, huh?" Without saying it, we both knew: we missed our home and our families, but what opportunities did we have there? Being traded for camels? Becoming some man's property? Struggling every day just to survive?

"No, but I have nothing here, either," I said. "My uncle was the ambassador, but now he's gone and the new man is coming. So this morning they kicked me out, and right this minute, I have no idea where I'm headed." I laughed.

She waved in the air to silence me, as if the movement of her hand could sweep away all my problems. "Look, I live around the corner at the YMCA. I don't have a big place, but you can come and stay for the night. I just have a room, so if you want to cook, you'll have to go to a different floor to make some food."

"Ooohh, that would be wonderful, but are you sure?"

"Yes, I'm sure. I mean, come on. What are you going to do otherwise?"

We walked together to her room at the Y. The YMCA was located in a modern brick high-rise normally occupied by students. Her room was a tiny space with a twin bed, a place for books, and Halwu's big, beautiful television. "Oh!" I threw up my hands. "Can I watch TV?"

The woman looked at me like I was from outer space. "Oh, yeah—sure. Switch it on." I plopped down on the floor in front of it and stared greedily at her TV. After four years, I could look at it without somebody chasing me out of the room like a stray cat. "Didn't you ever watch television at your uncle's?" she said curiously.

"Are you kidding? Sometimes I would sneak in, but I'd always get caught. `Watching TV again, Waris?' " I mimicked my aunt's snottiest voice and started snapping my fingers. " `Back to work, now, come on. We didn't bring you here to watch television.' "

My real education on life in London began with Halwu as my professor; the two of us became close friends. I spent that first night in her room, and the next, and the next. Then she suggested, "Why don't you get a room here?"

"Well, first of all because I can't afford it, and I need to go to school, which means I won't have time to work." I asked her shyly, "Can you read and write?"

"Yeah."

"And speak English?"

"Yeah."

"See, I can't do any of those things and I need to learn. That's my biggest priority. And if I start working again, I won't have time."

"Well, why don't you go to school part-time and work

part-time? Don't worry about what kind of job it is—just take anything until you learn English."

"Will you help me?"

"Sure, I'll help you."

I tried to get a room at the YMCA, but it was full with a waiting list. All the young people wanted to be there because it was cheap and very social, with an Olympic-size pool and fitness center. I added my name to the list, but in the meantime I knew I had to do something because I couldn't keep taking up poor Halwu's space. Right across from the YMCA, however, was the YWCA; it was full of elderly people, and fairly depressing, but I took a room there temporarily and set out to find a job. My friend suggested logically, "Why don't you start by looking right here?"

"What do you mean? Right where?"

"Right here. Right here," she said, pointing. "McDonald's is just next door."

"I can't work there—there's no way I can serve people. Don't forget, I can't speak English or read. Besides, I don't have a work permit." But Halwu knew the ropes, and following her suggestion, I went around back and applied for a job cleaning the kitchen.

When I began working for McDonald's, I found out how right she was. I thought that for the hard work I did the wages were poor and that perhaps the management took advantage of my illegal status. As long as you were a hard worker, the management didn't care about your story.

My career as kitchen help at McDonald's put to use the skills I'd learned as a maid: I washed dishes, wiped counters, scrubbed grills, and mopped floors, in a constant effort to erase the traces of burger grease. When I went home at night I was coated with grease and stank like grease. In the kitchen we were always short-staffed, but I didn't dare complain. None of that mattered because, at least now I could support myself. I was just grateful to have the job, and besides, I knew I wouldn't be there for long. In the meantime, I'd do whatever it took to survive.

I began going part-time to the foreigners' free language school, improving my English and learning how to read and write. But for the first time in years, my life wasn't only about work. Sometimes Halwu took me to nightclubs, where the whole crowd seemed to know her. She talked, laughed, and was hysterically funny—just generally so lively that everybody wanted to be around her. One night we went out and had been dancing for hours until I suddenly looked up to realize we were surrounded by men. "Damn!" I whispered to my friend. "Do these men like us?"

She grinned. "Oh, *yeah*. They like us very much." This notion astonished me. I scanned their faces and decided she was right. I had never had a boyfriend, or even the attention of any male other than my cousin Haji—which hadn't exactly flattered me. For the past four years I'd simply considered myself Miss Nobody—the maid. Now here were these guys lining up to dance with us. I thought, *Waris, girl, you have finally arrived!*

Oddly enough, even though I always liked the black men, it was the white guys who were most interested in me. Overcoming my strict African upbringing, I chatted away, forcing myself to talk with everyone—black, white, male, female. If I was going to be on my own, I reasoned, I had to learn survival skills for this new world, which were different from the ones I was raised with in the desert. Here I needed to learn English, and how to communicate with all sorts of people. Knowing about camels and goats wasn't going to keep me alive in London.

Halwu supplemented these nocturnal nightclub lessons with further instruction the next day. She went through the entire roster of characters we'd met the night before, explaining their motives, their personalities—basically giving me a crash course in human nature. She talked about sex, what these guys were up to, what to watch out for, and the special problems in store for African women like us. Nobody had ever discussed this topic with me in my life. "Have a good time talking, laughing, and dancing with these guys, Waris, then go home. Don't let them talk you into having sex. They don't know that you're different from an English woman; they don't understand that you've been circumcised."

After several months of waiting to get a room at the YMCA, I learned of a woman who wanted to share a room there. She was a student and couldn't afford the room by herself. This was perfect for me, because I couldn't either, and the room was large enough for the two of us. Halwu was a great friend, and I made others at the Y, because the whole place was swarming with young people. I was still going to school, gradually learning English, and working at my McDonald's job. My life was moving along, smooth and steady, but I had no idea how dramatically it was about to change.

One afternoon, I got off work at McDonald's and, still covered with grease, decided to leave through the front, passing by the counter where the customers ordered their food. And there, waiting for a Big Mac, was the man from All Souls Church School and his little girl. "Hello," I said, gliding by.

"Hey, it's you!" Clearly I was the last person he was expecting to see at McDonald's. "How are you?" he said eagerly.

"Fine, fine." To Sophie's friend I said, "And how are you?" I enjoyed showing off my English.

"She's fine," her father replied.

"She's growing quickly, isn't she? Well, I've got to dash. Byebye."

"Wait—where do you live?"

"Bye-bye," I said with a smile. I didn't want to talk to him anymore, because I still didn't trust this guy. The next thing I knew, he'd show up outside my door.

When I got back to the Y, I decided to consult the all-knowing Halwu about this mystery man. I grabbed my passport from the drawer, flipped through its pages, and pulled out Malcolm Fairchild's card from the spot where I'd stuck it the day I buried the little plastic bag in Uncle's garden.

Marching downstairs to Halwu's room, I said, "Tell me something. I have this card, and I've had it a long time. What is this man? I know it says fashion photographer, but what does that mean?"

My friend took the card from my hand. "It means somebody wants to put clothes on you and take your picture."

"You know, I'd really like to do that."

"Who is this man? Where'd you get this card?"

"Oh, he's this guy I met, but I don't really trust him. He gave me his card, then followed me home one day and started saying something to my aunt. She just got pissed off and started yelling at him. But I never really understood what he wanted."

"Well, why don't you call and ask him?"

"You *sure*?" I said, making a face. "Should I? Hey, why don't you come with me and you can talk to him—find out what's the story. My English is still not very good."

"Yeah, go call him."

It took me until the next day before I worked up the courage. As Halwu and I walked down to the pay phone together, my heart pounded a drumbeat in my ears. She put a coin in the slot, and I listened to it click. She held his card in one hand, squinting at it in the dim light of the dark hallway as she dialed. Then a pause. "Yes, may I speak to Malcolm Fairchild?" After exchanging a few opening comments, she got right to the heart of the matter: "You're not some kind of pervert or something, are you? You're not trying to kill my friend? . . . Yeah, but I mean we don't know anything about you—where you live or nothing . . . uh-huh, uh-huh . . . yeah." Halwu was scribbling something on a scrap of paper, and I strained to see over her shoulder.

"What's he saying?" I hissed. She waved at me to be quiet.

"Okay, then. Fair enough . . . we'll do that."

Halwu hung up the phone and took a big breath. "Well, he said, 'Why don't you both come by my studio, and see where I work, if you don't trust me? If you don't want to—well, that's okay, too.' "

I covered my mouth with both fists. "Yes. And? Are we going to go?"

"Shit, yeah, girl. We might as well check it out. Let's find out who this guy is that's been following you around."

11.

THE MODEL

The next day Halwu and I went down to inspect Malcolm Fairchild's studio. I had no idea what to expect, but when we opened the door, I stumbled into another world. Hanging everywhere were enormous posters and billboards featuring pictures of beautiful women. "Oh . . ." I said quietly, spinning around the room, looking at their elegant faces. And I just knew, like I'd known the day when I first heard Uncle Mohammed telling Auntie Sahru back in Mogadishu that he needed a girl to take to London—*this is it*. This is my opportunity—this is where I belong—this is what I want to do.

Malcolm came out and said hello; he told us to relax and gave us a cup of tea. When he sat down, he said to Halwu, "I just want you to know that all I want to do is take her picture." He pointed at me. "I've been following this little girl for over two years, and never have I had such a hard time just to take a photograph."

I stared at him with my mouth hanging open. "That's it?

That's it—you just want to take my picture—a picture like this?" I waved at the posters.

"Yes," he nodded emphatically. "Believe me. That's it." With his hand he drew a line down the center of his nose. "I just want this half of your face"—he turned to Halwu—"because she has the most beautiful profile."

I sat there thinking: All that time wasted! He followed me for two years and it took him two seconds to tell me he just wants to take my picture. "Well, I don't mind doing *that*." But suddenly I became wary, remembering some of my past experiences alone with men. "But she's got to be here, too!" I put my hand on my friend's arm and she nodded. "She's got to be here when you take the picture."

He looked at me with an expression of bafflement. "Yeah, okay. She can come too . . ." By this point I was so excited I was barely touching the chair. "Come day after tomorrow, ten o'clock, and I'll have someone here to do your makeup."

Two days later we returned to his studio. The makeup woman sat me down in a chair and started to work, coming at me with cotton, brushes, sponges, creams, paints, powders, poking me with her fingers, and pulling my skin. I had no idea what she was doing but sat quietly all the same, watching her perform these strange maneuvers with these strange materials. Halwu leaned back in her chair, grinning. Occasionally I would look at her and shrug or make a face. "Be still," the makeup woman commanded.

"Now'—she stepped back and put one hand on her hip and looked at me with satisfaction—"look in the mirror." I stood up and stared in the glass; one side of my face was transformed, all golden, silky, and light with makeup. The other side was plain old Waris.

"Wow! Look at me! But why did you just do one side?" I said in alarm.

"Because he only wants to photograph one side."

"Oh . . ."

She led me out to the studio where Malcolm positioned me on a stool. I swiveled around, studying the dark room full of objects I'd never seen before: the view camera, the lights, the battery packs, the cords hanging everywhere like snakes. He twisted me in front of the camera till I was at a ninety-degree angle to the lens. "Okay, Waris. Put your lips together and stare straight ahead. Chin up. That's it . . . beautiful—" Then I heard a click, followed by a loud pop which made me jump. The flashes went off, the lights blazing for a split second. Somehow, the lights popping made me feel like a different person; suddenly in that moment I imagined myself as one of the movie stars I had seen on the television, smiling into the cameras as they exited their limos at the premieres. Next, he took a piece of paper from the camera and sat looking at his watch.

"What are you doing?" I asked.

"Timing it." Malcolm motioned for me to walk over into the light and pulled off the top layer of paper. As I watched, a woman gradually emerged from the sheet of film as if by magic. When he handed me the Polaroid, I barely recognized myself; the shot showed the right side of my face, but instead of looking like Waris the maid, I looked like Waris the model. They had transformed me into a glamorous creature like the ones posing in Malcolm Fairchild's lobby.

Later in the week, after Malcolm had the film developed, he showed me the finished product. He put the transparencies up on a light box, and I loved them. I asked if he could make more pictures for me. He said it was too expensive, and unfortunately he couldn't afford it. But what he could do was have prints made for me of the shot he'd already taken.

A couple of months after Malcolm had taken my picture, he called me at the Y. "Look, I don't know if you're interested in modeling, but there's some people who want to meet you. One of the modeling agencies saw your photo in my book and said you should call them. If you like, you can sign with their firm and they'll get you jobs."

"Okay . . . but you have to take me there . . . because, you know, I don't feel comfortable going alone. Will you take me there and introduce me?"

"No, I can't do that, but I'll give you the address," he offered.

I carefully chose the ensemble I would wear for my important meeting with Crawford's modeling agency. As it was summer-time, and hot, I put on a red V-necked dress with short sleeves. The dress was not short, not long, but hit me squarely in the middle of the leg and was god-awful ugly.

I walked into the agency wearing my cheap red dress and white sneakers, and thinking: *This is it. I'm happening!* In reality I looked like shit. But even though I cringe whenever I think back to that day, it's just as well that I didn't realize how wrong I looked, because I was still wearing my best outfit. I certainly didn't have the money to go out and buy a new one.

When I arrived the receptionist asked if I had any pictures and I said I had one. She introduced me to a classically beautiful woman, elegantly dressed, named Veronica. Veronica called me into her office and motioned for me to sit down opposite her desk. "How old are you, Waris?"

"I'm young!" These were the first words that came to mind and I blurted them out. "Really—I'm young. These wrinkles' —I pointed to my eyes—"I was born with them."

She gave me a smile. "It's all right." Veronica began writing down my answers, filling out forms. "Where do you live?"

"Oh, I live in Y."

"What, now . . ." She frowned. "Where do you live?"

"I live in YMCA."

"Do you work?"

"Yes."

"What do you do?"

"McDonald's."

"Okay . . . Do you know about modeling?"

"Yes."

"What do you know about it—do you know much?"

"No. I know I want to do it." I repeated this last phrase several times for emphasis.

"Okay. Do you have a book—pictures?"

"No."

"Do you have any family here?"

"No."

"Where is your family?"

"Africa."

"Is that where you're from?"

"Yes, Somalia."

"Okay, so no one here."

"No, none my family here."

"Well. There's a casting right this minute and you have to go."

I was really struggling to understand her, and paused for a minute trying to decipher what she meant by her last statement. "I don't understand, sorry."

"A c-a-s-t-i-n-g." She drew out the word slowly.

"What's casting?"

"You know, it's an interview—when you go for a job and they interview you? Okay? Interview? You understand?"

"Yeah, yeah." I was lying by then. I had no idea what she was talking about. She gave me the address and told me to go straight over.

"I'll call them and tell them you're on your way. Do you have money for a taxi?"

"No, I can walk."

"No, no—it's too far. *Too far*. You have to take a taxi. *Taxi*. Okay? Look, here's ten pounds. Call me when you're finished. Okay?"

Riding crosstown in the taxi, I was in complete euphoria. *Oh, oh, oh, I am on my way now.* I'm going to be a model. Then I realized I forgot one thing: I didn't ask her what the job was. *Oh, well, it doesn't matter. I'll be fine because I am one good-looking bitch!*

When I arrived at the casting, I walked into another photographer's studio. I opened the door to a place crawling with professional models—room after room packed full of women with legs up to their necks. They strutted around like lionesses circling for the kill, preening in front of mirrors, bending at the waist to shake their hair, smearing makeup on their legs to make them look dark. I flopped down and said hello to one of the girls sitting next to me. "Um, what is the job?"

"Pirelli calendar."

"Mmmm." I nodded my head wisely. "Prulli calendar. Thank you." *What the hell is that—Prulli calendar?* I was a complete nervous wreck, unable to sit still, crossing and uncrossing my legs, twisting around in my chair until an assistant came out and told me I was next. Then I froze for a minute.

Turning to the girl beside me, I shooed her toward the assistant. "You go. I'm waiting for my friend." I repeated this move each time the assistant came out, until the entire place was empty. Everyone had gone home.

Finally the woman came out, leaned tiredly up against the wall and said, "Come on. You can go now." I stared at her for a minute and I said to myself, *Enough now, Waris. Are you going to do this thing or not? Come on, get up, let's go.*

I followed the woman into the studio and a man with his head glued to the back of a camera yelled out, "Over there. There's the mark." He motioned with one hand.

"Mark?"

"Yeah, stand on the mark."

"Oh, okay. Stand here."

"Okay. Take off your top."

I thought, *Surely I'm not hearing this man right*, but by now I felt ready to vomit. "My top, you mean my shirt?"

He brought his head out from under the drape, and stared at me like I was an idiot. With great irritation he said, "Yeah. Take off your shirt, you know, *why you're here?*"

"But I don't have a bra."

"That's the idea, so we can see your breasts."

"NO!" *What is this shit—my breasts!* Besides, I wasn't wearing a top. All I had on was my red dress. *What does this jerk think I'm going to do, just whip it off and stand there in my fucking underpants and tennis shoes?*

"No. No? Everybody's dying to come to this casting, and you're telling me no?"

"No, no, I'm sorry. Mistake, mistake. I make mistake," and in a panic I headed for the door. When I passed a series of Polaroids scattered across the floor, I bent down to examine them.

The photographer looked at me for a few seconds with his mouth open. Then he turned and called over his shoulder, "Oh, Lord, have we got something in here! Terence, we've got a little problem."

A heavy, robust man with thick gray hair and rosy jowls walked into the room and looked at me curiously. He smiled slightly. "Ah, yes. So what do we have here?"

I stood up straight and tears came to my eyes. "No. That's nothing I can do. I don't do this." I pointed at a photo of a woman nude from the waist up. At first I was simply disappointed. There went my big excitement, my big dream of being a model. *The first job I get and they want me to take my clothes off!* Then I became angry—furious—and I started to cuss them all in Somali. "You dirty fucking men! You shit! You pigs! Keep your fucking job!"

"What are you saying? Look, I'm far too busy for this now—" but by this time I was running out the door, slamming it nearly off the hinges. I cried all the way back to the Y, saying to myself, *I knew there was something sad, something deeply disgusting, about this whole modeling business.*

That evening I was lying on my bed, limp with misery, and my roommate said, "Waris, phone for you."

It was Veronica from the modeling agency. "It's you!" I yelled. "I don't want to talk to you people! You—you embars— embress—" I was trying to pronounce *embarrassed* but I couldn't even choke out that word. "It was terrible. It was very bad; I don't want to do this. I don't want to do this. I don't want to be with you no more!"

"Okay, now calm down, Waris. Do you know who that was today, the photographer?"

"No."

"Do you know who Terence Donovan is?"

"No."

"Well, do you have a friend who speaks English?"

"Yes."

"Well, anybody who speaks English will know who that man is. When we get off the phone, you ask them. He takes pictures of the royal family, Princess Di, and all the big name models. Anyway, he wants to see you again, he's interested in photographing you."

"He asked me to take my clothes off! You didn't tell me that before I went!"

"I know—well, we were in a big hurry; I just thought you were perfect for the job. I explained to him that you couldn't speak English and this sort of thing was against your culture. But this is the Pirelli calendar, and after this job comes out you will get much more work. Do you ever buy the fashion magazines, like *Vogue* and *Elle*?"

"No, I can't afford them. I look at them at the newsstand, but I always put them back."

"Okay, but you've seen them? That's the type of work you're

going to be doing. Terence Donovan is the best; if you want to be a model, you need this job. After this you'll be making all kinds of money, and do whatever you want."

"I'm not taking off my top."

I heard her sigh. "Waris, where did you say you work?"

"McDonald's."

"How much do they pay you?"

I told her.

"Well, he's paying you fifteen hundred pounds for one day."

"All for me? All mine?"

"Yes, and you get to travel, too. The job's in Bath; I don't know if you've been there, but it's a beautiful place. You'll be staying at the Royalton," she added, like I knew what that meant. "Look, do you want to do it, or not?"

By this point she had convinced me. Making this kind of money, I could quickly earn enough to help my mother. "Okay, okay! When can I go back to him?"

"How about tomorrow morning?"

"And I just have to take my top off—that's it? I mean, are you sure for fifteen hundred pounds I don't have to sleep with this man?"

"No, no. It's no trick. Nothing like that."

"Or . . . you know, like he wants me to spread my legs or some shit? If so, tell me now."

"Only take your top off. But remember, he's just doing a Polaroid tomorrow, then he'll tell you if you got the job. So be nice. . . ."

The next day when I got there, Terence Donovan looked at me and started laughing. "Oh. It's you again. Come here. What's your name?" From that moment on, he was very patient with me. Terence was a father, and he realized that I was just a frightened kid who needed help. He brought me tea, and showed me all his work, photos he'd taken of the most beautiful women in the world. "Okay. I'm going to show you some pictures. Come with me." He led me into another room full of shelves and drawers, and lying on a table was a calendar. He flipped through the pages, and on each page was the photograph of a different, stunningly gorgeous woman. "You see this? This is last year's Pirelli calendar. I do it every year. Except this year it's going to be different—just African women. Some pictures you'll be wearing clothes, but some might be no clothes." He went over everything with me, explaining how the whole process worked. By that point I felt comfortable that he wasn't just some dodgy, dirty old man. He said, "Okay, we're going to take the Polaroid now. Are you ready?"

As soon as Veronica told me how much I'd make I was ready, but now I was relaxed as well. "Yes, I'm ready." And from that moment on I was a complete professional. Stood on the mark—*whoosh*—off went the top, and I stared into the camera with confidence. Perfect! When he showed me the Polaroid, it reminded me of being back home in Africa. The shot was black and white, and very simple and honest—nothing tarty and corny; there was nothing pornographic about it. Instead, it was Waris as she'd grown up in the desert, looking just like a little girl child, tiny breasts exposed in the heat.

When I came home that night, I received the message from the agency saying I got the job and would be going to Bath next week. Veronica had left her home number. I called to explain that I was scheduled to work at McDonald's and couldn't afford not to, since I had no idea how long it would be before I'd see the money from my modeling job. But she saved me by saying if I needed money, she could give me an advance.

Since that day, I've never set foot in a McDonald's again. After I talked to Veronica, I hung up the phone and ran all over the Y. I told not only my friends about my new enterprise, but any stranger who would listen. Halwu said, "Oh, come on! Stop showing off, for God's sake! You're showing your tits, right?"

"Yeah, for fifteen hundred pounds!"

"For those little things? You should be ashamed," she laughed.

"But this is not like that. This is really nice! Not that nasty stuff . . . and we're going to Bath and stay in a big hotel."

"Well, I don't want to hear it—just stop telling everybody in the building about it, all right?"

The night before we left, I couldn't sleep at all, wishing it were morning; my packed duffel sat by the door. I still couldn't believe it—I'd never been anywhere, and these people were paying me money to go! Terence Donovan was sending a limousine to pick me up and bring me to Victoria Station. There the group—the photographers, assistants, art director, four other models, the makeup artist, hairstylist, and me—would assemble to take the train to Bath. I was the first person to arrive, because I was so nervous about missing the train. The next person who got there was Naomi Campbell.

When we arrived in Bath, we checked into the Royalton, which was like a palace; I was stunned to find out I'd have a huge room all to myself. But that first night, Naomi came to my room and asked if she could sleep with me. She was very young, and sweet, about sixteen or seventeen, and frightened to stay by herself. I said sure, because I enjoyed having the company. "Don't tell them, okay? They're going to be mad if they find out they're wasting all that money on my room and nobody's sleeping in it."

"Don't worry about it—just stay in my room." After years of experience, it came naturally to me to play the mother. In fact, my friends called me Mama, because I always wanted to mother everybody. "I'm not going to say anything, Naomi."

When we started to work in the morning, two girls would go first and get their hair and makeup done. Then, while they were on the set getting their pictures taken, the next two would get ready, and so on. The first morning that the hairstylist started working on me, I told him to chop it all off. Back then, I was pretty chunky for a model; I had all that nice juicy McDonald's meat on me. So I wanted my hair short, to make me look more fashionable. The stylist kept cutting and cutting, until almost nothing was left—my hair was about one inch long all over my head. Everyone said, "Ooohh, you look so different." But I decided I really wanted to shock people, and I said to the hairstylist, "You know what I'm going to do? I'm going to bleach my hair blond."

"Oh, God! Well, I'm not going to do it. You'd look wicked—mad!"

Naomi Campbell laughed and said, "Waris, you know what? One day you're going to be famous. And don't forget me then, okay?" Of course, the reverse came true, and she's the famous one.

We went on working like this for six days, and I couldn't believe I was getting paid for it. As soon as I got off in the evening, and the group would ask me what I wanted to do, my answer was always the same: go shopping. They would let me take the car, and the limo driver would drop me wherever I wanted, then come back and pick me up. When the job was done, my picture wound up being selected for the cover, which was a surprising honor and got me even more publicity.

We took the train back to London; as soon as we arrived, I jumped in the limo, and the driver asked where to drop me. I told him to take me to the agency. When I walked in the door, they said, "Guess what? There's another casting for you, and it's right around the corner. But hurry up—you have to go right now."

I protested about this, because I was tired. "I'll go tomorrow," I said.

"No, no. Tomorrow will be too late; it's over then. They're

looking for Bond girls for the new James Bond movie, *The Living Daylights*, with Timothy Dalton. Leave your bag here and let's go. We'll walk you over and show you where it is."

One of the guys from the agency took me around the corner and pointed to the building: "You see that door there, where all the people are going? That's the place." I went in, and it was a repeat of the day I went to Terence Donovan's studio, except worse. Inside was an army of girls, standing, leaning, sitting, gossiping, strutting, and striking poses.

The assistant said, "We're asking everybody to say a couple of words." This news sounded ominous to me, but I kept telling myself I was a professional model now, right? I'd worked for Terence Donovan on the Pirelli calendar. This was nothing I couldn't handle. When my turn came they ushered me into the studio and told me to stand on the mark.

I said, "I just want to tell you guys that I don't speak very good English."

They held up a cue card and said, "That's okay, you just have to read this." *Oh, my God—now what? I have to tell them I can't read? No, it's too much, it's too humiliating. I can't do it.*

Instead I said, "Excuse me. I have to go—I'll be right back." And I just walked out of the building and went to the agency for my bag. God knows how long the casting people waited for me before someone realized I wasn't coming back. At the agency I told them I hadn't gotten in yet; I just wanted to pick up my bag first, because it looked like it was going to be a long wait. This was around one or two in the afternoon, but I went home, dropped off my bag, then went out searching for a hairdresser. I wandered into a shop close to the Y, and a gentleman asked what he could do for me.

"Bleach my hair," I said.

The stylist raised his eyebrows. "Well, you know we can do it, but it's going to take a long time. And we close at eight."

"Okay. Then we have till eight."

"Yeah, but we have other appointments ahead of you." I

begged him till he finally gave in. He applied the peroxide and I immediately regretted my begging. My hair was so short that the chemicals started burning my head, and I felt like big hunks of my scalp were peeling away. But gritting my teeth, I waited it out. When the hairdresser washed my hair, it turned orange. So he had to do it again because the peroxide needed to stay on longer to remove the color. The second time it came out yellow. The third time I finally became a blonde.

I loved it, but as I walked back to the subway, little kids grabbed their mother's hands and cried, "Mommy, Mommy, Mommy, what is that thing? Is that a man or a woman?" I thought, *I'll be damned. Maybe I made a mistake here? I'm scaring the children.* But by the time I reached the Y, I decided I didn't give a shit, because my hair wasn't meant to impress the children. Being blond was something I wanted to try for *me* and I thought it looked bloody fabulous.

When I got home, I had message after message waiting for me from the agency. *Where are you? Everyone at the casting is still waiting for you. Are you coming back? They still want to see you. They're still waiting* . . . But the agency was closed, so I called Veronica at home. "Waris, where on earth did you go? They thought you went to the bathroom! Promise me you'll go back tomorrow?" She made me agree I'd go back the next morning.

Of course, what I had neglected to tell Veronica, the casting people noticed immediately: that yesterday I was an ordinary black woman, today I was a Somali with blond hair. The whole production stopped to stare at me. "Wow! That is amazing— you just did that last night?"

"Yeah."

"Oh, my. Love it. Love it—don't change it again, all right?"

I said, "Believe me, I'm not going through that torture again any time soon. By now my scalp is blond."

We picked up with the test where we'd left off the day before. "Are you worried about your English—is that the problem?"

"Yeah." I still couldn't bring myself to admit that I couldn't read.

"Okay. Well, just stand there, look right, look left. Say your name, where you're from, what agency you're with, and that's all." That much I could handle.

Afterward, since I was right around the corner from Crawford's, I decided it would be fun to drop by the agency and show them my hair. They went berserk. "What the fuck have you done to your hair!?"

"It's nice, isn't it?"

"Oh, my God, no, it's not nice! We can't book you now! You've got to consult with us before you do something like this to your appearance, Waris. The client has to know what they're getting—this isn't just *your* hair anymore that you can do anything you want with."

The casting people did, however, like my hair, and I got the Bond Girl job. But from that day forward the folks at the agency had a nickname for me: Guinness. Because I was dark with a white head on the top.

I was very excited about my new movie career, until one day I went by the agency and Veronica said, "Well, great news, Waris. *The Living Daylights* will be filmed in Morocco."

I froze.

"You know, unfortunately, I have something to tell you, which I really would rather not have to tell you. Remember the day you hired me and asked me if I had a passport? Well, I do, but I don't have a current visa, so if I leave England, I can't get back in."

"Waris, you lied to me! You have to have a valid passport to be a model or we can't use you; you have to travel all the time. God—you're not going to be able to do the job. We'll have to cancel."

"No, no. Don't do that—I'll think of something. I'll figure it out." Veronica gave me a disbelieving look, but said it was up to me. For the next few days I sat in my room thinking and thinking but nothing came to mind. I consulted all my friends, but the only solution anyone could think of was that I might marry someone, and I certainly had nobody to marry. I felt terrible, not only that my career was being flushed down the toilet, but that I'd lied to Veronica and let the agency down.

One night in the midst of this dilemma, I went downstairs to the pool at the Y. My friend Marilyn, a black woman who was born in London, worked there as a lifeguard. When I first moved in, I would come to the pool and just sit there and stare at it because I love the water. Finally, one night Marilyn asked me why I never went in, and I told her I couldn't swim. "Well, I can teach you," she said.

"Okay." I went to the deep end of the pool, took a deep breath, and dived in. I figured since she was a lifeguard, she could save me. But guess what? Underneath the water, I swam like a fish all the way to the other end of the pool.

I came up with the biggest grin on my face. "I did it! I can't believe, I did it!"

But she was angry. "Why did you tell me you couldn't swim?"

"I never swam in my life!" After that episode, we became good friends. She lived with her mother on the other side of the city, and sometimes, when she got off work late at night, she'd be too tired to make the long journey home. So she would stay in my room.

Marilyn was a generous, lovely person, and as I swam in the pool that evening, trying to forget my passport troubles, the solution came to me. I came to the surface and pushed up my goggles. "Marilyn," I panted, "I need your passport."

"What? What are you talking about?" I explained my problem. "You're out of your fucking mind, Waris! Do you know what's going to happen? They're going to catch you, deport you for life, and put me in jail. Now, what am I risking all that for? So you can be in some stupid James Bond movie? I don't think so."

"Oh, come on, Marilyn. It's fun, an adventure—take the risk. We'll go to the post office and I'll apply for a passport in your name; I'll forge your signature, and put my picture on it. I don't have much time, but I can get a temporary passport in just a couple of days. *Please, Marilyn!* It's my big chance to be in the movies!"

Finally, after hours of pleading and begging, the day before I was scheduled to fly to Morocco, she gave in. I had my photo taken, then we went to the post office; an hour later I had my British passport. But all the way home, she was worried sick. I kept saying, "Cheer up, Marilyn. Come on, it'll be okay. You've just got to have faith."

"Faith my ass. I have faith that this one stupid incident can ruin my whole life." That night we went to her mother's house to spend the night. I suggested that we rent some videos and get some Chinese takeout and relax. But when we got to Marilyn's, she said, "Waris. I can't do it. It's too dangerous. Give me back the passport." I sorrowfully handed it to her, watching my movie career disappear into the realm of lost fantasies. "You stay here— I'm going to hide it," she said. She took it upstairs to her room.

I said, "Okay, girl. If it makes you feel like this, there's no point in suffering. If you think something will go wrong, then we shouldn't do it." But that night, as soon as she went to sleep, I started scouring her room. She had hundreds of books in there, and I knew that's where it had to be hidden. One by one, I opened them and shook them. The car was coming to her house in the morning to pick me up and take me to the airport, so I was moving fast. And suddenly the passport fell out at my feet. Grabbing it up quietly, I stuck it in my duffel, then went to bed. In the morning I woke up and sneaked downstairs before the driver came to ring the bell, so he wouldn't wake anybody up. It was cold outside, but I stood on the sidewalk shivering until the car came at seven, then headed to Heathrow.

Getting out of England was no problem. In Morocco, my movie career consisted of a couple of scenes where I was supposed to be what the script called "a beautiful girl lying around the pool." Then I was in another scene where we were sitting inside this fantastic house in Casablanca having tea, yet for some reason all the women were naked. James Bond flew through the bloody roof, and we threw our hands up to our faces and screamed, "Ahhh, oh, my God!" But I thought, *Well, I'm not complaining. Since I didn't get a speaking part, at least that means I don't have to worry about the fact that I can't read.*

The rest of the time we just lounged around the house, sat by the pool, ate and ate, and did nothing at all. I stayed in the sun the whole time, so thrilled to see it again after living in foggy London. Not knowing how to mingle with the movie people, I stayed mostly by myself; they were all very handsome and intimidating, spoke perfect English, and seemed to know each other—gossiping about this job and that job. I was just thrilled to be back in Africa again; in the evening, I'd go sit outside with the mamas cooking colorful food for their families. I couldn't speak the language, but we'd smile, and I'd say one word of Arabic, they'd say one word of English, and we'd laugh.

One day the film crew came around and said, "Anybody want to go to the camel races? Come on, we're getting a group together." After standing around watching the races for a while, I asked one of the Arab jockeys if I could ride, too. In a mangled combination of Arabic and English we communicated; he informed me that, oh no, women weren't allowed to ride the camels.

"I bet I can beat you," I said. "Come on, I'll show you— you're afraid for me to ride because I'm going to win!" This infuriated him—that this little girl would challenge him—and that's when he decided to let me race. The word spread through the movie crew that Waris was going to enter the next race; everybody gathered around and a few people tried to talk me out of it. I informed them to get their money out and bet on Waris, because I was going to teach these Moroccan guys a lesson. There were about ten Arab men seated on their camels at the starting line, and me. When the race began, we took off and flew. It was a terrifying ride, because I was not familiar with this camel and didn't really know how to make him "kick." Camels not only hurtle forward at a fast clip, but bounce up and down and side to side, so I was hanging on for my life. I knew if I fell, I would be trampled to death.

When the race was finished, I had come in second place. The James Bond people were astonished, and I could tell I'd gained a new, if weird respect, especially as they collected their winning bets. "How did you know how to do that?" one girl asked me.

"Easy. When you're born on top of a camel, you know how to ride one," I laughed.

However, the camel race demanded no courage compared to what was awaiting me when I returned to Heathrow. As we exited the plane, we lined up for customs; as the line inched forward, everyone got their passports out. The officials would yell out, "NEXT!" and each time it was the most excruciating torture to hear that word, because it meant I was one step closer to being arrested.

The British officials are always harsh enough letting you into England; but if you're African and black, they're doubly tough. You know they'll be scanning your passport with razor eyes. I felt so sick I wanted to faint—and began to fantasize about lying down on the floor and dying so I wouldn't have to go through this agony anymore. *God*, I prayed, *please help me. If I live through this, I promise I'll never do anything this stupid again.*

I was almost there, if my knees didn't give out. Then suddenly an obnoxious male model named Geoffrey grabbed my passport from my hand. He was a smart-aleck bastard anyway, who delighted in making other people miserable, and this time he couldn't have found a more vulnerable target. "Oh, please, please—" I tried to grab it back from him, but he was much taller than I was and held it up where I couldn't reach it.

Everyone throughout the trip had called me Waris; they all knew my name was Waris Dirie. Geoffrey opened the passport and shrieked, "Oh, my God. Listen to this—listen to this, everybody. Guess what her name is? MARILYN MONROE."

"Please give that to me—" I was shaking by now.

He ran around in circles, doubled over laughing, then began showing the whole gang my passport. "Her name is Marilyn Monroe! Check this shit out! What the fuck? What's the story here, girl? No wonder you bleached your hair!"

I had no idea there was another Marilyn Monroe. To me, she was simply my friend, the lifeguard at the Y. Luckily, I didn't even know about the added concern that I was walking around with a passport bearing my photo and the name of a famous movie star. At that moment, my biggest worry was that my passport said I was Marilyn Monroe, born in London, yet I barely spoke a word of English. *I'm dead . . . It's over . . . I'm dead . . . It's over . . .* were the words ringing through my brain as my whole body poured a river of sweat.

All the James Bond people joined in the game: "Hey, so what's your real name? Now, really—where are you from? Did you know that people born in the middle of London don't speak English?" They were just ribbing the piss out of me. This Geoffrey jerk finally handed back my passport. I went back to the end of the line, letting all of them go through ahead of me, hoping they'd be gone by the time it was my turn.

"NEXT!"

As the rest of the film crew went through customs, no one went on about their business, running off to hop in the car as they normally would have after a long trip. No. They waited, huddled around in a group just beyond the customs booth, to see how I was going to get out of this one.

Pull yourself together, Waris, girl. You can do it. I walked up and handed the customs clerk my passport with a dazzling smile. "Hello!" I called out, then held my breath. I knew better than to say one more word, because then he'd find out my English was a joke.

"Nice day, isn't it?"

"Umm." I nodded and smiled. He handed me my passport and I sailed by. The James Bond crew stood there looking at me in astonishment. I wanted to collapse, exhale, and fall down on the floor, but I flew past them too, knowing I wasn't safe until I got out of the airport. *Just keep moving, Waris. Get out of Heathrow alive.*

12.

THE DOCTORS

While I was still living at the YMCA, I spent an afternoon in the pool downstairs, swimming laps. After I finished, I dressed in the locker room, and was heading back upstairs when I heard someone calling my name from the Y's little café. It was a guy I knew who also lived in the building. His name was William and he motioned for me to come in. "Waris, have a seat. Would you like something to eat?"

William was eating a cheese sandwich, and I said, "Yeah, I'll have one of those, please." My English was still pretty weak, but I could make out the gist of what he was saying. While we ate, he asked me if I'd like to go to the movies. This was not the first time he'd asked me out. William was young, handsome, white, and always very sweet. But as he talked, I stopped hearing what he was saying. Instead I sat staring at him, watching his lips move, and my mind began running like a computer:

Go to the movies with him

If only he knew about me
Oh, imagine what it would be like to have a boyfriend
It might be nice
Someone to talk to
Someone to love me
But if I go to the movies
He'll want to kiss me
Then he'll want to have sex
And if I agree
He'll find out I'm not like other girls
I'm damaged
Or if I disagree
He'll be angry and we'll have a fight
Don't go
It's not worth the heartache
Say no
If only he knew about me, he'd realize it has nothing to do with him.

I smiled and shook my head. "No, thanks. I have too much work." The hurt look that I knew would come, came, and I shrugged, saying to both of us: *There's nothing I can do.*

This problem began when I moved to the Y. When I lived with my family, I was normally never around strange men unchaperoned. A man who came to my parents, or Auntie Sahru's, or Uncle Mohammed's, would either know our culture and not attempt to ask me on a date, or would be dealt with by the family. But since I left my uncle's house, I had been alone. And for the first time I was forced to cope with these situations by myself. The Y was a building chock-full of young, single men. Going to clubs with Halwu I met more men. Modeling I met more men still.

But I was interested in none of them. The thought of having sex with a man never crossed my mind, but unfortunately, after some of my awful experiences, I knew it crossed theirs. Although I've always wondered, I can't imagine what my life would be like if I hadn't been circumcised. I like men and I'm a very emotional, loving person. At that time, it had been six years since I ran away from my father, and the loneliness had been hard for me; I missed my family. And someday I hoped to have a husband and family of my own. But as long as I was sewn up, I was very much closed to the idea of a relationship, shut away into myself. It was as if the stitches prevented any man from entering me—physically or emotionally.

The other problem that prevented me from having a relationship with a man came up when I realized I was different from other women, particularly Englishwomen. After I arrived in London, it gradually dawned on me that not all girls had had done to them what had been done to me. When I lived with my cousins at Uncle Mohammed's house, sometimes I would be in the bathroom with the other girls. I was amazed when they peed quickly in a heavy stream, whereas it took me about ten minutes to urinate. The tiny hole the circumciser had left me only permitted the urine to escape one drop at a time. "Waris, why do you pee like that—what's wrong with you?" I didn't want to tell them because I assumed when they got back to Somalia they would be circumcised, too, so I just laughed it off.

However, my periods were no laughing matter. From the very beginning, when I was around eleven or twelve years old, they were a nightmare. They began one day when I was alone out tending my sheep and goats. The day was unbearably hot, and I sat weakly under a tree, feeling even more uncomfortable because my stomach hurt. I wondered, *What is this pain? Maybe I'm pregnant? Maybe I'm going to have a baby? But I haven't been with a man, so how can I be pregnant?* The pressure grew and grew, and so did my fear. About an hour later I went to pee and saw blood. I thought I was dying.

Leaving the animals grazing in the bush, I flew home, and

ran to my mother crying and screaming, "I'm dying! Oh, Mama, I'm dying!"

"What are you talking about?"

"I'm bleeding, Mama—I'm going to die!"

She stared at me hard. "No, you're not going to die. It's all right. It's your period." I had never heard of periods—knew nothing about any of it.

"Can you please explain this to me—tell me what you're talking about?" My mother explained the process as I writhed around in misery, holding my abdomen. "But how do I stop this pain? Because, you know, it *feels* like I'm dying!"

"Waris, you can't stop it. You just have to let it go. Wait until it's ready to leave."

However, I wasn't prepared to accept that solution. Looking for something that would bring me relief, I went back into the desert and started digging a hole under a tree. The motion felt good and gave me something to take my mind off my pain. I dug and dug with a stick until I had a spot deep enough to bury the bottom half of my body. Then I climbed in, packing the dirt in around me; the underground hole was cooler, sort of like an ice pack, and I would rest there during the heat of the day.

Digging a hole in the ground became the method I would use for coping with my period each month. Oddly enough, later I found out that my sister Aman had done the same thing. But this treatment had its drawbacks. One day my father came walking by and saw his daughter half buried under a tree. Viewed from a distance, I looked like I'd been cut off at the waist and had been sat on the sand. "What the hell are you doing?" On hearing his voice, I automatically tried to jump out of the hole, but since the dirt was packed tightly around me, I didn't get very far. Struggling out, I clawed with my hands to get my legs free. Papa started laughing hysterically. I was too shy to explain why I did it, and afterward he kept making jokes about it. "If you want to bury yourself alive, do it properly. I mean, come on, what was that halfway business?" Later, he asked my mother about my strange behavior. He worried his daughter was turning into some kind of burrowing animal—a mole obsessed with tunneling underground—but Mama explained the situation.

However, as my mother had predicted, there was nothing I could do to stop the pain. Although I didn't understand it at the time, the menstrual blood backed up in my body the same way the urine did. But since it was continuously flowing—or trying to—for several days, the pressure of the blockage was excruciating. The blood came out one drop at a time; as a result, my periods usually lasted for at least ten days.

This problem reached a crisis while I was living with my uncle Mohammed. Early one morning, I prepared his breakfast as usual. Then carrying the tray from the kitchen to the dining room table where he waited, I suddenly blacked out, and the dishes crashed to the floor around me. Uncle ran to me and started slapping my face, trying to bring me around. I began to regain consciousness and, as if he were far away, I heard him crying, "Maruim! Maruim! She's fainted!"

When I came to, Aunt Maruim asked me what was wrong, and I told her I'd gotten my period that morning. "Well, this is not right, we have to take you to the doctor. I'll make an appointment with my doctor this afternoon."

I told Auntie's doctor that my periods were very bad, and whenever I got them, I started passing out. The pain paralyzed me, and I didn't know what to do about it. "Can you help me? Please—is there something you can do? Because I can't stand it anymore." However, I didn't mention to him that I'd been circumcised. I didn't even know how to begin a discussion of that topic. Back then I was still a girl, and all the issues associated with my physical condition were mixed with ignorance, confusion, and shame. And I wasn't sure my circumcision was the source of the problem, since I still thought what happened to me happened to all girls. My mother hadn't thought my pain unusual, because all the women she had ever known had been circumcised, and they all went through this agony. It's considered part of the burden of being a woman.

Since the doctor didn't examine me, he didn't find out my secret. "The only thing I can give you for pain is birth control pills. That will stop the pain because it will stop your periods."

Hallelujah! I began taking the pills, even though I didn't really like the idea. I'd heard from my cousin Basma that they were bad for you. But within the month, the pain stopped and so did much of my bleeding. Because the drug tricked my body into thinking it was pregnant, other unexpected things happened also. My breasts grew; my ass grew; my face filled out, and my weight exploded. These drastic changes in my body seemed extremely weird and unnatural. Deciding I'd rather deal with the pain, I stopped taking the pills. And deal with the pain I did, because it all came right back again, fiercer than ever.

Later, I visited a second doctor to see if he could help. But that experience was a repeat of the first; he wanted to give me birth control pills as well. I explained that I had tried that option, but I didn't like the side effects. However, without the pills I couldn't function for several days each month; I simply went to bed and wanted to die so the suffering would stop. Did he know of another solution? The doctor said, "Well, what do you expect? When women take birth control pills, for the most part their periods stop. When women have periods, they have pain. Take your pick." When the third doctor repeated this same advice, I realized I needed to do something besides visit new doctors.

I said to Auntie, "Maybe I need to see a special kind of doctor?"

She looked at me sharply. "No," she said emphatically. "And by the way—what are you telling these men?"

"Nothing. That I just want to stop the pain, that's all." I knew the unspoken message of her comment: circumcision is our African custom—and not something you discuss with these white men.

I began to understand, however, that this was exactly what I was going to have to do. Or suffer and live like an invalid for one third of each month. I also understood that this action would never be accepted by my family. My next step became clear: I would have to secretly go back to the doctor, and tell him I'd been circumcised. Perhaps then one of them could help me.

I chose the first doctor, Dr. Macrae, because he was located in a big hospital and, I reasoned, would have the facilities if I needed surgery. When I called for an appointment, I had to wait a whole agonizing month before I could get in. When the day came, I made some excuse to Auntie for my absence, and went to Dr. Macrae's office. I said to him, "There's something I haven't told you. I'm from Somalia and I—I—" It was terrible for me to try to explain this horrible secret in my broken English. "I been circumcised."

He didn't even let me finish the sentence. "Go get changed. I want to examine you." He saw the look of terror on my face. "It's okay." He called in his nurse, and she showed me where to change, how to put the gown on.

When we went back into the examining room, I really questioned what I'd gotten myself into this time. The thought that a girl from my country would sit in this strange place, spread her legs, and let a white man look in there . . . well, it was the most shameful thing I could imagine. The doctor kept trying to get my knees apart. "Relax. It's all right—I'm a doctor. The nurse is right here—she's standing right there." I craned my neck around to look in the direction his finger was pointing. She smiled reassuringly at me and I finally gave in. I forced myself to think about something else, pretend I wasn't here, but was back walking in the desert with my goats on a beautiful day.

When he finished, he asked the nurse if there was someone in the hospital who could speak Somali; she said yes, there was a Somali woman working downstairs. But when she came back, she brought a Somali man instead, because she couldn't find the woman. I thought, *Oh, beautiful! Here's the rotten luck, to discuss this horrible business using a Somali man to translate! How much worse could it get?*

Dr. Macrae said, "Explain to her that she's closed up way too much—I don't even know how she's made it this far. We need to operate on her as soon as possible." Right away, I could see the Somali man wasn't happy. He pursed his lips and glared at the doctor. Between the fact that I did understand some English, and the Somali man's attitude, I sensed that something was not right.

He said to me, "Well, if you really want it, they can open you up." I just stared at him. "But do you know this is against your culture? Does your family know you're doing this?"

"No. To tell you the truth, no."

"Who do you live with?"

"My aunt and uncle."

"Do they know you're doing this?"

"No."

"Well, the first thing I'd do is discuss it with them." I nodded, thinking: *That's the response of a typical African man. Thanks for your good advice, brother. That will put an end to the whole business.*

Dr. Macrae added that he couldn't do the operation right away; I'd need to make an appointment. I realized then that I couldn't do it, because Auntie would find out. "Yeah. I'll do that—I'll call for an appointment." Of course, over a year went by and I never called.

Immediately after my family returned to Somalia, I called and made an appointment, but the soonest I could get was two months. As the two months ticked by, I remembered the horror of my circumcision. I thought the surgery would be a repeat of that process, and the more I thought about it, I decided I couldn't go through that again. When the day came, I simply never went to the hospital and never called.

By this point I was living at the Y. The problems with my periods hadn't decreased, but now I was having to earn my living outside the home. You couldn't just miss a week of work each month and hope to keep a job. I struggled along, but my friends at the Y saw I was in bad shape. Marilyn kept asking me what was wrong. I explained to her that I'd been circumcised as a girl in Somalia.

But Marilyn was raised in London, and she couldn't fathom what I was talking about. "Why don't you show me, Waris? I really don't know what you're talking about. Did they cut you here? This? That? What did they do?"

Finally one day I pulled my pants down and showed her. I'll never forget the look on her face. Tears poured down her cheeks as she turned away. I felt so desperate, because I thought: *Oh, my God, is it really that bad?* The first words out of her mouth were "Waris, do you feel *anything?*"

"What are you talking about?"

She just shook her head. "You know, do you remember how you looked when you were a little girl? Before they did this?"

"Yes."

"Well, that's how I am now. You're not the same." Now I knew for sure. No longer did I need to wonder—or maybe even hope—that all women had been mutilated the way I had. Now I knew for certain that I was different. I didn't wish my suffering on anyone else, but I didn't want to be on my own. "So this hasn't happened to you, to you and your mother?"

She shook her head and began crying again. "It's horrible, Waris. I can't believe that anybody would do this to you."

"Oh, come on, please don't make me feel sad."

"*I* feel sad. Sad and angry. I'm crying in a way because I can't believe there are people in the world who would do this to a little girl."

We sat there in silence for a few moments, and while Marilyn continued to sob quietly I couldn't look at her. Then I decided I'd had enough. "Well, fuck it. I'm going to have this surgery. I'm going to call this doctor tomorrow. At least I can enjoy going to the bathroom. That's all I can enjoy, but at least that much."

"I'll go with you, Waris. I'll be right there. I promise."

Marilyn called the doctor's office and made the appointment for me; this time I had to wait a month. During that time, I kept saying, "Girl, you sure you're coming with me?"

"Don't worry. I'm coming. I'll be right there." When the morning came for surgery, she got me up early and we went to the hospital. The nurse led me into the room. Ah, there it was: the table. When I saw the operating table, I nearly turned around and ran out of the building. It was better than a rock in the bush, but I had little hope the procedure would feel much better. However, Dr. Macrae gave me an anesthetic for pain— something I wished I'd had when the Killer Woman butchered me. Marilyn held my hand while I went to sleep.

When I woke up, they had moved me into a double room with a woman who had just given birth. This lady, along with all the people I'd meet at lunchtime in the cafeteria, kept asking me, "So, what are you here for?"

What could I say? Confess, "Oh, I came to have surgery on my vagina. My pussy was just way too tight!" I never told anyone the truth. I said I had a stomach bug. And even though my recovery process was greatly improved over that of my circumcision, some of my worst memories of that time were repeated. Every time I had to pee, the same old thing: salt and hot water. But at least the nurses let me have a bath and I'd soak in the hot water. Ahhhh. They gave me painkillers, so it wasn't so bad, but I was really glad when it was over.

Dr. Macrae did a fine job, and I've always been grateful to him. He told me, "You know, you're not alone. Let me tell you,

I have women come in here with this same problem all the time. A lot of women from the Sudan, Egypt, Somalia. Some of them are pregnant and they're terrified because trying to give birth while they're sewn up is dangerous. There can be a lot of complications—the baby can suffocate trying to exit the tight opening, or the mother can bleed to death. So, without the permission of their husbands or their family they come to me, and I do my bit. I do my best."

Within two or three weeks I was back to normal. Well, not exactly normal, but more like a woman who hadn't been circumcised. Waris was a new woman. I could sit down on the toilet and pee—*whoosh!* There's no way to explain what a new freedom that was.

13.

PASSPORT DILEMMA

When I returned from my movie debut as a Bond Girl, I told the driver to take me straight to Marilyn Monroe's house. Like a coward, I hadn't called my friend after I'd left for Morocco, but instead had decided to let her cool off until I returned. Standing on her stoop with a sack full of presents, I nervously rang the bell. She opened the front door, grinned from ear to ear, then rushed forward to hug me. "You did it! You crazy bitch, you did it!" Marilyn forgave me for stealing the fraudulent passport; she said she was so impressed that I had the guts to pull the whole caper off that she couldn't stay mad. But I agreed never to put either one of us through the danger of using her passport again, especially after my torture passing through customs at Heathrow.

I was glad that Marilyn forgave me, because she was indeed a good friend. And once again, I had to call on that friendship. When I returned home to London, I thought my modeling career was just beginning—especially after the back-to-back successes of working with Terence Donovan and being in a

James Bond movie. But as if by magic, my modeling career vanished over night, disappearing as suddenly and mysteriously as it had begun. No more working at McDonald's for me, but also no more living at the YMCA. With no work, I couldn't afford to keep my room there, and was forced to move into the house with Marilyn and her mother. This arrangement pleased me much more in many ways—living in a real home, and being part of their family. I wound up staying with them for seven months, and even though they didn't complain, I knew I'd outstayed my welcome. I got a few little modeling jobs here and there, but still was not making enough money to support myself. I moved in with another friend, a Chinese man named Frankie, who was a friend of my hairdresser. Frankie owned a big house—well, to me it was big because it had two bedrooms. He generously offered to let me stay there while I tried to get my career going.

In 1987, shortly after I moved in with Frankie, *The Living Daylights* came out. A couple of weeks later, another friend took me out on Christmas Eve; everyone in London was celebrating, and caught up in the mood, I came home very late. As soon as my head touched the pillow, I was asleep. But a steady tapping on my bedroom window woke me. Looking outside I saw the friend who'd just dropped me off, holding a newspaper. He was trying to say something, but I couldn't understand him, so I opened the window.

"Waris! You're on the cover of *The Sunday Times*!"

"Oh . . . " I rubbed my eyes. "Honestly—I am?"

"Yeah! Take a look." He held up the paper and there was a three-quarter shot of my face filling the whole cover. It was larger than life-size, with my blond hair ablaze and a determined look on my face.

"That's nice . . . I'm going back to bed now . . . sleep," and I stumbled to my bed. By noon, however, I'd realized the possibilities of that publicity. Surely being on the cover of *The Sunday Times* of London would generate some action. In the meantime, I hustled. I ran all over London going to castings, pestered my booker, and finally switched modeling agencies, but nothing improved.

My new agency said, "Well, Waris, there's simply not much of a market for a black model in London. You have to travel for jobs—Paris, Milan, New York." I was all for traveling, except for the same old problem: my passport dilemma. The agency said they'd heard of an attorney, Harold Wheeler, who had been able to help several immigrants with their passports. Why didn't I talk to him?

I went to this Harold Wheeler's office and discovered that he wanted an extortionate amount of money to help me—two thousand pounds. Still, I reasoned, since I would be able to travel and work, I could make that money back in no time. As it stood now, I was quickly going nowhere. I scraped together the money from every possible source, eventually raising the two-thousand-pound fee. But I was concerned about giving him all my borrowed cash, then finding out he was a crook.

Making sure to leave my cash at home, I made my second appointment, and took Marilyn with me for her opinion. I rang the intercom and Wheeler's secretary answered, then buzzed us into the building. My friend waited in the lobby while I met with Wheeler in his office.

I spoke bluntly: "Tell me the truth. I just want to know if this passport I'm getting is going to be worth two thousand pounds. Am I going to be able to travel all over the world legally? I don't want to wind up stranded in some godforsaken place and get deported. And where are you getting this thing from?"

"No, no, no, I'm afraid I can't talk about my sources. You must leave that to me. If you want a passport, my dear, I can certainly get you a passport. And you have my word, it will be perfectly legal. After we begin the process it will take two weeks. My secretary will give you a ring when it's ready." *Great! That means two weeks from now I can just bugger off anyplace I like, anytime.*

"Well, okay, that sounds good," I said. "What do we do next?" Wheeler explained how I would marry an Irish national, and he just happened to have such an individual in mind. The two thousand pounds would go to the Irishman in return for his services. Wheeler would keep only a small fee for himself. He wrote down the date and time of my appointment; I was to meet my new husband at the registry office, and bring one hundred and fifty pounds in cash for additional expenses.

"You'll be meeting a Mr. O'Sullivan," Wheeler advised in his proper British accent. He continued to write as he talked. "He is the gentleman you'll be marrying. Oh, and—by the way—congratulations." He glanced up and gave me a slight smile.

Later, I asked Marilyn if she thought I should trust this guy. She said, "Well, he has a nice office in a nice building in a nice neighborhood. He has his name on the door. He has a professional secretary. He looks legitimate enough to me."

My trusted friend Marilyn also came with me as a witness on my wedding day. Waiting outside the registry office, we watched an old man with a withered red face, unruly white hair, and ragged clothes zigzag down the sidewalk. We were laughing until he started up the registry steps. Marilyn and I looked at each other in shock, then back at him. "Are you Mr. O'Sullivan?" I ventured.

"In the flesh. That's me name." He lowered his voice. "Are you the one?" I nodded. "You got the money, lass—did you bring the money?"

"Yes."

"One hundred fifty quid?"

"Yes."

"Good girl. Well, then, hurry up, hurry up. Let's go. Time's a-wastin'." My new husband-to-be reeked of whiskey, and was obviously completely and thoroughly soused.

As we followed him inside, I muttered to Marilyn, "Is he going to live long enough for me to get my passport?"

The registrar began performing the ceremony, but I was having a hard time concentrating. I was constantly being distracted by Mr. O'Sullivan weaving unsteadily on his feet; and sure enough, as the registrar said, "Do you, Waris, take this man—" he collapsed to the floor with a heavy thud. At first I thought he'd died till I realized he was breathing heavily through his open mouth. I knelt down and started shaking him, yelling, "Mr. O'Sullivan, wake up!" But he refused.

I rolled my eyes at Marilyn and cried, "Oh, great, my wedding day!" and she fell against the wall laughing, holding her stomach. "Just my luck! My dear husband-to-be passes out on me at the altar." Presented with such a ridiculous situation, I figured we might as well have some fun, and I twisted it for all I could get.

The registrar put both hands on her knees and bent down to examine my fiancé, peering over the top of her tiny half glasses. "Is he going to be all right?"

I wanted to shout at her, "How the fuck should I know?" but realized that would be giving away the game. "Wake up, come on, WAKE UP!" I had resorted to slapping his face fairly soundly by now. "Please—somebody get me some water. Somebody do *something*!" I pleaded with a laugh. The registrar brought a cup of water and I threw it in the old man's face.

"Ugh . . ." He began snorting and grunting and finally his eyes flickered open. With some serious tugging and pushing we were able to get him to his feet.

"My God, let's get on with it," I mumbled, worried that he'd keel over again. I held on to my beloved's arm with an iron grip until we finished the ceremony. Back on the sidewalk, Mr. O'Sullivan asked for the one hundred fifty pounds, and I got his address, just in case I had any problems. He lunged off down the street singing a little ditty with the last of my money in his pocket.

One week later Harold Wheeler himself called to say my passport was ready; I gleefully rushed down to his office to pick it up. He handed me the document: an Irish passport with a photograph of my black face and the name Waris O'Sullivan. I was no expert on passports, but it looked a little weird. No, it looked *really* weird. Rinky-dink, as if somebody had made it in the basement. "This is it? I mean, this is a legal passport? I can travel with this?"

"Oh, yes." Wheeler nodded his head emphatically. "Irish, you see. It's an Irish passport."

"Ummm." I turned it over and examined the back cover, flipped through the pages. "Well. So long as it does the job, who cares how it looks?"

I didn't wait long to put it to the test. My agency set up bookings for me in Paris and Milan and I applied for my travel visas. But a couple of days later, I received a letter. When I glanced at the return address, I felt ill. The letter was from the immigration office, saying they wanted to see me right away. I considered all kinds of wild options, but in the end I knew there was nothing to be done, except go see them. I also knew they had the power to deport me immediately—or send me to jail. Good-bye, London. Good-bye, Paris. Good-bye, Milan. Good-bye, modeling. Hello, camels.

The day after I received the letter, I took the tube from Frankie's house to the immigration office, and wandering through the huge government building, I felt like I was walking into a tomb. When I found the right office, I was met by the most deadly serious faces I'd ever seen. "Sit here," ordered a stone-faced man. They put me in a completely isolated room and began asking me questions. "What is your name? What was your name before you married? Where are you from? How did you get this passport? What was his name? How much money did you pay?" I knew one little wrong answer and they would be putting handcuffs on old Waris. Meanwhile, the immigration officials were recording every word I said. So I trusted my instincts and didn't tell them much. When I needed to stall and think of an answer, I relied on my perfectly natural talent, pretending to be confused by the language barrier.

Immigration kept my passport and told me that in order to get it back I had to bring my husband in for an interview—not what I was hoping to hear. In the end, though, I was able to get out of their office without telling them about Harold Wheeler. I figured to get my money back from this thief before the government picked him up, or that would be the end of my two thousand pounds.

I left immigration, marched straight to his swanky office, and rang the intercom. When his secretary answered, I said it was Waris Dirie to see Mr. Wheeler and it was urgent. But surprisingly, Mr. Wheeler was not in, so she refused to open the door. Day after day I came to his office and called on the phone screaming, but his loyal secretary protected the rat. Playing private detective, I hid outside his building all day long, waiting to pounce on him when he walked by. But he had disappeared.

In the meantime, I had to produce Mr. O'Sullivan for the immigration board. His address was in Croydon, south London, an immigrant neighborhood where a lot of Somalis live. I took the train as far as I could, then had to take a cab the rest of the way, because trains don't go there. Walking down the street alone, I kept looking over my shoulder, really not happy to be there. I found the address, a broken-down tenement, and knocked on the door. No answer. I walked around the side of the house and strained to look in the window, but couldn't see anything. Where could he be—where would he go in the daytime? I wondered. Ah—the pub. I started walking, and when I came to the closest pub, I went inside and found Mr. O'Sullivan sitting at the bar. "Remember me?" I asked. The old man looked over his shoulder, then quickly resumed his position staring straight ahead at the bottles of liquor behind the bar. *Think fast, Waris*. I had to tell him the bad news, and beg him to come to immigration with me; I knew he wouldn't go for it. "Here's the story, Mr. O'Sullivan. Immigration took my passport away. They want to talk to you, just ask you a couple of quick questions before they'll give it back. Make sure we're really married, you know. I can't find this damn attorney—he's disappeared, so I've got nobody to help me." Still staring straight ahead, he took a swig of whiskey and shook his head. "Look, I gave you *two thousand pounds* to help me get my passport!"

This got his attention. He turned to stare at me, his mouth open in amazement. "You gave me one-fifty, love. I never had two thousand pounds in me life, or I wouldn't be hanging around the likes of Croydon."

"I gave Harold Wheeler two thousand pounds for you to marry me!"

"Well, he didn't give it to me. If you're foolish enough to give that man two thousand quid that's your problem—not mine." I kept begging, pleading with him to help me, but he wasn't interested. I promised I'd take him in a cab, he wouldn't even have to take the train to the immigration office. But he wouldn't budge from his bar stool.

Searching for the right approach to motivate him, I offered, "Look, I'll pay you. I'll give you more money. After we visit immigration, we'll go to the pub, and you can drink all you want." This offer received skeptical interest, as he turned to me and raised his eyebrows. Push it home, Waris. "Whiskey, lots and lots of whiskeys, shots lined up all the way down the bar. Okay? I'll come to your house tomorrow, and we'll take a taxi to London. It will only take a few minutes, a couple of quick questions— and then we'll head straight for the pub. Right?" He nodded his head and went back to staring at the bottles of spirits behind the counter.

The next morning, I returned to Croydon and knocked on

the old man's door. But there was no answer. I walked down the deserted street to the pub and went inside, but the only person there was the barkeep, wearing a white apron and drinking a cup of coffee while he read the paper. "Have you seen Mr. O'Sullivan today?"

He shook his head. "Too early for him, love." I walked quickly back to the lying bum's house and pounded on the door. Still no answer, so I sat down on the front steps, which reeked of piss, and I put my hand over my nose. While I sat there trying to decide what to do next, two tough-looking guys in their twenties walked up and stopped in front of me.

"Who're you?" one of them grunted at me. "And why are ya sittin'' on me old man's stoop?"

"Oh, hi," I said pleasantly. "I don't know if you know, but I'm married to your father."

They both glared at me, and the bigger of the two shouted, "What! What the fuck are ya talking about?"

"Look, you know, I'm in a complete mess and I need your father's help. All I want is for him to come with me to this office in the city, and answer a couple of questions. They took my passport away, and I need to get it back, so please . . ."

"Piss off, you fucking cunt!"

"Hey, look! I gave that old man all my money," I said, pointing to his front door, "and I'm not leaving without him." However, his son had other ideas. He jerked a club out of his coat and pulled it back menacingly, like he was going to break my skull.

"Oh, yeah? Well, we're going to fuck you up. We'll teach you to come around here telling your lies—" His brother laughed and grinned, and I stared at his smile, missing a few teeth. That was enough for me. I knew these guys had nothing to lose. They could beat me to death right here on the doorstep, and nobody would know—or care. I jumped up and ran. They chased me for a couple of blocks; then, satisfied that they'd scared me away, they stopped.

But when I got home that day, I decided to go back to Croydon again, and keep going back until I found the old man. I had no other choice. By this point, Frankie was not only letting me live with him without paying rent, but he was buying my food, too. Added to that, I was borrowing money from my other friends for expenses, and that situation couldn't go on much longer. I'd thrown away all my money on that crook posing as an immigration attorney, and without a passport, I couldn't work. So what did I have to lose? A few teeth if I wasn't careful, but I decided I had to be smarter than those punks, and that didn't seem too difficult.

I went back the next afternoon and quietly circled the neighborhood, making sure not to stop in front of the old man's house. I found a little park and sat down on a bench, and in a few minutes Mr. O'Sullivan himself came strolling past. For some unknown reason, he was in a jolly mood and happy to see me. He quickly agreed to get in a taxi with me and head to London. "You're going to pay me, yeah?" I nodded. "And then you'll buy us a drink, lass?"

"I'll buy you all the drinks you need when we're finished. But first you have to be a little bit normal when you talk to these immigration people. They're complete bastards, you know. *Then afterwards* we'll go to the pub. . . ."

When we walked into immigration the agent took one look at Mr. O'Sullivan and, with a very grim face, said, "This is your husband?"

"Yes."

"Okay, Mrs. O'Sullivan, let's stop playing these games. What's the story?" I sighed, realizing that there was no point going on with this charade. I poured my heart out, and told them the whole business, about modeling, about Harold Wheeler, about my so-called marriage. They were quite interested in Mr. Wheeler; I provided all the information I had about him, including his address. "We'll contact you about your passport in a few days after we finish our investigation." And that was it; they dismissed us.

Now, out on the street, Mr. O'Sullivan was raring to go to the pub. "Okay, you want money? Here . . ." I reached in my bag, pulled out my last twenty pounds and handed it to him. "Now get out of my sight. I can't stand to look at you anymore."

"This is it?" Mr. O'Sullivan shook the note at me. "This is all I get?" I turned and started walking down the street. "WHORE!!" he screamed. He bent double at the waist. "YA FUCKIN" WHORE!" People walking past on the sidewalk turned to stare at me. They probably wondered why, if *I* was the whore, I was paying *him*.

In a few days immigration called and requested I come back to their office. They said they were investigating Harold Wheeler, but so far they hadn't learned much. His secretary said he'd gone to India, and it was unclear when he'd be returning. However, in the meantime, they gave me a temporary passport that was good for two months. Here was my first break in this whole ugly mess, and I vowed to make the most of those two months.

I decided to travel to Italy first, since I spoke a little of the language, having lived in a former Italian colony. True, most of my Italian consisted of Mama's cusswords, but they might come in handy. I went to Milan and loved it, doing runway work in the fashion shows. During this time I met another model, named Julie. Julie was tall, with blond shoulder-length hair and a great body; she did a lot of lingerie work. We had such a great time exploring Milan that when the shows finished there, we decided to move on and try our luck in Paris together.

These two months were fabulous for me, traveling to new places, meeting new people, eating new foods. And even though I didn't make any serious money, I still made enough to get by while I was touring Europe. Then, when the work ran out in Paris, Julie and I returned to London together.

When we got back, I met an agent from New York, who had come to England searching for new talent. He urged me to come to the States, saying he could get me lots of modeling jobs there. Of course, I was anxious for that, because everyone agreed that New York was the most lucrative market of all, especially for a black model. My agency made the arrangements, and I applied for a visa to the States.

The American Embassy reviewed my papers, then immediately contacted the British government. The upshot of that communication was a letter announcing I was being deported from England in thirty days and sent back to Somalia. In tears, I called my friend Julie, who was staying with her brother in Wales.

"I'm in trouble—big trouble. It's over for me, girl. I have to go back to Somalia."

"Oh, no, Waris. Well, why don't you come here for a few days and relax? You can take the train. It's not too far from London, and it's beautiful here. It'll do you good to get out in the country for a while, and maybe we can figure something out."

When I arrived, Julie picked me up at the station and drove through the velvet green countryside to the house. We sat down in the living room and her brother, Nigel, came in. He was short and very pale, with long fine red hair, and his front teeth and fingertips were stained with nicotine. He looked older than I expected, probably early fifties. He brought us tea on a tray, then sat there chain-smoking while I told my nightmare story of the passport dilemma, and how it was all coming to a sad end.

Leaning back in the chair with his arms folded, Nigel suddenly said, "Don't worry, I'll help you."

Shocked at this statement from a guy I'd known only about thirty minutes, I said, "How are you going to do that? How are you gonna help me?"

"I'll marry you."

I shook my head. "Oh, no. No. I've been through all that.

And that's what got me into this mess. I'm not going through that again. Enough. I can't deal with this shit. I want to go back to Africa, be happy; my family's there, and everything I know. I don't know nothing about this crazy country. Everything here is just madness and confusion. I'm going home."

Nigel jumped to his feet and ran upstairs. When he came back, he was holding up *The Sunday Times* with my picture on the cover—which had come out over a year ago, long before I ever knew Julie. "What are you doing with that?"

"I saved it because I knew one day I was going to meet you." He pointed at my eye in the photograph. "The day I saw this picture, I saw a tear here in your eye, water running down your cheek. When I looked at your face, I saw you crying and I knew you needed help. Then Allah told me—Allah said it was my duty to save you."

Oh, shit. I stared at him with my eyes open wide, thinking: *Who is this crazy motherfucker? He's the one who needs help.* But during the course of the weekend, both Nigel and Julie kept assuring me that if he could help me, why not? What future did I have back in Somalia? What was waiting for me there? My goats and camels? I asked Nigel the question that kept coming to mind: "What's in it for you, man? Why do you want to marry me, and put yourself through all this?"

"I told you—I don't want anything from you. Allah sent me to you." I explained that marrying me wasn't just a simple matter of hopping down to the registry office. I was already married.

"Well, you can divorce him, and we'll tell the government blokes we're planning to get married," Nigel reasoned, "so they won't deport you. I'll go with you. I mean, I'm a British citizen—they can't say no. Look, I feel bad for you and I'm here to help. I'll do whatever I can."

"Well, thank you very much . . ."

Julie added, "Look, if he can help you, Waris, might as well. You might as well take a chance, because what else have you got?" After listening to them for days, I decided at least she was my friend, and he was her brother. I knew where he lived, and could trust him. She was right: might as well take a chance.

We concocted a plan where Nigel would come with me to talk to Mr. O'Sullivan about a divorce, since I certainly didn't want to run into his boys again alone. I figured—as usual with everything concerning this old man—he'd want some money before he'd consent to do anything. I sighed; just thinking about it made me tired. But my friend and her brother kept urging me on, and I began to feel more optimistic about the whole plan. "Let's go," Nigel said. "We'll drive down to Croydon tomorrow."

The next day the two of us drove to the old man's neighborhood, and I gave Nigel directions to the flat. "Watch yourself," I warned as we drove. "These guys—his sons—are crazy. I mean, I'm scared to get out of the car." Nigel laughed. "I'm serious. They chased me and tried to beat me—they're mad, I tell you. We've got to be really careful."

"Come on, Waris. We'll just tell the old guy you're getting a divorce. And that's that. It's no big deal."

By the time we reached Mr. O'Sullivan's house, it was late afternoon and we parked out front on the street. As Nigel knocked on the door, I constantly looked over my shoulder up and down the street. No one answered, but I wasn't surprised. I figured we'd have to make another trip to the corner pub.

Nigel said, "Come on, let's go around and look in the window, and see if he's home." Unlike me, he was tall enough to look inside easily. But after walking to several windows without any success, he looked at me with a confused expression on his face. "I feel like something's wrong." I thought, *Oh boy, now you're getting the picture. I get that feeling every time I have anything to do with this creep.*

"What do you mean 'something's wrong'?"

"I don't know . . . I just feel . . . maybe if I can get in through this window'—and with that statement he started pounding one of the windows with the palm of his hand in order to open it.

The next-door neighbor came out and yelled, "If you're looking for Mr. O'Sullivan, we haven't seen him for weeks." As she stood there watching us with her arms folded over her apron, Nigel banged the window open a crack, and a horrid smell rushed out. I covered my mouth and nose with both hands and turned away. Nigel put his eyes down to the level of the crack and peered in. "He's dead—I can see him lying there on the floor."

We told the neighbor lady to call an ambulance, jumped in the car, and took off. I hate to say it, but all I felt was relief.

Shortly after we discovered Mr. O'Sullivan rotting in his kitchen, Nigel and I were married. The British government stopped proceedings to deport me, but made no secret of the fact they thought our marriage was a crock. And, of course, it was. Still, Nigel and I agreed that until I got my passport, it would be best for me to stay at his place in Wales.

After living first in Mogadishu, then London, for seven years, I'd forgotten how much I enjoyed nature. And even though the leafy-green countryside scattered with farmland and rivers was completely different from the deserts of Somalia, I enjoyed spending time outside again as opposed to being in high-rise buildings and windowless studios. In Wales I was able to resume some of my favorite pleasures from my nomad days: running, walking, picking wildflowers, and peeing outside. Occasionally someone would catch me with my ass poking out of the shrubbery.

Nigel and I had separate rooms and lived like roommates— not husband and wife. We had made an agreement that he would marry me so that I could get my passport, and although I offered to help him financially when I started making money, he insisted he expected nothing in return. Nigel only wanted the joy received from following Allah's advice to help another human being in need. One morning I got up earlier than usual, around six, because I was headed to London for a casting. I came downstairs and put the coffee on while Nigel remained asleep in his room. I had just pulled my yellow rubber gloves on and begun washing the dishes when the doorbell rang.

Still wearing my gloves dripping soapsuds, I opened the door and found two men standing there. They wore gray suits and serious gray faces, and carried black briefcases. "Mrs. Richards?"

"Yes?"

"Is your husband here?"

"Yes, he's upstairs."

"Step out of the way, please. We're here on official government business." As if anybody else would walk around looking like that.

"Well, come in, come in—hey, you want a coffee or something? Sit down, and I'll get him." They sat down in Nigel's big comfortable living room chairs, but didn't permit their backs to rest against the furniture. "Oh, darling," I called sweetly. "Come downstairs, please. We have some visitors here."

He came down still half asleep, his blond hair tangled. "Hello." Nigel knew immediately by the way they looked who they were. "Yes, can I help you?"

"Well, yes, we'd just like to ask you a couple of questions. First of all, we want to make sure you and your wife live together. Do you live together?"

I could see from the look of pure disgust on Nigel's face that things were going to get interesting and leaned up against the wall to watch. He spat out, "Well, what does it look like to you now?"

The two agents looked nervously around the room. "Umm. Yes, sir. We believe you, but we still need to have a look around the house."

Nigel's face grew dark, ominous, like a storm cloud. "Look.

You're not going through my house. I don't care who you are. This is my wife, we live together, you see how it is. You came in unannounced—we didn't dress up for you—so get out of my house!"

"Mr. Richards, you don't have to get so angry. By law we're required to—"

"YOU MAKE ME SICK!!!" *Run, boys, run while you can.* Instead, they just sat there glued to their chairs with looks of astonishment on their pasty faces. "GET OUT OF MY HOUSE! If you ever come around here or call me again, I'm gonna get my gun, I'm gonna fuckin' shoot you, and I'll—I'll die for her," he said, pointing at me.

I just shook my head, thinking. *This guy is crazy. He is really, really falling for me, and I'm in deep trouble. What in the hell am I doing here? I should have gone back to Africa—I would have been better off.* After living there a couple of months, I was saying, "Nigel, why don't you clean yourself up, get some decent shoes, and get a girlfriend? Let me help you."

And he would respond, "Girlfriend? I don't want a girlfriend. For God's sake, I have a wife—what would I want with a girlfriend?"

When he would say this, I would go berserk. "Go put your fucking head in the toilet, you psycho, and flush it! Man, wake up and get out of my life! I don't *love* you! You and I made an agreement—you wanted to help me—but I can't be what you want me to be. I can't pretend I love you just to make you happy." But even though Nigel and I had made an agreement, he broke it and made his own. When he was screaming himself purple at the agents who visited his house, he wasn't lying. In his mind, every word of it was true. And things became even more complicated because I depended on him, liked him as a friend, was grateful to him for helping me, wanted no part of him romantically, and seriously wanted to kill him when he started acting like I was his beloved wife and personal property. Quickly I realized I had to get away, and the sooner the better.

But the passport dilemma dragged on. As Nigel realized I was dependent on him, the sense of power drove him to be more and more demanding. He became obsessed with me—where I was, what I was doing, whom I was with. He constantly pleaded for me to love him, and the more he begged, the more I loathed him. Sometimes I would get jobs in London, or go to visit friends. I took every chance to get away from Nigel in an attempt to remain sane.

However, I was losing my ability to remain sane while I was living with a man who I thought was insane. I grew tired of waiting for my passport—my ticket to freedom—and one day, heading to London, I stood on the platform wanting desperately to throw myself in front of the oncoming train. In those few minutes, I listened to its roar, felt the cold wind of its force blow my hair, and thought about what those tons of steel would feel like as they crushed my bones. The temptation to end all my worries was strong, but finally I asked myself: *Why waste my life because of this man?*

To his credit, after waiting for over a year, Nigel went to the immigration office and created a spectacular scene that finally got them to issue me a temporary passport. He cried, "My wife is an international model, and she needs at least a temporary passport so she can travel for her career." BAM! He slammed my portfolio of modeling shots down on the desk. "I am a fucking British citizen, and for you to treat my wife like this— well, I'm appalled, I'm ashamed to say this is my country. I demand this be sorted out NOW!" Shortly after his visit, the government confiscated my old Somalian passport, and sent me a temporary travel document that permitted me to leave the country but had to be constantly renewed. Stamped inside were the words: "Good for travel anywhere except Somalia." They were the most depressing words I could imagine. Somalia was at war, and England didn't want to take a chance on my visiting a nation at war while I was under its care. As a British resident, they would be responsible for me. As I read the words "Good for travel anywhere except Somalia," I whispered, "Oh, my God, what have I done? I can't even go to my own country." Now I was completely alien.

Had anyone told me what my options were, I would have said forget it, give me back my Somalian passport. But no one discussed it with me. And now it was too late to go back. Since I couldn't go back, there was only one direction to go and that was forward. I applied for a visa to America, and booked a flight to New York—alone.

14.

THE BIG LEAGUE

Nigel kept insisting that he had to come to New York with me. He'd never been there before, yet he knew all about the city: "That place is totally crazy. And you, Waris—you don't know what you're doing, where you're going—you'll be completely lost without me. And it's not safe for you to be there alone—I'm going to protect you." Yeah, but who was going to protect me from Nigel? One of his more endearing traits was that in an argument, he would repeat his warped logic—over and over and over and over and over . . . like a crazy parrot, until he wore you down, no matter what you said to him. There was no reasoning with him. But I was not giving in this time. I looked at this trip as a big opportunity for my future, not only for my career, but as a fresh start, away from Britain, away from Nigel and our whole sick relationship.

In 1991, I arrived in the States alone, and the booker at my New York agency gave me his apartment while he stayed at a friend's. The apartment was in the Village, right in the heart of everything exciting in Manhattan. There wasn't much in the studio except a big bed, but that simplicity suited me fine.

My agency had lots of jobs lined up for me when I got there, and I immediately began running in a way I never had before, and making money in a way I never had before. I worked every day that first week I arrived. After having struggled for four years to get work, I wasn't complaining.

Everything was going great until one afternoon when I was on a shoot. During a break, I called the agency to check on the next day's appointments. My booker said, "And your husband called. He's on his way and will meet you at the apartment tonight."

"My husband—you gave him the address where I'm staying?"

"Uh-huh. He said you were so frantic before you left, you forgot to give it to him. Your husband was so cute, he said, 'I just want to make sure she's all right, because, you know, it's her first time in New York.'" I slammed down the receiver and stood there for a minute breathing hard. I couldn't believe it. Yes, I could, but still he had gone too far this time. I didn't blame this poor guy at the agency; he had no idea that Nigel wasn't a *real* husband. And how could I explain it to him? *See, we're married and everything, but I just married him for his passport because I was an illegal alien then and they were deporting me to Somalia. Got it? Now, about those appointments for tomorrow—* The scariest part was that I really *was* legally married to him.

When I finished work, I came back to the apartment that evening, with my mind made up. As I'd been forewarned, Nigel arrived and knocked on the door. I let him in, and before he could take his jacket off, I said in a deadly, no-nonsense tone, "Come on, let's go. I'll take you out for dinner." Once we were safely seated in public, I spelled it out for him: "Look, Nigel, I can't stand you. *I can't stand you.* You make me sick! I can't work when you're around me. I can't think. I'm frustrated. I'm tense, and I just want you to go away." I knew what I was saying to him was horrible, and it gave me no pleasure to hurt him. But I was desperate. Maybe if I was cruel enough, mean enough, I could finally get through to him.

He looked so sad and pathetic that I felt guilty. "Okay, you've made your point. I shouldn't have come. I'll take the first flight home tomorrow."

"Good! Go! I don't want to see you in that apartment when I get home from the studio. I'm working here—this isn't a holiday. I don't have time for your craziness." But when I got home the next evening, he hadn't budged. He was sitting there looking out the window of the dark apartment—listless, lonely, miserable—but there all the same. When I started screaming, he agreed to go the next day. And the next. Finally he left and went back to Wales, and I thought: *Thank you, God; finally I can have some peace.* My stay in New York lengthened as the work continued to pour in. However, Nigel didn't permit me any peace for long. He flew back to New York again twice more, three times in all, each time showing up unannounced.

In spite of the absurd situation with Nigel, everything else in my life was heavenly. I was having a great time meeting people in New York, and my career took off like a rocket. I worked for Benetton and Levi's, and appeared in a series of commercials for a jeweler, Pomellato, wearing white African robes. I did makeup ads for Revlon, then later represented their new perfume, Ajee. The commercial announced: "From the heart of Africa comes a fragrance to capture the heart of every woman." These companies were utilizing the thing that made me different—my exotic African look, the same look that had kept me from getting modeling jobs in London. For the Academy Awards, Revlon filmed a special commercial where I appeared with Cindy Crawford, Claudia Schiffer, and Lauren Hutton. In this spot, each of us kept asking and answering the same question: "What makes a woman revolutionary?" My answer summed up the bizarre reality of my life: "A nomad from Somalia becoming a Revlon model."

Later, I became the first black model ever to be featured in ads for Oil of Olay. I made music videos for Robert Palmer and Meat Loaf. These projects kept snowballing and soon I was in the big fashion magazines: *Elle*, *Allure*, *Glamour*, Italian *Vogue*, French *Vogue*. Along the way, I got to work with the biggest photographers in the business, including the legendary Richard Avedon. In spite of the fact that he's more famous than the models he photographs, I loved Richard because he's so down-to-earth and funny. And even though he's been doing this for decades, he would constantly ask my opinion about shots: "Waris, what do you think about this?" The fact that he cared enough to ask meant a lot to me. Richard joined my first great photographer, Terence Donovan, as a man I respected.

Through the years, I've developed a list of favorite photographers. It sounds easy to have a job taking pictures all day, but after I became more experienced, I started to see a huge difference in quality, at least from my perspective of being the subject of those photographs. A great fashion photographer is one who is able to bring out the true individuality of the model and enhance it, instead of imposing a preconceived image on her. Part of my appreciation may be that as I get older, I appreciate more who I am and what makes me different from the women I constantly work with in the modeling business. To be a black in this industry, where everybody's six feet tall and has silky hair down to her knees and porcelain-white skin, is to be an exception. And I've worked with photographers who used lighting and makeup and hair stylists to make me look like something I wasn't. But I didn't enjoy it, and I didn't like the end result. If you want Cindy Crawford, you should definitely use Cindy, instead of taking a black woman and slapping a long wig and a bunch of light foundation on her to make a weird, black Cindy Crawford look-alike. The photographers I enjoyed working with appreciated the natural beauty in women and tried to seek out that beauty. In my case, they no doubt had their work cut out for them, but I respected the effort.

As my popularity grew, my commitments grew, and my schedule was packed with castings, shows, and shoots. All of it was very difficult for me to keep track of, with my bias against wearing a watch. I discovered problems trying to tell time the old way; it was tough to observe the length of my shadow amidst Manhattan skyscrapers. I started to get in a lot of trouble for showing up late for appointments. I also discovered that I was dyslexic when I kept showing up at the wrong address. My agency would write down the address for me, and I would always reverse the numbers. They'd give me an address, 725 Broadway, and I'd show up at 527 Broadway wondering what happened to everybody. I had done this in London, too, but since I was working so much more in New York, I began to realize this was a constant problem.

As I became more experienced and confident in my career, my favorite part of modeling emerged: the runway. Twice a year, the designers hold shows to announce their new line. The circuit for the fashion shows begins in Milan and lasts for two weeks. Next it's on to Paris, then London, then New York. My nomad days prepared me well for this life: traveling light, moving on when the work did, accepting what life had to offer and making the most of it.

When the shows begin in Milan for the season, every woman and girl in modeling heads there, along with every woman and girl who's ever dreamed of becoming a model. Suddenly the city is mobbed by extremely tall mutant women, running everywhere like ants. You will see them on every street corner, at every bus stop, in every café—models. *Oh, there's one now. There's another one. Yes, there's one.* There's no mistaking the look. Some are friendly. "Hi!" Some just look each other up and down. "Um-hmmm." Some know each other. Some are complete strangers, there for the first time all alone and scared to death. Some get along. Some don't. There are all kinds, all types. And anybody who says there's no jealousy, well, that's complete bullshit. There's plenty of that going on, too.

The agency sets up your appointments, then the models run around Milan going to castings, trying to secure a spot in the shows. This is when you realize that modeling is not all about glamour. Hardly. You might have seven, ten, eleven appointments in a single day. And it's very, very hard work, because you're running around all day; you don't have time to eat because you have one appointment and are late for two others. When you finally make it to your next casting, thirty girls are lined up waiting. And you know that every single one of them has to go before you do. When it's your turn, you show your book—your portfolio with your photographs. If the client likes you, he'll ask you to walk. And if he really likes you, he'll ask you to try something on. Then that's it: "Thank you very much. Next!"

You don't know if you made it or not, but you don't have time to worry about it, because you're on to the next one. If they're interested, they contact your agency and book you. Meanwhile, you better learn quickly not to dwell on the job, or get upset about losing jobs you really wanted, or feel hurt being rejected by your favorite designers. When you start thinking, *Oh, did I get it? Am I going to get it? Why didn't I get it?* you drive yourself absolutely crazy, especially when you're turned down for assignments. If you let it bother you, you'll soon start falling to pieces. Eventually you realize the whole casting process is mostly about disappointment. In the beginning, I used to worry, *Well, why didn't I get that one? Damn, I really wanted that job!* But I later learned to live by my motto with this business: *C'est la vie.* Well, shit, *it just didn't work.* They didn't like you, simple as that. And it's not your fault. If they were looking for somebody seven feet tall with long blond hair who weighs eighty pounds, well, they're not interested in Waris. Just move on, girl.

If a client books you, you go back and do the fitting for the clothes you'll wear in the show. All this activity is going on, and we haven't even gotten to the show yet. You're getting run-down and exhausted, and you haven't slept well, and you don't have time to eat right. You're looking tired and skinny. And then skinnier and skinnier, while every day you're fighting to look your best, because your career depends on it. Then you're wondering, Why am I doing this? Why am I here?

When the fashion shows begin, sometimes you're still doing castings at the same time, because the whole process only lasts two weeks. On the day of the show, you have to be there about five hours before it begins. All the girls are packed in, you get your makeup done, then you sit around, then you get your hair done, then you sit around waiting for the show to start. Next, you put your first outfit on, then you stand around, because you can't sit down and wrinkle the clothes! And when the show starts, suddenly it's chaos—complete madness. "Whoa! Where are you? What are you doing? Where's Waris? Where's Naomi? Come here. Come front—hurry up. You're number nine. You're next." You jerk your clothes on in front of all these strange people you don't know. "Ah, ah, I'm coming, yeah—hold on." Everybody's pushing everybody. "What are you doing? Get out of my way—I'm on!"

And then, after all that hard work is the best little bit: you're on. You're next, standing off stage. Then BOOM! You walk out on the runway, and the lights are blazing, and the music's blasting, and everybody's staring, and you're sashaying down the walk for all you're worth, thinking, *I AM IT. ALL OF YOU—LOOK AT ME!* You've had your hair and makeup done by the best in the business, and you're wearing an outfit that's so expensive you could never dream of buying it. But for a few seconds it's yours, and you know you look like a million bucks. The rush shoots through you, and when you leave the runway, you can't wait to change and get back out there again. After all that preparation, the whole show lasts only twenty or thirty minutes, but you may do three, four, five shows in a day, so you have to tear out and head to your next one as soon as you're finished.

When the two weeks of insanity is finished in Milan, the colony of designers, makeup artists, hairstylists, and models moves on to Paris like a band of gypsies. Then the whole process repeats itself, before they go on to London and New York. By the end of the circuit, you're barely hanging on, and when you finish in New York, you better take some time off. You're ready to go to some little island somewhere with no telephones to try and relax. Otherwise, if you don't, if you try to keep working, you'll go absolutely mental from being worn out.

While modeling is fun—and I admit to loving the glamour and glitter and beauty of it—there's a cruel side that can be devastating for a woman, especially a young one, who's insecure. I've gone in for jobs and had the stylist or photographer exclaim in horror: "My God! What is wrong with your feet! Why do you have those ugly black marks all over them?" What can I say? They're referring to the scars caused by stepping on hundreds of thorns and rocks in the Somalian desert; a reminder of my childhood, when I walked for fourteen years with no shoes. How can I explain that to a designer in Paris?

When they'd ask me to try on a miniskirt at a casting, I'd immediately feel sick. I'd walk out and stand on one foot, twisting around, hoping they wouldn't notice my problem. I've got bowlegs—the legacy of growing up in a nomadic family without proper nutrition. And I've been fired from jobs because of these bowlegs, a physical ailment I had no control over.

I used to be so ashamed, so hurt, because of my legs that I once went to a doctor to see if he could fix them. "Break my legs," I ordered him, "so I won't have to feel humiliated anymore." But thank God, he said I was too old, the bones were already set, and it wouldn't work. As I got older, I thought,

Well, these are my legs, and they're a result of who I am and where I'm from. And as I got to know my body better, I came to love my legs. If I had broken them so that I could do some runway show for five minutes, I would be very, very angry with myself today. I would have broken my limbs for what—so I could make some guy's clothes look good? Now I'm proud of these legs because they have history; they're part of the history of my life. My bowlegs carried me thousands of miles across the desert and my slow, undulating walk is the walk of an African woman; it speaks of my heritage.

Another problem with modeling is that the fashion business, like any other industry, has its share of unpleasant people. Maybe because so much is at stake in some of the decisions, people let the stress get to them. But I remember working with a particular art director at one of the major fashion magazines, who—for me—epitomized the bitter, bitchy attitude that made a photo shoot feel like a funeral. We were in the Caribbean, shooting on a beautiful little island. This place was like paradise, and all of us should have been having a great time, since we were getting paid to work in a setting most people would pay dearly to visit for a holiday. But not this woman. From the minute we arrived she was on my back. "Waris, you really need to get yourself together. You need to get up and get moving—you're just lazy. I can't stand working with people like you." She called the agency back in New York and complained that I was just a moron and refused to do any work. They were quite mystified, but no more so than I was.

This art director was a heartbreakingly sad woman. She was obviously frustrated, she didn't have a man, no friends, nobody to love. And all her life, love, and passion were poured into this business because she had nothing else going for her. So she took all her frustration out on me, and I'm sure I wasn't the first one—or the last. After a few days of this, however, I lost my sympathy for her. I looked at her and I thought, *There are two things I can do to this one: I can slap her across the face, or I can just look at her and smile and say nothing.* And I thought: *It's best to say nothing.*

The saddest thing is to see a woman like this art director get hold of young girls who're just starting out in the business. Sometimes these girls, who are no more than children, leave Oklahoma or Georgia or North Dakota and fly to New York or France or Italy alone and try to make it. Often they don't know the country or the language. They're naive and get taken advantage of. They can't deal with the rejection and fall apart. They don't have the experience or wisdom or inner strength to realize the fault doesn't lie with them. Many wind up coming back home sobbing, broken and bitter.

Crooks and con artists also abound in this business. Many young girls want desperately to be models, and they fall into these scams where a so-called agency charges them a fortune to put a portfolio together. Having been a victim of this type of thief when I met up with Harold Wheeler, this outrages me. Modeling is about making money, not paying money. If a person wants to be a model, the only money she needs is bus fare to visit the agencies. She can look in the Yellow Pages, call up, and make an appointment for a visit. And if the agency starts talking about fees—she should run! If a legitimate agency thinks someone has the right look, the look for the times, they'll help her put together a book. And then, they'll book her appointments and castings, and she's working.

If some of the people in modeling are unpleasant, some of the conditions are not always the best either. I accepted one project that I knew involved a bull, but until I had flown from New York to Los Angeles, then taken a helicopter into the desert, I didn't know exactly how much bull.

We were completely isolated in the California desert, just me, the crew, and a monstrous black bull with long pointy horns. I went into the little trailer and had my hair and makeup done. When I finished, the photographer led me outside to this animal. "Say hello to Satan," he said.

"Ohhh, hello, Satan." I loved him. "He's beautiful. Fantastic. But, is he safe?"

"Oh, yeah, of course. This is the owner." The photographer pointed at a man holding Satan's lead. "He knows what to do." The photographer explained the project to me. The shot would appear on a liquor bottle label. I would be sitting on top of the bull. Naked. This news was a big shock indeed, because I'd had no idea about any of this before I arrived. But I didn't want to make a big fuss in front of all these people, so I figured I might as well get it over with.

I felt sorry for the bull because it was miserably hot in the desert, and his nose was dripping. All his feet were manacled in position so he couldn't move, and this huge beast stood there humbly. The photographer put his hands down to act as a step to boost me up on the bull's back. "Lie down," he commanded, waving his arm. "Stretch out across the bull—put your upper body down across the bull and stretch your legs out." The whole time I was trying to look beautiful and relaxed and playful and sexy, I was thinking: *If this thing bucks me off, I'm dead*. Suddenly I felt his furry back flex beneath my naked belly, and I saw the landscape of the Mojave fly by as I sailed through the air and hit the baked dirt with a thud.

"Are you all right?"

"Yeah, yeah." I was playing tough now, trying not to act shook up. I didn't want anybody to call Waris Dirie a coward—afraid of an old bull. "Yeah, let's go. Help me back on top again." The crew picked me up and dusted me off, and we started again. Evidently the bull was not enjoying the heat, because he bucked me off twice more. On the third landing I sprained my ankle, which began to swell and throb immediately. "Well, did you get the shot?" I called from the ground.

"Oh, it would be beautiful if we could get one more roll . . ."

Fortunately, that bull shot never appeared. For some reason they never used it, and I was glad. The thought of a bunch of old men sitting around drinking liquor and looking at my naked butt was very sad. After this project, I decided not to do any more nude shots, because I simply didn't like it. The money was not worth the feeling of being vulnerable, standing there in front of people feeling completely awkward and helpless, waiting for a break when I could run grab my towel.

Although the bull job was probably my worst, most of the time when I'm modeling, I love it; it's the most fun career anybody could ask for. I could never get used to the idea, from the time Terence Donovan took me to Bath and stood me in front of a camera, that anybody would pay me simply for the way I looked. I never really thought that I'd be able to make a living from something that seemed so little like work. Instead the whole business just seemed like a silly game to me, but I'm glad I stuck it out. I've always felt grateful that I got the opportunity to succeed in this business, because not every girl can get that break. Sadly, so many young girls try so hard, and often it just doesn't work out.

I remember when I was young, working as Uncle Mohammed's maid, and dreaming of being a model. And that night I finally worked up the courage to ask Iman how to get started. Ten years later, I was working on a Revlon shoot in a New York studio when the makeup artist came in and said Iman was next door photographing her new line of cosmetics. I rushed out and went to see her. "Oh, I see now you're doing your own product line. Why didn't you use me, a Somali woman, to pose in the ads for your makeup?" I asked.

She looked at me defensively and mumbled, "Well, I can't afford you."

I said to her in Somali, *"I would have done it for you for free."* Funny, she has never realized that I'm the same little girl, the maid, who used to bring her tea.

The odd fact is that I never went in search of modeling, it came to me; maybe that's why I never took it too seriously. The thrill didn't lie in being a "supermodel" or a "star," because I still can't understand why models have become so famous. Each day, I watch the whole fashion scene become more and more frantic with magazines and TV shows about supermodels, and I wonder: *What is it all about?*

Simply because we're models, some people treat us like goddesses and some people treat us like idiots. I've run into this last attitude plenty of times. It's as if because I make my living with my face, I must be stupid. With a smug expression, people say, "You're a model? Oh, too bad—no brains at all. All you have to do is just stand there and look pretty for the camera."

However, I've met all types of models, and yes, I've met some who were not very bright. But the majority are intelligent, sophisticated, well traveled, and as knowledgeable about most subjects as any other worldly person. They know how to handle themselves and their business, and act completely professional. For people like that insecure bitchy art director, it's tough to handle the fact that some women can be beautiful *and* smart. So there's a need to put us in our place by talking down to us, as if we're just a flock of gawky dimpled dimwits.

I find the moral issues surrounding modeling and advertising incredibly complicated. I believe the most important priorities in the world are nature, personal goodness, family, and friendship. Yet I make my living by saying, "Buy this because it looks beautiful." I'm selling stuff with a big smile. I could be cynical about it all and say, "Why am I doing this? I'm helping destroy the world." But I believe almost anybody in any career could say that about their work at some point. The good that comes from what I do is that I've met beautiful people and seen beautiful places and experienced different cultures that have made me want to do something to help the world instead of destroy it. And instead of being another poverty-stricken Somali, I'm in a position to do something about it.

Instead of wanting to be a star or celebrity, I've enjoyed modeling mostly because I felt like a citizen of the world, and was able to travel to some of the most phenomenal places on the planet. Many times when I was traveling for work, we'd go to some beautiful island and I would escape to the beach every chance I got and just run. It felt so wonderful to be free in nature, back in the sun again. Then I would sneak off into the trees and sit quietly and just listen to the birds singing. Ahhh. I would close my eyes, smell the sweetness of the flowers, feel the sun on my face, listen to the birds, and pretend I was back in Africa. I would try to recapture that feeling of peace and tranquillity I remember from Somalia, and pretend I was back home again.

15.

BACK TO SOMALIA

In 1995, after a long stretch of photo shoots and fashion shows, I escaped to Trinidad to relax. It was Carnival time and everyone was in costume, dancing and rejoicing, reveling in the sheer joy of life. I was staying at the home of a family I knew; I'd been there a couple of days when a man came to their door. The matriarch of the family, an elderly woman we called Auntie Monica, went to answer the door. It was late afternoon, and the sun was hot outside, but the room where we sat was cool and shady. The man standing at the door was in silhouette against the bright light; I couldn't see him, but I heard him say he was looking for somebody named Waris. Then Auntie Monica called, "Waris, you have a phone call."

"Phone call? Where is the phone?"

"You have to go with this man. He'll take you there."

I followed him back to his place. He was a neighbor of Auntie Monica's who lived a few doors away and was the only person in the area with a telephone. We walked through his living room to the hall where he pointed to a receiver lying off the hook. "Hello?" It was my agency in London.

"Oh, hello, Waris. Sorry to trouble you, but we've been contacted by the BBC. They say it's urgent you get in touch with them right away. They want to talk to you about making a documentary."

"Documentary about what?"

"About being a supermodel, and where you came from and, you know, how does it feel living your new life."

"That's not a story. I mean, for goodness sake, can't they find something better?"

"Well, anyway, you talk to them about it. What time should I tell them you'll call?"

"Look, I don't want to talk to anybody."

"But they really want to talk to you right away."

"Hey, whatever. Just tell them I'll talk to them when I get to London. I have to go back to New York when I leave here, then fly to London. I'll call them when I get there."

"All right, then. I'll tell them."

But the next day, while I was out carousing around town, the man came back to Auntie Monica's again, saying there was another phone call for Waris. I completely ignored this news. Again, the next day, another phone call. This time I went back with the gentleman, because obviously they were going to wear him out running over to get me. Of course, it was my agency again. "Yeah, what is it?"

"Yes, Waris, it's the BBC again. They say it's very urgent they talk to you; they're going to call you tomorrow at this same time."

"Look, it's my break time, okay? No way I'm talking to anybody. I've escaped from all that, so leave me alone and quit bothering this poor man."

"They just want to ask you a couple of questions."

I sighed. "For God's sake. All right. Tell them to call me tomorrow at this number." The next day I spoke with the director, Gerry Pomeroy, who makes films for the BBC. He asked me questions about my life.

I replied curtly: "First of all, I don't want to talk about this now. I'm supposed to be here on holiday. You know? Can't we talk another time?"

"I'm sorry, but we have to make a decision, and I need some information." So I stood in a stranger's hallway in Trinidad, telling the story of my life to a stranger in London. "Okay, great, Waris. We'll get back to you."

Two days later the man came to Auntie Monica's again. "Phone call for Waris." I shrugged at him, shook my head, and followed him down the street. It was Gerry from the BBC. "Yes, Waris, we really want to do a documentary of your life. It will be a half-hour episode for a show called *The Day That Changed My Life.*

In the meantime, between the first phone call from my agency and the second call from the BBC, I'd been thinking about all this documentary business. "Well, listen, uh, Gerry— I'll make a deal with you. I'll do this with you guys if you take me back to Somalia and help me find my mother." He agreed, thinking my return to Africa would make a good conclusion to the story. Gerry told me to call him as soon as I got back to London; then we'd sit down and plan the whole project.

Returning with the BBC would be the first opportunity I'd had to go home since I left Mogadishu, because of my myriad passport problems, tribal wars in Somalia, and my inability to locate my family. Even if I'd been able to fly to Mogadishu, it wasn't exactly as if I could call my mother and tell her to meet me at the airport. From the moment the BBC promised to take me, I could think of nothing else. I had numerous meetings with Gerry and his assistant, Colm, to plan the project and elaborate on the story of my life.

We started filming in London right away. I returned to all my old haunts starting with Uncle Mohammed's house—the Somalian ambassador's residence—which the BBC got permission to enter. They filmed All Souls Church School, where I was discovered by Malcolm Fairchild. Later they interviewed him on camera, asking why he was so interested in photographing an unknown servant. The crew filmed me doing a photo shoot with Terence Donovan. They interviewed my good friend Sarah Doukas, the director of Storm, a London modeling agency.

The heat on the whole project was turned up considerably when the BBC decided to follow me on a gig hosting *Soul Train*, a TV program that features the best in black music. I had never done a project like this before and was a complete nervous wreck. Added to that was the problem that when we got to L.A., I had a terrible cold and could barely talk. And the whole time I was traveling from London to Los Angeles, blowing my nose, reading my script, getting ready for the show, riding in the limo, I was being filmed by my constant shadows: the BBC film crew. The insanity was multiplied when we went to the studio and the BBC documentary crew was filming the *Soul Train* crew filming me. And if there was ever an act that I didn't want to have documented, this had to be the one. I'm sure I was the worst host in the history of *Soul Train*, but Don Cornelius and the production crew were so patient with me. We started at ten in the morning and worked till nine that night. I think it was their longest day ever. My old difficulty with reading still plagued me, as it had in my James Bond film debut. Although my skill was much improved, I still struggled reading aloud. And trying to read from cue cards in front of two film crews, dozens of dancers, and a handful of internationally famous singers, while lights blazed in my eyes, was more of a challenge than I was up for. They were screaming, "Take twenty-six . . . Cut!" "Take seventy-six . . . Cut!" The music would start playing, dancers would start dancing, and everybody would start filming, then I'd bungle my lines: "Take ninety-six . . . Cut!" The dancers would freeze, then let their arms flop down to their sides and glare at me as if saying, "Who *is* this stupid bitch? Oh, God, where did you find her? We just want to go home."

My host's duties included welcoming Donna Summer, which was a big honor for me, because she's one of my all-time favorite singers. "Ladies and gentlemen, please put your hands together and welcome the lady of soul, Donna Summer!"

"CUT!!"

"WHAT NOW?"

"You forgot to say her label. Read the cue card, Waris."

"Ohhhh, Fucking-A! Will you pick this shit up, pick it up? I can't see it. And don't put it down. Put it up straight—these lights are right in my eyes. I can't see a thing."

Don Cornelius would take me into the corner and say, "Take a deep breath. Tell me how you're feeling." I explained to him that this script just wasn't working for me—it wasn't my groove—the way I speak.

"How do you want to do it? Go ahead. Take over—take it all." They were amazingly patient and calm. Don and the crew let me take over and make a mess out of everything, then helped me fix it up again. The best part of that whole experience was working with them and Donna Summer, who gave me an autographed CD of her greatest hits.

Then the BBC and I moved on to New York. They followed me out to do a job on location where I was being photographed in the rain, walking up and down the streets of Manhattan— wearing a black slip and a raincoat and holding an umbrella. On another night, the cameraman sat quietly in the corner filming while I cooked dinner with a group of friends at an apartment in Harlem. We were having such a good time that we forgot he was there.

The next phase required me and the whole crew to meet in London and fly to Africa, where I would reunite with my family for the first time since I'd run away. While we were filming in London, Los Angeles, and New York, the BBC staff in Africa began searching diligently for my mother. In order to locate my family, we went over maps, and I tried to show them the regions where we usually traveled. Next, I had to go over all the tribal and clan names of my family, which is very confusing, especially for Westerners. For the past three months the BBC had been searching—without success.

The plan was that I would remain in New York working until the BBC found Mama, then I'd fly to London, and we'd all go to Africa together and film the conclusion of my story. Shortly after the BBC began looking for Mama, Gerry called one day and said, "We found your mother."

"Oh, wonderful!"

"Well, we think we found her."

I said, "What do you mean 'you think'?"

"Okay, we found this woman, and we asked her if she had a daughter named Waris. She said, yes, yes, she has a daughter named Waris. Yes, Waris lives in London. But she seems awfully vague on the details, so our people in Somalia aren't sure what's going on—if this woman is the mother of another Waris or what." After further questioning, the BBC disqualified this woman, but 'the search was just beginning. Suddenly the desert was alive with women claiming to be my mother; they all had daughters named Waris who lived in London, which was especially odd, considering I have never met another human being with my name.

I explained what was going on. "See, these people are so poor over there, they're desperate. They're hoping if they say 'Yeah, we're her family,' you'll come to their little village and make a film, and they can get some money, get some food. These women are pretending to be my mother, hoping they'll get something out of it. I don't know how they think they're gonna get away with it, but they'll try."

Unfortunately, I had no pictures of my mother, but Gerry came up with another idea. "We need some kind of secret that only your mother would know about you."

"Well, my mother used to have a nickname for me, Avdohol, which means small mouth."

"Will she remember that?"

"Absolutely."

From then on, Avdohol became the secret password. When the BBC was interviewing, these women would make it through the first couple of questions; then they'd always flunk out on the nickname. Bye-bye. But finally one day they called me and said, "We think we've found her. This woman didn't remember the nickname, but she said she has a daughter named Waris who used to work for the ambassador in London."

I hopped a flight out of New York the next day. When I got to London, the BBC needed a few more days to make preparations. We would take a flight to Addis Ababa in Ethiopia, then charter a small plane to take us to the Ethiopia-Somalia border. The trip would be very dangerous. We couldn't go into Somalia because of the war, so my family would have to come across the border to us. The place where we were landing was in the middle of the desert; there was no landing strip, just rocks and brush.

While the BBC was getting ready for the trip, I stayed in a hotel in London. Nigel came to visit me. I tried to remain on cordial terms with him because of my precarious circumstances. By this time, I was paying the mortgage on his house in Wales, because he had no job and refused to look for one. I even got him a job working for some people I knew but they fired him after three weeks, and told him not to come around again. From the beginning, when Nigel first learned of the documentary, he started pestering me to go to Africa with us. "I want to come. I want to make sure you're all right."

I said, "NO, you are not coming. How am I supposed to explain you to my mother? Who are you supposed to be?"

"Well, I'm your husband!"

"No, you're not! Forget it. All right? Just forget about it." One thing was for sure, he was not the type of person I wanted to introduce to my mother. Certainly not as my husband.

Back when I was having the initial planning sessions with the BBC, Nigel had insisted on tagging along. Quickly, Gerry had enough of him. We'd usually meet up for dinner, and Gerry would call that day and say, "He's not coming with you tonight, is he? Please, Waris, let's leave him out of this."

When I came back to London, Nigel came to my hotel and started in again on his campaign to come to Africa. When I refused, he stole my passport. Of course, he knew that in a few days, we were supposed to leave the country. Nothing I said could persuade him to give it back to me. Finally, in desperation, I met Gerry one night and told him, "Gerry, you're not going to believe it. He took my passport and won't give it back to me."

Gerry put his forehead down on his hand and closed his eyes. "Oh, my God, I'm really getting fed up with this, Waris. I'm so sick of dealing with this shit, I've just—I've really had enough." Gerry and the other guys at the BBC tried reasoning with Nigel. "Look, act like a grown-up—be a man. We're almost at the end of this project; you can't do this to us. We need this story to end in Africa, which means we've got to take Waris there. Now, for God's sake, please —" But Nigel wasn't interested. He went back to Wales with my passport.

I made the trip to Wales alone and begged him. Again and again, he refused to give it to me unless he got to go to Africa with us. It was a hopeless bind for me. I'd prayed for the chance to see my mother again for fifteen years. With Nigel there, the whole experience would be ruined. No doubt about it—he'd make sure of that. If I didn't take him, I had no chance of seeing her, because I couldn't travel without my passport. "Nigel, you can't be following us around and making a bloody headache for everybody. Don't you see—it's my chance to see my mother for the first time in fifteen years!"

He was so bitter that we were going to Africa and it had nothing to do with him. "I swear, you're just being so fucking unfair!" he cried. Finally, in the end, I convinced him to give me my passport by promising I'd take him to Africa some day, when this job was done—just the two of us. It was a cheap trick, and I wasn't proud of it, because that was a promise I knew I'd never keep. But when it came to Nigel, being a decent, reasonable adult never worked.

The twin-engine bush plane landed in Galadi, Ethiopia, a tiny village where Somali refugees had gathered across the border to escape the fighting at home. As we hit the red desert soil strewn with rocks, the plane bounced wildly. You must have been able to see the trail of dust for miles, because the entire village ran toward us. They'd never seen anything like this before. The BBC crew and I all climbed out of the plane, and I began trying to speak Somali to the people hurrying to meet us. I was struggling to communicate with them, because some were Ethiopians and some were Somalis, but they spoke a different dialect. Within a few minutes I gave up.

I smelled the hot air and the sand and suddenly I remembered my lost childhood. Every little thing came flooding back to me and I began to run. The crew was yelling, "Waris, where are you going?"

"Go on . . . go wherever you have to go . . . I'll be back." I ran and touched the ground and rubbed the earth between my fingers. I touched the trees. They were dusty and dry, but I knew it was time for the rains soon, then everything would blossom. I sucked the air into my lungs. It held the scents of my childhood memories, all those years when I lived outside and these desert plants and this red sand were my home. Oh, God, this was *my* place. I started to cry with the joy of being back home. I sat down under a tree and felt at the same time overwhelming happiness that I was back where I belonged, and deep sadness that I missed it so much. Looking around me, I wondered how I could have stayed away so long. It was like opening a door that I hadn't dared open before today, and finding a part of me that I'd forgotten. When I walked back to the village, everyone gathered around me, shaking my hand. "Welcome, sister."

Then we found out that nothing was what we expected. The woman who'd claimed to be my mother was not, and nobody knew how to find my family. The guys from the BBC were despondent; they didn't have the money in their budget to come back a second time. Gerry kept saying, "Oh, no, without this portion, there's no ending. And without this ending, there's no real story to the whole film. It's all wasted. What are we going to do?"

We combed the village, asking everybody if they'd heard of my family, or had any information about them. People were all anxious to help, and word of our mission spread quickly. Later that day, an older man walked up to me and said, "Do you remember me?"

"No."

"Well, I'm Ismail; I'm the same tribe as your father. I'm a very close friend of his." And then I realized who he was and felt ashamed for not recognizing him, but I hadn't seen him since I was a little girl. "I think I know where your family is. I think I can find your mother, but I'll need money for gas." Right away, I thought, *Oh, no. How can I trust this guy? Are all these people trying to con us? If I give this guy some money, he's just going to bugger off and we'll probably never see him again.* He went on, "I have this truck here, but it's not much. . . ."

Ismail pointed to a pickup truck—the type you'd never see anyplace but Africa or a junkyard in America. On the passenger's side the windshield was shattered; on the driver's side it was missing altogether. This meant that all the sand and flies in the desert would come sailing into his face as he drove. The wheels were warped and dented from driving over rocks. The body looked like someone had taken a sledgehammer to it. I shook my head. "Hold on a minute, let me talk to the guys."

I went to find Gerry and said, "This man over here thinks he knows where my family is. But he says he needs some money for gas to go look for them."

"Well, how are we going to trust him?"

"You're right, but we have to take a chance. We have no choice." They agreed and gave him some cash. The man hopped in his truck and took off immediately, raising a cloud of dust. I saw Gerry staring after him with a depressed look on his face, as if to say, "There went more money wasted."

I patted him on the back and said, "Don't worry. We're going to find my mother—I promise you. By the third day." My prophecy did little to ease the crew's minds. We had eight days here before the plane would come back to pick us up. And that was it. We couldn't say to the pilots, "Uh, yeah, we're not quite ready, try us again next week." Our tickets were scheduled for return from Addis Ababa to London; we would have to leave, and that would be the end of it, Mama or no Mama.

I had a good time hanging out with the villagers in their huts, sharing their food, but the English guys did not fare so well. They found a building with busted-out windows to sleep in, and rolled out their sleeping bags. They had brought some books and a flashlight, but they couldn't sleep at night because the mosquitoes drove them crazy. The BBC crew was living on canned beans, and complaining they were sick of their food, and there was nothing else to eat.

One afternoon, a Somali man decided he'd give them a treat and brought around a beautiful little baby goat; the guys were all petting it. Later, he brought it back skinned, and proudly presented it: "Here's your dinner." The guys looked shocked, but didn't say anything. I borrowed a pot and built a fire, then cooked the goat with some rice. When the Somali man left, they said, "You don't think we're going to eat that, do you?"

"Yes, of course. Why not?"

"Oh, forget it, Waris."

"Well, why didn't you say something?" They explained they

felt it would be rude, because the man was trying to be polite, but after petting the little goat, they couldn't eat it. They never touched it again.

My three-day deadline for finding Mama passed with no sign of her. Gerry grew more anxious by the day. I tried to reassure these guys that my mother was coming, but they thought I was being ludicrous. I said, "Look. I promise you my mother will be here tomorrow evening by six o'clock." I don't know why I had this belief, but it just came to me, so I told them.

Gerry and the guys started ribbing me about my latest prediction. "What? Yeah? How do you know that? Oh, yes, Waris knows! She predicts everything. She knows! Just like she predicts the rain!" They were laughing because I kept telling them when it was going to rain, because I could smell it.

"Well, it did rain, didn't it?" I demanded.

"Oh, come on, Waris. You were just lucky."

"It has nothing to do with luck. I'm back in my element now—I know this place. We survived here on our instincts, my friends." They started looking sideways at each other. "Okay. Don't believe me. You'll see—six o'clock."

The next day I was sitting talking to an elderly lady when Gerry jogged up at about ten minutes to six. "You're not going to believe it!"

"What?"

"Your mother—I think your mother is here." I stood up and smiled. "But, we're not sure. The man is back and he's got a woman with him; he says it's your mom. Come have a look."

The news had spread like a brushfire through the village; our little drama had definitely been the biggest thing to happen here for God knows how long. Everyone wanted to find out: Is this Waris's mother or just another impostor? By now it was nearly dark and a crowd gathered around us till I could barely walk. Gerry led me down a little alleyway. Up ahead was the man's pickup truck with the hole in the windshield, and a woman was climbing down from the seat. I couldn't see her face, but from the way she wore her scarf I could tell immediately that it was my mother. I ran to her and grabbed her. "Oh, Mama!"

She said, "I drive for miles and miles with this awful truck—and oh, Allah, what a horrible ride that was! And we're driving two solid days and nights—all for this?"

I turned to Gerry and laughed. "It's her!"

I told Gerry that they had to leave us alone for the next couple of days, and he kindly agreed. Talking to Mama was awkward; my Somali, I discovered, was pathetic. Tougher than that was the fact that we'd become strangers. At first, we just discussed little everyday things. But the gladness I felt at seeing her overcame the gap between us; I enjoyed just sitting close to her. Mama and Ismail had driven for two days and two nights straight, and I could see she was exhausted. She had aged a great deal in fifteen years—the result of a relentlessly hard life in the desert.

Papa wasn't with her. He was off searching for water when the truck came. My mother said Papa was getting old, too. He would go off chasing the clouds looking for rain, but he desperately needed glasses because his eyesight was terrible. When Mama left, he'd been gone for eight days, and she hoped he hadn't gotten lost. I thought back to how I remembered Papa, and realized how much he'd obviously changed. When I left home, he'd been able to find us even if the family moved on without him, and even on the blackest night with no moon.

My little brother, Ali, was also with her, along with one of my cousins, who happened to be visiting my mother when Ismail came. Ali wasn't my little brother anymore, however. At six four he towered over me, which pleased him no end. I kept holding Ali, and he would cry, "Get off now! I'm not a baby no more. I'm getting married."

"Married! How old are you?"

"I don't know. Old enough to get married."

"Well, I don't care. You're still my baby brother. Come here—" And I'd grab him and rub his head. My cousin laughed at this. I said to him, "I used to whip your ass!"—I used to baby-sit him when he was little and his family came to visit us.

"Yeah? Well, come try it now." He started shoving me and dancing around.

"Oh, no, don't!" I cried. "Don't even try. I'll beat you up." My cousin was getting married soon, too. "If you want to make it to your wedding day, boy, don't mess with me."

At night, Mama slept in the hut of one of the families there in Galadi who had taken us in. I slept outside with Ali—just like in the old days. As we lay there at night, I felt such a state of peace and happiness. We'd stare at the stars and talk deep into the night: "Remember the time we tied up Papa's little wife?'—and then both of us would roar.

Ali was so shy at first, but he confided, "You know, I really miss you. You've been gone for so long. It's so strange to think you're a woman now and I'm a man." It felt wonderful to be back with my family again, and talk and laugh and argue in my language about familiar things.

All the villagers were incredibly generous to us. We had invitations to a different home each day for lunch and dinner. Everybody wanted to spoil us and show us off, and hear all the stories about where we'd been. "Oh, come on, you've got to meet my child, meet my granny"—and they'd drag us off and introduce us. And none of this was about my being a "supermodel," because they had no idea about any of that. I was one of them—a nomad—and I'd come back home.

My mother, bless her heart, couldn't understand what I did for a living, no matter how hard I tried to explain. "Now, what is it again? What's modeling? You do what? What does that mean exactly?" At some point, someone traveling through the desert brought my mother a copy of *The Sunday Times* of London with my picture on the cover. Somali people are fiercely proud, and they were delighted to see a Somali woman on the cover of this English newspaper. Mama looked at it and said, "It's Waris! Oh, my daughter!" She carried it around showing all the villagers.

She got over her shyness after that first night, and quickly warmed up enough to boss me around: "You don't cook like *that*, Waris! Tsk-tsk, come, now! Let me show you. Don't you cook in that place where you live?"

Next, my brother started asking me what I thought about this and that. I'd tease him, "Oh—please shut up, Ali. You're just stupid, ignorant bush people. You've lived here too long and you don't know what you're talking about."

"Oh, yeah? You're famous, so you come home and put on your bullshit Western attitude? Now you live in the West and you know everything?"

We argued back and forth for hours. I didn't want to hurt their feelings, but I figured if I didn't tell them certain things, who else was going to? "Well, I don't know everything, but I've seen a lot and learned a lot I didn't know living back in the bush. And it's not all about cows and camels. I can tell you other things."

"Like what?"

"Well, for one thing you're destroying your environment by cutting all the trees. You cut all the little trees before they have a chance to grow, using the saplings to make pens for these stupid animals." I pointed at a nearby goat. "It's not right."

"What do you mean?"

"Well, the whole land is a desert now because we've cut all the trees."

"The land is a desert because it doesn't rain, Waris! It rains in the north and they've got trees."

"That's why it rains there! It rains *because* there's a forest there. And every other day you're cutting any little twig, so no forest ever has a chance to grow here." They didn't know whether to believe this bizarre idea or not, but there was one topic they felt confident I couldn't argue with.

My mother started. "Why are you not married?" This subject was still an open wound with me after all these years. As far as I was concerned it was the issue that had cost me my home and family. I know my father had meant well, but he'd offered me a terrible choice: do what he said, and ruin my life by marrying that old man, or run away, and give up everything I knew and loved. The price I paid for my freedom was enormous, and I hoped I'd never have to force a child of mine to make such a painful decision.

"Mama, why must I marry? Do I *have* to be married? Don't you want to see me a success—strong, independent? I mean, if I'm not married, it's just because I haven't found the right man yet. When I find him, *then* it will be time."

"Well, I want grandchildren."

Now they decided to all gang up on me. My cousin joined in: "Too old now. Who'd want to marry you? Too old." He shook his head at the horror of anybody marrying a twenty-eight-year-old woman.

I threw my hands up. "And who wants to get married if you're going to force them to? Why are you two getting married?" I pointed at Ali and my cousin. "I bet somebody pushed you into it."

"No, no." They both agreed.

"Well, okay, but just because you're boys. But as a girl, I have no say. I'm supposed to marry who you tell me to, when you tell me to. What is that shit? Who came up with that idea?"

"Oh, shut up, Waris," my brother groaned.

"You shut up, too!"

When we had two days left, Gerry said we had to start filming. He got several scenes of me with my mother. But Mama had never seen a camera before and she hated it. She said, "Get that thing out of my face. I don't want that," and she'd swat at the cameraman. "Waris—tell him to get that thing out of my face." I told her it was okay. "Is he looking at me? Or is he looking at you?"

"He's looking at both of us."

"Well, tell him I don't want to look at *him*. He's not going to hear what I say, is he?" I tried to explain the process to her, but I knew it was hopeless.

"Yeah, Mama. He hears everything you say," I said with a laugh. The cameraman kept asking me what we were laughing about. "Just the absurdity of it all . . ." I answered.

The crew spent another day filming me, as I walked through the desert alone. I saw a little boy watering his camel at a well, and I asked him if I could feed it. I held a bucket up to the animal's mouth for the crew. Throughout all this, it was hard for me to hold back my tears.

The day before we left, one of the women in the village did my fingernails with henna. I held my hand up to the camera, and it looked like I had mushy cow poop globbed on the tip of each finger. But I felt like a queen. These were the ancient beauty rituals of my people—the type they normally save for a bride. That night we had a celebration and the villagers were all dancing, clapping, and singing. It was like old times I remembered from childhood, when everyone would rejoice over the rain—such an uninhibited feeling of freedom and joy.

The next morning before the plane came to get us, I got up early and had breakfast with my mother. I asked her if she would like to come back and live with me in England or the States.

"But what would I do?" she said.

"That's precisely it. I don't want you to do anything. You've done enough work in your time. It's time for you to rest—put your feet up. I want to spoil you."

"No. I can't do that. First of all, your father's getting old. He needs me. I need to be with him. And second, I have to take care of the children."

"What do you mean, children? All of us are grown!"

"Well, your father's children. Remember what's-her-name, that little girl he married?"

"Y-e-s-s."

"Well, she had five kids. But she couldn't take it anymore. I guess our life was too tough for her, or she couldn't handle your father. Anyway, she ran away—disappeared."

"Mama . . . how dare you. You're getting too old for that kind of stuff! You shouldn't be working that hard—chasing kids around at your age."

"Well, your father's getting old, too, and he needs me. Besides, I can't just sit around. If I sit down, I'm going to be old. I can't stay still after all these years—that would drive me crazy. I have to keep moving. No. If you want to do something for me, get me a place in Africa, in Somalia, that I can go to when I'm tired. This is my home. This is all I've ever known."

I gave her a big hug. "I love you, Mama, and I'm coming back for you, don't you forget that. I'm coming back for you . . ."

She smiled and waved good-bye.

Once we got aboard the plane, I broke down. I didn't know when or if I'd ever see my mother again. While I was staring out the window crying, watching the village, then the desert, slip away, the crew was filming a close-up shot of me.

16.

THE BIG APPLE

In the spring of 1995, I finished the documentary with the BBC, which they titled *A Nomad in New York*. And I was indeed a nomad after all these years, since I still didn't have a real home. I moved around, following the work: New York, London, Paris, Milan. I'd stay with friends, or in hotels. What few things I owned—a few photos, some books and CDs—were stashed away at Nigel's house in Wales. Since most of my work was in New York, I spent more time there than anywhere. At one point I actually rented my first apartment—a studio in SoHo. Later, I had a place in the Village, then a house on West Broadway. But I didn't like any of these places. The place on Broadway was total madness—it drove me crazy. Every time a car passed by, it sounded like it was inside my house. There was a firehouse on the corner, and I heard sirens going off all night. I couldn't get enough rest, and after ten months I gave up and went back to my nomadic existence.

That fall I did the runway shows in Paris, then decided to skip the shows in London and come straight to New York. I felt it was time to get my own place and settle down a bit, and while I was apartment hunting, I stayed in the Village with one of my closest friends, George. While I was there one night, another friend of George's, Lucy, had a birthday. She wanted to go out on the town to celebrate, but George announced he was too tired, and he had to get up early in the morning for work. I volunteered to go out with Lucy.

We walked out of the house, with no idea of where we were going. On Eighth Avenue, I stopped and pointed out my old apartment. "I used to live up there, above that jazz place. They always played good music, but I never went in." As we stood there, I listened to the music coming out the door. "Hey, come on, let's go in. You want to?"

"Nah. I want to go to Nell's."

"Oh, come on. Let's go in and just check it out. I really like this music they're playing—I feel like dancing."

Reluctantly, Lucy agreed to go in. I walked down the steps into a tiny little club, and straight ahead was the band. I walked up to the stage and stopped. The first person I saw was the drummer; the light was shining on him in the otherwise dark room. He was banging away, and I just stood there staring at him. He had kind of a big seventies Afro, with a funky style. When Lucy caught up to me, I turned to her: "No, no, no. We're staying. Sit down, have a drink. We're staying for a little bit." The band was really jamming and I started dancing like crazy. Lucy joined in, and soon all the other people, who had been kind of subdued, sitting around just watching, got up and started dancing with us.

Hot and thirsty, I got a drink and stood next to a woman in the audience. I said, "Oh, this is bright music. Who are they, anyway?"

She said, "I don't know because they're all freelancers, but my husband is the one playing sax."

"Uh-huh. And who's the one playing drums?"

She smiled slowly. "Sorry, but I don't know." In a few

minutes the band took a break, and when the drummer walked by, this lady grabbed his arm and said, "Excuse me, but my friend would like to meet you."

"Oh, yeah? Who's that?"

"Her"—and with that she pushed me forward. I was so embarrassed I didn't know what to say.

Finally, after standing there frozen for a few moments, I said, "Hi." *Play it cool, Waris.* "I like the music."

"Thanks."

"What's your name?"

"Dana," he said, and looked around shyly.

"Oh." And he just turned and walked away. Damn! But I wasn't letting him get away that easily. I followed him to where he sat down with his buddies from the band, yanked up a chair, and sat next to him. When the drummer turned around and saw me, he jumped. I scolded, "Wasn't I just talking to you? That was rude. You walked away from me, you know?" Dana looked at me, bewildered, then cracked up laughing and doubled over the table.

"What is your name?" he said, when he straightened himself up.

"It doesn't matter now, anyway," I replied in my cockiest manner, sticking my nose in the air. But then we began to talk about all kinds of things until he said he had to play again.

"Are you leaving? Who are you here with?" he asked.

"My friend. She's in the crowd over there." On his next break, he said the band only had a couple of more sets, and if I wanted to, after they finished we could go somewhere. When he came back, we sat talking and talking about anything and everything. Finally, I said, "It's too smoky in here. I can't breathe. You want to go outside?"

"Okay. We can go outside and sit on the steps." When we reached the top of the stairs he stopped. "Can I ask you something? Can I have a hug?"

I looked at him like it was the most natural request in the

world, like I'd known him forever. So I hugged him really tight, and I knew that was it, just like I knew about going to London, and I knew about modeling. I knew this shy drummer with the funky Afro was my man. It was too late to go anyplace that night, but I told him to call me the next day and gave him George's number. "I have appointments in the morning. But call me *exactly* at three o'clock. Okay?" I just wanted to see if he would call me when I told him to.

Later, he told me that on the way home that night, he went to catch the subway to his place uptown in Harlem. When he was entering the station, he looked up and there was a huge billboard of my face staring down at him. He'd never noticed it before, and had no idea I was a model.

The next day the phone rang at twenty past three. I jerked up the receiver. "YOU'RE LATE."

"I'm sorry. Do you want to meet me for dinner?" We met at a little café in the Village and again talked and talked. Now that I know him, I realize how unlike him that was, because he's phenomenally quiet with anyone he doesn't know. Finally I started laughing. Dana looked startled. "What are you laughing about?"

"You're going to think I'm crazy."

"Go ahead. I already think you're crazy."

"I'm going to have your baby." He did not look pleased to find out he would be the future father of my child. Instead, he stared at me with a look that said, *This woman is really crazy, not just hey, let's party, crazy*. "I know you think that's strange, but I just wanted to tell you. But anyway, drop it. Let's forget it."

He sat silently staring at me; I could see he was shocked. And no wonder. I didn't even know his last name. Later, he said he was thinking, *I don't want to see her again. I've got to get rid of this woman. She's like that loony stalker in* Fatal Attraction.

Dana walked me home after dinner, but he was very quiet. The next day I was thoroughly disgusted with myself. I couldn't believe I'd said something so obviously uncool. But at the time, it just seemed like the most normal thing to say, like "Oh, it's going to rain today." Not surprisingly, I didn't hear from him for a week. Finally, I gave in and called him. "Where are you?" he asked.

"At my friend's. You want to get together?"

"Oh, God. Yes, all right. We can go for lunch."

"I love you."

"I love you, too." I put the phone down in absolute shock and horror that I'd just told this man I loved him after I swore to myself I'd be good. No more talk about babies—any of that—and now here I go and tell him I love him. *Oh, Waris, what is wrong with you?* Always, when any man was interested in me, I ran. I would disappear. Now here I was, chasing this man I barely knew. The night I met Dana, I was wearing a green sweater and had my hair in a wild Afro. He later told me that everywhere he turned that night, all he could see was GREEN SWEATER WITH AFRO. I explained that if I wanted something I went after it, and for some reason—for the first time in my life—I very much wanted a man. The thing I couldn't explain was why I felt like I'd known him all my life.

Dana and I met for lunch and again talked and talked and talked about everything in the world. Two weeks later I was living with him at his place in Harlem. After six months we decided we wanted to get married.

After we'd been together nearly a year, one day Dana said unexpectedly, "I think you're pregnant."

I cried, "What are you talking about, for God's sake!"

"Come on, we're going to the pharmacy." I protested, but he was not giving in. We went to the pharmacy and bought a home pregnancy test. It turned out positive.

"You don't believe this piece of shit, do you?" I asked, pointing at the box.

He picked up the pack and pulled out another one. "Do it

again." That one was positive as well. I had been feeling sick, but I always felt sick when it was time for my period. But this time was different. I felt worse than usual, with even more pain. However, I didn't think I was pregnant. I thought something critical was wrong with me—I thought I was going to die. I went to the doctor and explained the situation. He did a blood test and I waited an agonizing three days to hear from him. *Hell! What is going on here? I've got some horrible disease and he just doesn't want to have to tell me?*

Finally, I came home one afternoon and Dana said, "Uh, yeah, the doctor called."

My hand flew to my throat. "Oh, God, what did he say?"

"He said he'd talk to you."

"Didn't you ask him any questions!?"

"Look, he said he'd call you tomorrow around eleven or twelve."

That was the longest night of my life, lying there wondering what my future would hold. The next day when the phone rang, I grabbed it. The doctor said, "I have news for you. You're not alone." *There you go—that's it! Not alone—full of tumors all over my body!*

"Oh, no. What does that mean?"

"You're pregnant. You're two months pregnant." And when I heard those words I just flew over the moon. Dana was delighted, too, because all his life he'd wanted to be a father. We both knew instantly the baby was going to be a boy. But my first concern was about the baby's health. I went to an obstetrician the second we found out I was expecting. When the doctor did the ultrasound, I told her not to tell me the sex.

"Please, just tell me, is the baby okay?"

She said, "It's a fine baby, perfectly fine." Those were the words I was waiting to hear.

Of course, there was one very large barrier to my happy marriage to Dana: Nigel. When I was four months pregnant, we decided to go to Wales together and deal with him once and for all. By the time we arrived in London, I was ill with morning sickness and a bad cold. We stayed at a friend's house, and after I recuperated a couple of days, I got up the nerve to call Nigel. But when I called him he said he had a cold, too, so I'd have to postpone my visit.

Dana and I waited in London for over a week before Nigel was feeling up to a visit. I called and gave him the train schedule so he could pick us up at the station, and said, "I just want to let you know that Dana is coming with me. And I don't want any problems, okay?"

"I don't want to see him. I'll tell you that now. This is between me and you."

"Nigel—"

"I don't care. I don't care. This has nothing to do with him."

"It has a lot to do with him now. He's my fiancé. He's the man I'm going to marry. Okay? And whatever I have to do here, he's doing it with me."

"I don't want to see him and that's it." So Nigel had it in his head that I was taking the train to Wales alone. When I got off, he was waiting, leaning up against a post in the parking lot, smoking a cigarette as usual. He looked worse than the last time I'd seen him. His hair was longer now, and he had dark circles under his eyes.

I turned to Dana and said, "Okay, there he is. Now be cool."

We walked over to him, and before I could get a word out of my mouth, Nigel said, "I told you I didn't want to see him. I told you that. It was very clear. I made it very clear. I want to see you alone."

Dana dropped the bags on the pavement. "Look, you don't talk to her like that, and you don't talk to me like that. Why do you want to see her alone? What is the deal here? You want to see her alone? Well, I don't want you to see her alone. And if you say it one more time, I'm going to kick your fucking ass!"

Nigel turned even paler than he already was. "Well . . . there's not enough room in the car."

"I don't give a fuck about your car. We can take a cab. Let's just get this thing over with."

By now Nigel was moving rapidly toward his car, calling over his shoulder, "No, no, no. That's not how I do things." He jumped in, started the engine, and roared past us as Dana and I stood there next to our bags, watching him drive by. We decided it was best to find a hotel. Luckily, there was a bed-and-breakfast right by the station. It was a depressing little dump, but under the circumstances, that was the least of our worries. We went out and ordered Indian food, but had no appetite, so we basically just sat there staring at it glumly, until we decided to go back to our room.

The next morning I called Nigel again. "I just want to get my things. Okay? If you don't want to deal with this, then forget it. Just give me my stuff." No deal. Now Dana and I had to move to a hotel because the bed-and-breakfast, where we had spent the night, was booked solid, and it looked like we better get comfortable. With Nigel, only God knew how long this process would take. We found another place to stay, and after we'd moved, I called again. "Look, why are you being such an asshole? Why are you doing this? How many years has this been going on? Seven? Eight? Now, come on."

"Okay. You want to see me, all right. But just you. I'll pick you up from the hotel, but if he comes out, that's it. I'll drive away. No, just you." I sighed, but couldn't see any other way out of this mess so I agreed.

I hung up the phone and explained the situation to Dana. "Please, Dana, just let me go over there alone and see if I can talk to him. Just do this for me."

"All right, if you think it's going to work. But if he touches you, he's had it. I'm telling you now, I don't like this shit, but if that's what you want to do, I can't stop you." I told Dana to stay around the hotel and I'd call him if I needed him.

Nigel picked me up and we drove to the cottage he was renting. We went inside and he made me a cup of tea. I said,

"Look, Nigel. This is the man I'm going to marry, and I'm pregnant with his child. There's going to be no more bullshit of your little fantasy world where I'm your precious wife and we have a life together. It's over. Okay? Got it? Now, come on, let's just get on with it. I want a divorce now, this week. And I'm not going back to New York until we get this garbage straightened out."

"Well, first of all, I'm not divorcing you unless you give me all the money you owe me."

"Um, I owe *you* money? How much? Who's been working and giving you money for years now?"

"That all went to pay for the food you were eating."

"Oh, I see. When I wasn't even here. Well, since you're so obsessed with this money, how much is it?"

"At least forty thousand pounds."

"Hah!! Where am I going to get that kind of money? I haven't got it."

"I don't care. I don't care. I don't care. I mean, this is how it is. You owe me money, and I'm not going anywhere, and I'm not giving you a divorce or anything else. You're never going to be free, unless you come up with the money you owe me. I sold my house because of you."

"You sold your house because you couldn't pay the mortgage, and I got sick of paying it. All you had to do was get yourself a job, but you couldn't even do that."

"What? Job to do what? What kind of job was I going to get—work at McDonald's?"

"If that's what you had to do to pay your mortgage, why not?"

"That's not what I do best."

"What the fuck did you ever do best?"

"I'm an environmentalist."

"Yeah, right. I got you a job and they sacked you and told you not to come back. You've got nobody but yourself to blame, and I'm not putting up with this shit. And I'm not giving you a fucking penny. You know what? You can take your stupid passport and shove it up your ass. There's obviously no point talking to you anymore. Ours was never a real marriage, and it wasn't legal, because we were never intimate."

"That's not true. Not now. That's not how the law reads now. You're married to me and I'll never let you go, Waris. Your baby is going to be a bastard for the rest of his life."

I sat there staring at him, and any pity I ever felt hardened into hatred. I realized the awful irony of the situation. I decided to marry him when he was so eager to help me "because it was Allah's will." Since his sister was a good friend of mine, I felt if there were any problems, she'd intercede. But she wasn't around. "I'm getting a divorce, Nigel, with or without your consent. We have nothing else to talk about."

He looked at me solemnly for a minute, then said quietly, "Well, if I don't have you, I have nothing. I'll kill you, then kill myself."

I froze, trying to decide my next move, then started bluffing. "Dana is coming here to get me. I wouldn't try anything if I were you." I knew I had to get out of there immediately, because this time he'd really gone over the edge. I bent over to pick up my bag from the floor, and he shoved me from behind. I went crashing into the stereo face first, then rolled off onto the hardwood floor, landing on my back. I just lay there, scared to move. Oh, my God—my baby! I was so paralyzed with fear that I'd harmed my baby. Slowly I got to my feet.

"Oh, fuck, are you all right?" he cried.

"Yeah. I'm okay," I said calmly. I realized now what a fool I'd been to come here alone, and just wanted to get out in one piece. "It's okay. I'm all right." He helped me up. Pretending to be very collected, I put my jacket on.

"I'll take you home. Get in the fucking car." Now he was angry again. While he was driving, I sat there thinking: *He hates this baby and nothing would make him happier than to see it dead. Maybe he's going to try to drive us off a cliff?* I put my seat belt on. In the meantime, he was screaming, cursing, calling me every name he could think of. I just sat there, quietly staring straight ahead, afraid to say a word or he'd hit me. By this point, I was so numb, I didn't even care about myself, but I cared deeply about my baby. I'm a fighter, and if I hadn't been pregnant, I would have ripped his balls off.

When we got to the hotel, he screamed, "That's it? You're just going to sit there and say nothing—after all I've done for you!" The second he stopped the car, he reached across me, opened the door, and pushed me out onto the ground. One of my legs was still inside, lying across the floorboard; I struggled to untangle myself from the car and ran inside and up to our room.

By the time Dana opened the door, tears were pouring down my face. "What happened? What did he do to you?"

I could see it all clearly: if I told Dana the truth, he'd kill Nigel, then he'd go to prison and I'd get to raise my baby alone. "Nothing. He's just being an asshole, as usual. Wouldn't give me my stuff." I blew my nose.

"That's it? Oh, Waris, forget that shit. That's not worth crying over." Dana and I took the first flight we could get back to New York.

Now, looking back on this time, despite the way he behaved towards me at the end, I feel grateful for the fact that he often went to battle on my behalf and helped me so much when I was really alone in Britain.

When I was eight months pregnant, an African photographer heard I was having a baby and said he wanted to photograph me. He asked me to come to Spain where he was working. By this point I felt great, so I wasn't afraid to travel. I knew I wasn't supposed to fly after six months, but I wore a loose sweater and sneaked on board the flight. He did some brilliant shots for *Marie Claire*.

But I had to fly pregnant one more time. Twenty days before I gave birth, I flew to Nebraska to be with Dana's family so they could help me with the baby after he was born. I stayed with Dana's parents in Omaha. He had gigs scheduled playing in the clubs, and planned to fly out the following week. Shortly after I arrived, I got up one morning and noted my stomach felt funny; I kept wondering what I'd eaten the night before that would cause such indigestion. This continued for that day, but I didn't mention it. By the next morning I had a really bad stomachache. Then it occurred to me that maybe this wasn't a stomachache. Maybe I was having the baby.

I called Dana's mom at work and said, "Look, I've got this weird pain and it comes and goes. It was happening all day yesterday and last night. But it's getting worse. I don't know what I could have eaten, but it feels strange."

"Waris, for God's sake. You're having contractions!"

Oh! Then I was really happy, because I was so ready to have the baby. I called Dana in New York and told him, "I think I'm having the baby!"

"No, no, no! You can't have it till I get there. HOLD THAT BABY! I'm coming, I'm getting on a plane."

"You fucking come and hold it! How am I supposed to do that? Hold the baby!" God, silly men! But I did want Dana to be there for the delivery of our first baby, and I was going to be disappointed if he didn't see it. After I had talked to his mother earlier, she called the hospital, and the nurse called to check on me. She said if I wanted to have the baby, I should walk around. I figured if I *didn't* want to have the baby, that meant I should do the reverse, so I lay absolutely still.

Dana didn't arrive until the following evening. By this time I'd been having contractions for three days. When his father went to pick him up at the airport, I was panting hard. "Oh, oh, oh, EEE! AH! SHIT! OH GOD!"

"Count, Waris, count!" Dana's mom yelled. We decided it was time to go to the hospital, but we couldn't go because

Dana's father had the car. When he drove up, they didn't even make it into the house before we started yelling, "Get back to the car, we're going to the hospital!"

We arrived at the hospital at ten o'clock; at ten o'clock the next morning, I was still in labor. "I want to swing upside down from the tree!" I kept screaming. This I knew was pure animal instinct, like a monkey's instinct, because that's how animals do it. They move around, they sit, they squat, they run and swing until they give birth. They don't just lie there. And since that day, Dana still calls me Monkey. In a falsetto voice he'll cry, "Ahhh, I want to swing upside down from the tree!"

While we were in the delivery room, the expectant father would coach, "Breathe, baby, just breathe."

"FUCK! Get the fuck away from me. I'll fucking kill you, you motherfucker!" Oh, my God, I wanted to shoot him. I wanted to die, and before I died, I wanted to make sure I killed him.

Finally, at noon, the moment came. I was so grateful to that doctor in London who operated on me, because I couldn't even imagine trying to go through that delivery when I was still sewn up. And then, after waiting nine months and suffering for three days, magically there he was. Ooooh! After all this time, I was so glad to see him—this little, little thing. He was so beautiful, with silky black hair, a tiny, tiny mouth, and the longest of feet and fingers. He stretched over twenty inches but weighed only six pounds and thirteen ounces. Immediately my son said, "Ah," and began looking around the room, very curious. *This is what it's all about, then? This is it? This is the light?* Must have felt good after being in the dark for nine months.

I had told the staff that as soon as the baby was born, I wanted them to lay him on my chest, with all that goo and everything. They did, and in that instant I first held him, I realized that the old cliché that every mother told me was true: When you hold that baby, suddenly you forget the pain. In that moment, there is no pain. There is only joy.

I named the baby Aleeke, which in Somali means strong lion. But right now, with his tiny bow mouth, chubby cheeks, and halo of curls, he looks more like a little black Cupid than a lion. His big, smooth forehead looks exactly like mine. When I talk to him, he puckers his mouth like a tweety bird preparing to sing. Since the moment he was born, he's been eternally curious, quietly looking at everything and exploring his new world.

When I was a little girl, I so much looked forward to coming home at night after tending my animals, and lying in Mama's lap. She would stroke my head, giving me such a feeling of peace and security. Now I do this to Aleeke, and just as I did, he loves it too. I'll massage his head and he immediately falls asleep in my arms.

From the day he was born, my life changed. The happiness I get from him is everything to me now. I pushed aside all the stupid little things that I used to complain and worry about. I realized that none of that matters at all. Life—the gift of life— is what matters, and that's what giving birth to my son made me remember.

17.

THE AMBASSADOR

In my culture, a woman earns a badge of respect when she becomes a mother. She has brought another human being into this world, contributed to the gift of life. When Aleeke was born, I, too, was a mama, a woman who had come of age. After going through the cycle of womanhood that began prematurely with my circumcision at age five, and came full circle with my baby's birth when I was about thirty, I had even more respect for my own mother. I understood what incredible strength the women in Somalia possess to bear the burden they carry simply because they're born female. As a woman living in the West, I struggled to do what I had to do, and some days didn't think I'd make it: trying to work scrubbing floors at McDonald's when my periods were so painful I thought I'd pass out. Having surgery to open the crude scars of my genitals so that I could urinate properly. Waddling around nine months pregnant, taking the subway uptown to Harlem, climbing the stairs, and shopping for food at the market. Spending three days in labor and thinking I would surely die right there in the delivery room in front of the doctors.

The reality is that I'm the lucky one. What about the girl back in the bush, walking miles and miles to water her goats, while she's in such pain from her period that she can barely stand up straight? Or the wife who will be sewn back up with a needle and thread like a piece of cloth as soon as she gives birth, so her vagina will remain tight for her husband? Or the woman nine months pregnant hunting for food in the desert to feed her other eleven starving children? Or what happens to the new wife who's still sewn up tight, and it's time for her first baby to be born? What happens when she goes out into the desert alone, as my mother did, and tries to deliver it by herself? Unfortunately, I know the answer to that question. Many bleed to death out there alone, and if they're lucky, their husbands will find them before the vultures and hyenas do.

As I grew older and more educated, I learned that I was not alone. The health problems I've coped with since my circumcision also plague millions of girls and women throughout the world. Because of a ritual of ignorance, most of the women on the continent of Africa live their lives in pain. Who is going to help the woman in the desert—like my mother—with no money and no power? Somebody must speak out for the little girl with no voice. And since I began as a nomad just like them, I felt it was my destiny to help them.

I could never explain why so many things happened in my life by pure chance. But I don't really believe in the concept of pure chance; there has to be more to our lives than that. God saved me from a lion in the desert when I ran away from home, and from that moment on, I felt he had a plan for me, some reason to keep me alive. But if it was for a reason, what was that reason?

Some time back, a writer for the fashion magazine *Marie Claire* made an appointment to interview me. Before our meeting, I gave a lot of thought to what I wanted to say in the article. When I met the writer, Laura Ziv, for lunch, I took one look at her face and liked her right away. I said, "You know, I don't know what kind of story you wanted from me—but all of that fashion model stuff's been done a million times. If you promise to publish it, I'll give you a real story."

She said, "Oh? Well, I'll do my best," and switched on her tape recorder. I began telling her the story of my circumcision when I was a child. Suddenly, halfway through the interview, she started crying and turned off the tape.

"Oh, what's the matter with you?"

"I mean, it's horrible . . . it's disgusting. I never dreamed such things still happen today."

"Now there you go. That's the whole point, people in the West don't know. Do you think you can put that in your magazine—your fabulously glossy, gorgeous magazine, which nobody reads but women?"

"I promise I'll do the best I can. But the decision will be up to my boss."

The next day after the interview, I felt stunned and embarrassed at what I'd done. Everybody would know my business now. My most personal secret. Even my closest friends didn't know what had happened to me as a little girl. Being from a very private culture in Somalia, it simply wasn't the type of thing I could ever talk about. Now here I was talking about it to millions of strangers. But finally I decided: Let it be. Lose your dignity if that's what it takes. So I did. I removed my dignity, as if I were taking off my clothes. I put it to the side and walked around without it. But I was also worried about the response of other Somalis; I could imagine them saying, "How dare you criticize our ancient traditions!" I could imagine them echoing my family when I saw them in Ethiopia: "You think because you moved to the West, you know everything?"

After much thought, I realized I needed to talk about my

circumcision for two reasons. First of all, it's something that bothers me deeply. Besides the health problems that I still struggle with, I will never know the pleasures of sex that have been denied me. I feel incomplete, crippled, and knowing that there's nothing I can do to change that is the most hopeless feeling of all. When I met Dana, I finally fell in love and wanted to experience the joys of sex with a man. But if you ask me today, "Do you enjoy sex?" I would say not in the traditional way. I simply enjoy being physically close to Dana because I love him.

All my life I've tried to think of a reason for my circumcision. Maybe if I could have thought of a good reason, I could accept what they'd done to me. But I could think of none. The longer I tried to think of a reason without finding one, the angrier I became. I needed to talk about my secret, because I kept it bottled up inside me all my life. Since I didn't have any family around me, no mother or sisters, there was no one I could share my grief with. I hate the term "victim" because it sounds so helpless. But when the gypsy woman butchered me, that's exactly what I was. However, as a grown woman, I was no longer a victim, and I could take action. By doing the *Marie Claire* article, I wanted the people who promote this torture to hear what it feels like from at least one woman, because all the females in my country are silenced.

It occurred to me that after people learned my secret, they were going to look at me oddly when they saw me on the street. I decided I didn't care. Because the second reason for doing the article was the hope of making people aware that this practice still occurs today. I've got to do it not only for me but for all the little girls in the world who are going through it now. Not hundreds, not thousands, but millions of girls are living with it and dying from it. It's too late to change my own circumstances, the damage has already been done; but maybe I can help save somebody else.

When my interview "The Tragedy of Female Circumcision" came out, the response was dramatic. Laura did a great job, and publishing it was a courageous act on the part of *Marie Claire*. The magazine and Equality Now, an organization that fights for women's rights, were swamped with letters of support. Like Laura the day I told her, the readers were obviously horrified:

> One month ago today I read with horror the story in the March issue of *Marie Claire* on female "circumcision," and have not been able to get it off my mind. I would find it difficult to believe that *anyone*, male or female, could forget or pass off something as cold and inhuman as this treatment of the gender which God created as man's friend and companion, his "helpmate." The Bible says men are to "love their wives." Even if living in a culture where God is not known to exist, people cannot help but realize that by the pain, trauma, and even death this inflicts on their women that it is SO WRONG! How can they continue to allow this to happen to their wives, daughters, and sisters? Surely they must know they are destroying their women in so many ways!
>
> God help us, we have to DO SOMETHING. I wake up thinking about it, I go to bed thinking about it, and throughout the day I cry about it! Surely with World Vision or another such organization these people can be educated and taught how their marriages and intimacy could be so much better for the men as well as for the women, *as it was meant to be*, and that women were born with certain body parts for good reason, just as men were!

And another:

> I just finished reading your article on Waris Dirie, and am sick to my soul that such torture and mutilation is still endured by little girls. I can hardly believe that something

this sadistic is being practiced today. The problems these women face their whole lives resulting from this are incredible. Tradition or not, these outrages against females worldwide need to end. Let me slice open one man's genitals and sew them back up and I can guarantee this practice would stop. How can you want to be with a woman physically when her pain is severe and never-ending? This story has brought me to tears and I am writing the Equality Now organization for information on how to help.

Another letter addressed to me read:

There are a lot of tragic stories that have been told, and there will be more told in the future, but Waris, there are not any more to be told of an entire culture that can be more horrifying than what these people are doing to their children. I cried and felt deeply when I read this. I want to do something to change things, but I don't know what one person can do.

I was relieved by the letters of support; I received only two negative responses criticizing me, and not surprisingly they came from Somalia.

I began giving more interviews and speaking at schools, community organizations, and basically anywhere I could to publicize the issue.

Then another stroke of fate occurred. A makeup artist was on board a plane flying from Europe to New York; she picked up *Marie Claire* and read my interview. During the flight she showed it to her employer, and said, "You should read this." Her employer happened to be Barbara Walters. Barbara later told me that she couldn't finish the article because it was so disturbing. However, it was a problem she felt needed to be addressed. She decided to do a segment for *20/20* using my story to make viewers aware of female circumcision. Ethel Bass Weintraub produced the award-winning segment titled "A Healing Journey."

While Barbara was interviewing me, I wanted to cry; I felt so naked. Telling the story in an article somehow put a distance between me and the reader. I only had to tell Laura, and we were just two women in a restaurant. But when they were filming me for *20/20*, I knew the camera was doing a close-up of my face as I revealed secrets I had guarded my entire life; it was if someone had cut me open and exposed my soul.

"A Healing Journey" aired in the summer of 1997. Soon after that I received a call from my agency saying they had been contacted by the United Nations. The UN had seen the *20/20* segment and wanted me to contact them.

Events had taken another amazing turn. The United Nations Population Fund invited me to join their fight to stop female circumcision. Working with the World Health Organization, they had compiled some truly terrifying statistics that put the extent of the problem in perspective. After seeing those numbers, it became clear that this wasn't just my problem. Female circumcision, or as it is more aptly referred to today, female genital mutilation (FGM), occurs predominantly in twenty-eight countries in Africa. The UN estimates that this practice has been performed on 130 million girls and women. At least 2 million girls are at risk each year of being the next victims—that's 6,000 a day. The operations are usually performed in primitive circumstances by a midwife or village woman. They use no anesthetic. They'll cut the girl using whatever instruments they can lay their hands on: razor blades, knives, scissors, broken glass, sharp stones—and in some regions—their teeth. The process ranges in severity by geographic location and cultural practice. The most minimal damage is cutting away the hood of the clitoris, which will prohibit the girl from enjoying sex for the rest of her life. At the other end of the spectrum is infibulation, which is performed

Waris and Aleeke

Tea time

Nomadic
Somali home

Somali village

Waris and Ragge
visiting the school

The front of
the school

Laundry Day

Nhur, Burhaan's wife

Mohammed Inyer

Waris and her mother

on 80 percent of the women in Somalia. This was the version I was subjected to. The aftermath of infibulation includes the immediate complications of shock, infection, damage to the urethra or anus, scar formation, tetanus, bladder infections, septicemia, HIV, and hepatitis B. Long-term complications include chronic and recurrent urinary and pelvic infections that can lead to sterility, cysts and abscesses around the vulva, painful neuromas, increasingly difficult urination, dysmenorrhea, the pooling of menstrual blood in the abdomen, frigidity, depression, and death.

When I imagine that this year two million more little girls will go through what I went through, it breaks my heart. It also makes me realize that each day this torture continues, angry women like myself will be produced, women who can never go back and recapture what was taken from them.

In fact, instead of dwindling, the number of girls being mutilated is growing. The large numbers of Africans who have emigrated to Europe and the United States have taken the practice with them. The federal Centers for Disease Control and Prevention estimates that 27,000 New York State women have had or *will* have the procedure performed. For this reason, many states are passing laws to make FGM illegal. Legislators feel that separate laws are necessary to protect the children at risk, because the families will claim it is their "religious right" to mutilate their daughters. Many times an African community will save enough money to bring a circumciser, like the gypsy woman, all the way from Africa to America. Then she'll cut a group of little girls all at once. When this is not possible, families take matters into their own hands. One father in New York City turned up the stereo so his neighbors couldn't hear the screams. Then he cut off his daughter's genitals with a steak knife.

With great pride, I accepted the UN's offer to become a Special Ambassador and join its fight. One of the highest honors of my position will be working with women like Dr. Nafis Sadik, the executive director of the UN's Population Fund. She is one of the first women who took up the fight against FGM, raising the issue at the International Conference on Population and Development in Cairo in 1994. I will travel back to Africa again soon to tell my story, and lend support to the UN.

For over four thousand years African cultures have mutilated their women. Many believe the Koran demands this, as the practice is nearly universal in Moslem countries. However, this is not the case; neither the Koran nor the Bible makes any mention of cutting women to please God. The practice is simply promoted and demanded by men—ignorant, selfish men—who want to assure their ownership of their woman's sexual favors. They demand their wives be circumcised. The mothers comply by circumcising their daughters, for fear their daughters will have no husbands. An uncircumcised woman is regarded as dirty, oversexed, and unmarriageable. In a nomadic culture like the one I was raised in, there is no place for an unmarried woman, so mothers feel it is their duty to make sure their daughters have the best possible opportunity— much as a Western family might feel it's their duty to send their daughter to good schools. There is no reason for the mutilation of millions of girls to occur every year except ignorance and superstition. And the legacy of pain, suffering, and death that results from it is more than enough reason for it to stop.

Working as a UN ambassador is the fulfillment of a dream so outrageous that I never dared dream it. Although I always felt I was different from my family and fellow nomads when I was growing up, I could have never foreseen a future for myself as an ambassador working for an organization that takes on solving the problems of the world. On an international level, the UN does what mothers do on a personal level: it gives comfort and provides security. I guess that's the only past inkling of my future role with the UN; during my early years my friends constantly referred to me as Mama. They teased me because I always wanted to mother them and look after everybody.

Many of those same friends have expressed concern that a religious fanatic will try to kill me when I go to Africa. After all, I'll be speaking out against a crime many fundamentalists consider a holy practice. I'm sure my work will be dangerous, and I admit to being scared; I'm especially worried now that I have a little boy to take care of. But my faith tells me to be strong, that God led me down this path for a reason. He has work for me to do. This is my mission. And I believe that long before the day I was born, God chose the day I will die, so I can't change that. In the meantime, I might as well take a chance, because that's what I've done all my life.

18.

THOUGHTS OF
HOME

Because I criticize the practice of female genital mutilation, some people think that I don't appreciate my culture. But they're so wrong. Oh, I thank God every day that I'm from Africa. Every day. I'm very proud to be Somali, and proud of my country. I guess some other cultures might consider that a very African way of thinking—you know, being proud for nothing. Arrogant, I guess you'd call it.

Other than the circumcision issue, I wouldn't trade with anyone the way I grew up. Living in New York, although everyone talks about family values, I've seen very little of them. I don't see families getting together like we did, singing, clapping, laughing. People here are disconnected from one another; there's no sense of belonging to a community.

Another benefit of growing up in Africa was that we were part of pure nature, pure life. I knew life—I wasn't sheltered from it. And it was real life—not some artificial substitute on television where I'm watching *other* people live life. From the beginning, I had the instinct for survival; I learned joy and pain at the same time. I learned that happiness is not what you have, because I never had anything, and I was so happy. The most treasured time in my life was back when my family and I were all together. I think of evenings when we'd sit around the fire after we'd eaten, and laugh about every little thing. And when the rains began and life was reborn, we celebrated.

When I was growing up in Somalia, we appreciated the simple things in life. We celebrated the rain because that meant we had water. Who in New York worries about water? Let it run from the tap while you walk away and do something else in the kitchen. It's always there when you need it. BOOM, you turn on the faucet and out it comes. It's when you don't have something that you appreciate it, and since we had nothing, we appreciated everything.

My family struggled every day to have enough food. Buying a sack of rice was a big occasion for us. In this country, however, the volume and variety of food is astonishing to anyone who comes here from a Third World nation. Yet, sadly, so many Americans are preoccupied with *not* eating. On one side of the world we're struggling to feed people. On the other side of the world, people are paying money to lose weight. I watch commercials on TV for weight-loss programs and I scream, "You want to lose weight—go to Africa! How about that? How about if you lose weight while you're helping people? Do you ever think about that? You'll feel good *and* different, too. You'll accomplish two powerful things at one time. I promise you, when you come back you will have learned so much. Your mind will be much clearer than when you left home."

Today, I cherish the value of the simple things. I meet people every day who have beautiful homes, sometimes several homes, cars, boats, jewels, but all they think about is getting more, as if that next thing they buy will finally bring them happiness and peace of mind. However, I don't need a diamond ring to make me happy. People say, oh, that's easy for you to say now that you can afford to buy what you want. But I don't want anything. The most valuable asset in life—other than life itself—is health. But people ruin their precious health worrying about all kinds of pointless little irritations—"Oh, here comes that bill, and another bill, and bills flying in from every direction, and . . . oh, how am I going to pay them all?" The U.S. is the wealthiest country in the world, yet everybody feels poor.

And more than bankrupt of money, everyone is bankrupt of time. Everybody's got no time. No time at all. "Get out of my way, man, I'm in a hurry!" The streets are packed with people rushing here and there and chasing God only knows what.

I *am* grateful that I've experienced both lives—the simple way and the fast way. But without growing up in Africa, I don't know if I would have learned to enjoy life the simple way. My childhood in Somalia shaped my personality forever, and has kept me from taking seriously trivial issues like success and fame that seem to obsess so many people. Frequently I'm asked, "How does it feel to be famous?"—and I just laugh. What does that mean, famous? I don't even know. All I know is that my way of thinking is an African way, and that will never change.

One of the greatest benefits of living in the West is peace, and I'm not sure how many people realize what a blessing that is. True, there is crime, but that is not the same thing as having a war raging around you. I have been thankful for shelter here and the opportunity to raise my baby in safety, because Somalia has seen constant fighting since rebels ousted Siad Barre in 1991. Rival tribes have fought for control ever since, and no one knows how many people have been killed. The beautiful city of white buildings that the Italian colonists built, Mogadishu, has been destroyed. Nearly every structure bears the marks of seven years of nonstop fighting, with buildings bombed or shot full of bullet holes. There is no longer any hint of order in the city—no government, no police, no schools.

It is depressing for me to know that my family has not escaped this fighting. My uncle Wolde'ab, my mother's brother who was so funny and looked so much like Mama, died in Mogadishu. He was standing by a window when his house was sprayed with gunfire. The entire building was shot full of holes, and a bullet came through the window and killed my uncle.

Even the nomadic people are affected now. When I saw my little brother, Ali, in Ethiopia, he had been shot also, and narrowly escaped getting killed. He was walking alone with his camels, when poachers ambushed him and shot him in the arm. Ali fell down and pretended to be dead, and the poachers made off with his entire herd.

When I saw my mother in Ethiopia, she told me she was still carrying a bullet in her chest after being caught in crossfire. My sister had taken her to the hospital in Saudi, but they said she was too old for them to operate. Surgery would be dangerous, and she might not survive. Yet, by the time I saw her, she seemed strong as a camel. She was Mama, tough as always, and cracking jokes about getting shot. I asked her if the bullet was still inside her, and she said, "Yeah, yeah, it's in there. I don't care. Maybe I melted it down by now."

These tribal wars, like the practice of circumcision, are brought about by the ego, selfishness, and aggression of men. I hate to say that, but it's true. Both acts stem from their obsession with their territory—their possessions—and women fall into that category both culturally and legally. Perhaps if we cut their balls off, my country would become paradise. The men would calm down and be more sensitive to the world. Without that constant surge of testosterone, there'd be no war, no killing, no thieving, no rape. And if we chopped off their private parts, and turned them loose to run around and either bleed to death or survive, maybe they could understand for the first time what they're doing to their women.

My goal is to help the women of Africa. I want to see them get stronger, not weaker, and the practice of FGM simply weakens them physically and emotionally. Since women are the backbone of Africa, and they do most of the work, I like to imagine how much they could accomplish if they weren't butchered as children and left to function maimed for the rest of their lives.

In spite of my anger over what has been done to me, I don't blame my parents. I love my mother and father. My mother had no say-so in my circumcision, because as a woman she is powerless to make decisions. She was simply doing to me what had been done to her, and what had been done to her mother, and her mother's mother. And my father was completely ignorant of the suffering he was inflicting on me; he knew that in our Somalian society, if he wanted his daughter to marry, she must be circumcised or no man would have her. My parents were both victims of their own upbringing, cultural practices that have continued unchanged for thousands of years. But just as we know today that we can avoid disease and death by vaccinations, we know that women are not animals in heat, and their loyalty has to be earned with trust and affection rather than barbaric rituals. The time has come to leave the old ways of suffering behind.

I feel that God made my body perfect the way I was born. Then man robbed me, took away my power, and left me a cripple. My womanhood was stolen. If God had wanted those body parts missing, why did he create them?

I just pray that one day no woman will have to experience this pain. It will become a thing of the past. People will say, "Did you hear, female genital mutilation has been outlawed in Somalia?" Then the next country, and the next, and so on, until the world is safe for all women. What a happy day that will be, and that's what I'm working toward. *In'shallah*, if God is willing, it will happen.

DESERT DAWN

To You

To sit and dream, to sit and read,
To sit and learn about the world
Outside our world of here and now—
    Our problem world—
To dream of vast horizons of the soul
Through dreams made whole,
Unfettered, free—help me!
    All you who are dreamers too,
    Help me to make
    Our world anew.
I reach out my dreams to you.

Langston Hughes

Africa You are Beautiful

Has anyone told you
      you are beautiful
Africa?
      Your full body
and sensuous lips
      have kissed my soul
and Africa, I am bound to you
      by the drumbeat of
my heart that pumps the
      blood of my birthright
and you are mine.

Rashidah Ismaili

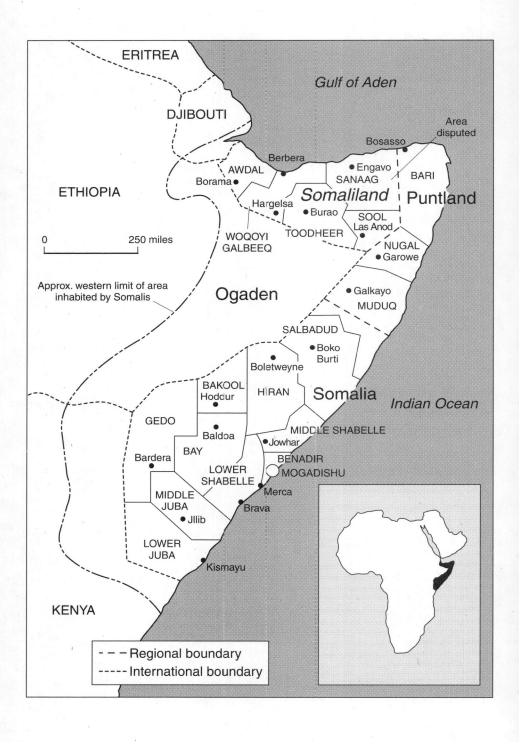

ERITREA

Gulf of Aden

DJIBOUTI

Area disputed

Bosasso

Berbera

ETHIOPIA

Engavo
SANAAG   BARI

AWDAL
Borama   *Somaliland*   Puntland

Hargelsa   Burao
SOOL
Las Anod

0   250 miles

WOQOYI
GALBEEQ   TOODHEER

NUGAL
Garowe

Approx. western limit of area
inhabited by Somalis

Ogaden

Galkayo
MUDUQ

SALBADUD

Boko
Burti

Boletweyne

BAKOOL
Hoddur   HIRAN   *Somalia*   *Indian Ocean*

GEDO
MIDDLE SHABELLE

Baldoa
BAY

Jowhar

Bardera
BENADIR
LOWER   MOGADISHU
SHABELLE

MIDDLE
JUBA   Merca
Jllib   Brava

LOWER
JUBA

Kismayu

KENYA

– – – Regional boundary
----- International boundary

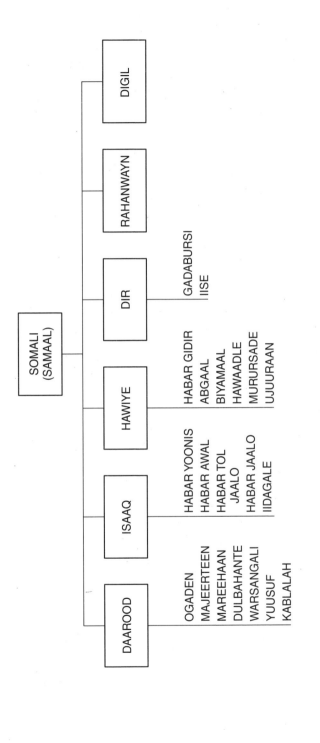

I

desert dreaming

A man came to God's Messenger and said, 'O Messenger of God, who is the most entitled to the best of my friendship?' The Prophet said, 'Your mother.' The man said, 'Then who?' The Prophet said, 'Your mother.' The man further said, 'Then who?' The Prophet said, 'Your mother.' The man said again, 'Then who?' The Prophet said, 'Then your father.'

Somali Traditional Saying about the Prophet Mohammed

In Somalia the devils are white. They are called *djinn* and they are everywhere. Everywhere! They crawl inside people and animals and make them sick. They play tricks and make you crazy. When you put something down and then suddenly it's gone when you turn around, you know that a *djinn* is sitting on it. My mother shouted at them, 'Hey! Devil! Get away from my things! They are not for you; you are not wanted around here.' My mother knew all about the *djinn* and how to get rid of them. She knew the special chants and exactly what tree leaves or bark would get the *djinn* out when we were sick. She cooked flowers and roots or gave them to us raw to chew on and kept special leaves and fungus in a leather pouch. She could read smoke, the wind and the stars and knew when the time was right. She was well-respected because she was gifted with many magic powers. I remember when I was a little girl people brought sick animals to her.

I was born in the Somalian desert. I don't know how many children my mother had. Many were babies born to be buried. Like most Somalis, we cared for camels and goats and lived on their milk. Following tradition, my brothers usually took care of the camels, and the girls watched over the smaller animals.

My family never stayed in one place for more than three or four weeks. After the animals ate the grass we had to move and find something else for them to eat.

One day when I had lived for about eight *gu* or rainy seasons, I was looking after our goats not too far from where my family was camped. That morning I scrambled down and back up the steep sandy banks of the *tuug* or dry river bed to a place I had seen the day before. It had some fresh grasses and a few acacia trees. The bigger goats would stand up on their hind legs and pull branches down so they could eat the bottom leaves. In the rainy season goats stay around the settlement without much care, but in the dry season you have to search for the grassy spots and you can't take your eyes off the animals for a split second because predators are lurking behind every bush. I sat in the shade during the hot afternoon singing little songs to myself, and playing with the dolls that I had made out of sticks. I always knew what I wanted to be. Even as a little child I had a vision. I knew the man I was going to marry. I played that I had a house. I used little rocks for my goats and bigger rocks for my camels and cattle. I built a big round house with sand. Wet sand was the best because I could make it exactly like our own little hut, only mine was better because I could make it just the style I wanted. My mother built our house and covered it with mats she wove from long grasses so it could be quickly loaded on our camels when we moved. My play house was safe and nice like hers. I had a husband and children and we lived far away from my family.

The sun's heat seemed to keep everything in place in the middle of the day. I could see up and down the sandy *tuug* for a long way in both directions. In the evening, on my way back to our camp, I had seen the wicked yellow eyes of a pack of hyenas watching me and the goats. I was scared because hyenas are clever and if you aren't on your guard they will get between you and one of the goats. You have to make yourself big and fearless so that they won't sense that you are afraid.

Whitey, my mother's favorite goat, looked up and sniffed the air so I looked too. I saw a man walking along the edge of the *tuug* pulling a camel after him with a braided rope. Usually camels follow along behind a lead camel who wears a wooden camel bell. It makes a hollow sound and the others follow single file like elephants holding on to each other's tail with their trunks. This funny camel was twisting and turning to one side in a strange way. It was not fighting, it was shaking and frothing at the mouth. Every now and then it would stop entirely and tremble. That animal had a *djinn*, there was a devil in it for sure. I watched the man yank the poor thing along the ridge of the hill. Suddenly, it fell over, all scrambled up in a heap. He shouted and yelled at it to get up. He started hitting it with a stick right on its belly but that camel just lay there twitching like crazy in the sand. I thought it must be a *hahl* or female and that she was pregnant, a valuable animal. The man sat down and put his

247

head in his hands. I was surprised to see a grown man sit in the dirt. Nomads will stand and rest with one foot braced up against the other thigh and their arms draped over a stick across their shoulders, or sometimes we squat on the ground. I had never seen anyone beat a camel like that. In my family, camels were valuable. A man who owns camels is one with power. He can sell or trade them for a wife and buy anything else he wants. They are magic animals. My father and uncles were firm with our herd but they never beat them unless they were obstinate and would not obey them. Camels are mean and I knew to stay away from kicking feet and biting teeth.

I didn't let him see me watching, I was afraid he would hit me too. I wanted to run home and tell my mother but I didn't dare leave the goats. My father would be furious and whip me if the animals wandered off or a hyena got one of them. I stood as still as a baby gazelle surprised in the bush and hardly dared to breathe.

Finally the *hahl* stopped shaking. She looked around for a moment and seemed to realize she was lying on the ground. She jerked to put her legs underneath her belly then got up all of a sudden. Although she was graceful, like most camels, drool and foam were dripping from her mouth. The stranger got up then too – almost as though he had been through this many times – and started pulling at her again. They went down into the *tuug* and up the other side towards our camp. I thought he must be worried about this sick camel. If she died he would lose both the camel and baby and the opportunity for more.

It had been dry and hot for longer than I could remember. I knew my parents were worried even though they didn't say anything. We didn't have much water because the wells in the *tuug* were dryer and dryer. We had moved our camp several times to find water for the animals. A newly born camel had died during the night. My younger brother, who we called Old Man because he was born with white hair, found her in the morning. Old Man always seemed to know things before anyone else did even though he was so young. My father poked the tiny thing. It was all legs and neck. Father stared at the cloudless sky. When it was dry he constantly looked to the sky and Allah for rain. We couldn't eat the meat from the calf because in our Muslim religion it is unclean to eat an animal that has not been properly slaughtered with a knife to the throat. Vultures were already circling above us so boldly that their long wings cast a shadow every time they passed overhead. I remember the sound of the dry wind and the low murmur of my mother praying.

My mother would never miss any of her daily prayers no matter how desperate the situation. If a person is sick they only have to pray three times a day instead of five and they don't have to prostrate themselves, but my mother always prayed five times. Before Muslims pray they wash so they are clean and pure when they talk to God. *Allah, let this washing cleanse my soul* . . . We barely had enough water to stay alive or give the animals, so there was no water to wash. When Mama couldn't find water she washed herself with sand. Five times a day, she carefully dug some earth out from under a bush so that no people or animals had walked on it. She put it between her hands and washed herself just like it was water. She rubbed it on her face and her feet. Then she would roll out her woven prayer mat and face the East, towards the holy city of Mecca, and pray, bowing and kneeling and chanting. *There is no God but God and Mohammed is His prophet* . . . The sun was our only clock. We kept time with the five daily prayers, at dawn, noon, before sunset, after sunset and night.

When my mother finished her song to Allah she rolled up her mat and put it inside our round house. She built it herself out of the long roots of the *galol* tree. She dug the flexible roots out of the ground and arched them into a dome. These were then covered with the mats she wove out of grasses. My mother was the worker in our family. She cooked the food, nursed the babies, built the house, wove the mats we slept on and made baskets and wooden spoons. She was the cook, the builder, the doctor, and my only teacher. My mother didn't say anything about the dead baby camel, she just got on with the day. 'God willing the goats will have milk this morning,' she said. She said that every day when we went to milk the goats and the camels. My mother had a way with animals. They stood quietly when she touched them. I had to put the animal's head between my legs into the folds of my dress and bend over its back to keep it from kicking or shitting in the bowl when I tried to milk them. But with Mama they seemed to want to stand next to her, to let her touch their silky teats. Mama would joke and sing while she milked.

Whitey had the most milk that morning and mother divided it for the eight of us. She looked at my father right in the eyes, something she rarely did, and when she put her bowl of milk in his hands they held it together for a moment. My papa was so strong he could pick up the biggest goat we had. He was Daarood, the biggest and toughest clan in all of Somalia. The nickname for Daarood is *Libah,* or Lion. He was taller than any man I knew and had eyes so sharp he could tell a male gazelle from a female across the plain. I knew he was handsome because I saw how women joked with him to get his attention.

I watched the stranger lead the camel into our camp. I knew I couldn't leave the goats but I really wanted to know what was happening with the bitter man and his strange camel. Suddenly I saw Old Man walking along the other side of the *tuug* looking for wood. '*Calli, calli*, come here, come here,' I called, cupping my hand towards him. I wondered why he was looking for firewood. He bounded down and stood at the bottom of the *tuug*.

'What's going on?' I called to him.

'Mama wants a bigger fire,' he said. 'A cousin brought a sick camel to see if she can heal it.' Old Man had a sweet face under his startling white hair, and round golden brown eyes, the color of frankincense. He looked like my mother who was the real beauty in our family. No one would say so though because as soon as you did it would attract a *djinn* and something bad was bound to happen to him.

'Old Man,' I called, 'come over here and I'll let you watch the goats. I need to see Mama.' My brother hesitated, but he was eager to be considered old enough to look after goats. Boys work their way up to herding camels, the most prestigious job, by looking after sheep and goats when they are small. Usually I wouldn't let him near them saying he would scare them. Today I wanted to see what was happening enough to risk a beating if Old Man did lose one of the goats.

I worried that someone would notice that I left my duty and so I crept cautiously towards our house. However, nobody took any notice of another skinny little kid. I could smell smoke from the fire and tea. I saw my older sister pour the tea into one of our two glasses. She held the pot up high and poured it in a long thin stream to release the spicy smell into the air. She served it to my father and the stranger. She never looked directly in their faces, only at the ground, like a proper woman. I wondered why Mama wasn't serving the tea to the men.

251

The camel by the side of our hut began jerking and twitching again. The camel was having a fit! My mother crouched nearby in the long afternoon shadow of our hut and watched. She followed everything that animal did, studying it as if she was going to buy it. The camel was light brown, almost the color of a lion's mane, and her belly was swollen with a baby. Her flesh was torn and her knees were bloody from falling down. Mama looked so hard at this animal it seemed like she was transfixed – but not with fear. I squatted silently behind my mother, I wanted to be a healer and I wanted to find out what she did.

My mother looked over at the men drinking tea. The man was a distant cousin of my father. He was not as tall as Papa and he had an odd-shaped head and a long neck like an ostrich. She watched him drink his tea and talk with my father about some political party, and fighting in the Ogaden. She was seeing what kind of a person he was. Mother looked at the camel's dried blood and hairs on the end of his stick. She got up and slowly approached the camel, cooing softly '*Allah Bah Wain*'; 'God is Great,' she chanted. She put her outstretched hand on the camel's cheek then slowly, delicately, drew her fingertips down the long neck, over the top of the shoulder to the belly. The camel didn't move away but kept shaking the whole time. Mama ran her hand all over the big stomach feeling the new life within. The animal was so thin that her ribs stood out even though she was carrying a baby. Mama put her ear on the beast's belly and listened for the heartbeat of a new life. She slowly backed away and then wiped her hand through some of the froth dripping out of the animal's black lips. She rubbed it back and forth in her fingers and tasted it. She opened the camel's mouth and looked at the teeth and the thick tongue. When the animal peed she picked up some of the wet sand and smelled it. She seemed to be waiting for the right time and watched the sun slowly sink behind the distant hills. She knew how the stars moved and when the seasons would change from the *gu* rains to the *hagaa* or dry season. She knew just when things needed to be done and when it was better to wait.

Mama took the braided halter and tugged on it backwards. She coaxed the camel to *faardisimo* or sit. I saw its long ears turn one after the other in the direction of my mother's voice. The beast sat down heavily. First it knelt on its front knees, then the back legs folded up and she sat down with her legs tucked under her. Camels are trained to kneel because they are too tall to load standing up. Mama squatted down so that the camel's head was at exactly the same height as her face.

Everything in the camp got very quiet. The men stopped talking, women stopped banging the cooking pots. Even the smoke from the fire seemed to be waiting. Mama reached up and placed her hands on either side of the animal's face as if it were a human child. She looked at it right in the eyes – then she slapped the camel with gentle slaps. 'Get out you devil, get out of here! You are not wanted.' She knew exactly how many times to slap and just how hard to get the *djinn* to move on. She took the leather amulet she wore around her neck and with holy words from the Koran touched it to the animal's nose, the entrance to the soul. The animal kept absolutely still for several breaths. Then the trembling stopped and it started chewing like camels do when they are resting.

Mama got up and covered her face with her headscarf before she went to my father and his cousin. She looked at the ground and told them that a bad spirit, a certain *djinn*, had got into the camel and caused it to have fits. 'She will deliver her baby soon,' Mama told them, 'before the moon is dark. The shaking *djinn* has gone now, but the camel needs to rest and to have extra food and water until she delivers her child. That will help her to fight off the *djinn* if it comes back.'

'She won't eat,' the cousin said.

'She is frightened of the devil,' my mother explained. 'You must pet her and talk calmly to her, then she will eat and get fat.'

'*Hiiyea,* I see,' my father and his cousin nodded at the same time.

'We shall slaughter a goat, make a feast, and say many prayers to Allah to keep away this *djinn*,' Father said. I must have jumped when he said goat because he looked over and saw me. He reached out and grabbed my arm before I could run away. He drew me over to him and slapped me so hard that I could taste the blood running out of my nose. Before he could hit me again I wriggled free and raced back to the grazing area. The bottom of the *tuug* was darker than the sky and I couldn't see in the growing darkness. I tripped over jagged rocks and the thorns on the *galol* bushes tore at my skin. In the darkness I heard Baby, one of the goats, bleating. We called him Baby because he always made so much noise. Old Man was walking in the *tuug* with the goats obediently following along behind him. I was so glad to see his silver hair in the shadows I cried and couldn't stop. It felt like my arm was broken and I knew my father would beat me again when we returned. I wanted my mother's hands on my face instead of that vicious slap. Why was a camel more important than a daughter?

Several years later, when I was considered old enough to be married off, I ran away from my father and the harsh Somali life, but in many ways the Western world was harsher. A father's slap was better than the loneliness I found in the modern world. When I found myself alone in a hotel, in America or Britain, with devils spinning the room all around, I longed for a human touch – even a slap – from hands that loved me. My eyes would be burning and swollen from crying. I felt that I was lost and that my life had no direction. In Somalia, family is everything; relationships are as essential as water and milk. The worst insult you could hurl was 'May gazelles play in your house.' It means: may your family disappear. Gazelles are shy and would never come near a house unless it was abandoned. For us, to be alone is worse than death. I had no family nearby and my relationship with my fiancé, Dana, had deteriorated. I wanted to find my mother, but when I asked a Somali man about Somalia, he said, 'Forget about Somalia. It does not exist any more.' His eyes were flat, as if the light had gone out of his heart. It was as if he said I didn't have a mother. It can't be true. If there is no Somalia, then what am I? My language, culture and customs are unique, even the way we look is particular to us. How could a country disappear like water in a *tuug*?

Now it was 2000, nineteen years after I had run away. My country was torn apart by famine and war and I didn't know what had happened to my family. I was in Los Angeles to give a talk about female genital mutilation. I agreed to speak even though it was difficult for me. In 1995 I had broken a strong traditional taboo and talked publicly about my own circumcision. I had become a United Nations spokeswoman on the subject, but every time I spoke it brought back painful emotional and physical memories. As a child I actually begged my mother to have it done because I heard it would make me clean and pure. When I was only as tall as a goat, my mother held me while an old woman cut off my clitoris and the inner parts of my vagina and sewed the wound closed. She left only a tiny matchstick-sized opening for urine and menstrual blood. At the time I had no idea what was going on because we never, ever talked about it. The topic is taboo. My beautiful sister Halimo died from it. Although no one in my family would tell me, I am certain she bled to death or died from an infection. The *midgaan* women who do the circumcision use a razor blade or a knife sharpened on a stone for the cutting. They are considered untouchables in Somali society because they come from a tribe that is not descended from the Prophet Mohammed. They use a paste of myrrh to stop the blood but when things go wrong we don't have penicillin. Later, when a girl is married, the groom tries to force open the bride's infibulation on the wedding night. If the opening is too small, the girl is opened with a knife. After years of struggle I realized that this is actually mutilation but I still felt anxious when I spoke out about it – I was afraid something bad would happen to me for breaking the code of silence.

It was late when I got to the hotel where the conference was being held and I didn't know there were events going on in many different rooms. I had trouble figuring out where I was supposed to be. Finally someone directed me to the ballroom. When I opened the double doors I was stunned to see five or six hundred people in the giant room. The chair, Nancy Leno, was already sitting on the stage with the other panelists. In situations like this, I have learned to act as if I know exactly what I am doing. Taking a deep breath, I held my head high and walked up the little stairs on the side of the stage. Nancy got up and came over to greet me. She was reassuring and her graciousness calmed me down.

I spoke on a panel with an attorney who specialized in securing asylum and a Sudanese doctor. Both women had facts and numbers to back up everything they said. It is estimated that some 70 million women have been victims of the ancient tradition, though the roots of the procedure are lost in its great secrecy. Different levels of severity are practiced around the world. *Sunna* is the removal of the clitoris. Excision removes the labia as well. Girls in Somalia suffer the most severe form of female genital mutilation called Pharonic circumcision or infibulation. The clitoris and the inner lips of the vagina are cut off and the wound is sewn shut leaving only a small opening for blood and urine. The doctor said that female genital mutilation (FGM) was performed on 84 percent of Egyptian girls between three and thirteen. It is no longer limited to Muslim countries either – over 6,000 young girls in Western countries now suffer this procedure.

I tried to explain what had happened to me as a little girl in Somalia and my difficulties with urination and menstruation. My mother told me not to drink so the opening would remain small and to sleep on my back so the wound would heal flat and clean. She believed this would ensure my future because girls with intact genitals are considered unclean and sexually driven sluts. No mother would consider such a girl a proper wife for her son. My mother believed, like all my people, that infibulation was ordered in the Koran. Talking about my genital mutilation was both a blessing and a curse. I was glad people wanted to do something about this cruel custom, but over and over I had to relive all the pain and misery it caused in my life. Every time I spoke out about female genital mutilation I spoke against something my mother, my father and my people believe. I denounced my family and a tradition that was very important to them. I wanted to heal women who had been through this painful experience but it made me an enemy in my own country. If I still lived with my family I would never have dared to say anything in public. It made me frightened and anxious every time I spoke about female genital mutilation. There are things you don't talk about in my culture; we do not speak about the dead or say that someone is beautiful. We have many secrets because if you talk about it openly, you are sure that something terrible will happen. It upset me when the attorney said that female circumcision was actually torture. My mother did not have me tortured. She thought she was making me a pure woman. One who would be a good wife and mother to her children and an honor to her family.

After I spoke, many people in the audience wanted to know more, but I was ashamed and I felt like I couldn't say anything else. I felt my part of the presentation had been terrible. I left the auditorium by the side door, got on the elevator and pushed the button for the nineteenth floor. It always scares me to go up so high in buildings. As a child my world was flat and open, and feeling my body go straight up in a little box always makes me anxious, it is so unnatural.

My hand shook as I pushed the cardboard key thing in the slit and I put the 'do not disturb' sign on the door. I closed the brown drapes to keep out the sunshine. It was a clear cloudless day and it reminded me of my home in the south of Somalia. I looked in the minibar and a *djinn* smiled at me. It said, 'Welcome! Welcome!' I gathered up the little bottles of gin and rum and scotch and crawled into the bed with them. Every bottle was a different devil and I drank them all – one after the other.

My mother could have kept the devils away but I had no

idea where she was or if she would even know me any more. She didn't understand photographs let alone modeling. Our clan would tear my eyes out if they knew what I was saying about our culture. I wanted to be a healer like my mother, but speaking out against FGM insulted her. She taught me never to say anything mean because you send it out to the universe, it's out there and you can never get it back. A black angel, Malick, sits on one shoulder, and a white devil, Behir, sits on the other. When Behir made my mother say something unkind she would ask Malick to take it back. 'Take it back, take it back,' she would say right away, before it got too far. 'I take it back, I take it back,' I cried, but I knew it was too late. All of the terrible things I said about my people were all over the universe. There was no taking it back.

I wanted to stay in that room forever. I put the sheets over my head and burrowed down like a tortoise. I was frightened and alone – a worthless failure. Big sobs started in my chest and pushed themselves right out of my mouth; they had been stuffed down my throat for a long time. Fear punctured every thought. When I finally fell asleep I dreamed that I couldn't find the goats, they had wandered off and I looked everywhere. My feet were bleeding from stumbling over the rocks and thorn bushes. I could hear them bleating, but I couldn't find them. When I woke up I found that I was the one crying.

Even though I really didn't care what happened to me, suicide was unthinkable. My mother told me she knew a girl of fifteen who burned herself to death because her parents refused to allow her to marry the boy she loved. They did not bury her and even the vultures would not approach the body. When I turned on the water in the gleaming tiled bathroom to take a shower, all I could think about was my mother washing herself with dirt and here I

259

let gallons of water flow down the drain. I stared at myself in the wall of mirrors. My mother is an extraordinarily beautiful woman but she has never seen her reflection. She has no idea what her face looks like. I looked at my body and felt ashamed of my legs. They are bowed due to childhood malnutrition and I have been fired from modeling jobs because of them. Like the devils who wait at crossroads, the threat of starvation is always there in Somalia. I wondered if anyone in my family was still alive. News was rare and always terrible. My brother, Old Man, was dead, and my sisters Aman and Halimo were too. Stray bullets that came through the kitchen window in Mogadishu, during the political struggles between tribes, had killed my mother's funny brother, Uncle Wold'ab, who looked just like her. My mother had been shot but she lived. I didn't know about anyone else.

I had run away when I was about thirteen years old because my father tried to marry me off to an old man. In Somalia men must pay a bride price for a virgin and this balding old man leaned on a walking stick and offered several camels for me. A woman doesn't have much choice in the matter; women have to get married. There is no other way to live in the desert; there are no jobs for single women other than prostitution or begging. Somehow, I knew that herding goats and waiting on an old man was not for me. I defied my father and ran away. My mother helped me; I don't really know why. Perhaps she didn't want me to have a bad husband. She taught me the song:

> *It is you who travels into the dark night*
> *Only to marry an ill-chosen husband*
> *Who beats you with a shepherd's crook*
> *In the scuffle it is your headscarf that comes undone.*

Now, alone and drunk with devils all around me, I longed for Mama. I knew that she could help me. After I had my son Aleeke, I ached for my own mother, for her arms around me and her voice low in my ear whispering, 'It's going to be all right.' No matter how much has passed between you, no matter how different your life's journey – you want your mother when you have a child. Every time I held my little Aleeke, now three years old, I missed my home in Africa, and my mother who is part of Africa.

My mother believes in Allah with every drop of blood in her body. She can't breathe or do anything without Allah. She can't pound the grain or milk the goats without saying thank you to God. That's how I was taught to live and that's what I love about her. Living in the West I'd lost the kind of life where you are in touch with God at every step. I began to feel I'd lose everything if I didn't go back to my soul's home in the desert.

My name, Waris, means Desert Flower in Somali. The oval petals of the desert flower are sort of yellowish-orange and this little bush bends low to hold Allah's earth between her roots. In Somalia sometimes it can be a year between the blessing of rains and yet somehow this plant stays alive. When the rains finally do come you will see flowers blooming the very next day. They appear out of the cracks in the earth as if they were nomadic butterflies. These delicate little blossoms decorate the desert when nothing else survives. Once I asked my mother, 'How did you find that name for me?'

My mother just made a kind of joke about it, she said, 'I guess because you are special.'

The thing that comes to my mind about my name is that I am a survivor, like the desert flower. My soul says it too. After all I have been through I feel like I'm 130 years old – sometimes more. I know I have been here before over and over. When I considered all the good and bad things in my life, I knew without a doubt that somehow I would manage to survive. I don't know why my mother chose that plant, I don't know why Allah chose me – but the two go together perfectly. I know that.

If you are raised in Somalia, then you know what it is to get up and walk when you have no strength. That's what I did, I got out of that bed and I moved on. I knew that I wanted to find my mother. I wanted to return to the place where I was born and see it with new eyes. I just didn't know how to do it, it seemed impossible to find my family – almost as impossible as a camel girl becoming a fashion model.

2

alone

A woman without relatives dances with her children on her back

Somali proverb

Back in New York, the travel agent looked at me like I was crazy. My friends said, 'Have you seen the newspapers? Mogadishu is a war zone.' Dana flatly refused to even talk about going to Somalia. He wanted his band to be famous and worked all the time on his music. I desperately wanted to see if I could find my family again, but no one in New York City was helpful or supportive of the idea. 'You better call the state department and see if it's safe,' the agent said. 'Did you know that Somalia is one of the world's most dangerous places?' When I got the information about Somalia I found terrible warnings: the United States warns against all travel in Somalia. Somalia has no functioning government. The present political situation is one of anarchy, marked by inter-clan fighting and random banditry. Kidnapping, rape and murder are frequently reported. There is no national government to offer assistance, nor any police protection. The northern region, the self-declared Republic of Somaliland, which formed in 1991, is less dangerous but there is no diplomatic presence in the country.

The airline agent didn't know if there were flight connections into Somalia. 'I have no idea how you could even make such a trip,' he said. 'We don't handle that sort of thing – I can't find a scheduled flight.' He also explained that in order to travel to Africa I would need to be vaccinated for yellow fever, smallpox, typhoid, hepatitis B and polio. He read from his computer screen, 'Recently there have been cases of smallpox in Somalia. You will need to take malaria pills.' It was so discouraging that I didn't even show him my passport. My British travel documents specifically forbid travel into Somalia. When I got the papers in London they did not want to be responsible for a British citizen in Somalia. 'How about a nice island in the Caribbean?' he suggested. 'Get away for a while and relax.' I didn't want to get away – I wanted to find my family.

I called people I know at the United Nations. They advised me that it was much too dangerous for me to travel in Somalia. They said I would need an armed escort everywhere I went and advised me to hire guards and a truck for the entire trip. They were concerned that fundamentalist Muslim groups might target me for an attack or kidnapping due to my public opposition to FGM.

Discouraged, I went back to my apartment. As usual, it was messy and dirty. The sink was full of dishes and take-out containers and most of a large pizza was just left on the kitchen table. I hated to see food wasted like that. When I was a child we didn't have enough to eat every day. Once my brother finished his drop of camel milk and reached over to take some of mine. I shoved his arm away and he punched me in the chest so hard I fell over and dropped the cup. That delicious milk spilled on the dirt and was gone. You couldn't lick it back out of the ground. The only thing left to drink was tears.

The kitchen faucet had not been turned off hard enough so water was dripping down the drain. I will never understand letting water run like that. In my childhood water was so precious we never wasted a drop. I still can't let the water run when I brush my teeth or wash dishes. It's a matter of respect for me; respect for the blessing of water. Nobody had opened a window; no incense was burning to add a little freshness to the air. Frankincense and myrrh come from Somalia and we always burn it to welcome a guest, for a bride or a new baby. When her husband comes back from a journey a woman will stand over the little burner and fill her skirts and her hair with the scent.

Dana was out and Aleeke was with his grandmother. I picked up the mail and bills from the floor to see what needed to be paid so things would not be shut off. That apartment was full of *djinn* and troubles. When Dana finally did come back we had one gigantic and all-out row. It ended with me shouting 'Get out, you are not wanted here!' Then I went to see my friends and had some beer to calm down. Alcohol is strictly forbidden to Muslims and my mother has never touched it. I felt guilty about drinking but first my family in Somalia was lost, now it seemed my family in the West was lost as well.

In Somalia everyone tries to keep a couple together for the good of the clans who are involved. Women do not have the same rights as men to divorce. Men decide when a marriage is over and the woman can lose her children and be left to beg without any other way to support herself. A man can say 'I divorce you' to his wife, her family and his family. If the families cannot get him to reconsider, then the marriage is over. A woman is allowed to leave if he doesn't provide for her but where will she go? What can she do? Men are required to give a bride a number of goats or sheep as her own. This is all she can take with her when they separate.

'Waris, good for you,' my girlfriends said, 'you have to stand up to men or they will take advantage of you.' I was surprised, I expected them to say, that's how men are, and watch out he will beat you when you go back. My friend Sharla said, 'Hey, come and stay with me for a few days.' She had watched Dana and I argue before, and thought that this would blow over, but I didn't think so. It had gone too far. The truth was I wasn't feeling this relationship any more. It was like an empty ostrich egg or a dry river bed; the life had gone out of it. There was a song the women used to sing and I remembered parts of it.

> *Goats need to be tended with tenderness*
> *Camels need to be tied to their tethers*
> *Your children have many needs*
> *A husband needs you to run errands for him*
> *And needs to beat you for uncommitted wrongs*

When I returned Dana wasn't home. There would be no apologies and no making up. Aleeke was still with his grandmother and I felt alone with the *djinn*. They were waiting and jumped in my head to keep me tossing all night. I spent a sleepless night angry and anxious about everything again. I knew that this was really it for us.

When Dana came home I asked him to move out. He looked at me and shook his head. 'No, I'm not going anywhere. If anybody is leaving it is you.' Dana said it with

such determination I knew he meant it. I stood in the doorway and watched him for a long time while he pretended
that I wasn't even there. He was really saying: I'm going to
make you suffer, Waris. If I have to move out, I am going to
make you move too.

Moving was something that I hated to do even though I
once lived a nomadic life. We all hated moving. When the
goats and camels had eaten the grasses and we needed to relo-
cate our camp, my father's tactic was to move in the middle of
the night so we could get to the water and new grass before
other people had touched it. We would all be sound asleep
and he would start shaking us and telling us to get up and
pack so we could load the camels. It was pitch black and everyone would stumble around in the dark trying to find things
except my father. Somehow he could see in the dark.

'Get the cooking pot, Waris.'

'I can't find it.'

'On the other side of the fire pit.' I scurried to find it by
feeling along the ground hoping I wouldn't step on a hot
coal.

My mother and he would load the camels with our few
little things. Women braided leather ropes out of animal
hide and they were very strong. Mama tied the braided
ropes under the camel's belly and from behind its ears to
under the tail. She tied our things to the ropes. Then she
coaxed the animal to kneel down so she could easily reach
the animal's back. She put our blankets over the hump first
as a base. Everything had to be tied tightly and carefully
balanced so that it would not fall off or shift around during
the long hike. It was hard to see in the dark and sometimes
the whole load would come undone and my father would
beat my mother for it with the bottom of his shoe. Mama
loaded heavy things, like our milk baskets, on either side,

and then added our cooking pot and smaller baskets. On another camel she fastened the mats that covered our round house, rolled up and tied on to either side. Mother built the load like a little house and made it comfortable for the camel to carry. In the middle you can put a young child or a baby animal that can't walk fast enough to keep up. We'd been told stories of children who didn't keep up and were left behind to die in the desert. We tripped and fumbled; scared to leave something behind, scared we might be left behind. My mother sang the work song or *salsal* while she and my father loaded the camels.

> *Nagging and worry are the companion*
> *Of a husband with many wives.*

I don't think my father liked that song but it was one all the women sang, so what could he say? After the camels were loaded, my family would walk all night and most of the next day. My people do not ride camels. Only a baby, an old relative or a sick person will ride on a camel's back.

I had to choose between moving out myself or putting up with Dana to see who would back down first. I went into my office, sat down in my chair and took a deep breath to calm down. This was my apartment; I paid the rent and the utilities every single month. In Somalia grievances are discussed and worked out by the men who are involved. There are no bosses; each man is given an opportunity to speak. A woman is not considered a member of her husband's tribe so her brothers or relatives will present her side when they are involved in a dispute. When my mother married my father she did not become a member of the Daarood because of the marriage, her alliances remained with the Hawiye. The men gather under a big tree and discuss the problem for as long as it takes to reach a decision that everyone can live with.

I didn't live in Somalia any more, I lived in Brooklyn where I had rights. But it turned out that since Dana's name was on the lease, he didn't have to move out. When I had found the apartment I was near my due date with Aleeke and I flew out to Omaha to have the baby near Dana's family. I was nervous about signing a big long legal paper like that. It's hard to read and I really didn't know what it was all about. So Dana stayed behind with my cheques and met with the landlord to lease the place for us.

A home is very important to nomadic people because our surroundings change frequently, but I looked around the place and decided, well this isn't a place where my soul is nourished anyway. I couldn't live somewhere with a dead spirit, a dry waterhole, an empty den. It was time to move on; the grass was gone and the place was full of *djinn*. There was trouble everywhere!

I knew that I needed to change myself – that I was a lot of the problem but I didn't know what to do. I have always been wary around men, not only because of my father, but due to other things that have happened to me. Many encounters with men in my life have been awful and I am guarded and suspicious. I thought it would be different with Dana because he was so shy and sweet when we first met, but I ended up feeling taken for granted. I thought I left all those lazy men who let their wives do everything behind in Somalia but I found the same thing in the West. Too many men have taken advantage of me and worse.

A friend of my father's came to live with us when I was quite young. He was called Guban. He stayed with my family during the dry season and didn't leave until the *gu* rains came. He came from Galkayo where he got into a fight with a man from another clan. Guban had a knife and almost cut off the other man's arm. Everyone in the clan is held responsible when blood is drawn so our clansmen paid the *diya* – the price to settle the dispute. They sent Guban to stay with us in the bush until tempers were not so hot.

Guban was funny and always teased me; he reached out long arms and secretly snatched at my *guntino*, my wraparound dress, when I walked by. He looked at me right in the eyes. I loved it and thought he was a special person. One evening he said, 'Waris, do you want me to come with you and help you round up the lambs?' I was flattered that he was interested in me – a little girl.

Halimo said, 'Don't trust him,' but I didn't listen to her, she was always telling me to do this or that. We walked out into the bush – down the *tuug* and back up the other side to call the lambs as the sun slipped behind the end of distant hills. He found a pretty acacia tree and said, 'Let's take a rest here in the shade.' He took his jacket off and told me to come and sit down next to him.

There was something strange about him and I said, 'No, let's get the lambs and go,' but he insisted that I sit on his jacket. I sat down on the very edge of it and he lay right next to me. He was so close that I could smell his sweat. I watched the lambs for a while chewing on the grass and nuzzling the ground to get the good young shoots.

'Listen Waris,' he said. 'I'm going to tell you stories. Lie down and look up at the stars starting to come out.' I liked that and lay right down on the edge of the jacket away from him.

He turned on his side and faced me with his head propped up on his hand. He tickled my neck and told a story about a girl who had a big nose. He touched my nose, and then he said she had a thick neck and a big belly and big breasts. He fondled me every time he told me about the woman in the story. One minute I was lying next to him and he was telling me a story then he was pulling at my *guntino* and he grabbed me and untied the knots. He pulled me underneath him even though I yelled and told him to get off. Of course nobody could hear because we were so far away from the camp. He reached down and pulled up my dress and rolled over on top of me. His *maa-a-weiss*, the cloth he wore wrapped around his waist, was open and he pushed my legs apart and sprawled on top of me. He was poking my vagina with this thing and I screamed, 'Stop it, stop it! What are you doing?' He put his huge hand right in my little mouth and the next thing I knew he squirted something. He rolled off then started laughing and I had this sticky stuff all over me. I never smelled anything like that in my life and I still hate that smell, I hate that smell. I stood up, wiped myself and ran all the way home. I grabbed on to my mother's leg and smelled her – she smelled clean like the earth. I didn't know what to say because I didn't know what happened. I didn't know anything about sex. We never talked about it. That man did something wrong but I didn't know what he did. I couldn't explain in words so I just held on to my mother's leg.

She stroked my head and said, 'Baby, calm down, what is the matter darling? What's the matter? Did a hyena chase you?' I couldn't cry, I couldn't talk, I couldn't say anything. I just stood there – I couldn't let her go. I felt dirty and shamed but I didn't understand why. I hated that man because he did something bad to me, one of the family who helped him.

Breaking up with Dana didn't solve my problems. I was a single mother with no place to live and no family to help me. Getting him out of my life was supposed to help, but it only made things worse. The more alone I felt the more I

271

wanted my mother. But my dream to find my family again seemed impossible. Only terrible news about Somalia made the newspapers. In October 1992 I read, 'Up to two million Somalis are said to be in danger of starving to death and already are dying at a rate of 2,000 a day.' There are only four and a half million people in Somalia so I believed the news reporters when they said, 'Somalia descended into hell.' I didn't know what had happened to my family in the years of famine and clan warfare since I left. I knew that the government had totally collapsed after Muhammad Siad Barre ran away in 1991. Almost ten years later a new government had not been able to establish peace among the warring factions.

My mother didn't even know I had a son; Aleeke was three years old and there was no way to tell her about him. What limited mail service once existed in Somalia had been destroyed and my family never lived by a post office. No one in my family could read or write so even if there was a postal service I couldn't send a letter or an e-mail, or a fax. My poor little country has not kept up with technology, it has gone backwards.

I was a person without relatives, as good as dead and gone.

3

bush telegraph

Good Fortune is riding on God's wing
On its flanks a good omen is in view
Regain your calmness my son and don't despair.

Somali Song

The phone rang one cloudy afternoon and I knew I had to answer that call. I just had a feeling about it. It was somebody calling for Oprah Winfrey. She is a powerful businesswoman and I respect that.

'We are putting together a program on sanctioned violence against women around the world,' the voice on the other end of the line said. 'We would like to have you on the show. Part of the broadcast will be on empowering women.'

'Do you want me to talk about FGM?'

'Female genital mutilation will be one of the issues we cover,' she said, 'but Calista Flockhart is going to interview women in Africa about that.'

'Calista Flockhart?' I said.

'She's the actress who plays Ally McBeal on television.'

'Oh,' I said, but I thought, what does she know about FGM?

If it wasn't FGM I couldn't imagine what I could say or why Oprah would want to hear anything from me.

'We would like you to do the segment called: *Remember Your Spirit.*'

'Spirit?' I asked, 'not FGM?' I didn't get it; I felt like an elephant trying to see its backside.

'Yes,' the woman said, 'we think you would be perfect for our segment on remembering your spirit.'

I was astonished that they didn't want me to do FGM. The last thing I had at that time in my life was spirit. I was a milk basket in a drought, all dried up with nothing good inside. I couldn't understand why Oprah Winfrey wanted me to talk about spirit and have a white girl who was never infibulated talk about FGM. What kind of spirit did I have to remember anyway? It seemed like everything I tried to do had dissolved in my hand like salt. I told her I would think about it and get back to them. My heart and mind were overflowing with troubles and problems I couldn't seem to solve.

That same week, very early in the morning, the shrill sound of the phone woke me up and I looked over at the clock next to my bed to see what time it was. It said five o'clock but I was still sleepy and I couldn't remember if it was five when the clock said five, or six. Maybe it was four when the clock said five. A friend had warned me about daylight saving and the time change but I couldn't get it straight – especially half asleep.

'Now why do we have to change the clock?' I asked him. 'How can time change?'

'It's fall back and spring forward,' he said. 'You set the clock back an hour in the fall because the sun is rising later and later. We want it to be the same time when the sun comes up.'

'Why don't you just get up with the light?'

In Somalia, nobody tells the sun what to do. Near the equator daylight is pretty much the same all year round and I could tell how long until sunset by the length of the shadows. What did clocks have to do with the sun? In Western cities there are so many lights that it doesn't make much difference whether it's night or day and it's so cloudy and polluted you can't see the sun most of the time. In Somalia the sun ruled our lives, when it was dark you slept; when it came up it drove you out of bed. He mentioned something about the farmers in Michigan getting up to milk the cows. Goats wake up when the sun rises, why don't cows in Michigan do the same thing?

I had a feeling that call was from somebody in my family. In Africa people joke about the bush telegraph. Communication happens without telephones or paper; there's a sixth sense I can't describe in English. Often you know that someone is coming, or someone is sick. In the West we have the cell phone, the fax and the answering machine. They are nice but I believe that as long as you are in touch with God, you are in touch. People ask me all the time, 'Do you have your fax on? I have so many things to send you.'

'No.'

'Well do you have e-mail?'

I tell them, 'I am a little bit behind with the technology in your world.' There are important ways to be in touch with those you love that have nothing to do with technology.

That morning when I stumbled out of bed and picked up the phone, I found it was my oldest brother, Mohammed, calling from Amsterdam where he lives. '*Nihyea*, woman,' he said and it snapped me awake. He needed money and I told him I would send it. Waking me up at five in the morning is typical of my brother. I love him but when he needs money, he doesn't keep quiet about it. Mohammed told me he had met some relatives who just returned from Somalia. Not only had they been there without trouble, they had visited family members who lived near our mother! They were going back and Mohammed wanted to try and get some money to her. In my family if someone has money, you share – that's the way we are.

Mohammed was raised in Mogadishu with my father's wealthy brother so I didn't really know him. This kind of arrangement is not unusual for my people. A family member who has money is often asked to help the children of poorer relatives. Even the ostrich lays her egg in another nest. The unsuspecting mother sits on all the eggs and raises the chicks. Sometimes you will see thirteen eggs in one nest.

When Mohammed and I were growing up, the military dictator, Siad Barre, had taken over the Somali government. He was quickly named *Afweine* or Big Mouth. He was eager to make changes in the country. Somali was not a written language because the religious people and the government could not agree on a script. Educated people favored a Latin script, but the sheiks insisted that Arabic letters were better because the Koran was written in Arabic. Siad Barre negotiated aid from the Russians and the Chinese and he wanted to please both countries. Chairman Mao told a Somali delegation to China that he favored the Latin script and wished that the Chinese had used it from the very beginning. The Russians were also in favor of the Latin script. Siad proclaimed that Somali would be written with Latin script. This resolved the dispute and Somali was written for the first time. The government declared a cultural revolution and insisted that everybody learn to read within two years. New schools opened in Mogadishu and that's where Mohammed studied in Somali, Italian and Arabic. Arabic is the language of the holy Koran, every student studies it; meanwhile the southern part of Somalia was once an Italian colony so most of the government papers were still in Italian.

As Mohammed grew up, the city fell apart. The schools and hospitals paid for with foreign aid were never built. The only thing that grew was the army. Siad Barre was Daarood and there were plenty of opportunities for someone from the Daarood clan with the military. The army had a big demand for *khat* and Mohammed became a *khat* dealer. *Khat* is a green leaf that secretes an amphetamine like speed. Originally religious leaders chewed it when they recited the Koran all day and night. Later older men sat around all afternoon and tore little green leaves from bundles of *khat* branches while they discussed issues and politics. They chew the leaves into a sort of paste and collect it on the side of their mouths until they have a big fat cheek. Eventually all of their teeth turn black from it. I could never understand what anybody saw in it. It doesn't taste good and it looks even worse; men have green juice dripping down the side of their mouth. Mohammed smuggled *khat* into the country from the highlands of Ethiopia and Kenya where it grows and sold it to the army.

For teenage boys in the military *khat* was hip. After chewing the drug restless soldiers became more and more agitated and less rational. For the first two hours the chewer feels happy but later depression, fatigue and distrust kick in but it's impossible to sleep.

After Siad Barre took power in the early 70s, I remember

my Uncle Ahmed came from Galkayo to check on his camels and goats. He seemed agitated and talked to my father for a long time. My mother and I were braiding rope out of long strips of camel hide and we sat near enough to listen.

'Siad Barre's soldiers are looking for young boys.'

'What do they want with them?'

'They will take any boy they find to a place where they train them to be soldiers. Believe me, many boys are already gone, kidnapped! There is going to be a war with Ethiopia over the Ogaden territory they stole from us. I don't want my sons to fight, they are too young. I am going to hide them.'

'Where will they get the guns to give little boys? Who would give a gun to a young boy?'

'*Afweine* is getting money from everybody! Italy, the United States, Germany, Russia and China give him money and he uses it to buy equipment for his army. He has the weapons – he needs soldiers.' Uncle sipped his tea and spat. 'I have heard this from many relatives,' he warned. 'Young boys disappear while they are out in the bush with the camels. Soldiers kidnap them for the army and steal the livestock too.'

After he left, my father and mother thought they would dig a hole and hide my brothers. Eventually my father sent the boys to live with relatives in the North, and taught me to help him with the camels. I was proud and determined to do a good job, usually only boys had the honor of caring for the camels.

Every few days I took the camels to the well along a path my father found for us. He could always find water even when no one else could. Camels don't store water in the hump; the hump stores a kind of fatty food, like a power bar, that camels can live on. The lead camel knew the route and the rest ambled behind following the sound of her wooden camel bell. I carried a goatskin my mother had sewn into a flat bucket with a long rope to pull the water out of the well. One day my path was blocked – army tents and trucks were everywhere. My heart stopped because I knew that the soldiers would rape girls and steal any animals they found. I climbed up a little hill and crouched down to watch the soldiers wearing brown uniforms walking around with their long rifles and bigger machine guns on the back of trucks. I let the camels go and hoped they would eventually head towards the waterhole. I crawled on the ground, detouring miles so the soldiers would not see me. The camels arrived before me. I pulled up water for them and then spent a dark night crawling back to our camp in fear of those soldiers.

My rich uncle decided to move away from Mogadishu. He said the city was falling apart. 'People live by *baksheesh,* bribing, and finding ways to steal and loot,' he told my father. 'Mogadishu is full of *muryaan,* street children, with nothing to do but cause trouble.'

'Hunger-driven men with no honor will eat anything and do anything to get food,' my father said.

'They are people who have no home and no way to make a living. We left that city and I never want to go back. The government is just a bunch of people out for themselves. Ordinary people are not safe there anymore.'

The war with Ethiopia did come in 1974, and from then on Somalia was troubled by civil war and later by famine. By 1991, Barre's forces had been defeated and the opposition took control over parts of Mogadishu. But they failed to agree on who would be president and this resulted in yet more inter-clan fighting.

I ran away from home and went to London shortly after his visit. News about my family was rare and soon there was no word at all. In December 1992, just after I came to live in New York from London to further my modeling career, I saw the *New York Times* Sunday magazine. A friend brought a copy to me and I could hardly stand to look at the pictures. A famine in Somalia had killed more than 100,000 people. It was not due to a drought but because of the civil war that broke out when Siad Barre's regime was overthrown. Now there was no government and gangs who cut deals with other gangs ran the place. Nobody could grow any food and most of the animals were gone as well. The pictures were black and white photographs of starving people. The relief agencies couldn't feed those who were starving because bandits looted the food intended for women and children. The pictures showed crying children with sunken eye sockets and their cheekbones sticking out of the sides of their heads. A woman who looked like a broken old umbrella was crumpled in a heap by the road. I heard that one out of every four children died in those terrible years. Of course the people to suffer the most were the women and the children. There was simply no way to find out about my family. The newspaper said, 'The lucky ones are those who have died in this forgotten land racked by war, drought and famine.' I watched the TV reports about Operation Restore Hope and the increasingly desperate efforts to rid the cities of armed and lawless soldiers.

A million Somalis fled the country and my brother Mohammed was one of the lucky ones who escaped. He called me when he arrived in Amsterdam. I was so happy that he was alive I flew right over to him.

When I saw Mohammed I couldn't believe this stick

person was my brother. His lower lip was split right down to the bone from going long periods without water. His collarbones showed through his shirt and he had a hollow look like part of him was dead or like he was empty inside. I grabbed him and held him tight. 'Mohammed, what happened, what happened to you?' My brother looked haunted.

'They locked me up in a wire enclosure and I was held there in prison for months and months. They didn't give us enough water or food.'

'Why did they do this to you?'

'Waris, it was a crazy time. The soldiers were drinking, and chewing *khat* all day long. They chewed *khat* for breakfast, lunch and dinner. They had stupid arguments and shot off their guns for fun while they drove around the city.'

'*Hiiyea*,' I wondered what Mohammed had seen.

'In the early evening they are high and reckless and the officers suspected anybody who was sober when everybody else was drunk or high. If you even said, "Hey, calm down. There might be people over there," they would yell at you.'

'The army was used to enforce government decisions, no discussion was allowed. The government declared that women had the right to inherit property and many religious leaders protested that this was against Islamic tradition. Ten sheiks were executed right in their mosques by *Afweine*'s private troops, The Red Berets. Those who demonstrated against the murder of their religious leaders were slaughtered in the streets. Soldiers shot off their guns and raped women and little girls like it was a game.'

Over the next few days Mohammed explained how *Afweine* became suspicious of anyone from the Majeerteen, Hawiye or Issaq clans. He recruited clansmen from his family clan, the Mareehaan, for the SRC or Supreme Revolutionary Council and they did whatever he wanted.

One night my brother was accused of insufficient loyalty to the president and sent to prison.

'They became suspicious of anyone from the Majeerteen and one night they dragged me out of bed, beat me up and then chained me in a dark room for over a week. No trial, nothing – just punishment for nothing.' Mohammed didn't really want to talk about it.

'How did you eat?' I asked him. He was so thin his eyes were sunk into his head.

'They never fed us, we got a little rice and a cup of water to wash.'

'Oh, my God, Mohammed,' I said. 'How did you get out?'

'Everybody was high or something all the time and Uncle got enough money to bribe the guards so I could escape. They knew that if I stayed in Somalia I was a dead man. Relatives somehow got enough money for me to get out of Mogadishu and put me on a transport to Kismayu on the Southern coast. *Afweine*'s clan was not so powerful there. From there I took a dhow to Mombassa and a plane out of Africa.'

After all the horror he had been through my brother remained connected to Somalia, even eight years after he'd escaped. His early morning call to me came when I had almost given up on the whole idea of going to Somalia, and I do believe it was a message from Allah. It was a miracle he called at just that time. If anyone could help me, he could. He told me that my mother was living near the Somali border with Ethiopia in a village where it was pretty quiet and safe. My father now lived in the bush near Galkayo but, even though he was still too proud to live in a village, he was no longer a nomad. The constant warfare had claimed most of his camels and he had trouble with his eyes. He lived with the two wives he married after my mother.

'Mohammed,' I said, 'I have been dreaming of going back to Somalia.' My brother had heard me say this before and he didn't believe me.

'Yes, yea, yea woman,' he said. 'You ran away twenty years ago, how are you going to go back now? It's better to try and send them money.'

'No, Mohammed, this time I really mean it. I want to go home but I am worried and not sure how to go about this. Would you help me?'

'*Hiiyea*,' he assented.

Hiiyea? Like everybody else I expected him to give me a whole bunch of warnings about how dangerous it is and why would you ever want to go back there. *Hiiyea* means something like 'I hear you'. It was as if someone lit a match in the dark.

'Do you think it's safe enough to travel? Do you think I would find anybody that I know? I haven't even spoken Somali for years,' I said, anxious and excited at the same time. Back in 1995 I agreed to do a documentary for the BBC because they would help me track down my mother. I saw her for three days in Galadi in Ethiopia, near the Somali border. I didn't go into Somalia because of the danger. I'd struggled with the language then.

I was serious about going to Somalia; I wanted to go for it. Mohammed agreed to go with me if I would pay his expenses. He has a small stipend from the government and no extra money for a trip like this one. He speaks excellent Somali, useful for me in case mine didn't come back. I felt safe going with my brother and I could leave Aleeke with his wife and their children in Amsterdam. I decided to do it the very next week. News about the area where my mother lived could change and the door might close forever. When Mohammed said he thought we could also find our father the phone went sweaty in my hand. Just the thought of my father made me anxious even after all these years. Mohammed was also anxious about the trip. He barely escaped with his life, and memories of his vicious treatment in Mogadishu filled his dreams. It had taken him years to even get official refugee status in Holland and he was not allowed to study or to work. What did he have? The opportunity to wait. He was looking to find solutions for himself as much as I was.

That afternoon I called Oprah's people back and told them that I had to decline because I would be in Somalia while they were filming the show. I didn't want to pretend I was full of a beautiful spirit when I really had a hole in my heart.

Once I made the decision to go and find my family I was in a panic about it. The women in my family are proper Somali women, they don't wear tight pants and a T-shirt with a baseball cap. I had thrown away all the raggedy Somali dresses back in London like a caterpillar shedding its cocoon. Now I wanted my cocoon back. I hunted all over New York City, the garment capital of the world, but could not find any Somali dresses or *dirah*. These are floor length to cover the legs completely and made of a light gauzy material. The dresses have flowers or colorful geometric designs and are simply made. You measure four yards of cloth by holding it in your outstretched arm to your nose. Village tailors with foot pedaled sewing machines take the cloth, fold it in half the long way and cut a round hole for the neck. They sew up the sides leaving a few inches for the armholes, stitch the neck circle and put a hem at the bottom. Underneath you wear a petticoat. I didn't know anyone with breasts big enough to need a bra, especially me! Women cover their heads with a long scarf which is pulled over the face when going out or talking to a man other than your husband or father. Legs, however, are considered highly provocative and any women who would dare to wear shorts or tight pants would be stoned or worse.

I asked my friend, Sharla, and she sent me to Banana Republic. 'What do you have for the desert?' I asked.

'We have some nice cargo pants, khaki shorts, and safari hats.'

'I need things that are loose and flowing, no zippers, or waistbands,' I said. 'Pants are hot in the desert.' She showed me a long black dress and I asked if she had anything more colorful. 'I like colorful clothes, I don't want to look like the desert,' I said.

The only thing I could find were Indian saris. Some of the cotton cloth was similar and I thought I could make a *guntino* out of it though that really isn't what the women in my family wear. The sari material is much longer because it's wrapped around the waist under the little bodice, Somali dresses fall straight down from the shoulders.

I wanted to bring presents for everybody in my family, especially my mother. However, as soon as I started shopping I got stuck. What could I bring? Nomads don't have things just to have them and I had no idea what anyone really needed or wanted.

My family would not know what to do with tin silhouettes of the skyline of New York, or plastic models of the Statue of Liberty. My mother wouldn't appreciate a big pencil with a tassel on the end or a T-shirt with pictures of the Empire State building. They would only appreciate things they could actually use or eat. So I bought baby oil, cocoa butter and coconut oil because it's always good to have something for dry skin in the desert. I also bought combs, yellow soaps in the shape of a fan that smelled good, hair oil, toothbrushes and toothpaste. We used a tooth stick to brush our teeth when I was a girl and I wondered if my family could still find those special bushes that the sticks came from. We don't have dentists in Somalia and so I thought toothbrushes would be very useful. For my mother I bought the most beautiful mirror I could find. I wanted her to see herself, to see how beautiful she was. I walked up and down the aisles in the stores thinking, no, no, no. Food and water are essential, the animals are essential and travel is essential. Things are not important to my family. We don't use tissues, paper towels, disposable diapers, toilet paper or tampons or sanitary pads. When women have their periods they wear an old dark dress and stay in the house. We don't wear lipstick, face powder, eyebrow pencil or mascara. We don't have electricity for hair dryers, or toasters. I thought about clothes but nomads wear only what they have on their back. They don't have a closet full of different things to wear and I have never been interested in owning a lot of clothes myself. I like to model things, but I have never been interested in keeping them.

In the end I decided on colorful scarves for the women and sandals for my mother and father. We don't eat candy and food would be spoiled by the time I got there – so I forgot about bringing anything edible. I bought razors for my brothers so that they could shave. I bought my father a comb and brush set then I took it back to the store because he would hate it. He had always rejected me. I will never forget when he said, 'I don't know where you came from. You are not one of us.' How do you present a comb and brush to someone like that? All the tears I never cried because I had to survive were still there, trapped in my heart. But now I didn't have time to cry, I had a journey to make.

4

differences

Men protect one another's flank
Thus they become brothers
Shall we aid each other
Or part company?

Somali Working Song

To get to Amsterdam, the travel agent in the American
Express office told me that I could buy a twenty-one day
advance purchase or I could leave on Tuesday or Wednesday
and return on Wednesday or Thursday with a Saturday night
stay-over. I explained to her that my brother had found out
where my mother was but that she might have to move on,
so if I'm going to do this I have to do it now. The woman
stared at me from the other side of the desk like I was very
strange. When I came in I noticed that she had an enormous handbag on her desk. She took out a giant economy
size bottle of lotion and squirted some on her hands just
before I sat down. Why women walk around all day carrying
an entire drugstore full of things they don't need is a

---

mystery to me. Somebody like that could never understand a nomad so I said, 'I need two tickets for next week, one adult and a child.' When she asked me about the dates for our return, I told her, 'I'm going from Amsterdam to Somalia and I really don't know how we are going to get there and back but, God willing, everything will be OK and we will get back safely.'

Her eyes got very wide and she said, 'I didn't know you could go to Somalia.'

'I'm going to try,' I said. 'My mother is there.'

Her eyes softened and she nodded at me. She explained that she had to have a specific return date and time or the tickets would cost more. She also told me I might have difficulties with immigration if we had an open ticket so I booked our return to arrive the day before I had a meeting at the United Nations. I used a credit card to pay for the tickets and told her I didn't want the clerk in the airport to say he couldn't find something on the computer that I never had in writing either. I wanted to have a ticket I could hold in my hand and show to the person at the airport.

She laughed and confided, 'I feel the same way.'

We left on a Tuesday night and I called Mohammed that afternoon to tell him what time to meet us. He still didn't believe me and said, 'Really! I'll believe it when I see you at the gate,' even though I assured him we were on our way to the airport.

I was so proud of Aleeke on the airplane. He sat there like a little man and looked at the people or drew for the whole trip. My son likes to fly or ride in a car even if it means he can't run around and jump on everything like he does all day at home. When he had to go to the bathroom he got up and walked down the aisle and into the little room as if he did it every day. He is a traveling nomad like me.

Sitting next to him in the seat I could clearly see the top of his little head. He had a skin problem and I hadn't been able to figure out what was wrong. His soft fuzzy hair was falling out in clumps and I could see he had little white lumps on the back of his head. I had tried everything to get rid of them. I took pure oil of eucalyptus, added a drop of water, and rubbed it on the bumps. I pounded oregano into a paste to kill the germs and made an ointment of honey and myrrh. After I ran out of herbal remedies I took him to my pediatrician but he just said, 'Children get these all the time.' The doctor prescribed some white sticky cream but it didn't make any difference; the white lumps were still there. Here I was on my way to leave my child with someone I didn't know and he was sick.

Mohammed's wife, Dhura, and I had never met. I had last seen Mohammed when he escaped from Mogadishu and got to Amsterdam. He hadn't met Dhura then. She was also from Somalia. After talking to her on the phone for the last two years I felt that I knew she was a good woman and a caring person. She pushed my brother to do things and take care of the family. Once when he and I had an argument and we weren't talking to each other she told him to call me. 'Don't be stupid,' she told him, 'you are the oldest. Come on, call your sister – say hello – tell her the news from Africa.' I knew in my heart that she would be good to my son.

Just because someone is a relative doesn't mean that they will care for your children. When I was a girl, about up to my mother's breasts, I went to stay with an aunt. Unfortunately I got very sick the day after I arrived. First I was hot then I was cold and my head ached all the time and I was so weak I could hardly talk. Probably it was malaria. My aunt was not helpful – she just let me lie there while she went out to gossip with her friends. She told me to take care of her children even though I couldn't stand up without getting dizzy. I wanted my mother so badly I prayed for Allah to tell her. Mama knew what to do when people were sick and she made everyone feel better with the bark she gathered and pounded into a powder while singing special healing prayers. Sometimes a touch and a cool rag can heal as well as an antibiotic. My aunt didn't make any special teas for me; she acted as if she might catch my disease herself. I had a feeling about Dhura however, and I knew that she would take care of my child as if he were her own child. It was very important to me that Aleeke learn Somali ways. He wasn't going to learn them from Dana who didn't understand African thinking.

When I met Dana he was proud that I was from Africa. He thought I was special and exotic, later we disagreed over most of my ways of doing things. We had the same skin color, but we came from two different worlds. Dana is an African-American and he would say, 'Let's grab a slice of pizza on the way to the movies.' In Somalia we don't do that sort of thing – food is a gift from Allah. We wash and say a little prayer before we begin to eat. We eat with our hands and food is taken slowly and respectfully. It always offended me that Americans would push food into their mouths while walking down the street. Did Dana and I disagree because I was raised in Africa? Was it because I made money? Because I was well-known? Was it because of my modeling?

When I first walked into the club where Dana was playing with his band I knew there was something about him. I started to dance so that I could watch him. That night I was wearing a green sweater with high-heeled boots and I had my hair all wild in an afro. He told me, he couldn't take his eyes off the girl in the green sweater with the afro. Later I teased him, 'I am going to have your child.' He really got scared like I was a nut or something. When I was pregnant with Aleeke I reminded him of that. The very first time I saw that man something told me that he was the one for me.

Dana impressed me with his spirituality right away. He grew up in the Midwest and he was sensitive and shy. He struck me as an honest, good-hearted person. It's not easy for me to trust men and Dana's caution was magical. In addition to my infibulation, my earliest memories of sex between my parents are scary. One night when I was very little I heard noises I didn't understand and I saw my mother lying on her sleeping mat on the other side of our round hut. My father was on top of her. She didn't say anything but he pushed and sighed and grunted. I got up to see what was going on and went over to them. I reached out to get my mother's attention and the next thing I knew I was flying across the room. My father had grabbed my leg and pitched me up in the air backward. I was so stunned I didn't even cry out, it knocked the wind right out of me. My big sister, Halimo, took me in her arms. 'Be quiet, Waris,' she whispered. 'Leave Mama alone now.' When I asked my mother about it in the morning she shooed me away. Sex was a secret thing.

Dana was gentle and refreshing like rain in the morning. The more comfortable and safe I felt with him the sexier I felt. He would brush my hand and I would feel excited. I don't believe that infibulation kills all sexual desire, but it has made me very cautious, very reticent. However, once I feel safe and secure I want to be held and touched all over my body. My family and my people are very affectionate. Although men and women are never together in public, it's not unusual to see two men holding hands and walking together through town. Somali men express their friendship

by touching in the same way that women do with close
friends. In the West you only hug when you greet an old
friend, so it felt wonderful to be physically close to Dana.
Women who've had a breast removed because of cancer can
still feel sexy. Part of my body was cut away but nothing
important was missing when Dana kissed me. For me sex has
to do with how I feel about my partner. An orgasm begins in
my head and ends in my heart. I am easily spooked, but
Dana touched me shyly and I fell in love with him.

After Aleeke was born our differences were more obvious.
We don't use diapers on little babies in Somalia. Mothers
are so close that they know when the baby is going to make
water. You sit down on the ground and straddle the child
over your open legs. The baby goes in the sand and you can
use a leaf to wipe the baby's bottom. Allah's handiwipe. The
whole time you talk to them and tell them what they are
doing so they associate the action with what you are saying.
When children start to walk it's easy to get them to squat
down on their own and go by themselves. All of the little
children just wear a T-shirt until they are three years old or
so. They are very proud when they are old enough to wear
shorts or a dress.

Dana didn't understand this and neither did his grandmother. She was the one who raised Dana and we visited her
all the time. She felt that the child needed to be wearing a
diaper at all times. I can understand that when it is cold out
but around the house I let Aleeke go with just a shirt on as
soon as he was crawling. Dana felt letting Aleeke run around
without a diaper on was wrong. I think a little baby's body is
beautiful and wonderful to see; children are so physically
perfect. Dana's family thought it wasn't correct to allow a
child to be naked. The comments they made were hurtful
but I wanted to be accepted by Dana and his family so I

dressed my son in shirts, pants, shoes and socks. However, I couldn't get over disposable diapers. What a waste! All that paper from so many babies just thrown away? Where does all that paper and plastic end up?

Even though Dana and I were not married when I had Aleeke, his grandmother, whom we both called Granny, never did anything but love my child. She was so happy to have such a great grandson. She reminded me in some ways of my own grandmother because of her self-reliance, strength and old-fashioned values. I guess she is a typical American grandma. My grandmother in Mogadishu was a very correct Somali lady. She never went out of her house without covering her face. 'How can you see in there?' I always asked her. She had to raise her children by herself and she did things properly. Dana's grandma's manners were very different to mine. She always questioned every-thing I did and how I did it. She didn't seem to want to know about African ways, she wanted me to learn her ways. Granny lived in Omaha, Nebraska all her life and she had never even seen the ocean. I used to joke that one day I would take her to dip her two chicken feet in the ocean and then she would understand my world.

I always dreamed of breast-feeding my children, even before I could take care of the goats. My mother breast-fed my brothers and me until we were three or four years old and she was having another child. In Somalia we don't have baby bottles and if we did, there wouldn't have been the spare water necessary to cleanse them. When my mother cleans her wooden milk bowl she rinses it out with fresh goat urine. Then she takes a glowing coal from the fire and sterilizes the inside of the bowl. She uses ashes and sand to scrub the inside of the dishes after they are used. My mother's breast was my only nourishment as a baby; it was both food and comfort. When I got older I watched my mother and the other women breast-feed and I wanted to try that too. I wondered what it would feel like; it looked nice and close. A baby sleeps with its mother and is carried on her back so that whenever it cries she can swing the baby around to the front to nurse.

One day when I was too small to see over the tall grasses, I watched my aunt's tiny baby while she went to gather some firewood in the bush. He was only as big as a camel's head and his arms and legs were still tucked up next to his body. The protective amulet he wore was almost bigger than his soft baby belly. He started to scream and I thought, let me try something. I wanted to see how it felt to have a baby suck at your breast. When I put him next to my flat little chest; he reached for it with his little mouth and made a circle shape with his lips. It was a bizarre feeling. At first he looked surprised that I was different than his mother. I pushed him closer to me so he could get a better grip. He tried but there was nothing to take into his mouth. He got really mad then and screwed up his face like a camel hissing. He arched his back away from my trick and started to scream. I couldn't get him to stop until I finally tied him on my back so he couldn't see me and he quieted down. I decided it must be easier with your own children.

One of my sisters died shortly after she was born. My mother's breasts were full of milk for her and they began to hurt. She tried to milk herself like a goat but not much came out. After a few days they were big and red and hot when you touched them. The veins stuck out like tree bark. My mother started to cry from the pain and I was frightened and scared. I had never seen my mother cry even when my father beat her. 'Mama,' I pleaded, 'let me help you. I can suck it out of you.' I sucked the milk out of her breasts and spat it out on the ground. I sucked and spat and sucked and spat until she felt better. It didn't taste like the milk I used to drink; it had a bad smell and an acid taste.

When I found out that I was pregnant I wasn't worried, not the least little bit. I had watched so many mothers and babies, I felt like I had been pregnant over and over again. When I was eight months pregnant I traveled to Spain for a photo shoot. Dana's family was horrified – like pregnancy was some kind of an illness. They didn't want me to jump on an airplane and go to Europe. But my mother and my aunts didn't stop working because they were pregnant, I had never heard of that idea. I wasn't afraid to work and I put on a baggy sweater and got on the plane. The pictures show a woman who is full to the brim with joy. It was a beautiful pregnancy; I loved my big belly and the movement within. It was a blessing to be filled with life, an honor that Allah would allow me to create a new family. I felt powerful and confident that nothing would harm me.

Every time I went to the doctor for a check-up he would ask, 'Do you want to know the sex of the baby?'

'I don't want to know that,' I told him. 'I have a feeling. I know what this child is going to be.' I knew the personality, what the baby would look like, and how he would see the world. 'Will this child have two legs, two arms and two eyes?' That was all I cared about. Every day I would pray on my life for a healthy baby. I saw the babies born to be buried when I was a girl. My mother wrapped them in white and Father buried them on a shelf until Allah took them. When Aleeke came out of my body into the world I knew my hunch was right. Aleeke is my little brother, Old Man, come back to life as a spirit guide. The moment he was born, when the nurse handed him to me, we looked at each other, right in the eyes. 'Oh,' I said to him, 'it really is you, Old Man.' Aleeke looked right back at me and I know he knew too. I don't know how to thank God for giving me such a gift and bringing my little brother back into my life.

We had Aleeke circumcised in the hospital a day after he was born. This is very different from female genital mutilation; that should never even be called circumcision – it's not. In males it's done for medical reasons – to ensure cleanliness. I could hear Aleeke crying when they did it but he stopped as soon as I held him. Despite my strong feelings about FGM, I knew it was the right thing to do. My son has a beautiful penis. It looks so good and so clean. The other day he told me he had to go to the bathroom. I said, 'You can do that alone, you are a big boy now,' but he wanted me to come and see him. His little penis was sticking up straight and clean. It was lovely to look at!

Sad to say, I didn't have much success breast-feeding Aleeke. He was a healthy baby but he didn't seem to get enough milk. He would scream and cry and I didn't know what to do. My breasts were so huge I couldn't believe I didn't have enough milk in there but he just cried and cried. He arched his back and pulled away from me. I couldn't think what my mother or my aunts did, it seemed so easy, they never had a problem. The baby just sucked as far as I knew. Granny and Dana both said, 'Give him a bottle, it's better for him.' After I hadn't slept for three days I gave him the bottle and he took it just like that. He was content and full so I had to give up nursing. Granny said, 'Formula is better for babies.' I didn't want to argue with her, I wanted my baby to have a happy smile and a full belly. Dead children are wrapped in white, the devil's color, the color of mourning.

When my mother needed to go to the bathroom or pray she would hand my baby brother to me or my sisters or my aunts. We don't have high chairs, or baby seats or play pens. That was one thing I couldn't believe! A caged child is like a trapped lion or tiger. I always held my son and sang Somali lullabies even though they made me long for Africa.

Father camel is walking
Far, far away
Don't worry Baby
Allah will bring him
Back to our tribe

Sometimes I sang this one:

Father is traveling, traveling, traveling
Auntie is traveling, traveling, traveling
Brother is traveling, traveling, traveling
When Father returns he will bring many presents
When Auntie returns she will bring many presents
When Brother returns he will bring many presents
All for the good baby boy!

I taught Aleeke to drink from a cup when he was two months old because that is what I learned as a child. I poured a little milk in a cup and sat him in my lap then pressed his two cheeks together so his mouth was open a little bit. I carefully poured a drop or two into his mouth. Granny said, 'No, Waris. It's too early for that baby to learn to drink from a cup.' Well, that is interesting, I thought, because he is doing just fine. But I let her take him and feed him with a bottle.

She saw me washing him in my lap with a warm wash-cloth and offered to show me how to give him a 'good bath'. Granny thought it was better to put the poor little thing in the sink where you wash the dishes. Leeki got scared and screamed when she put him down in that metal basin. He threw his arms back and his legs out until I picked him up and swayed with him back and forth.

After cleaning her children my mother used *subaq ghee* or butter on the babies' skin. When Mama had enough goat or camel milk she poured it into her milk basket or *dhill*. A *dhill* is an elongated oval basket woven so tightly that not a drop, even of sweat, could leak through. Outside, branches bent into a U, surround it. Mama tied the top on tightly and let it sit for a day or two until the milk was thick like yogurt. She put a little blanket under the *dhill* so it could be easily rocked. That whole day one of the children had the job of rocking the *dhill* back and forth. When Mama came back home in the afternoon she would open the little hole in the top to test it. If milk came through the hole it meant that it wasn't ready. If nothing came out it meant that the butter was thick and done. Mama opened the *dhill* and collected the clumps of *subaq* from the bottom and the sides. It is wonderful butter! Then she would give us the milk that is left to drink. Whenever my mother made *subaq* it was a specially happy day – usually there was not enough milk to make it. You also use the *subaq* to fry meat and as an ingredient in cooking. We put it on our pancakes and in tea. We use it as a face and body lotion and in our hair. My mother massaged it into the babies' skin to keep it smooth and soft.

One crisp fall day when I was staying with Dana's family, I put Leeki on my back with a length of cotton cloth. He was about two or three months old. It was a bit chilly so I had my green jacket on too. When I carried my brothers and cousins on my back they loved it and I knew just how to do it. I used my headscarf because it is tightly woven like a bed sheet but not as wide. Mine is bright yellow, with a green and red African pattern. I bent over and gently put Aleeke on the flat of my back. You hold one of the baby's arms under your armpit so they won't fall while you tie the cloth around you and the child. It goes over one shoulder and under the other arm and you tie it right in the middle of your two breasts. It's comfortable, it's not heavy, and you are so close you can feel every breath the baby takes. I never could understand how people put a little baby all alone in a carriage. Even before he was born, Aleeke's grandmother said we would have to buy a stroller.

I answered, 'We won't be needing that.'

She looked very surprised and said, 'Well, what do you mean? How are you going to go shopping and take the baby outside for a walk?'

I said, 'I'm going to carry my child differently.'

She said, 'Listen Waris, take my advice, this is your first child and you really don't know what you are doing. You will need a stroller. You can't walk around carrying the baby everywhere.'

I said, 'I understand how you do things, but we carry our children in a different way.'

She got a stroller anyway, a huge gray ugly one. I hated it so much I stopped using it a few weeks later. Not so much because of her, I loved her, but because it was as big as a cow. I felt funny pushing it in the street. There isn't a lot of space in New York City and here I was taking up the whole sidewalk so everybody had to get out of my way. It was bad enough shoving the thing up and over the curb but getting inside the shops was impossible. You had to lean way over to push the door open, then quickly drag the stroller in after you. I always worried that the door might close and crush my baby. There was no way you could take the subway, you had to walk everywhere no matter how far it was. Then I had to leave it downstairs while I carried Aleeke up to the apartment, leave him alone and rush back down to drag the stupid thing under the steps where people could still trip over it in the outside hall. That is a so-called convenience I can do without.

Anyway I came running downstairs that morning with Aleeke on my back. The habits of my desert childhood remain and I am always running even when I have no destination. His itty-bitty head was hiding under my jacket, I felt so fine. I saw Granny in the kitchen washing up the breakfast dishes and I said, 'See you later Granny.'

She called, 'Wait a minute. Where is the baby? You said you were going for a walk with the child. Where is he?' She came out into the hallway and stood there holding the dishtowel.

'He's on my back,' I said.

She honest to God could not believe what I was saying. I moved Aleeke under my arm to the front, and pushed my jacket open and said, 'Here he is.' He looked at her with a big, happy baby smile. The woman had a fit, she didn't know how the child was hanging there. She had never seen such a thing and she couldn't understand how the baby was so comfortable. She kept insisting that he was suffocating and repeating, 'I am begging you to take it off.'

I laughed a little and told her, 'We are going for a walk, I will see you later.' But it bothered me, I needed support and reassurance, not somebody telling me I was suffocating my child. I wanted her to ask me, how do you do that, not assume it was bad because it was African.

5

endless flights

Closest are the tongue and the teeth, and even they fight

Somali Proverb

The plane dropped out of the clouds and landed next to the gray flat terminal in Amsterdam and I smiled even though the day was dreary and dark. I could see a tall figure sticking up like a thorn in the crowd waiting outside the gate. Sure enough it was my brother, over six feet four inches tall. Mohammed was there with a friend and he had the biggest smile on his face I ever saw. His eyes are the color of Africa, dark brown and deep with secrets. When Mohammed first escaped from Mogadishu he looked starved – starved of food, of water, and of hope. Now he was not as thin, but he still had a haunted, hungry look about him. He had the split in his bottom lip from extended thirst and I don't think that scar from the prisons in Mogadishu will ever heal. Mohammed wore round glasses and he watched us coming down the hall like a camel waiting for water at a well.

It was good to hold my brother again, to hug him and to greet him in Somali. With wide-open eyes Aleeke looked up at his tall uncle. Mohammed grabbed him and put him high in the air on his shoulders. Aleeke shrieked with delight.

Dhura was standing at the door when we got to Mohammed's simple flat an hour's drive outside of Amsterdam. My sister-in-law was exactly what I expected, exactly the way I visualized her. She has a round face and eyes that shine when she laughs. She is tall like my brother; they make a good couple. Dhura was wearing a long Somali dress and her hair was covered by her headscarf. She reached for me when I came in the door and held both my hands when Mohammed introduced us. She linked her arm in mine and held me close while she showed me the flat and where we would sleep. I could feel her warmth and strength. Dhura is also Daarood and has two children from a previous husband, a boy and a girl. Her son's name is Mohammed. She followed Somali tradition and named her first boy after the Prophet. He is about eleven. Her daughter, Zhara, is ten and already growing tall like her mother. Dhura's first husband disappeared somewhere in the madness of Mogadishu and even his family didn't know where he was. One night a mortar shell hit the building where she lived and the entire side of it crumbled into the street. Dhura took her children and fled to Kismayu and from there by boat to the refugee camps in Mombassa. When she arrived in Holland she gave up trying to find her husband and divorced him. She announced it to the people in his clan and they agreed with her.

Both children had soft eyes and they stood shyly behind

her long dress. They peeked out at Leeki with big smiles. He ran off with them to play and didn't look back at me. I was so happy I almost cried. I wanted him to have a big bunch of cousins to run around with and cause trouble like I did when I was little. He joined right in as though he knew them his whole life.

Dhura and I sat down to have some cardamom tea together. 'I am worried about leaving Aleeke to go on this trip,' I confided.

'Waris,' she said patting my hand, 'he'll be fine with my children.'

'He's got some lumps on his head and they won't go away,' I told her. I called Leeki over and he let Dhura feel his head and pop one of the bumps so the pus came out. They didn't seem to bother Leeki, he just wanted to go back and run around with his cousins.

'My Mohammed had this,' Dhura said, 'and if it doesn't clear up in a few days I can take him to a doctor here in Holland. The medical care is free and the doctors are very nice to us.'

'Free?' I was surprised. 'I paid over a hundred dollars to the doctor in New York and the cream he gave me didn't help.'

'The doctors are free and we have money for food and the flat but Mohammed is not allowed to work because he only has an F-1 refugee status. That means we can only stay until things are better in Somalia – we are not considered permanent residents. We are waiting and waiting and I don't have much hope that he will ever be allowed to study or get a job. Mohammed doesn't really want to go back to Somalia to live.'

Oh, I thought. There is no salt in the tears he cries about Somalia.

The next morning when Mohammed and I left the house to arrange our flights to Africa I put on a long wraparound cotton skirt that could sometimes open at the front when the wind blew to reveal my legs. I had a sweater and my jacket on and I was wearing socks and boots because it was cold. As we walked out of the flat my brother looked at me sideways and said, 'You're going to wear that?'

I said, 'Yes. Why?'

'I don't like that skirt.'

'I can go back and put on my jeans.'

He rolled his eyes and groaned, 'No! That's worse.'

I stopped walking and looked him dead in the face. 'What is the matter?' I asked.

He said, 'Is that all you have to wear? A pair of jeans and that skirt!'

'Well, brother,' I said, 'we live in wintry countries. I don't know what you want me to wear. This is what I wear, these are my clothes.'

He sighed and fumed, 'We are going to a Somali office where they deal with plane tickets and travel to Somalia. You will embarrass me if you show your legs off like that. You don't have something else to put on under it?'

I said, 'You know, this is going to be some trip because you and I have already started and we hardly left the house on the first day. I am not going to act like a Somali woman, cover my body completely and not say anything. I see how you tell Dhura to do this, do that, but let's get it straight right now: I am not taking it.'

'Waris, you don't know how things are here,' he started to say.

'You shut up,' I said to him. 'I left home when I was young – I raised myself and neither you nor any other man is going to tell me how to dress or anything. I pay my own bills, and you are asking me for money all the time. I know that in Somalia the legs are considered the sexiest part of the body and are always covered, but we are in Holland, so adapt already.' Mohammed looked very surprised. I don't think any woman he ever met talked right back to him. His eyes were as round as his glasses.

Before I left New York I bought American Express travellers cheques because we were going so many places. I didn't want to take a chance and carry cash, so the first thing we had to do was go to the bank. I needed to exchange at least four grand. We took a train into the city and went to the biggest bank in Amsterdam. It was all white with big columns in front and a brass door. Inside there was a long queue to change money. When my turn came, I gave the teller the travellers cheques and my passport. This pale man with a thick neck and a red nose looked at me over the top of his glasses and said, 'Are these your cheques?'

'Yes, of course they're mine.'

'Could you just sign here for me?' he said and pushed a piece of paper over from his side of the counter. I signed my name and after he turned it over several times in his hand he said, 'No, I'm afraid that these signatures don't go together.'

'This is my passport; it's the same name and it's the same signature.' I had at least five thousand dollars' worth of travellers cheques still in my backpack and I asked him if he wanted to see the rest of them. Even though I never went to school or had a teacher show me how to write properly, I can sign my name correctly.

His neck turned red and he said, 'No, I will not authorize this transaction. You will have to go somewhere else to cash these cheques.'

'There is nothing wrong with my signature.'

He stared at me and slowly repeated, 'They don't match.'

I stood up very tall and replied, 'I would like to see the manager.'

His eyes got very narrow like he just walked out into the sun and he said officiously, 'I am the manager.' I knew that he was no manager and what he was trying to do.

Mohammed touched my arm and started to get up to go. 'Let's go,' he whispered. 'You see the signature doesn't match, let's get out of here.' When I didn't move he started to get nervous. 'The two signatures don't go together, don't you see,' he said picking up the cheques from the counter. 'Come on, never mind, let's get out of here.'

I couldn't believe he would give up so easily. 'Stop it,' I told him. I wanted to beat him up for being such a baby. I hissed under my breath, 'Do not speak to me in this way any more! I know what I am doing.' I turned to the so-called manager and asked him, 'Well, where do you suggest I go?'

The self-proclaimed manager said, 'There is an American Express Bank on the other side of town. That is where they will be able to check the authenticity of your cheques.' He told us to take this train to there and then another train over across this and walk six blocks, turn left, and in the middle of the block . . .

I said, 'We have to waste all this time running all over the place because you don't believe this is my signature!' He glared at me and when I didn't move, he started motioning for the next person in the line to come forward. Mohammed was already backing out towards the door. I knew I could either make a big scene or walk away. I realized there was nothing I could say to that kind of person so I just walked away.

All the way to the other bank my brother huffed and puffed that it was my fault. 'You just don't listen,' he grumbled. 'You should always watch and see what is going on. The signatures looked different.'

'Well it was a different kind of pen,' I muttered. 'I think I used my left hand in New York and this time I used my right.'

It took us a long time to get to the other bank because of all the trains and waiting each time we had to change. Mohammed was all over me the whole time but I didn't say anything. I think you have to stand up for yourself and not let people push you around for no reason, but I didn't want to start another fight and I knew my brother was not going to listen to me.

The other bank was a branch of American Express and they had no problem with the signature on my travellers cheques. The clerk took the cheques and asked me, 'How do you want the money?' That's all he asked. I questioned him about what happened at the other bank. He was surprised. 'Really! Why wouldn't they cash your travellers cheques? What was the problem?'

'I don't have any idea. Maybe he didn't like Africans.'

From there we rushed to this place where my brother said we could get a cheap ticket. Again I didn't ask why we were in such a hurry or anything. I just let him direct me around.

Mohammed took me to a Somali office where they had Somali music and maps and other things. I wanted to see what sorts of things they had but my brother's got no patience whatsoever. 'Sit over there,' he said, 'in case I need you.' I had never seen anything like it – because I had really never seen him in action. He paced back and forth, back and forth, talking to a friend of his and some other men. He never sat down – his arms were constantly waving at no big thing I could figure. He jiggled his leg even when he was standing. I couldn't watch all that agitation and went outside even though it was chilly and damp. Mohammed came out with his friend, Ali, and hurried us over to a nearby travel agent. The tickets cost about two thousand dollars each and I gave the cash to Mohammed for them. That was my job – hand over the money. We purchased plane tickets to Bosasso, an airport on the northern coast of Somalia. I asked if we could leave tomorrow and fly directly there because I only had thirteen days before I had to be back in New York. The ticket agent told me there are no direct flights to anywhere in Somalia; there is no such thing. He explained that we would have to wait until Saturday. We would take an early flight to London and we had a couple of airplane changes on the way to Bosasso.

There are only a few flights each week between Nairobi and Mogadishu and they are canceled if there is any fighting in the capital. There is no safe way to get overland from Kenya or Ethiopia into Somalia unless you are part of a refugee aid convoy and I had not been able to arrange anything like that through my contacts at the United Nations. Recently gunmen had attacked government officials on their way to a peace conference and nine people were killed. Mohammed had heard stories from refugees in Amsterdam about the dangers of traveling overland. There are *shifta* bandits all over the place and they have lots of guns and even bigger weapons. They prey on people trying to get out of the country – especially if they think they have any money. You either pay what they want or you will be killed on the spot. Mohammed's friends told us that this flight into Bosasso was the most reliable because the further north you go the less trouble you are likely to encounter. Mohammed and Ali insisted this was the best way to go and so I bought the tickets.

'How are we going to get from Bosasso to our family?' I asked my brother.

'We can hire a car at the airport and drive to Galkayo. Mama is living in a village not too far outside of Galkayo,' my brother said. 'I want to stay away from Mogadishu.'

Mohammed didn't want to go anywhere near Mogadishu. He didn't even want to fly over it. 'Those rag-tag army commanders in Mogadishu don't know the difference between a passenger plane and a military fighter,' Mohammed said. 'They shoot at anything if they are high or bored – anything except *khat* smugglers.'

'So what do they have to shoot with?'

'Waris, they have Scud missiles,' he told me like I was stupid or something. 'They are old and dangerous to begin with, and they are in the hands of desperate people with no training and crazy people telling them what to do.'

'Mohammed,' I asked. 'What happened to Mogadishu?' I thought it was the most beautiful city in the world when I was a girl. Hammawein, the original part of the city, sits on the shores of the Indian Ocean. I used to go and stand out on the sand at the edge of the sea and look back at the two and three story buildings all gleaming white in the moonlight. I had never even seen stairs until I went to Mogadishu. My uncle said it was more beautiful than Mombassa or Zanzibar. Of course, I had no reason to question him. Sultans who traded with China, Persia and India in dhows that went up and down the Indian Ocean built many of the houses. One house was called 'milk and honey'. The Sultan who built it was so rich he had milk and honey mixed into the mortar for the bricks. It was a light golden color and faced that blue, blue ocean. They said it would never ever fall down because of the mortar. My aunt told me that the top floor was a long hall with four carved wooden doors on either side and that the Sultan kept the women from his harem in those rooms and they could only be opened from the outside.

'Waris,' Mohammed sighed, 'most of the city is ruined. There are piles of rubble where the buildings were and the streets are full of burned out trucks and piles of rocks left over from barricades. Soldiers would get high on *khat* and go out and aim at a building with a grenade for fun, to see if they could hit it. They liked to watch things fall apart, those idiots.'

'Allah!'

'Everybody was so crazy from *khat* and drugs they didn't know what they were doing and they didn't want to think about it. The city would be quiet all afternoon while they chewed the *khat* then the trouble started after the sun went down. After the effects of the drugs wore off everything was quiet again.' Mohammed's eyes were flashing and I could feel deep anger and rage in this man. He looked old and drained of joy when he talked about it. Something about him was ended, finished. Maybe that was why I didn't see Dhura's belly swollen with a new life, a child of Mohammed.

When we got back to Mohammed's flat I could hear Aleeke in the back room running around with his cousins. Even though they are much older he was right in there chasing everybody around. My son is completely a warrior little boy, he is so very Somali and African. The word for a man in Somali is *warrior*. Being with my brother reminded me of what Somali men are, and I had one in my son. In the bush, when I was growing up, men were either fighters or herders. We consider the warrior to be the best, and my Aleeke is definitely a warrior.

I was afraid he would grow up to feel different and alone like I did – that he would not understand the family heritage he comes from. He is a member of a powerful and

important clan. I wanted to take my son home and to introduce him to my mother, his grandmother, so he would know
more than my mother's name. Her personality, her relationship to life and her wisdom; that's what I wished he
could know. How could he be proud of himself if he wasn't
proud about where he came from? I wanted him to know his
family in Africa but, at that time, I knew that there was no
way I was taking my precious boy that I loved more than
myself. I just hoped we would get there safe and back and
that it would be a peaceful and successful trip. The more
Mohammed talked about bullets in Mogadishu and bandits
on the border with Ethiopia the more anxious and nervous
I felt.

Enshallah, God willing, I'll bring Aleeke another time. I
want my mother to see that Aleeke is the spitting image of
Old Man, my little brother who died, in every way everything about him reminds me of my little brother. She
wouldn't believe me though; I knew she would have to see it
for herself so I wasn't going to say anything about it.

When I showed Dhura the clothes I packed we laughed
about the problems I had finding anything to wear in New
York.

'Mohammed would never let me wear that wraparound
skirt,' she said.

'I thought he didn't want to go back to Somalia to live,' I
said. 'Why don't you dress like the Dutch women?'

Dhura nodded and smiled at me. 'We'll see,' she said. I
asked her if there were places to buy Somali dresses nearby.
She said that the women made them and offered to lend me
some of her Somali clothes to wear on our trip. One *dirah*
had flowers in bright yellow, my favorite color. She handed
me a slip embroidered in blue and silver threads for underneath and a flowered silk scarf that matched to cover my

head and face. I put everything on and Dhura announced that I looked like a proper Somali woman – only my eyes showed. I walked around the room and lowered the scarf so she could see my smile. The long dress swished around my feet and I almost tripped over Aleeke who ran in to see what all the laughing was about.

As a girl I always battled with those long dresses. One night my father woke us and said we needed to move our camp to a fresh pasture. My mother and I rolled up the grass mats that covered the curved frame of our house. She pulled the frame poles out of the earth and loaded everything on one of the camels. We strapped the milk baskets and water skins on another camel. My father led the camels and the rest of us followed behind herding the goats. We walked quickly without stopping from the middle of the night until the sun started to sink behind the blue hills. Finally my father halted the caravan at a new little land. We knew we would stay there until the moon was full again. The place was grassy and my father said he knew a well that was not far away and belonged to our clan. As soon as you stop you have to make an enclosure for the animals so my father said to me, 'Waris, we must go and cut brush to make a corral for the camels and goats tonight.' In Somalia, it seemed to me that every single tree or bush had thorns so I knew I was going to be scratched all over carrying them with my hands.

My father used his long knife to hack down the trees and told me to tear the branches off.

'Carry that pile back to where your mother is putting up our house,' he said walking swiftly over to a thicket a little distance away. The wind was blowing and my dress kept catching on the thorns whenever I tried to grab the bushes. I had to be careful not to rip it when I pulled it out of the thorns because it was my only dress. As soon as he was out of sight I tucked my dress between my legs so it wouldn't catch and started carrying the pile of brush back to camp. My father called, 'Waris, wait for me,' and I knew he would not let me walk around with my dress up over my knees like that. I took a big thorn and scratched myself, and then I wiped the blood all over my face and arms and pretended that I was bleeding all over. When my father caught up with me he saw my bloody arms and face and said, 'What's the matter?'

I said, 'Oh it's all right. It's all right. I'm OK – but look Father, I'm already bleeding all over the place and you want me to carry these branches and walk back with this dress blowing out and catching on every bush and tripping me. I can't do this!'

He said, 'Well OK, keep the dress tucked up for now but don't let anybody see you like that. As soon as you are finished put it back down. Don't forget to put it back down and cover your legs, *Afdokle*.' That was my nickname, *Afdokle*, Little Mouth.

I said, 'All right, all right.' I was so pleased that I got away with tucking that dress up. I ran ahead of my father and leapt all the way back to our camp. What could he do? We both had our arms full of branches.

My brother Mohammed drove me crazy for the two days we waited for our flight. I could hear him shouting at Dhura, 'Bring me my checked shirt. Where is the case for my glasses?' He couldn't sit still for a minute. It broke my heart and made me angry at the same time. He paced all day long and kept coming in to ask if I was packed. The day before we left I was holding Aleeke in my lap and giving him a little drink of milk. Mohammed saw what I was doing but he said, 'Are you ready yet?'

313

I said, 'Hey, brother, listen *warrior*! You know what time the flight leaves? It's nine o'clock in the morning. We are going to sleep here tonight, you know. We got all night before we have to leave.'

'How are you going to get everything ready?' he asked. 'You have things all over the place.'

I said, 'I'm not packed, Mohammed, but I have most of my things ready and I'm not worried about it.'

'Don't take that,' he said pointing his finger at the duffel bag I brought from the States with all my presents. 'They don't need your garbage. We should only take certain things with us.'

I said, 'That is mine and I am bringing it.'

'Well I don't know how you are going to carry all that or get it on the planes,' he shrugged.

At five o'clock that night he had his brown suitcase all ready. We didn't leave for the airport until five o'clock in the morning but he was already packed and his stuff was sitting at the door. I went into the back room and finished arranging everything in my cases. At one-thirty in the morning I was packed. I tucked in my little Aleeke for the last time, stroked his head and sang a little song to him. 'Mama is going to Africa,' I sang, 'she won't be here when you wake up but she will be back soon.' He was sleeping so sweetly, I didn't know if I could bear to leave him. Sometimes in your life you just have to put one foot in front of the other. Before the next sun rose we would begin our journey.

I couldn't get to sleep that night and just as I drifted off Mohammed pounded on the door. I still had not adjusted to the change in times between Europe and New York and it really was the middle of the night for me.

'Get up, it's time to go,' he called.

'Hey, we got time.'

'Waris, we have to go,' he said, all upset. 'We have to get to the airport.' Mohammed was panicked about missing the flight for some reason so I got up and hurried into the car. We left my brother's house before five o'clock in the morning and drove for over an hour and a half through the sleeping city. We arrived two hours before we had to board the plane. I watched the sun come up through clouds the color of an elephant's hide and I prayed to Allah to bless us with a safe trip. We boarded our flight to London. As soon as the plane started to move down the runway Mohammed wanted to get up and go to the bathroom. He was suddenly desperate and started acting like a little child. The fasten seatbelt sign was on but he kept whining, 'I want to go to the toilet. I have to go to the bathroom.'

I said, 'Hang on for a second, Mohammed. The sign will be turned off any minute. As soon as the plane is in the air they will turn it off and you can go.'

He moaned, 'I can't wait, I can't wait!' rocking back and forth in his seat and wriggling all over the place.

Finally I told him, 'Well, if you really can't wait, then just get up and go. Go if you must go.' Mohammed started to get out of his seat but one of the flight attendants rushed over and told him to sit back down.

'No, no, mister,' she said. 'Sit down, you can't get up now.'

He sat back down but started crossing his legs and holding his stomach. I looked at him and thought Aleeke would do better. My son would just get up and tell the stewardess to get outta his way. My brother sat there moaning louder and louder. People started to look at us and I hissed at him, 'Hey, brother, you are embarrassing me, and you are acting like a child. If you have to go – just go. Pee on the bitch if you have to – but go.'

'They won't let me,' he whined.

'She has no right to do that – if somebody has to go, they just go,' I told him. 'Why are you listening to her?' She was treating him like some ignorant little man but why he waited until the last minute I do not know. Every time he got up she would look at him and he would sit back down. I couldn't understand why he let her tell him what to do.

At Heathrow airport we boarded a plane that took us all the way to Bahrain. After over seventeen hours of flying plus all the time between planes and getting to the airport I had no idea what time it was – where I was, or how long we had been traveling because of all the time changes. I was tired, annoyed and fed up with little seats, no room and terrible food. When we finally got off the plane in Bahrain I asked Mohammed how much longer it would be until I saw my mother.

'We are not even halfway there yet,' he told me. He got out the tickets and pointed to a section. 'We have to change planes again here and fly to Abu Dhabi.'

'Abu Dhabi? I didn't know we had to go to Abu Dhabi.' I had bad memories of that place. Our sister was there, but the last time I was there I had so much trouble with my papers that I couldn't go out of the airport to see her.

'Yes,' he said. 'But the flight to Abu Dhabi will only take another hour. From there we go to Somalia.'

On those endless flights my heart was filled with doubts. Who would I see? Who would be healthy? Who would still be alive in that home to battles, starvation, jagged rocks and whirlwinds? How would my mother accept that I never married the father of my son? A single mother with a child in Somalia is only one thing – a prostitute.

I wanted my father to see me, to look at his daughter right in the face. People all over the world have looked at pictures of my face. Photographers and magazines have paid a lot of money to take photographs of me – to capture my face on film. I wondered if my father even knew what I looked like. When I was a girl, all of his attention was for the boys. Girls were supposed to bring the tea and go away. I was never to speak to a man unless I was spoken to; I was barely allowed to stay nearby when the adults were talking. Now I had lived in a place where men and women talked directly to each other. I didn't believe that it was wrong or that something bad would happen to you or a *djinn* would be attracted to the trouble.

'Waris, look down when you are talking to your father,' my mother taught me as soon as I could carry a milking bowl.

'Why?' I asked, looking into her eyes.

'*Ebwaye, ebwaye!*' she repeated – shame, for shame. She said the same thing if I sat with my legs open or my skirt was up. She would never answer my questions, or give me any reasons. Why is it shameful? What does that prove or mean? That is the way things are in Somalia. When I was a girl I didn't like it; now that I had lived in the West, I hated it. I respected my culture, but I wanted to look my father in the eyes. I knew that he would never look away from me – he would expect me to look down, to demonstrate my respect for him. I was not going to do that! I was going to look right at him, stare at him, and hold his gaze with my eyes. He would see me, Waris, the daughter he sold to an old man for a few camels who now earned her own money. He would have to look at the girl he never sent to school who became a writer. The girl who was a United Nations special ambassador for women's rights.

FGM was another thing I wanted to talk about. My family's intention was not to harm me; it was something my mother and her sisters and her mother went through themselves. They honestly felt it had to be done in order for me to be pure. They believed that it was specifically ordered in the Koran. I know better now, this ritual practice is not even mentioned in the Koran, but that is not what they were told by the *Wadaddo,* the religious people. Nobody could read the Koran or the Hadith – my mother listened to the sheiks, she didn't question what she was told.

My father told me, 'Waris, you are too strong and wild. You have to get married now or no man will want you.' He thought that getting married would stop me from speaking out, from acting like a boy. The choice of a husband is not based on love. It is made by the parents to ensure support, tighten clan alliances and produce children. The price a man pays for the woman shows that he can support a wife. If he has nothing to offer and his clan will not contribute some livestock, then he has no connections and should not have the responsibility of a wife.

'She will bring many she-camels and white goats for her bride price,' my aunts always said about my older sister, Halimo.

'*Hiiyea*!' my mother would answer lifting up Halimo's dress to show off her legs when only women were present. Everyone would grab at her dress to tease her. She would whirl around and flash her sexy little ankles. 'This one will not go for less than twenty camels, I'll tell you that,' Mama bragged. She didn't pick up my dress to show off my legs. They had a funny shape and stuck out to the side. My legs weren't pretty but they were strong and I was fast. When you are taking care of camels you have to move quickly. You must take big strides or you will never get to where you have to go before it gets dark and the hyenas can see better than you. I thought my father would be proud of me because I could move as fast as any man, but I was always in trouble for talking back or tucking my skirts up. No matter what I did I was only a girl.

We always used to hide behind my mother when my father was angry. Once we moved our camp in the middle of the night, arrived in a new pasture and unpacked. My father sent me right out to watch the goats. I was so tired from walking all night long that I fell asleep in the shade of a tree. I was only a little girl and I couldn't keep my eyes open. When I woke up the sun had moved and I wasn't in the shade any more. One side of me was blistered black and the animals were gone! Gone! Terrified I looked for hoof prints but there were too many and I couldn't tell which way they went. Finally I climbed the biggest tree around and from there I could see little heads off in the distance in high grasses. When I ran to the animals, I jumped through the grass like a gazelle. Relieved to find any of them, I didn't even want to know how many were missing. I pretended like nothing had happened and went back to our camp.

My father counted every single animal in the evening before he put them in the corral and every morning before he let them out to graze. As soon as he started to count I stood behind my mother. He slowly counted those animals, *koe, laba, suddah, afra, shun,* up to fifty. The higher he counted the closer I stood to my mother. I wished I could climb inside of her. My father counted them twice but there were two animals missing, a baby sheep and a goat. He called my name, 'Waris, come over here.' I didn't move and he walked towards me. 'Did you hear me calling you?'

I said, 'Sorry, Papa. I didn't know you wanted me.'

He said, 'Come here.'

I knew if I went near him I would be crushed and there was no way I would move away from my mother. I said, 'No!' No one ever said no to my father. No one. I knew I was going to get killed anyway so I might as well take a chance – anything. I thought about running but where would I go?

My father grabbed a stick and Mama put her hands up and asked him to calm down. 'Don't beat her, she is just a baby. Let's just think about where the animals could be,' she said. In one split second, he hit my mother so hard it knocked her across the corral. She crumpled in a heap on the ground and blood ran out of her nose and mouth. I knew that if I didn't stay away from my mother he would kill me as well as her.

When my father was mad he reminded me of an angry lion. He had no mercy – nothing stopped him. Lions are like kings or queens. They sit there in silence all day and when they are hungry they kill gracefully, elegantly. They go directly for the muzzle or the throat and death is almost instant. Usually they are calm and dignified but there is one thing that they hate – being bothered, especially by hyenas. Once I watched a hyena tormenting a golden lion. He sat there quite calmly but all of a sudden, he had enough. He leapt up and in one single bound caught the pest in the middle of its back and crushed it. He shook the hyena in his mouth and threw it away.

I intended to go back and educate my father about what a woman could do – how a woman could make a good life for herself.

The minute we landed in Abu Dhabi my stomach turned into a big knot like we had come to a dry well after days of walking. I had such terrible memories of that airport and the United Arab Emirates. I hoped that nothing bad would happen this time, but Mohammed and I did not see any of our bags. We waited until the very last suitcase was picked up off the conveyer belt and I almost cried right there. I knew we had problems, and I was afraid of missing our flight to Somalia. First I thought that we had waited at the wrong place. Everything was in Arabic and I couldn't understand it.

'Mohammed,' I asked, 'are you sure that this is the right conveyer?'

'Yes,' he said, 'I saw other people from our flight.'

'Well, what could have happened to our things?'

'Let me take care of this.' Mohammed announced in Somali, 'I can deal with it.'

'Mohammed let me talk to them, I've been through this before, and I've traveled a lot.'

He insisted, 'No, no, I can do this.' He went to see a woman in a little office outside the baggage area. Waiting outside I could see that she was not in the greatest mood and he couldn't explain to her what had happened. She shook her head and pointed upstairs several times. I didn't think she had anything to do with baggage and certainly didn't know where our bags were. Mohammed got so frustrated that he started yelling at her in Somali and stormed out.

'Brother,' I told him, 'let me talk to these people, you are getting nowhere.' I went back to the office and the woman told me to go up to another floor and look for an information desk.

'We are looking for our bags,' I informed the man behind the counter when it was my turn. He didn't even look up or say anything to me, he just gestured over to another section of the airport. 'Excuse me,' I said. 'Do you speak English?' He waved again. I decided he could not help us and went to find someone else.

Another man in a little uniform said, 'Go talk to the agents at the gate,' so we walked all the way back up to the gate. The dress that Dhura lent me was too long and I kept forgetting to pick it up in the front. Every time I started to move I would trip – it was like being haltered. When we got back to the gate area the person just looked at us like we were crazy.

———

'Hey, wait a minute,' I said. 'They told us upstairs to come here for our bags. What is going on! I'd like to get some answers here.' He just shrugged and looked at Mohammed before he turned his back on us and began to walk away. I started to shout, 'Well what are we supposed to do? Just go with nothing? When are my bags going to get here?'

'I don't know when your baggage will arrive,' the clerk said to Mohammed. 'Go and sit over there.' He pointed to a row of hard wooden benches. 'Someone will let you know.'

Flights came and went. People walked by greeting relatives and picking up babies. Almost every woman was totally covered in a black chador, the men were free to wear whatever they liked. Some had pants and shirts, others wore traditional Muslim robes. The sun set and I saw it grow dark outside. 'Mohammed,' I said, 'check the tickets and see what time our flight is to Somalia. I don't want to miss that.' Mohammed got out the tickets but had trouble figuring out the times. 'Let me have the tickets, I'm going to ask someone so we don't miss that flight.' I pulled my scarf up over my head and covered my face. It was silk and would not stay on my head, it slipped off no matter how I tried to tie it. I took our tickets back up to the airline counter. 'We have been waiting all day for our bags and I need to know what time our flight to Somalia leaves. I really need some kind of information so we don't miss our connection.'

'There are no more flights to Somalia today,' he announced, still sorting through papers on the counter.

'Excuse me,' I said, letting my scarf fall down around my shoulders. I didn't care if he thought I was not Muslim. 'Did we miss our flight? Nobody told us, nobody will help us. What is going on?'

'There are no flights to Somalia today,' he said, still looking down.

I tapped the counter to get him to look at me. 'That can't be, there must be a mistake.'

'Let me see your tickets,' he sighed as if I was too much trouble. I handed him our tickets. He started flipping the pages and then pointed to the numbers in the little boxes. 'See here,' he sneered, 'you people left on September twenty-ninth and you don't get to Somalia until October second.'

'What?' I stammered

'Today', he said clicking the words slowly on the top of his mouth, 'is September thirtieth. Your flight is October second, and that is two days from today.' He made me feel stupid and small the way he kept pointing to the numbers on the ticket. He pushed them back to me over the counter as though I was unclean or something.

'Mohammed,' I cried, 'do you realize that we have to wait in this stinking airport for two days! I didn't know that!' He looked confused and anxious. 'These people are treating me like a fucking yo-yo,' I said. 'They won't even talk to me because I am a woman. Well excuse me, but I am a Muslim myself.' Mohammed looked over at me from the wooden benches with his hands between his legs.

I started to breathe deeply and when I finally calmed down I remembered our sister, Fartun. She works for a Saudi family as a maid and lives not too far from the airport. 'Let's get a cab and go to Fartun,' I told Mohammed. 'At least we can see our sister and have a shower and a bed while we wait for the flight.' We gathered up our things and I went to the bathroom and washed my face. I tucked my scarf around my head in yet another attempt to keep it there. Having my head and face covered all the time was miserable. What had I done to deserve that kind of punishment?

When we got to the passport control exit Mohammed walked right through. He has travel documents from

Holland and he didn't need a visa. However, a customs clerk with a nose like a hawk took my passport and started to go through every single page.

'You do not have a visa to enter the United Arab Emirates,' he said very slowly like he was talking to a child. I couldn't believe it. My mouth went dry, I felt like I couldn't get a breath. I had been through this.

'Please, please help me,' I pleaded. 'I am on my way to Somalia with my brother and I have not seen my family for a long time. Our flight does not leave for two days and I just want to go and stay with my sister until the flight.'

That man tapped on the passport with fat fingers. 'You don't have a visa to enter the country,' he said.

'I'm just trying to go home to my mother in Somalia. Can't you see that I am Somali?' His face was turned toward me but he looked at the wall. He would not look in my eyes. 'Please sir,' I begged. ' I just want to see my sister for two days.'

'You do not have the proper documents to enter the country,' he repeated. 'You can't leave this airport.' He practically threw my passport back at me. He turned and motioned for the next person.

I will never understand this need for documents and papers. Why do they have all this power over people; why do they dictate what people can do? Nobody has papers in Somalia. We don't need to show a passport when we are looking for grass for the goats to eat. If you want to see someone you go, you don't have papers to keep some people in and others out. You do what you feel, what you need to do. You are a person, not numbers and letters written on a piece of paper. It doesn't matter to a nomad where he is from, what matters is where he is. Once I asked my mother about the year that I was born – but she didn't remember.

'I have a feeling,' she said, 'I think it was rainy, but was it?'
I said, 'Mama, do you remember or not?'

'Please child,' she said, 'I don't remember. What could be so important about that?'

I have a feeling that I was born in the rainy season. You know why? I'm very much attached to water and especially to rain. I love it very much and so I have a feeling that it was rainy but I don't know what year I was born or how old I am. I do not know.

Nearly twenty years ago when I was about fourteen years old, my uncle decided to take me to London as a house-girl. He said, 'If I'm going to take you to London you'll need a passport, right?'

I said, 'Yes I do,' but I really had no idea what this passport thing was.

He brought me someplace where we took a picture and the next morning he had the passport. I didn't look at the writing, I only looked at my picture. It was the first time I ever saw myself. I was looking up at the sky in the photograph, I wasn't looking at the camera. I didn't know where to look so when the photographer said, 'Open your eyes,' I just looked up. (Actually I was praying to God because I didn't know what was going on.) I didn't realize what a passport was until years later when I was in London. My uncle just put a birth date on the passport that he made up. I still don't know what it was.

I left my brother in the middle of the crowd. I just had to move, to do something, to go somewhere. I went upstairs and found out there was a hotel in the airport.

'Do you have any rooms available right now?' I asked the agent.

'Yes, we do have a vacancy,' he said, 'but you have to pay

in cash.' He acted like I couldn't have enough money for a room.

'I want a room,' I insisted.

'They are $150 for the night . . . in American dollars,' he added like it was a dare or something.

God, I thought, I'm glad I have money. I checked in to the hotel and I didn't care how much it cost because I was so tired. It was a crummy little room, with cheap thin towels and a dirty brown cover on the single bed. I threw myself down and started to cry. I was worried about my little boy. I left him with some sort of infection to go on this crazy trip to nowhere. He had freaking bald spots all over his sweet head. I didn't know what it was and I wondered if God had been trying to tell me something. Perhaps God was punishing me. I felt helpless and trapped.

The airport in Abu Dhabi brought back a miserable memory and here I was again. I'd been sent back from this same airport; from the same place. I decided that it must be a curse or something. I don't know. I'd been trying to see my mother that time too. Mama had been caught in cross-fire between rival clans. She was out getting firewood, not bothering anybody, and soldiers started shooting at each other. She tried to get out of the way but she took two bullets in her chest. I sent money to Fartun and they brought her to Abu Dhabi for medical treatment. Of course I hopped on the first plane I could to meet her there. People in New York assured me that I didn't need a visa. When I arrived, after an 18-hour flight, they would not let me leave the airport. An ugly fat man said I didn't have a visa and could not enter the country. My mother and sister were right outside in the lobby but I couldn't get to them. I was so determined that I flew all the way back to New York and went to the United Arab Emirates Embassy and got the visa.

I spent another $2704 to buy a ticket back to Abu Dhabi. When I got back, the same heartless, ugly, short, fat man was there. He had two front teeth missing and I would have kicked the rest of his teeth out myself if I could. He took my passport with the visa stamp and left me standing there in the customs area. I waited and waited for the entire day. I was afraid to get something to eat or go to the bathroom in case he came back and didn't find me. Finally I heard my name called and when I came forward he sneered at me and said I was not allowed to enter the country.

'Please,' I begged him. 'I went back to New York to get the visa you said I needed. What is the problem? Please tell me. My mother was shot. She is waiting for me. Please let me see her.'

He looked at me and snarled, 'I told you. You will not be allowed to enter the country.' He handed me my passport and said, 'Where do you want to go? You are to leave on the next plane.'

'I am not leaving until you explain what the problem is.'

He said, 'There is a flight to London boarding at this time and I am going to put you on that plane.'

I told him that I didn't live in London. 'Why send me there?' I asked him. 'I live in New York.' I cried and pleaded with him but he wouldn't listen to anything I said.

'Do you see those women over there?' he snarled. They were very mean looking and wore police uniforms. 'Either you get on the next plane out of here or they will hurt you, I will tell you that. They will put you on the plane and they will hurt you.' Those women walked me through the gate to the plane and I could hear everyone laughing at me as I passed by. I will never forget it.

Here I was trapped in the same airport, paying over three hundred dollars for two nights in a crappy hotel room and being treated like I wasn't a human being. It got into my throat; my skin; my blood. I couldn't think of words in any language to describe it.

Islam means submission and a Muslim is one who has submitted to God. I got on my knees and said to Allah, 'Please help me.' I wondered if there would be something joyful and good after all of this aggravation. '*Enshallah, Enshallah.* Allah will work it all out,' I repeated over and over. There is a reason for everything; I truly believe that, deep in my heart, and I hoped to God it was a good one.

6

the night ride

Prayer against Evils
Evils lurking behind us, be ye halted there.
Evils waiting before us, be ye forced to flee.
Evils hovering above us, be ye suspended still.
Evils rising beneath us, be ye blunted of spear.
Evils treading beside us, be ye thrust afar.

Somali Gebei

Songs about Africa drummed in my head when our flight
landed in my desert home after more than twenty years.
'Hello, Africa! How are you doing? I'm feeling good and I
hope you are too,' I sang with a big smile as I stepped out of
the plane and was greeted by the sky. I was home! I danced
down the metal stairs onto the runway. My heart was pounding at the look of the land and especially the desert sky. The
Somali sky is the home of the sun and the moon; it goes on
forever, all the way into tomorrow. The sky is so big it makes
you feel big too, not small. I stretched my arms out as far as
they would go just to feel the space, to touch the freedom.

The sun is so bright and powerful that everything stands out – and everything looks close. I could see the Indian Ocean and it seemed like I could walk right over and jump right in. It had been such a long, long time since I had heard the sweet sound the wind makes over the open desert – I almost forgot about it. I knew the acacia trees, the beetles and the termite mounds, the tiny *dikdik*, the ostrich and the raspy sound turtles make. As we walked off the runway I looked at the people, I understood their faces – what they were thinking – what they were doing. After all those years of being a stranger trying to figure out what was going on and desperately trying to fit in, it felt wonderful. I could smell something and I knew immediately it was *angella*; it's what we have for breakfast. It is the opposite of sugary cocoa puffs, it's a sour pancake that fills you up for the whole day. Tears filled my eyes, but it wasn't sadness – it was joy. Mama Somalia, I thought, I've missed you so. How could I stay away for so long – you are so special to me. What kept me away so long? Everyone at the airport looked right to me, they looked normal and I felt a wonderful sense that I belonged. This is where my dreams come from. I am a daughter of Africa and I wanted to see my mother right away – then I would know that I was really home.

The sun was almost directly overhead in a clear blue sky and it was hot, very hot, unbelievably hot. After living in London and New York the intense heat caught me by surprise. Waves of warmth rose off the ground and it was hard to catch my breath. The Indian Ocean shimmered in the distance and I was glad there was a gentle breeze off the water because I had to get used to the torrid temperature. You have to relax in heat, you can't run around tense and excited.

There were no public buses or trains from that tiny airport. Men with vehicles for hire waited outside the whitewashed brick terminal along the road. Women own many of the cars. They worked as prostitutes in Saudi Arabia rather than starving to death or begging in the refugee camps. They bought cars with the money they saved and shipped them back to Somalia. They hired drivers and ran taxi services. Women in Somalia don't drive but if you own a car you are considered really wealthy.

Mohammed said, 'I'll handle this,' and walked up and down the row of cars and studied everybody. He saw a tribal relative he had known in Mogadishu and announced, 'There is somebody we can hire. Abdillahi is Majeerteen.' Majeerteen is our father's clan.

'Brother, let's make sure we get someone with a good car that won't break down somewhere,' I pleaded.

My brother had already decided. 'You can trust people from your own clan,' he informed me. 'Let's see if he will take us to Galkayo.'

Abdillahi had an old, beat-up station wagon. It was dented in the front and looked like the hood was wired to keep it shut. The tires were worn smooth as a baby's face and the seats inside were worn out and ripped. Mohammed greeted Abdillahi and the two men gave each other the double Muslim handshake and stood arm in arm talking. Abdillahi was tall with a thin face that ended in a little goatee. He wore a white shirt over the traditional *maa-a-weiss*. That's a length of patterned cloth that men wrap around their waist and tuck into a pleat at the front. It comes to about mid-calf length and most of the men at the airport were wearing them. Mohammed and Abdillahi went into the building to pay the airport tax and retrieve our papers. The stewardess had collected them when we got on the plane. My papers are British travel documents and they state that I am not allowed to travel in Somalia. I was frightened that they would send me back or detain me but Mohammed insisted that he could take care of it. The sun beat down until I had sweat dripping down the back of my neck all the way to my waist. It felt like it was over 200 degrees. What is taking these guys so long I worried. I was tempted to rip the silk scarf off that stuck to my head and neck and I couldn't wait to get into a car and get going.

Finally they came out and I could see that Abdillahi was upset. 'Your brother started a fight with the police!' he told me.

'They had no right to keep our papers. They have to give them back after I paid the airport fees!' Mohammed insisted.

'What happened in there?' I asked Abdillahi who seemed more rational than Mohammed.

'Your brother got upset with the clerk and started shouting. He almost knocked a policeman over when he pushed him out of the way,' Abdillahi said. Mohammed was still agitated and pacing back and forth. Abdillahi turned to him with his palms in the air, 'Calm down, you have to calm down.'

'They can't talk to me like that,' Mohammed continued. 'I paid a special fee and he has no right.'

Abdillahi waved his hand in front of Mohammed's face. 'This is not Europe, my friend. Those guys have guns and they use them. They don't care who you are or what the problem is – you have to stay away from trouble – don't argue with anybody who has a gun. It won't make any difference who was right if they shoot you.'

Abdillahi had grabbed my brother and dragged him back to keep him from hitting anybody. The police had returned my documents but I was frightened and afraid they might change their minds.

'Abdillahi, do you think you can find my mother?' I interrupted their argument about police tactics and soldiers on drugs and *khat*, eager to get out of the airport and find my family.

'Well, your family lives near the border with Ethiopia,' Abdillahi said. 'I just came from that region and I drove all night to get here for the plane. Believe me, I can find them.'

Still worried I inquired, 'Do you have a map?'

Abdillahi looked at me funny and said, 'I am Somali.'

'He can find them,' Mohammed laughed. 'He doesn't need a map on paper, it's in his head.'

'How long will it take to get there?' I asked, suddenly excited. I wanted to hold my mother, to touch her face.

'It will take eight or nine hours to get there depending on the condition of the roads and any military checkpoints,' Abdillahi said, stroking his little beard as he talked.

'What do you mean eight hours!' I screamed. I couldn't believe it. Three days of my precious time had already been wasted in airplanes and a nasty hotel room. Now I had yet another whole day of travel and the sun was already halfway across the sky. I was hysterical and paced back and forth, tripping on my dress. I ripped off the headscarf because it was choking me around the neck. It was so hot I couldn't breathe and I needed to move around, to get this trip over with. Eight hours in a car would actually mean two more days I would not see my family because we would have to allow a day to come all the way back to Bosasso to get the return flight. Mohammed and Abdillahi stood there looking at me like I was crazy or something. Time didn't seem to matter to either one of them. They lived on some other planet, not the one I lived on – the one with deadlines and appointments. I had no choice though, I had to just calm down and do what had to be done.

***

'How much will you charge to take us?' Mohammed asked. Abdillahi wanted three hundred American dollars for the trip. Mohammed offered him one hundred and Abdillahi refused.

'Mohammed, let's just do it and get out of here,' I whispered. 'Let's not waste time with this.' My brother glared at me like I should stay out of his business and I stepped back to wait in the burning sun while they bargained.

'Three hundred is not right,' Mohammed said. 'We are Majeerteen, you and I. My sister and I are not foreigners.'

'I am poor and I need money for my children.'

'Listen Abdillahi, one hundred American dollars is a lot of money, I know it, and you know it. It's more than the going price for this trip. Besides that,' Mohammed joked, 'you already know that I am crazy!'

'That's for sure!' Abdillahi teased. 'I guess I better get you and your sister out of here before you get in any more trouble. I'd have to contribute something to the blood price if you hurt someone.'

'Good, one hundred dollars,' Mohammed said and they shook hands on the deal. I gave Abdillahi the money to take us across the middle of Somalia to the tiny village where my mother was last seen. He looked intelligent enough and he seemed to know what he was doing but I wouldn't call him a considerate person; he treated me like men treat women in Somalia. It didn't matter that I paid for the trip. Both he and Mohammed left me to drag my duffel bag and all of our other things over to the car while they went to see some other relatives. I watched them hugging and holding hands as they greeted men they knew.

As soon as we landed in Somalia and Mohammed started speaking Somali he became an entirely different person. He stood straight and tall, his chin was up in the air and he was aggressive and cocky. It reminded me of the way he acted when I was a kid and he came to visit us. He showed up at our camp one day and started drawing things in the dirt.

'Hey you,' this strange boy called to me, 'are you ready to learn your abc's?' He acted like he was in charge and knew everything. I was curious and went over to see what he was doing. 'Sit down,' he ordered but I was afraid of the stick in his hand and so I stood to make sure I could get away if he started to hit me. He was making letters in the dirt but I didn't know that. I hadn't even heard of reading or writing. Mohammed was making *a b c d e f* very quickly with a big stick. 'What's this?' he demanded. Of course I didn't know what it was. 'So what is this letter?' he yelled at me, flicking his switch in my eyes. I didn't know what he was doing so I just stood there and stared at this crazy boy making lines in the dirt. He started to scream at me, 'You are a stupid nomad girl. What are you looking at me for? Look at the letters. Say them.' I started to laugh because he was shouting so much and I ran away when he tried to hit me with the stick. 'You bush people are too lazy and dumb to learn to read and write,' he called after me. 'Forget it, I'm not teaching you. I'm not going to waste my time with girls.' He threw a rock and it hit me on the ankle. After that I had a big sore and my mother told me to keep away from him. I was sure I didn't want any more to do with reading or writing.

Now he was strutting and acting like he knew everything and I was still an ignorant nomad girl. It was hot in the car but when I opened the windows too many flies got in so I stood there in the burning sun. Mohammed came back and ordered me to get in the car like I was the one who kept everyone waiting. He got in the front seat, I got in the back. 'You owe me for this,' he turned and said to me as soon as we were on our way.

I didn't say anything, I looked out the window at the country I longed to see. That is the way men are in Somalia. They don't listen to women and it doesn't matter who or what the woman is. You adapt to life in Africa, you don't change it.

There was a sort of petrol station on the gravel road that led away from the landing strip. Abdillahi filled up the tank and two large ten-gallon containers of emergency petrol and placed them in the back of the ratty old car. I was nervous about going so far with no map and no protection. I hoped we wouldn't have trouble with roadblocks or soldiers somewhere on the way. 'Allah, grant us a safe trip,' I prayed. 'Please help me to find my mother.' It was the *hagaa* or dry season and everything was brown and parched. Dust billowed behind the car and crawled in the windows and settled on every surface, fold and indentation. The road started out bravely, it was even paved for a little while, but it turned into dirt tracks. Tire ruts wandered off in other directions. I hoped that Abdillahi knew which tracks to follow and that he could keep the car moving over deep sand drifts and boulders fallen or thrown into the path.

We hadn't gone very far when Abdillahi turned off the road near several small huts. 'I have to get some *khat*,' he said, 'I drove all night to get here and it will keep me awake.' People were sitting in the shade but ran towards us with *khat* branches in their arms. Green leaves on twigs, demon twigs, I call them. Devil leaves. I hate the stuff and believe it is ruining my country. Now here it was the first thing I saw when I got back. *Khat* doesn't grow in Somalia so all the money men spend to buy it goes to Ethiopia or Kenya. Abdillahi drove slowly past everyone and looked at the small bundles of twigs and leaves they showed him. He didn't like any of it and drove on. Ragged little boys without shoes puffed on cigarettes. They weren't more than six or seven years old and they were smoking the damn things. With arms and legs as thin as toothpicks, they looked like spider children. When they are hungry they chew the *khat* so they won't feel it. Abdillahi stopped again a little way up the road where the same thing happened. Little boys and old women ran towards the car with bunches of *khat*. He waved to a woman with branches wrapped in her *chalmut*. 'Come over here Mama, come here,' he called out the window. 'How old is this?' he asked her. 'Is this new? Is it fresh? Is it today?' *Khat* loses its potency after a day. There are many airplanes that fly *khat* into Somalia and smugglers never have problems getting a flight with fresh *khat*.

'Well,' she said, 'we had a bad drought but, yes, this just came from Ethiopia last night.' He ran his fingers through the leaves, examining and studying them to determine how old they were.

'Hey, Abdillahi,' I said. 'Just grab a tree, man. Let's go!'

'This is pretty good stuff,' he said. 'Why don't you give her twenty shillings for it.'

'No,' I said. 'I'm not paying for your *khat*.'

'It helps me drive, and we have a long way to go. You know, I've been up all night driving to meet the plane this week. *Khat* will keep me awake.'

'I already gave you a hundred American dollars. What do you need that stuff for?'

He said, 'You are not going to get there for another two days unless I drive you. I know the roads. I know where to find your family. If we have any trouble with police or soldiers I will give them some *khat*. That's all they want, drugs.'

I told him, 'I am not paying for that shit. You buy it yourself.'

Abdillahi backed down and purchased his bunch right

there to start the journey. He put it on the seat next to him, near the steering wheel and gave it a little pat when he put it down. He tore off leaves one at a time and shoved them into his mouth. He chewed them into a paste then carefully tucked it deep into the side of his mouth so he could chew more leaves. I knew that in a few hours his cheek would be bulging and green juice would drip down his chin. He would be high and full of energy. He had a little tape recorder and turned the sound up as loud as it would go. All afternoon Abdillahi sang along with the Somali songs, the *gebai*.

> *He who has lain between her breasts*
> *Can call his life fulfilled*
> *Oh God, may I never be denied*
> *The well of happiness.*

Abdullah's voice was high-pitched and shrill. He could only sing out of the corner of his mouth in order to hold the wad of *khat* in his cheek. On and on he sang:

> *When fate decrees that evil days*
> *A tribe shall meet,*
> *Even the clouds must flee the path*
> *The cursed ones take.*
> *Faltering the elders grow, and weak,*
> *And counsel fails.*
> *As a vessel is overturned to shield*
> *Sweet ripe dates,*
> *So from the tribe's eyes God conceals*
> *Wisdom and light.*

Suddenly the music stopped. A bad pothole had blown out the front tire. Abdillahi pulled the car over to the side of the road. There was no traffic at that point other than an occasional truck so there was no one to help us. While shoving *khat* leaves into his mouth Abdillahi found a jack and changed the tire as if he did this every day – all day. It was incredibly hot in the car and I got out to watch. There was no shade and nothing to do but watch him jack up the car, push leaves in his mouth, take off the flat and put his spare tire on and more leaves in his mouth. If we blew the spare we would have to sit there until someone came by to help us – or rob us – or worse. Abdillahi tried to avoid the big ruts in the road but it was the middle of the day, the hottest time and heat was rising off the desert like steam. He thought that the heat as much as the pothole had blown the tire. As soon as we came to a village he stopped and bought another tire. They would patch the one that blew and sell it to the next people who needed a tire. Allah what a waste of time! We changed at least four tires on that endless trip. We drove for over fourteen hours and had to stop constantly. Abdillahi probably spent most of the hundred dollars I gave him on tires that day.

Distance in the desert is nothing. You can see so far that it feels like it takes forever to pass anything. Except for the plume of dust following the car, it doesn't seem like you are moving. The road was rough and I was thrown back and forth all over the seat every time the car hit another rough spot. I felt that road, I was a part of every up and down in that landscape. We traveled in three dimensions – forward, up and down. We traveled through space as big as your mind, nothing was hidden or secret.

All day my heart was heavy because of things we saw along the way. Children, no taller than a camel's belly, stood by the side of the road wearing rags and looking hopeless and lost. Where were their parents? I saw men whose teeth were black from chewing *khat*. Once when we stopped to change a tire a silent old man stood and watched us from the top of a little hill. He never moved, he never swatted the flies that walked on his eyes. I looked for the lines of camels, beautiful golden brown camels, the ships of the desert. But we only passed ragged people without animals. The worst thing I saw was a thin woman with a child on her back out in the middle of nowhere. She waved at us for a ride. It was getting dark and we had not passed a village for hours. She only had the front half of a shoe. The heel had broken off and her feet were torn and bleeding. They looked like a camel's feet, with deep crusts and thick skin, not like they belonged to a human person. I couldn't stand it and I pleaded, 'Please stop. Stop for the sister. Stop for the mama!'

'What's the matter?' Mohammed asked.

'The entire back of her sandal is gone!' I said. 'Her feet are bleeding from walking barefoot.' Once I had feet like that – so hard and deeply cracked they looked like a mud hole in a drought. She obviously had a long, long way to go and soon it would be dark. The hyenas would be after that child for sure. Sometimes you have to sleep in the desert at night because it's too far to get where you have to get. It reminded me of running away from my father when I was all alone in the desert with the dust and flies for company. When I ran away from my family I had to spend many nights alone in the dark with no food and nothing to protect me. I was scared to death of falling asleep because I knew that hungry things were waiting for the night. A lion waited for me and I woke up to the smell of his breath in my face. 'Please stop,' I pleaded. 'She can sit back here with me. There is plenty of room here.'

Abdillahi just passed her by, saying, 'Don't worry.' He flicked his wrist and passed her like she was nothing. Both men kept saying, 'She's a woman. What do you need to pick her up for? She's used to walking.' I was almost in tears but they would not listen to me. All day long we passed women and little children, leaving them to choke on our dust.

Mohammed had heard through tribal relatives that my father might now be alone in the desert. Three rainy seasons ago our younger brother Rashid was herding my father's camels near our tribal wells in the Haud. He was just minding his own business and he sat down in the grass to rest with the animals grazing all around him. Suddenly he heard a noise and he stood up. The next thing he knew bullets were flying everywhere. He started to run and several men chased him and shot at him wildly. Rashid was hit by a bullet in the arm and collapsed into the grass and passed out. When he came to, all the animals, my father's entire herd, were gone. The desert was silent except for the empty wind. My father's life's work, the animals he raised from a single pair into a major herd and kept alive in times of drought and little food, his fortune, his property and his pride, had completely vanished. Rashid dragged himself back to our camp and my mother took care of him. Fortunately the bullet went right through the bottom of his upper arm, right through, and didn't even hit the bone, so he was all right, but my father was crushed. My father disappeared after that happened. We have a saying that a desperate man will look in a milk basket to find his camels. His lifeblood was gone and the spirit went out of him. He sat with his head in his hands for days then wandered off in the night, nobody knew where. They didn't know if he went to search for his livestock and to kill the men who stole them or was in such despair that he had given up and was just looking for some place to die.

7

mama

We traveled on and on towards blue hills on the horizon but
it felt like we would never get there. The sky stretched out in
an enormous circle above us; there was no end to it and no
end to the heat either. Abdillahi said it was hot enough to
kill people if they didn't get out of the sun. Every bush and
hill reminded me of my childhood, and especially of my
mother. I was one of those children who was obsessed by her
mother. I prayed every day that nothing would happen to
her and I followed her everywhere, even if she didn't know
that I was following her. Mama was my world and I don't
know how I ever got the courage to leave her. I guess I never
really thought I would and now one path had led to another
and another and I had lost her. In Somali we have a word,

nurro, it means instinct. Animals, and those who escape death, have the gift of *nurro* from Allah. It is how the termites build a home out of their own saliva, it's how a lizard knows to break out of its egg and find something to eat. I wanted to believe in my *nurro*, but I worried that I had been away too long. I didn't know how to read the signs any more. Maybe after this whole long journey we would not be able to find my mother at the end. It was all I could do to keep from crying with fear and frustration. Perhaps she was lost forever.

Night came as dark as a snake. I was discouraged and exhausted from the heat and from bumping and breaking down continually across those dirt tracks. Abdillahi worried me. What if he couldn't find the village and we were just lost, hopelessly lost. Without any warning he left the road and drove over a little hill. He turned off the engine and silence surrounded us like sleep. I could see a little encampment but there were no lights in any of the huts. Then Abdillahi announced, 'We're here. This is it.' Suddenly I was excited and full of energy. I jumped up in the back seat.

'Really! Are you sure? Is this where my mother lives?'

'Yes, Waris,' Abdillahi said, 'this is the place.'

'Thank you Allah!' I said. We had actually made it across the width of the country. Nobody had bothered us, only the heat and the tires had caused trouble. I got out immediately and leaned back on the car and smelled the air. Allah, how I love that smell. What is it? It's home.

Abdillahi pointed to a square house at the edge of the silent village and said, 'Your family is there.' He and Mohammed walked over and started knocking on the door. After a few minutes it opened and a tall man holding his *maa-a-weiss* around him answered. Mohammed said it was a cousin, Abdullah. He knew exactly where everyone lived.

He walked with us down a little street to another tiny square house. He knocked on the wooden window shutters and a pregnant woman answered. She stood in the doorway and stared at us with sleep in her eyes while Abdullah explained who we were.

'Who are you?' I asked.

'I'm your brother Burhaan's wife, but he isn't here,' she said. 'My name is Nhur.' When Mohammed explained that I was here to find my mother she quickly grabbed her scarf and took my hand in the darkness. She led us across a little path. The only sounds were our footsteps on the packed dirt.

Ahead of us, I could just make out the shape of a tiny hut. It was a one room shack made of upright sticks held together with twine and covered with bits of tin for a roof. We stopped in front and I took a deep breath.

'Wait a minute,' I asked my brother and Nhur. 'Don't say anything until I give her a hug and a kiss.'

Of course there were no locks. The door was just a thin sheet of tin fastened on to the side with pieces of wire for hinges in the top and bottom corners. The battered door leaned against the house and I had to pull it up and drag it across the ground to open it. My mother's house was so small that her feet were right next to the door and I bumped them when I opened it. My mother sat up and asked the shadows, 'Who's that?' I couldn't see anything but I crawled over the floor towards the sound of her voice. You had to bend way over to get into the hut, but Mohammed is so tall he bumped his head even though he ducked. That made another noise and my mother called again, 'Who is it?' I didn't want to say anything, I knelt there in the silence because I wanted to feel the moment. She called out, 'Who's that? Who is that?' Finally I found her head and I held her face in my hands and kissed it and then put my cheek next to hers so she could feel my tears running down my cheeks. She listened to my breathing for a moment, drew my face right next to her and whispered again, 'Who's this?'

'It's me, Mama. Waris.'

I could tell she recognized my voice, she kind of stopped breathing for a moment. Then she grabbed me and held me next to her like a baby snatched at the last second from falling into the fire. 'Waris? Is this really my daughter Waris?' she said and started to laugh and cry at the same time.

'Yes, Mama,' I said. 'It's really me, and Mohammed, he's here too.'

She reached up for him and held his hands and I felt her joyful tears on my arm. 'Where did you come from? I thought you were dead. Allah! Allah! My daughter, my son!' All of a sudden she snapped back and started rocking me back and forth and pretended to scold me, 'Allah – Allah! Waris, do you want to kill me! What are you doing creeping up on me like that!' Then she started laughing and crying again. 'You go right back where you came from,' she said. 'I'm too old for this.' Then she hugged me again and said, 'What are you doing here, child!'

I burst out laughing. She hadn't seen me for about five years, not since my short visit to Ethiopia, and now when I suddenly showed up in the middle of the night she could make a little joke. I thought, I hope that I have a little bit of my mother in me.

'Mohammed,' my mother said hugging him. 'I should have known it was Mohammed *Dehrie* when I heard you bump your head.' *Dehr* is my brother's nickname, it means the tall one because he stands as tall as a standing camel's head.

My mother was sleeping with a child but he never woke up with all our talk. 'Who is the little boy?' I asked.

'That is your brother Burhaan's oldest child, Mohammed *Inyer*, Little Mohammed,' Mother said stroking his sleepy head.

Abdillahi said he would take my brother Mohammed to sleep with my Uncle Ahmed and his family because there wasn't enough room for everyone to sleep in the tiny hut. Little Mohammed slept on after they left and my mother lit the little lantern we call a *feynuss*. It gives a soft light and I could see her dear face, her perfect nose and her eyes the color of cinnamon. She pulled me close as if I might be a dream and she had to keep touching me or she might wake up.

Nhur joined us and sat with us as we talked for a little while. Nhur said she had heard a car then voices of people she didn't know outside her house. That is what woke her. She hugged me and stroked my arm and dress. I told them all about our journey and how long we had been traveling. My mother rocked back and forth and hugged me and laughed in amazement as if we'd come on a magic carpet.

'Nhur,' I said, 'I am sorry for asking who you were. First of all, I didn't know you existed. I didn't know you were around! I didn't even know my brother was married the first time. I certainly didn't know that you are his second wife and already have a daughter and another on the way.' I felt embarrassed but – it's the way life is in Somalia.

Nhur patted my arm and said reassuringly, 'Really! I'm married to your brother for a long time now – and you didn't even know I existed.'

'I'm sorry,' I said. 'My hopeless brother Mohammed doesn't tell me anything.'

Nhur laughed again and teased, 'That means you didn't bring me any presents.'

I said, 'Yes, that's right and I am sorry.' I didn't have

anything for her, no baby presents nor anything for her little girl. I pointed to my bag and said, 'I'm sorry I didn't bring you anything but whatever you can find in this bag is yours.'

'What happened to Burhaan's first wife?' I asked.

There was a long silence and my mother said, 'She is with Allah in the garden of paradise.'

'I'm sorry, I'm so sorry,' I said. 'How did she die?'

'How do I know?' Mama announced firmly. 'It was her time and Allah took her.' Whenever you ask a Somali how someone died or passed away they say, 'Do you think I'm a God? God knows that, I don't know what happened.' That is all there is to it, when it's time to go, it is time to go. The Somalis believe there is a tree on the moon, the tree of life. When your leaf falls from the tree that is the moment that you will die. When you're dead, you go to heaven and good-bye. Death is between you and Allah. I knew that nobody was going to tell me what happened to that child's mother. My mother had taken in her grandson without a single thought; she saw somebody who needed her and she took him. He was about three years old and I could see that she was totally in love with that little boy. She was cuddled right up with him on the bed. He slept peacefully, soothed by the sound of her voice.

Mama looked like Mama – the person I knew all my life. She has skin like oiled ebony and when she smiles she is missing one of her front teeth. I think she lost it when my father beat her once, but she would never say. She has been through a lot and her skin is etched with lines of both wisdom and hardship. She didn't look old to me, the wrinkles around her forehead give her a great dignity. It tells you that hardship is not the same as worries.

Suddenly I heard drumming and pounding on the tin

roof. I jumped and said, 'What is that?' For a second I didn't know what it could be. It was so hard and so loud, and it didn't start slowly, it came all at once.

My mother and sister-in-law both laughed and said at the same time, 'Oh it's rain, Waris. Rain at last.'

Mama looked up and said, 'Thank you, Allah.'

Out of nowhere, it poured. In Somalia, rain is not the annoying little drizzle of the West, it's like a slap in the face. The rain really hits you on the head. It was drumming on the tin roof like dishes thrown on the floor.

'Oh Mama, it's going to cool down, because of the rain. It's really some beautiful rain.'

My mother looked at me in the lamplight. 'Child it hasn't rained for more than a year,' she said.

'Oh Mama,' I said, 'Mama, I brought the rain, I brought it.'

She clicked her tongue on the top of her mouth in disapproval, 'Waris, you are not God, so take that back. Don't you even say that – don't compare yourself to God. The rain came because Allah sent it – it doesn't have anything to do with you.'

I said, 'I'm sorry, I'll stop.' It was good to be reminded of the order of things in my mother's home. I was grateful to have that rain, I felt blessed by Allah himself.

My mother smiled and said, 'I knew you were coming.'

I was surprised at how certain she was. 'How did you know that?' I asked.

'I had a dream a couple of days ago about your sister. She was getting water and bringing it to me strapped on her back. She was singing the watering song and her voice got louder and louder. I knew one of my daughters was coming, but I didn't know which one it was.'

I sighed, 'Oh Mama.' My eyes filled up with tears because we are still so connected after all these years and all these troubles. What I missed more than anything else is the natural power and spirit that I used to know. I knew that I had to come back more often, I had to keep in touch with the powerful spirit in my mother's house. God willing, I would never stay away so long again. Now I knew the routes and how to get around.

My mother. I don't really know her – I was just a kid when I left, but I feel her, you know, like when you know something but you can't really put it into words. The last time I saw her in Ethiopia I begged her, 'Mama, come back with me to New York. I'm going to give you everything.'

She looked at me and asked, 'What do you mean, child? What is everything? I have everything that I need right here.' I felt, deep in my bones, that desert life was not right for me, so I ran off. Now I wanted to understand her life, to find her spiritual treasures and I never wanted to be without them again.

'Mama,' I said, 'do you know where my father is? Mohammed said he wandered off after his camels were stolen. And how is Rashid?'

'Oh, you heard about that trouble. Rashid is fine. The bullet went right through his arm, not like the ones that got stuck in my chest. Your father was determined to get his camels back but most of them were all gone. Probably shipped to Saudi Arabia or the thieves ate them. He finally gave up and came back. He's out in the bush, out that way,' she waved in the darkness.

Nhur explained that my father lived with another wife not too far from the village where we were. He insists on living in the desert with a few of the animals he did manage to get back. Each animal was clearly branded with his sign so, with the help of some tribal relatives, he was able to claim some of his livestock back. She thought maybe he had about five camels, some goats and a few sheep. My youngest brother, Rashid, was helping him to take care of them. I thought about all the empty hills we had passed on our journey here and I wondered if we would be able to find Papa. My mother still loved my father, but he had taken a second younger wife years ago when I was young. He lived with her in the bush most of the time. 'I heard that he had taken a third wife too,' I said, wondering what my mother's reaction to that had been.

'Well he did, but she ran away or he divorced her a while ago,' my mother stated.

'What? What happened?'

'Child, I don't know why she left. Maybe she didn't want to work,' Mama said flatly. The lantern started to smoke and she reached over and adjusted it. We say that billowing smoke tells secrets, but my mother's reaction to other wives remained a secret. Often another wife is a blessing because there is a lot of work for women and they can help each other. However, my mother was not going to talk about my father and his wives any more than she would talk about what happened to Burhaan's first wife.

'Your father was operated on two days ago somewhere in the bush,' Nhur whispered. 'Burhaan heard that it was bad and went to look for him.'

'An operation in the desert?'

'*Hiiyea.*'

'Two days ago,' I gasped. If only we had been able to get here sooner. I thought of that terrible room in Abu Dhabi and the days we wasted there. 'What kind of an operation?' I stuttered.

'His eyes, Waris,' Nhur said, softly. 'He was having trouble with them.'

'Allah, his eyes.' I had heard that he was having trouble

with his eyes, but I just thought he would get better like he always did. I assumed he had a little vision problem and maybe needed glasses. My father needed me but I had not been there to help him.

'We heard that he was blind and in terrible pain,' Nhur continued. 'Burhaan decided to see if he could find him and get him all the way to the nearest hospital in Galkayo. We don't know what happened yet, but I hope he is all right.'

Suddenly I was crazy with worry and fear. An operation in the middle of the desert? Who would do that! How could anyone do that? I couldn't believe it. How could he find his way around if he was blind? How could he take care of his animals or find water? From Nhur's description I suspected he had cataracts caused by years of blinding sun reflected on the sand. 'I am going to see if we can find him tomorrow,' I said. Even if it meant another endless journey, then so be it.

When I said, 'Mama can three of us share the bed?' she replied that we would not all fit. She only had some cloths spread out on a mat and a ragged piece of mosquito netting barely big enough for herself and Mohammed *Inyer*.

When I was a child we used to sleep outside under the stars because it is hot in the houses with no big windows to capture the air. Outside, there is usually a little breeze after the sun drops down over the edge of the world and the stars come out. What I really wanted to do was fall asleep outside with just a few little sheets. However, the mosquitoes could be fierce after the rain.

After the rain let up I went to sleep with my newfound sister-in-law. I shared a sleeping mat with Nhur and her little girl. The three of us shared it every night that I was there. My niece is almost two years old. Burhaan's house is square and made of whitewashed mud bricks. There are two rooms and a third that is not finished yet. The walls are about waist high and when it is completed I hope that my mother will agree to live there. Mama preferred to live in the ragged little stick thing she built with her own hands. She has lived all of her life in houses she built.

That night I was tired after such a complicated journey and emotionally exhausted from all my worries and fears but I couldn't fall asleep. I was excited that I would see everyone in the morning; I couldn't wait. I lay down next to my sister-in-law and her little daughter and waited for my mind to stop whirling. Listening to the last drops of rain drip off the roof I felt peace settling into my bones. We found my mother, I knew my father was alive, even if he was in a hospital, and I had relatives all around me.

Suddenly I thought I felt something and then I saw a dark shape on my leg below the knee. I was lucky I even saw this huge shadow, because it was very dark. I stared at what I thought might be a scorpion for a long time. Then I slowly whispered to Nhur, 'Is that what I think it is?' I tried to stay calm and not move, because we had been taught not to panic. Danger will snap at you so quickly that you will never know what happened to you. So we know not to move. Maybe the scorpion is just passing you by – you never know. You may think you can get him off faster than he can sting you, but I knew that you do not move before you are sure that you are really in charge. So I stared at it in the inky darkness and I said again, 'Is that what I think it is?'

She whispered in my ear, 'Oh, yes.'

We call it *hangralla*, scorpion. When it turned around I knew from the pointed poison tail – without a doubt – that it was a *hangralla*. He was the grandpapa or mama of them all. He'd come to welcome me home to Somalia. I jumped up and mashed it.

Even after that, I had no fear as I lay back down to sleep. I pushed away all my worries, all my stress and chaos. I let the Somali darkness and the deep silence surround me. People insist that Somalia is one of the most dangerous places in the world but I was at peace. It was a peace I have not felt anywhere else in my life.

I never slept more comfortably. Actually I feel quite comfortable on the floor. If you roll, you are going nowhere. If you kick, you can't break anything. It's good for the back too. I hadn't slept so well in years. Things in New York keep me up, or I wake up worried about something. When you know something, and I know the ways of the desert, you know that you are safe. You can let your fears go and slip away from your mind like water spilt on dry ground. I slept soundly every night I was there. I really did. I heard hyenas laughing in the distant hills like a wicked, wicked woman. Ha-ha-ha they tease each other. But we are not afraid, you know why? We know they wouldn't come. They aren't coming to the village to snatch people. God's hands are covering the village, keeping everybody safe so you don't have to worry about tomorrow or yesterday.

8

desert dreams come true

Liver with blood

2 cups blood
500g. liver
2 spoons *subaq ghee*

Wash the liver and cut into small pieces. Put the liver, blood
and *subaq ghee* into a small pan and cook slowly over glowing coals, stirring all the time. Do not fan the coals or the
ashes may get into the food. Simmer until the mixture is
tender and moist.

That morning I woke up in a different world. The dusty
gray plain had turned into dark red earth with big puddles
all over the place. Everything in my mother's house was
soaked. I looked up and you could see the sky through the
uneven parts of her corrugated tin roof. It wasn't like someone built her a roof; she had picked up scrap pieces of tin
here and there and placed them on top of the branches
she tied together to construct the four walls of her one

room. It was so small she had to sleep diagonally. Both she and Nhur had been up before the sun. Nhur had already been to the market and Mama was hanging her few little cloths on the fence of thorn bushes surrounding the house and on a rusty blue oil drum to dry. A battered truck tire leaning against the house had water inside and one of the goats was happily lapping it up. It looked at me out of the corner of yellow-brown eyes and kept drinking.

We don't feel miserable and complain that stuff gets wet when it rains, we say thank you to God. According to the Koran everything alive is made from water. Rain means that the grasses will turn green; the animals will fill their bellies, and so will we. In the desert water is precious; it's blue gold. We wait for the rain; we pray for the rain; we wash with the rain. Without rain there is no life. We don't have winter and summer, we have *jilaal*, the dry season and *gu*, the rainy season. In Somalia, a guest is greeted with water; it is a token of welcome and respect. I felt like Allah had offered me a greeting. The difficult journey, the long hot drive, and the hard days of drought were over; the *gu* rains had come and Allah blessed us with water. It started my visit to my family with joy and happiness.

I gave my mother a hug and kissed her good morning. 'God be with you, Mama,' I said. 'I am so happy to see you and to be here with you this beautiful morning.' I grabbed her and started squeezing her tightly. 'How I missed you! I love you so much Mama, I can't tell you how I love you!'

'Ohh,' she groaned, 'you are suffocating me.' She looked at me sideways with a wisp of a smile on the two ends of her mouth. She pretended to be annoyed but her eyes were shining with pride and delight. 'Waris,' she said, 'what a surprise to see you. I heard that you were dead. Somebody said that – then somebody said you were a prostitute. Now Allah brought you back and you are standing in my house, really I can't believe it.'

My mother has a special way of looking at life and it always catches me. She wears a string of black beads around her neck and a protective amulet. It is a little leather pouch with holy words from the Koran sewn inside. A *wadaddo* or holy man made it especially for her years ago and she never takes if off. It keeps her safe and protects her from evil spirits.

'Let me show you the presents I brought you from New York, Mama.'

She waved me aside with long expressive fingers and said, 'Go and see your uncle first.' That was so like my Mama, not to be at all interested in herself but in everybody else.

I knew from Nhur that my father's brother, my Uncle Ahmed, was not well and I needed to see him. Nhur said he had a *djinn* from the spirit world take over the left side of his body. I certainly didn't believe that. My uncle is older than my father – he could have a whole lot of things. When I was a child I watched after his goats for him. I remember that the thing I wanted most of all then was a pair of shoes. Now that I saw my home as an adult I understood why. Jagged rocks stuck up everywhere. How I remembered those rocks and thorns on my bare skin. Some thorns were so long they would stick right through your foot. When I was a girl I liked to leap and run; I had so much energy I couldn't stop moving. My feet were cut and bruised all the time, especially when I climbed all over the place after those goats. I envied their little hard hooves; nothing tore at their feet. My feet throbbed at night and bled all the time. I begged my uncle for a pair of shoes as payment for taking care of his goats. I watched his animals every single day and kept them safe. When it was hot and dry I had to take them off to distant places to find something to eat. Often I didn't get back until after dark and that is when I really tore up my feet. To this day I am obsessed with feet and shoes – it's the first thing I notice about people. I don't have a lot of clothes; I really don't care about them, but I love shoes. I buy comfortable ones though, not high-heels. They feel just like you are standing on rocks! Now why would you do that if you don't have to?

Finally Uncle Ahmed had agreed to bring me a pair of shoes from Galkayo. I dreamed about my wonderful shoes and felt they would be like a magic carpet. I could go any-where without hurting and run as fast as the ostrich do, throwing stones up behind them, or leap like the gazelle when they get the scent of a lion on the prowl. When my uncle finally came I danced for joy, and whooped and shouted, 'Shoes, shoes!' My father yelled at me to quiet down and leave the man alone but I would not go away, I was too excited. Uncle reached into his pack and handed me a pair of cheap rubber flip-flops, not the sturdy leather sandals I expected. I was so angry that I threw them in his face.

Nhur had built a fire and the tea for our breakfast was steaming. She had found some liver in the market that morning and had already cooked it for my mother. 'She can't eat many things because those bullets are still inside her,' she explained to me. 'Mama keeps throwing up.'

'She is too thin,' I agreed with her.

'I hope the liver will build up her blood,' she said, and carefully placed the bowl on the ground for my mother to eat. Mother sat down in front of it and started to say a prayer over the food. Mohammed *Inyer* danced in. He was hungry and wanted some of the liver. He is too little to wear pants and he squatted down with his bare behind right in front of my mother.

She looked up from her prayers and said calmly, 'Child, move your bottom from my breakfast.' I was still laughing when Ragge, my Uncle Ahmed's son, walked in.

My mother greeted him warmly then reminded me to see my uncle. 'You better go,' my mother warned me, 'or your uncle will think you are favoring my side of the family.' Ragge was a little boy when I left and I remembered taking care of him for my aunt. Now he was about twenty-two, tall and slender, and he spoke excellent English. I liked him immediately. He had an old-fashioned haircut, short around the side with a longer piece on the top. He carried an afro comb in his back pocket and every five minutes he was running it through his hair.

Ragge walked with me through the village to show me the way to his house. There were maybe sixty houses with one or two rooms in various stages of completion. People had cleared the desert brush and built basic shelters. Families who had enough money to buy building materials inhabited the best ones. They had walls of sun-dried blocks and roofs of corrugated tin. Other women had patched together huts out of whatever they could find: old tires, woven grasses and bits of tin. Some of the houses were square and fashioned of sticks, others were round Somali *occles* made of the long roots of the acacia tree, arched and covered with woven mats and pieces of plastic sheets. Old plastic bags stuck on the outsides of the houses fluttered in the wind. Nothing that was lightweight and might be useful was thrown out. We passed a house with the mats folded back to dry out the inside from the rain. Other dwellings were round with baked mud walls and thatched conical roofs. Different clans built different kinds of houses. None of the huts had running water and there were no sewage pipes or electricity lines or even plans for such a thing. Someone had built a little hut for the chickens. It was round with a little cone top and a reddish hen was sitting inside clucking at me to leave her alone. A little boy not more than two years old followed us. He was free to go exactly where he pleased – he was perfectly safe walking all by himself. He had on a T-shirt and nothing else. His teeth were gleaming white against his black face and his shy smile was as wide as a camel's mouth.

It was exactly the life that I remembered from my childhood so many years and experiences ago. The village reminded me of the tortoise. It draws its head and arms and legs deep into its shell and refuses to acknowledge you even if you poke it with a stick. It will simply wait until you get bored and move on, and then will continue on its journey without changing direction. This village had nothing to do with what happened in the rest of the world. Nothing much had changed since I lived here, but I certainly had. When I was a child I felt like I had every single thing that I needed, except sandals. I didn't have any idea that I was poor. I still find it hard to believe that Somalia is one of the five poorest countries on the planet. The morning sounds of chickens and crying babies and smells of wood smoke and wet mats in the village were waking up parts of me that I hadn't heard from in a long time. It felt wonderful to be there but at the same time I noticed that none of the children had shoes.

My uncle lived with his daughter Asha and her husband in a square house made of sun-dried mud bricks and a corrugated metal roof. The door was painted a gay blue and decorated with a big red diamond in the middle and smaller dark blue ones on either side.

Uncle Ahmed was sitting next to his house on a *michilis* or a short three-legged stool made of stretched hide. His hair was white as a goat and he wore the traditional checked Somali *maa-a-weiss* wrapped around the waist and tucked in with a fold in the front. His hat was round with a flat top. It is the kind often worn by men who have completed the prescribed *hajj* or trip to Mecca to pray.

'*Afdokle! Afdokle,*' Uncle said, rocking back and forth. He called me by my nickname, Little Mouth. 'Sit down, sit down next to me. Let me look at you. Oh my God, child. Don't you eat? You are so thin – are you sick?'

'No, Uncle,' I laughed. 'You don't have to have a big behind following you to be healthy.'

'Well,' he said, 'you look terribly thin to me. Are you hungry child?'

I said, 'Yes, Uncle. We just arrived here last night and I am really desperate for *angella*.' I could smell it when I got off the plane and that is the very thing that woke me up that morning; the wonderful smell of *angella* cooking. To make this sorghum pancake, women pound the grain in a tube hollowed out of a log and grind it into flour. Before they go to bed they mix it with water and beat it to make it smooth and full of air. As night falls throughout the village you can hear everybody beating the batter. It's a competition because the louder the sound the better it is. In the morning the batter has risen and the women build a fire and put three large stones around it. They balance a flat lid on the stones over the coals. When it's hot, they put a drop of batter on and gently smooth it all around with the spoon like the French make crêpes. You cover it and cook it for about three or four minutes.

Uncle Ahmed called his daughter, Asha. 'Bring *Afdokle* about ten of those pancakes and some tea. You can't eat *angella* without the tea. She is starving. Look at her! I thought they had plenty of food in America.'

'Uncle, I can't eat ten pancakes. Four will be plenty for me.'

Asha brought some spiced tea with goat's milk and the *angella* on a dented tin plate. I put a little tea on the *angella* to soften it. We don't use forks or spoons, food is carefully taken with the fingers.

I had not tasted this special sour flavor for many years and I was so excited that I didn't think when I picked up the first bite.

My uncle jerked up like an angry camel when I reached for those pancakes. 'No! Stop, stop,' he shouted. 'That's your left hand, my child, it's your left hand. That is not for the food.'

I said, 'Oh Uncle, I am so sorry. I forgot. Excuse me.' I was ashamed and embarrassed. I am left-handed and I took the food with my left hand because it doesn't make much difference in the West. However, it's very important in Somalia that you don't get confused about which hand goes where. The right hand is for everything but touching your genitalia. After you go to the toilet you use your left hand to wash yourself with water. We don't have toilet paper. Only the left is for washing your genitals. The right hand is for eating, throwing, cutting, touching others and everything else.

Uncle shook his white head at me. 'Have you been gone that long? Have you forgotten what you knew?' He looked at me, 'How dare you forget to be clean. You can forget anything else in Somalia but not that.'

I was so hungry I didn't think of anything but putting food in my mouth as fast as possible. I was acting like I was in New York. I forgot about how Somalis feel about food. We don't have 'fast food'. We don't even have a concept of eating food while you are doing something else. I was taught that food is a gift from Allah. It is a blessing and must be treated with respect. You don't eat something because it tastes good, you eat to fill your belly – to keep from dying. You don't grab food and shove it in your mouth without thinking about it. You sit down, you say a little prayer of gratitude and you taste every bite. So there I was not only grabbing the food without a prayer or proper respect, but taking it with my left hand.

I took a deep breath and started over; I said thank you to Allah for my uncle, for this day and for this food. I ate the *angella* slowly and carefully. It was delicious. As I ate I watched my uncle. He had a wisp of a mustache and a few white hairs left on his chin. He was wearing a gray and black plaid *maa-a-weiss*. I started looking closely and I noticed that he was leaning against the house in a strange way. His mouth drooped and he talked very slowly like it was hard to make the words. Mohammed kept saying, '*Hiiyea*?' asking Uncle to repeat what he said.

'What happened to your father?' I asked Asha when she brought us some tea. 'Why is he leaning like that?'

'He went to sleep one night and when he woke up he could not use his left arm or leg. The one side was fine, the other was just hanging there.'

'Oh my God!' I said, 'what did the doctor tell you about it?'

'We don't have a doctor here.'

'Did you take him to the hospital?'

'No. It's too far and he couldn't walk. Why would we take him so far away when he was sick?'

'What!' I couldn't believe it. The man wakes up half paralyzed and they don't take him to the hospital. 'When did this happen?'

'A few days ago,' Asha said. 'He is better today, *Alhamdillah.*' She didn't seem to be anything but resigned to what happened and grateful to Allah that he seemed a little better. I understand why my family believes that there is a day when it is your time to die, that is the will of Allah and we have to accept death as part of life. I understand that, but at the same time they don't know that when you are sick you can be cured. They don't believe in doctors or surgeons. I can appreciate the way they feel but I think it's because they have not realized that there are other things they can do.

'Uncle,' I said, 'tell me what happened.'

'I woke up and I couldn't move my left side.' He looked patient and resigned. 'It doesn't hurt, but I can't use my left hand or raise my arm. My leg drags when I walk.'

'*Hiiyea.*'

'Your mother gave me some tea she brewed from the powdered shell of an ostrich egg and cinchona bark.'

Even though I knew that my mother's medicine cured many things I still wanted to know what was going on with my uncle. I looked at Ragge and said, 'We are taking him with us when we go to the hospital to find my father.'

Ragge shrugged and said, 'What for? How are they going to help him?'

'Well at least I want to know what happened and get him some medicine or an operation if that is what he needs,' I told him.

Asha helped her father to wash. She brought a small bowl filled with water and washed his face and arms with a little cloth. She helped him to put on a blue shirt and a jean jacket. She lifted the useless arm and fitted it into the sleeve. A relative of Asha's husband had a taxi-car and I asked if he would take us to the hospital in Galkayo. Asha helped her father to get into the back seat of the car with me, Mohammed and Ragge sat in the front. We had to drive for over three hours to get to Galkayo, but I didn't care about getting right back in another car, after our long journey the

363

day before. There was a hospital where I hoped to find my father and a dispensary and doctors who might be able to help my uncle in Galkayo.

Sand in the Somali desert isn't like on a beach, it's dark red earth. White rocks and low-growing thorn bushes are all over, like spots on a leopard. Very quickly after it rains the desert plants start to push up out of the ground. Tiny leaves fringe the bushes and the acacia trees. Driving around that day I was surprised at how lovely it was. All of the terrible heat had evaporated with the rainstorm. The earth was a muted red, almost the color of blood, the air was so fresh and clean it felt good taking it into my lungs. Why don't the newspapers ever talk about this? It seems all they care about is chasing after trouble. Even though my poor little country has a lot of sadness, at the same time it is still beautiful. If only tears were rain.

Along the road we came to a checkpoint guarded by men who had big long guns slung over their shoulders. Ragge said there are always security forces when you cross the borders into a territory controlled by another clan.

'Hey,' I asked him in a whisper from the back seat, 'they don't use those guns do they?'

'You bet they will. They will look at what you are carrying or who is with you – believe me anything can go wrong. Maybe they just don't like you. If you are a different clan and they want money or something you better give them what they want. That's all they have to live on, it's not like they get paid or anything by the army.'

'I pray to God they don't bother us,' I said, my heart pounding. We stopped and one of the soldiers peered inside the car. We paid the toll and he opened the gate and waved us through and the other soldiers just ignored us.

When we were children we would tremble when we heard

the word, *Aba*, father. Just thinking about my father made me anxious. I had so many feelings about that man, and still I wanted to see him badly. I wanted to look my father in the face; I wanted him to look at me and see what had become of that little girl he used to order around. I wanted him to look at my face – a face that had been on magazine covers and in movies, a face that people recognized all over the world. I wanted him to remember what he said to me. 'You are not one of my children; I don't know where you came from.' That is what hurt me the most – maybe it's why I never came back all these years.

I don't know what I expected to find in the hospital in Galkayo, but my heart sank when I saw it. Most of the buildings were just walls halfway up and only a little dispensary was open. It looked like they had started working then quit before it was anywhere near being finished. There weren't piles of bricks or materials around to complete the buildings anywhere that I could see. Mohammed and Ragge helped my uncle to step out of the car and walk into the dispensary. He put one foot out and dragged the other to meet it leaning on his son and his nephew.

I looked around the place while we waited for the doctor. Only two little rooms were finished. One room had some equipment, a microscope and a few bottles of medicine. There were no cabinets of instruments or medicine or any supplies. Wooden shutters on the windows let in light and you could see just a few empty trays and bottles scattered here and there. The walls were painted with thin paint, light blue on the bottom and pink on the top. There was an eye chart on the wall in a wooden frame. The bathroom had stacks of tiles and a toilet that was not hooked up. This was it, the only medical facility for hours in any direction. What do the doctors do, how can they help people who are sick or hurt? It didn't look like they could take an X-ray or even give someone blood.

Finally a nurse came and said that my father was there and she would show us to the room where he was. Suddenly I felt very weak and scared. I had high hopes that I would see the king that I used to know but at the same time I was worried about what he'd become. I took a long deep breath and dragged slowly behind the boys.

The room was filled with people, all relatives of my father. They recognized Mohammed immediately and shouted and greeted him with hugs and shouts of joy. He turned around and said, 'This is my sister Waris,' and everybody started to call out to me but I couldn't breathe and I didn't want to see anyone but my father.

'Mohammed,' I asked him, 'don't say anything because I want to be the one who says hello to *Aba*.' I slipped between the people and went over to see my father.

He was lying on a narrow bed with two people sitting next to him. He was just lying there dozing with his eyes bandaged and his arms crossed over his body as if he was dead. I broke down. My tears came in a gush and I just sat and held his hand while they rolled down my cheeks. I didn't want anyone to see me cry or hear any sobs. I took a minute and then put my cheek next to his. He looked terrible but I thanked Allah that he was still alive and that I had found this man. I was angry with myself because I hadn't been there for so long, and so hadn't helped my family through their troubles. His hair was totally gray and he had only a small tuft of a beard. He was so thin that his cheeks sunk into his teeth. He looked fragile and broken, bewildered and lost.

Aba woke and said, 'Who is this?'

I kissed him and whispered, 'It's me Papa, Waris.'

'Who's that?' he said.

I said, 'Father, Father, it's Waris.'

'Waris?' he said slowly, 'I used to have a daughter named Waris but I don't any more – we don't know what happened to her. Please stop teasing me about that.'

'Papa, oh Papa! Really it's me.'

'What, Waris? She's been gone too long to suddenly arrive out of nowhere.'

'Father, it is me.'

'What? Is this really Waris? Oh, my daughter, my daughter. I thought you were dead and gone,' he said, turning his head towards me and squeezing my hand tightly. 'What happened to your eye?' I said, afraid to hear what he had to tell me.

'Oh, I'm all right, I'm all right. *Alhamdillah*, I am fine. Two days ago my eye was operated on.'

'Where did you have this operation? Did you go to a hospital?' I asked.

'It was done in the bush,' he said.

I couldn't believe it. 'What did they do to your eye?'

'He sliced it with his knife and look off the skin that was covering the eye.'

'Was he a doctor?' I asked. I was wondering who would slice open a person's eye outside of a hospital.

My father mumbled, 'He said he was a doctor.'

I patted his hand, 'Papa, did you have anything for the pain?'

'Child,' he said. 'What do you think? Of course I felt the pain. I could only see shadows with one eye and I am blind in the other. I felt him slicing me and I just had to lie there.'

'That is ridiculous,' I groaned out loud. 'To let somebody you don't know slice up your eye with a knife.'

'Waris! Waris, it is you – my daughter!' Father said really recognizing me. 'You haven't changed a bit. You always were a rebel and you are still making trouble.' After he said that, it brought back the way he used to be, strong and tough, a real warrior. I couldn't stop crying. 'Child, you cry when I'm dead,' he said, squeezing my hands. 'Right now I'm alive and looking for another big wife.'

That was my papa – that was the man I remembered. He joked even when he was blind and lying on a bed helpless. I looked at him for a long time, this old man who was my father. To me he was still handsome even though his age and difficult life had changed him. His face is a perfect oval and the strong creases running down either side accentuate the shape.

My father has been a nomad all his life. He has traveled from tribal wells to grasslands but never out of the Horn of Africa, never to a city with traffic or telephones. He had no way of knowing about modern medicine. He did what his family has done forever, he went to a bush doctor to cure his eyesight with a knife and a prayer to Allah. He was not angry about what happened, he accepted it and would accept whatever came next without tears and remorse. I suppose doctors and operations can't give you acceptance or peace in your heart.

I heard a voice next to me and there was my brother Burhaan. He has such a beautiful face that if he had been a girl my father would have been a happy man. He is so perfect that tribes would fight to offer the biggest bride price. He has a baby face with skin so smooth it looked like a painting. I reached up and touched him to feel the perfection and hugged him tightly. He was not quite as tall as Mohammed and he had evenly spaced features and was a perfect combination of my mother and father.

Burhaan explained that when he found *Aba* he was in bad shape due to the pain and swelling. The veins in his whole head were swollen and he was crazy with fever. Burhaan was afraid that he would die or wander off into the bush and be killed by the hyenas who waited for people like that. He brought him to the hospital and our relatives stayed with him and cared for him. In Somalia the family never leave a family member with strangers in a hospital, they camp right outside so they can say prayers and cook special foods.

I said, 'We want to take you back home with us, Papa. We have to get you home where we can take care of you. We have a car and you are in no condition to walk.'

'Home, which home?' *Aba* asked.

I said, 'You come and stay with Mohammed and me at mother's house.'

'No, I am not going to that woman's house,' he said.

'Papa,' I said, 'we have to take you with us so we can take care of you. Mohammed and I will only be here for a few more days. We love you, we want to look after you, we want you to be with us for the next ten days.'

'No,' he insisted. 'I don't want to go there. You visit me at my house.'

Burhaan reminded him that there was nobody to take care of him there and Mohammed pleaded with him until he finally agreed. We asked the doctor to release him and arranged to pick him up later that afternoon on our way back.

I then asked if a doctor could take a look at my uncle. The nurse asked us to bring him to the nearby dispensary. She wore a white lab coat and a headscarf of yellow the color of saffron rice, which covered her head and shoulders down to her waist. To me it seemed strange that a professional woman still covered her face at work. She showed us in to see the dispensary doctor and stood behind him in case he needed anything. The doctor took a blood sample from Uncle's arm. Uncle didn't even flinch when they punctured his arm with the needle. That would show weakness. He appeared calm and patient but I noticed that the veins on the side of his head stood out. The doctor looked in his eyes, took his blood pressure and tapped on his knee with a little silver hammer. He listened to his heart and looked in his ears. All that time Uncle looked at me, not the doctor. As long as I agreed with what was going on he would not say anything.

The doctor had a round face pock-marked with large moles on both cheeks. He had glasses on a chain around his neck and an enormous gold watch. It was a little too big for his wrist and moved when he gestured. He was calm and careful with everything he told me. He spoke excellent English and I felt more confident talking with him in English than in Somali. I didn't have the words to discuss modern medicine in Somali.

'What's wrong with my uncle?' I asked. 'Can you fix him?'

'We can give him some medical treatment,' he said.

'When will he be better?'

'He has hypertension and has suffered a hemorrhage in his brain.'

'Oh my God!' I said. I really didn't understand exactly what he meant but it sounded serious.

'He had a little stroke. It has caused the paralysis on his left side.' He asked my uncle to lift up his left arm. He could raise it to about shoulder height but it was a clumsy effort.

'Allah is curing you!' I said to encourage him.

'As the swelling in the brain goes down he should recover more,' the doctor said. He wrote out a prescription on a piece of paper and gave us a round bottle of pills. 'He needs to take this medicine every single day,' he told me, with an emphasis on the every. There were directions on the bottle and a flimsy paper inside. I think it was German or French but nobody back at the camp would be able to read that complicated paper.

'What will happen when the pills run out?' I asked. We had traveled for hours to get to Galkayo and I knew there were no pharmacies where my family was living, and no reliable way to get things delivered to them. You could give someone money to bring things but many times they took most of the money – or they would bring you the wrong thing.

'There are several pharmacies here in Galkayo,' the doctor told me. 'They have medicine from Europe.'

I hoped that Uncle would be better after taking the pills in the bottle because I didn't trust that he would get more. 'Is there anything he shouldn't eat?' Diet might be something he could control. 'How about sugar?' I felt like I had to push this man to tell me anything – he didn't explain things. I wanted to know how this happened, how someone can just wake up paralyzed, but he carefully picked every single word he said.

'No sugar, no salt. Anything else he can eat.'

'How long have you been here?' I inquired. Behind him a hand-written sign was taped on the wall. It said, Dr Ahmed Abdillahi. I wondered how much he knew about what nomadic people eat – as much milk and animal fat as they can get, because vegetables and fruits are not available most of the time.

'Here in Puntland?' he asked. He didn't say Somalia – or even Somaliland.

'Yes, here in Puntland.'

'I received my degree in Italy in 1970,' he replied. 'I am a neurosurgeon.'

I had to be honest with the man. I said, 'How can you help people with what you've got here, which is nothing.'

'This will be one of the finest hospitals in the Horn of Africa,' he said earnestly. 'We are constructing a new hospital with aid from the UK. When the hospital is fully open we will be able to do surgery.'

'What is the major medical problem you deal with?' I asked.

'I really can't say,' he told me.

'Is it AIDS?'

'We do see that but not too much.'

'Why can't you tell me what the major medical problem is?'

'I am a surgeon. You will have to ask someone else that question.'

I tried to find out more from some of the other people around the hospital, but nobody wanted to talk to me. I asked one doctor wearing a face-mask how long he had been here.

'Only one month,' he said.

'What is the major medical problem you have encountered so far?'

'TB,' he said and turned back to his Bunsen burner.

We decided to shop since we were in Galkayo. I had not been able to stop thinking about food since we arrived, since there wasn't much around. Getting food, eating food, having food around was suddenly very important. I forgot what it is like not to have cupboards full of pasta and flour and sugar, or a refrigerator with milk and eggs and bread. I looked for a corner store stocked with bread and cheese and canned things, but we didn't pass any. There is no refrigeration and everything has to be eaten the day you get it. Even if you had money there didn't seem to be much food around. The little stores were basically empty. Mohammed asked someone to direct us to the *suq* or market. 'Oh, that's all closed now. Everybody has gone away,' the man said. He was tall and had to lean over to look in the window, which he did for a long time. 'Who is that?' he asked Mohammed, offended because I didn't have my head covered. Though it was hot in that headscarf, I was embarrassed and pulled it up over my head until he left. Why did I respond to some old nomad I'll never see again? Because in my bones I'm a Somali woman.

We stopped in front of a little shop with an open door and empty metal barrels scattered around the front. A sleepy man in a turban got up and stood behind the counter when we came in. He had a few bolts of cloth on the shelves behind him, a box of batteries and some plastic shoes. He looked like he didn't trust strangers. Mohammed and I had changed a hundred dollars into Somali shillings in Abu Dhabi. They gave me 2,620 shillings in battered, ripped and dirty money for every dollar. The money had a picture of Siad Barre on it and I suppose it was the last official currency printed by the government. The shopkeeper wouldn't accept the shillings. 'That kind of money is for the other parts of Somalia,' he said and handed it back to Mohammed. 'We use the money from Puntland. It has a picture of Mohammed Egal, the head of the government of Puntland,' he said firmly.

'How can you have some people who only accept one kind of money, and others who won't let you buy anything if you have that kind of money?' I asked Mohammed when he sat back down in the car.

'That's the way things are here.' We found a woman willing to sell some green oranges, and some packets of tea and spices wrapped in newspapers tightly folded into squares. We bought rice in newspaper wrapped like a cone.

Late that afternoon everybody was tired and hungry so we stopped to eat in a little place that looked like a garage. Even though it was late in the day they still had lamb, goat meat, rice, and pasta. You could order tea, melon or papaya juice, or water. I was hungry and I had a delicious meal. I had a nice long glass of melon juice and lots of pasta. I didn't eat the meat because I am very suspicious of meat unless I cook it myself. The cook put a slice of meat on my tin plate but it was tough. One thing I didn't understand was why they didn't cook the meat well enough. When they cook it in a sauce it is tender and falls apart. I stuck to pasta and sauce. I was worried about getting sick and asked, 'Do you have any bottled water?' They even had bottles of Somali spring water! The waiter brought me a bottle of *Ali Mohammed Jama* spring water. 'Mohammed, we should do something like this, we should build a factory,' I told him. Mohammed wasn't interested and we ate quickly in order to get back to pick up my father and Burhaan at the hospital.

My brother, Mohammed, was in control of the money, or so he thought, so he paid the bill. I kept the dollars and he kept the Somali money. It was confusing because of the two presidents on the different kinds of money, one was from the Hawiye, the other was printed by the Daarood in the South. Each kind was worth a different amount. I had to keep asking, 'How much is this? How much is that?'

Mohammed usually replied, 'Never mind, I'll take care of it.' He knew what was what and I didn't want to be taken advantage of, so that was fine with me. My uncle was hot and tired so we stopped at a cousin's house to visit. He needed to rest for a while before we tried to go all the way back to the village over those rough roads. While we were in Galkayo, and Uncle was resting, I wanted to change some money at a bank.

I told Mohammed, 'I don't want you coming with me. You give me too much trouble.'

Mohammed started to argue with me as soon as I said it. My brother's eyes were flashing. 'I should come with you Waris, you don't know what you are doing.'

'Don't worry about it, Mohammed. Ragge and me will go. You stay here with Uncle.' Mohammed flipped out and walked away in a huff. When I tried to get him to tell me what was the matter he told me not to trust Ragge.

'He may be family but he is not as close as your brother,' he said. 'Don't give him the money to change at the bank, you don't know how much you will get in exchange.'

My brother and I are too much alike. I had had enough of him telling me what to do all the time. I walked out of the house with Ragge and we drove over to the bank.

Women don't go into a bank in Muslim countries so I waited outside. I gave Ragge about four hundred and fifty dollars and I sat in the car in front of the bank while he went in to change the money. The bank looked like a storage building, it was a big box with a door. Ragge came right back and gave me everything I asked for arranged in three stacks. I changed a hundred dollars for my father, two hundred and fifty to give to my mother, and one hundred dollars for our trip. Ragge gave me every shilling and he wrote the names on the different stacks. The money was a mixture of both currencies so we were prepared for people who would only accept one or the other.

When we got back to our cousin's house Mohammed was so angry he wouldn't talk to me for the first hour. He looked the other way and ignored me he was so mad. It didn't matter because people started to fill up the room. They had heard that we were visiting and came to say hello. I have a very big family, even relations I never heard of, never imagined, never dreamt about. Everybody wanted to meet me, to say hello. It felt wonderful and terrible at the same time. I loved being a part of such a big family, and meeting so many people who cared about me. However, many of the relatives I met needed or wanted something from me and that was hard. What could I do for them? My uncle Ali called to a little girl and told her to come and sit down next to me.

'This little child is very ill. She needs you to help her,' he said.

'What is the matter with her?' I asked taking her little hand in mine.

'She has a disease.'

'Do you know what the name of the disease is?'

'No, but all of her hair has fallen out and she is wasting away. She is a feather and does not grow.'

I couldn't see her to find out what was wrong because she was wearing a long dress and had a headscarf wrapped all around her head and face like most Somali girls.

'I want you to take her back to the United States and take care of her there.'

'Uncle,' I said, 'I would like to help you but I really can't.'

'Why won't you help this child?' he said. 'I know that if you take her she can get better. Here she cannot be cured – we have no medicine for this sickness. You have to take this child and look after her and save her,' he begged me.

'Please Uncle, I have so many problems and responsibilities of my own that you don't know about. Just because I live in the West doesn't mean that I live in luxury.'

'What problems could you have?' he said. 'Here we have fighting and crazy soldiers with guns. We don't have a proper hospital or enough food all the time. What kind of problems can be worse than that?'

There was no way he could understand that it would be impossible for me to take a sick child back to New York with me. I knew that I could not accept the responsibility for her. 'Uncle, I will pray for her but I can't take her back with me. You must try to understand.' I stroked her hand and hugged her then I got up and said that we really had to go and pick up my father. It was getting late.

When we left I sat in the back with my uncle. Mohammed was still angry and he would not even look at me. He sat in the front and stared at the road. We went right back to the hospital to pick up my father and Burhaan but it was dark by the time we left Galkayo and you couldn't see much of anything. It must have been over one hundred miles back to my mother's village. A little way out of town my father asked where we were going and when I explained, he said he had changed his mind and didn't want to come back with us to my mother's place.

'No, I am not going there,' he insisted, a helpless old man with his face covered in bandages and too weak to walk. My uncle tried to talk to him. He and my father were sitting next to each other and my uncle put his arms around his brother and talked to him softly, calmly. It was the first time I ever saw them hold each other, two old men, two brothers. It was a beautiful moment in the middle of such sadness for both of them. How time had bent them.

My father would not relent however, and I begged him to come and stay with us for a few days. 'I have not seen you for twenty years,' I said. 'Mohammed and I will only be here for a few days and if you don't stay with us I will not get to see you. Please come with us.' He finally agreed to stay with us but he wanted to go back to his little mud-brick house and get some things first.

'Father,' I asked, 'where is your place?'

'Just go that way,' he answered waving his left hand in the air.

I tried again. 'Father, it's pitch black outside and we can't see anything.'

He got very short and insisted in a loud voice, 'Just go where I tell you, child! I know what I am doing, just go where I tell you.' My brothers and I had to laugh at this old man sitting in the back seat who can't see or drive and was still insisting that the driver go where he says. Even Mohammed had to give up his anger and see the irony in the situation. Blind and helpless, my father still ruled the roost. The only lights were the car headlights and they showed nothing but rocks and dust. My father pointed to the left and so we turned off the road and traveled right into the rolling desert. All at once my father said, 'Turn here, turn here,' but there was a lot of nothing. 'Is there a termite mound over there? Can you see the *dadune*?' he said.

'Yes, I see them,' Mohammed said, surprised.

'Well you have to turn left,' Father said, as if he had driven this route every night of his life. I had no idea what he was doing – we could not see more than six feet in front of the car and we were driving with no road, no track, nothing but my father's blind directions.

After about fifteen minutes my father said, 'Can you see it?'

'See what, Father?' Mohammed asked.

'My house,' he announced with total assurance. 'My house is right over there.' Sure enough the car lights showed a couple of huts over a little hill. 'OK we're here,' he said calmly.

I said, 'Which one is it? Where is your house?'

My father made a face and said, 'I think it's the one with a red door.' Then he reconsidered, 'Was it red?'

I said, 'Father, we have no idea which one is your house.'

He said, 'Well, I think the door is red. Take the torch and look for red.' We had no idea what else to do so we just went over to the first house. Mohammed opened the door and shone the light inside on a poor woman with three kids. We said, 'Oh excuse us. Sorry.' We shone the torch on the second house. Sure enough, it had a red door. It was empty – nothing inside but a dirt floor.

I went back out to him in the car. 'I think we've found it, but what are we looking for Father?'

'My shirts.' I asked him where they would be and he said, 'I don't know child. They will be in there – sitting in the corner.' I bent over and crawled into the tiny house and felt around on the packed earth floor. Sure enough, there were two shirts and an army jacket. They were filthy lying there in the dirt. There were stains all over them from the sand and his sweat had left half-moon white shapes under the arms. The smell was terrible. I left them right there and told him, 'Father, you don't need those things, they are dirty.'

'Bring them,' he snapped at me. There were no locks on the door so we just closed it and went back to the car. As we were about to get in I noticed three little kids standing next to the car talking to my father. I asked him who they were and he replied, 'Say hello, these are your brothers.' He explained that the mother of these children was a woman he divorced last week. I asked them to come in front of the car, in the light, so I could see them. They were skinny things with trusting eyes all under ten years old. I had only a little moment in the car lights to see my half-brothers before we had to entrust them to Allah and the peaceful desert. My father didn't offer any explanation and I knew better than to ask. I hoped I could find out about them from my mother when we got back. But how my blind old father led us back to his house in the dark – that I shall never understand.

On the long journey home I sat between him and my uncle, holding on to both of them. I felt so blessed. I had my father and my uncle and my brothers and I was home in my beautiful country. Yes, I was tired and worn out, but I didn't care, other things were so much more important. I couldn't stop myself from thinking about all the differences between my life in New York, where food and comfort is everywhere, and the life my family leads, here in Somalia. Most people in the West have so many things they don't even know what they have. My parents could probably count every single thing they owned, and food was difficult to get, yet they were cheerful and happy. People on the street were smiling and talking to each other. I think that Western people are trying to fill themselves up with something that is missing. Everybody there is searching. They search in the stores and on the television. People have shown me a room in their house where they have candles for prayer and meditation. A whole room just for the candles. Here we all had to squeeze together so there was enough space on the sleeping mat for everyone. It was not a problem, it was joy to be all together; everyone kept saying thank you Allah that we are all together. In Somalia we don't have a special place for prayer, we pray even when we greet someone. 'May Allah be with you,' we say. In New York everyone says 'hello'. What does that mean? Hello. It doesn't mean anything that I know of, it's just something that you say. People say 'have a good day', but it's just something that you say. 'If God is willing, I'll see you later,' we say in Somali. God had been willing and my first day with my family was a good day, a very good day!

9

tribal talk

A woman's beauty is not in her face

Somali Proverb

When we finally arrived back in the village my mother was sitting near the fire petting her goats and telling stories to Nhur, her granddaughter, and Mohammed *Inyer*. When she saw my brothers guiding my father between them she said to me, 'Allah! You brought him with you? How is he?'

'Go and ask him yourself,' I said to her. She went over to them and said, 'Well, well, what have we here? Did you find a stray camel in the bush?' Then she gently touched my father's bandage and said, 'How are you doing in there?' with her wicked sense of humor. She asked me to go with her to get some cloths to make him a bed.

'I'm surprised that your father agreed to come back here,' my mother said when we were alone.

'Why? Is it because he didn't want you to see him like this?'

'No! Waris, Burhaan never paid the bride price for Nhur,' she whispered in my ear. 'Your father kept saying he would pay it when he got the money. She has been married to Burhaan for two years and she's on her second child. Her father and brothers have been complaining about it.'

'Oh. She is such a sweet person, I love her already.'

'She takes good care of me and Burhaan. Her father is worried about what would happen if Burhaan kicks her out – she was a clean new bride. Now they are demanding the money for her. Your father promised Burhaan that he would give him some camels for her but instead of doing that he went and told a cousin that she wasn't worth five camels. He said that she was lazy and didn't work and so he would not pay.'

'No! Nhur is the first one up in the morning – she works harder than everyone. That woman is a queen,' I said.

'Well, it got back to her family and they said they were going to find your father and beat him. Nhur heard what he said about her and now he is ashamed to face her.' My mother sighed. Maybe my father couldn't bear to part with the few camels he had left, but that was no excuse for not paying the bride price he promised to Nhur's family.

In Somalia, on their wedding night, brides are cut open to allow their husbands entry. A woman takes a knife and slices through her circumcision to make an opening big enough for intercourse. Her mother-in-law inspects her daughter-in-law in the morning to see if she is bleeding and has slept with her husband despite the pain. If the blood between her legs is fresh the women will dance through the village and announce it to everyone. Everyone in the village had heard my mother singing about Nhur's bravery and that she was a clean virgin when she married Burhaan. They knew how hard she worked. They knew that she had to be cut open in order to give birth to her daughter, then sewn shut again. It was obvious that my father just didn't want to pay the bride price. Everyone was calling him a coward and cheap. 'He has to go and tell them that his camels were stolen and he doesn't have the money,' I said. 'Not go around saying that she wasn't worth it.'

We went back out with our arms full of cushions just in time to see Nhur greet her husband. Although they would never kiss in public the look on her face showed how much she loved my brother. Nhur walked directly over to where my father was standing with Mohammed. She said, 'Welcome *Aba*, Father,' keeping her eyes on the ground in respect even though he could not see. He shrank back a little bit when he recognized her voice and she reached out to him and gently took his hands and reassured him, '*Aba*, you must be tired. Come with me, we have a nice bed for you.' What a beautiful woman my brother married. We are all lucky to have such dignity and grace in our family. My mother arranged most of the little cloths and pillows she owned outside her little house for my father. Nhur helped him tenderly and slowly to lie down. He was tired but would not show it until he collapsed into the pillows.

My brothers slept with my father like they had when I was a child. The women slept in the *occle* with the little children and the men and boys stayed outside to guard the animals.

The next morning when I got up it felt like a dream. I had ached for that morning – waking up with my whole family. All that was missing were my sisters and Aleeke. The men were all still sleeping and I laughed when I saw three pairs of long legs sticking out from underneath the sheets. They were all intertwined with each other and you couldn't tell whose legs were whose. It had rained during the night and since there was nowhere to go they tried to cover themselves with a sheet of plastic, but the edges of the sheets were soaked and muddy. My mother had already been out to gather firewood and Nhur had been to the market to get breakfast ready for everybody before they woke up. She left before the first light to make sure and get the best things that were available. She was making *angella* and the smell drove me crazy. When Mother came back from chasing her goats she had milk for the tea in her tin cup with a blue rim. She looked at the tangle of legs and remarked, 'Are those men going to sleep all day?' My mother never whispers – you can hear her voice everywhere. That got everybody up.

The first thing I did that morning was find my father's filthy shirts and wash them in a flat pan. You use a good scrub to clean things because we don't use a lot of water since it has to be carried a long way back to the camp. I got as much dirt out of the shirts as I could, then I wrung them a little and spread them out on thorn bushes to dry in the sun. My father was lying on his cloth near the house and he heard me. He called out, 'Who's there?'

I said, 'It's just me Father, Waris.'

He said, 'Come over here, Waris, I need to talk to you.' My father told me that he wanted to discuss the fight I had with Mohammed over Ragge and the money. I remembered that nothing passes by my father without him knowing about it. Even if you whisper right up next to someone's ear, he will hear it. He said, 'Last night I heard you and Mohammed arguing about Ragge.' My father told me not to trust Ragge with anything, especially money.

I said, 'Why not? Ragge is your own brother's son. Mohammed and Ragge were raised like brothers! Isn't my brother's brother, my brother too?'

He said, 'Yes, but you don't know anything about him, Waris. You just got here. He is showing you this face now, but you don't know him. Listen to me, I don't want you to have anything to do with him.'

'I don't understand why you are so against him,' I told him. Ragge spoke good English and I could really talk to him. He understood me and I could say things to him that Mohammed and Burhaan did not understand. Sometimes I didn't think my brothers wanted to understand me, it seemed like they were really trying to control me. I have lived on my own too long to back down when a man says this or that.

My father propped himself up with one hand and I could see that it was painful for him to move. 'Listen to me Waris: your blood brothers and you against your half-brothers. Your brothers and half-brothers and you against your cousins. Your clan against other clans. Your tribe against another tribe.'

'*Aba*, I don't believe all this clan and tribal stuff.' I sat down and took his hand. 'What is the problem with Ragge? What has he done to make you feel that he can't be trusted?'

'Ragge is a terrible son and he doesn't treat his father right,' my father insisted. 'He should be taking care of his father and the family herds. He is a conniver, you only just got here – you won't see that side of him.'

Mohammed and Burhaan returned and overheard what we were talking about. They both sided with my father and started lecturing me. 'You stupid blind girl. Listen to what *Aba* is telling you. Why are you arguing with him?'

'Don't call me that,' I said, and told the three of them to stop pushing me around to get me to believe in something I didn't. I knew what they were saying – that your own blood family is the most trustworthy, but I don't think that is always true. Just because someone is not a blood sibling doesn't mean they will take advantage of you. I couldn't understand what they were talking about, or why it was so important to spend all morning discussing it so intently, but that is how we are. Talk, discussion, argument, is the breath of life in Somali families.

Mama came around the corner and she had a funny look on her face and I knew something was up.

'Why are you smiling like that, Mama?' I said. She looked away like she had a big secret; her eyes were shining in the morning sun. I looked up and a man almost as tall as Mohammed came around the corner of the house. He stopped and started looking hard at me. I was staring at him too. My mother was cackling at the two of us.

'Don't you recognize your little baby brother?' she said.

This man had a very familiar posture and look about him but I could not place him. He squinted at me in the sun, and stuck out his tongue. It was my baby brother, Rashid, all grown up. He was a handsome man with a little mustache and a short beard under his chin. He had grown tall and straight with long arms and legs and a smile that showed off two rows of perfectly white square teeth. He was wearing a green *goa* with a bright gold pattern draped over his shoulders and a brown checked shirt. Rashid had been out in the bush herding my father's camels, or what was left of the herd, and had just come back from the desert to see if he could get some supplies. He didn't know that Mohammed and I were coming, but now here he was. What a miracle! No wonder my mother was smiling. I couldn't remember one time during my whole childhood when we were all together, my brothers and I. One or another would be off somewhere. Mohammed lived in the city, somebody was off looking for food or water or taking care of the camels in the bush. I ran away when my little brother Rashid was still a baby boy running around without pants.

I hugged him tightly and felt his strong bones in my embrace. He and Mohammed started hugging and kidding around. 'Let me get my camera, I want to take a picture of my beautiful brothers,' I said and went inside the hut and rummaged through my bags to find it. When I got back outside, both those boys had disappeared. My mother had gone to give the orange rinds and the *angella* she didn't eat from breakfast to her little goats. I started looking around for my brothers.

In the back of the house, a little distance from the village was a big termite mound. It looked like a giant brown thumb poking up out of the ground at an angle. Rashid was sitting on the top. I remembered climbing up on those things as a girl. My mother told me that the tiny termites build the enormous mounds from their own saliva. That is a tribe who works together she taught me. 'I used to climb ones five times as big,' I called. Rashid made faces at me and stuck out his long tongue again. I wished I could climb up there too but I was not wearing pants, I had on a long Somali dress and was finding it impossible to do anything with it. 'I wish I could take this damn blanket off and climb up there like I used to,' I said to him. As a child I used to grab hold of the back hem of the dress and pull it up to the front where I could tuck it into the waist and make a kind of pant. I was tempted to try it, but I finally decided I was too old for that and I didn't want to offend anyone.

I looked at Rashid climbing on the termite mound, and noticed that he had bare feet. Here he was, a grown man, and he didn't have a pair of shoes. My own brother didn't own a single pair. The bottoms of his feet were so calloused and cracked they looked like elephant hide. The one thing that I could not get over was how rough the ground was. It's covered with sharp jagged edged rocks, and I remembered how those rocks cut and hurt my feet. I didn't have shoes as a child, and here I was looking at my brother, twenty years old and still going around without shoes. I decided that he was having nice sturdy leather sandals no matter what. I would find them in a shop, or get a *midgann* to make them for him, but my brother was not going to walk back into the desert barefoot. I said, 'Rashid I'm going to make sure that you've got a pair of shoes to walk back.'

'Why don't you give me the money for the shoes?' he said. 'I'll buy my own.'

I was worried that he wanted the money to buy *khat* so I said, 'Let's go over to the market and you can pick out the ones you want.'

I thanked Allah that I was able to buy some shoes for Rashid, to get medicine for my father and my uncle. We walked together back to my mother's hut. She was using her little pile of firewood to make tea and some rice and beans for our meal.

'What did they do for Uncle Ahmed in the hospital?' Rashid asked me. 'I heard there is a *djinn* in one side of his body.'

'The doctor examined him and gave him a little bottle of pills,' I told him. 'I can't tell you much more than that. The people there didn't really want to talk to me – to spend any time with me.'

'Who was the doctor?' Rashid wanted to know.

'What do you mean?' I asked. 'He said he was trained in Italy and was a neurosurgeon.'

'No, I mean who are his clansmen?'

'Well, I don't know. What does that have to do with it?'

'If we are not related he is not going to take the same

time and care of you that he would for people in his own tribe.'

'He's a doctor and they don't care what tribe you are,' I said. 'I don't think he wanted to talk to a woman. He's used to dealing with men and he probably thinks that women are stupid.'

'*Hiiyea,*' Rashid replied. He had to agree with that. He saw my mother walk by and asked her who was wearing the shoes.

Everybody was constantly fighting over one pair of flip-flops. They only had one good pair in the whole house and I kept hearing, 'Where are the shoes? I need to go to the bathroom. It's almost time to pray, I have to wash.' Mama would have them on to get something outside, and Burhaan would have to wait until she came back and gave him the shoes so he could go to the bathroom. 'Who is wearing the shoes?' I heard all day – especially just before it was time to pray and everybody had to go and wash. Four people were fighting for one pair of rubber flip-flops. They were the cheap kind that fall apart two days after you buy them. The front piece that goes between your toes comes out and they won't stay on your feet any more. My mother was wearing two different colors when I met her and half of the bottom of one was missing. I said, 'Let's go to the market and see if we can get some more shoes then you won't have to waste so much time waiting for them.'

Rashid flashed a big row of pearly teeth in my direction, 'You don't own time, Waris. How can you waste it?'

I could see that he was a tease. 'Well, talking to you is a waste of time,' I joked. He and Ragge walked with me over to the outdoor market. Ragge wanted me to buy him a pair of black boots. I looked at him and said, 'Hey what are you going to do with boots? It's hot here, those are for London.'

My cousin's got his own unique fashion thing going on so I bought them for him. I bought two pairs of flip-flops and some incense and a mortar and pestle to grind fresh spices. Rashid didn't like any of the shoes in the market and we decided to look another day. He did like my sunglasses and I gave them to him. They would protect his eyes from the sun when he watched after my father's herds.

That night I had a big discussion about clans and tribes with my brothers and the rest of the family. My father is Daarood, the major tribe in the Central/Southern parts of Somalia. His sub-clan is Majeerteen. My family has always lived in the Haud, an area that is on the border with Ethiopia. My father's name is Dahee Dirie. My mother is from another major tribe, the Hawiye. She was raised in Mogadishu in what was once considered the capital of the whole of Somalia. When my father went to her mother and asked about marrying her he was turned down by her family. 'You are Daarood – you are a wild man – how will you support my daughter? You are not our people.' My mother ran away with him and she has never looked back. Now her brothers and sisters are all over the world. She is the only one lost in the desert.

There are four major clans in Somalia: Dir, Daarood, Isaaq and Hawiye. The majority of the Somali people belong to one of those clans and everyone is Muslim and speaks Somali. There are some smaller ones, the Rahanwayn and the Digil, but those people live mostly in the far south of the country near Kismayu. The people in our clan family were traditionally pastoral, only now more people are living in towns. As nomads move constantly the clan is more important than an address that changes all the time. This is not something that Europeans understand very well. When they decided the borders for Somalia they scattered Somalis around several different countries. The five stars on the Somali flag stand for Somalia, Somaliland, Djibouti and the Ogaden, as well as the Somalis in Kenya.

This clan business didn't seem all that important to me when I was growing up except I was proud to be a Daarood because it was the most fearless clan and I mean fearless. The nickname of the Daarood people is *Libah*, the Lion. Now I wanted to understand it. It was certainly important to my father and brothers and played a role in what was going on in my country. Siad Barre first said he was going to abolish tribalism then he started to provoke tribal conflict in an effort to distract everyone from the problems he was having. In 1991 after Siad Barre left the country and his government collapsed everybody got together with members of their clans to try to establish a base of power. These attempts to gain power left my country in a big mess. I think the whole clan thing is ridiculous and I told my brothers what I thought.

'The only thing that is destroying Somalia is tribalism,' I said.

'Daarood is the biggest and the strongest clan in this country,' said Burhaan. 'It is the major clan at this point, Waris.'

'Yes,' I replied, 'and it's also the proudest and the most fearless.' I knew that even if you are trying to save your life and you lie about being Daarood, they will know. 'Everybody should have a say in the government,' I told him.

'We should say what happens here,' he said, 'I'm not sharing power with anybody from those other clans.'

I told him, 'This clan business is keeping this country from solving problems. If you left Somalia you would see that we are all the same people! We all live in the same land, we all speak the same language, we look alike and we think alike. We have got to get together and end this feuding.' I was blazing mad about this now we were talking about it. To the rest of the world we are all Somali, but here, people could not get along with each other.

My mother brought us some tea and Rashid started to kid around with me.

'Waris, who are you? Can you recite your lineage?' he asked.

'I am Daarood,' I said.

'Yes, but what are you after that?'

'Well, Waris Dirie,' I said and they all started laughing. 'I take my father's name, Dahee, then my grandfather's name, Dirie, Mohammed, Sulimann.' They laughed at me because it goes on for thirty names and I couldn't remember more than the first three. I said, 'Hey, they are all dead.' My mother's name is Fattuma Ahmed Aden and she started reciting her father and her grandfather and her great grandfather and on and on. The children are given the father's names, but a woman keeps her own father's names when she marries. My brothers started trying to teach me all of my ancestor's names. I couldn't get it and they would not slow down so I couldn't even hear the way they were pronounced. They started reciting our lineage like rap music. The clan rap sheets all start with a common ancestor and you keep adding a name each generation. My family thinks that the more names (generations) you have, the more prestigious the clan.

Finally I said, 'I'll tell you, as soon as I left Somalia I didn't have any use for that and I never paid any more attention to any of it. What is so important about remembering a bunch of names?' I asked them. 'What difference has this made to you, Mohammed, in Amsterdam? All of this hasn't fed me or anything.'

Mohammed was quiet, like he was remembering something terrible. 'When *Afweine* first took over the government, he started a lot of different projects. He decided that Somali would be written in the Latin script and opened schools. When *Afweine* ran out of money to pay the teachers he suddenly decided that the students had to go into the bush and teach the nomads. He had a big literacy campaign.'

'I remember that,' I said. 'You tried to teach me and Old Man the letters.'

'Yes, but I was a city boy,' Mohammed said. 'I thought you were stupid nomads. I didn't want to come out to the bush and I didn't want to teach you anything.'

'I remember that too!' I said. 'You hit me with the writing stick.'

'*Afweine* turned out to be the biggest tribalist of all,' Mohammed sighed. 'If nine men wanted to meet with him he would only talk separately with members of each clan. There were a lot of murders of the Isaaq clan, just because they were Isaaq,' Mohammed muttered, and he stopped talking like he didn't want to remember it.

'Waris, your clansmen are the ones who are going to help you when you need it,' Burhaan said. 'That doctor in the hospital was not helpful because he is not one of our people.'

'He's supposed to help everybody,' I said.

'Consider how we got here in the first place,' Mohammed added. 'We got a driver to bring us because he belongs to our family. He has a reason to help us – he knows that when he needs something we are going to give it to him if we have it.'

Before that visit to Somalia in 2000 I was happy that they had a new president for the first time since 1991 and I thought that many problems could be solved. Now I saw that they still couldn't get behind one person. 'So how are you going to have a country if the clans won't work with each other?' I said.

Burhaan said, 'There are two countries.'

'Well, how does that work?'

'One is in the North, called Somaliland, and the other is Somalia in the South. Then there is Puntland in the north-east around Galkayo,' Burhaan said. 'That's why there are two different kinds of money, one is left over from Siad Barre in the South and the other is Mohammed Ibrahim Egal's money from Somaliland in the North.'

When I was a child the tribal elders solved problems. Suppose you fought with somebody and managed to knock out an eye. His clan would demand compensation for the loss of an eye from your clan. That is called *diya* – paying. Men from the two clans would meet under a big tree and they would sit there until they had figured out what the loss of an eye was worth. Of course if you knocked out a woman's eye that would be worth a lot less than a man's eye. Everybody would have to contribute and those animals would be distributed to the members of the blinded man's clan. Nowadays people would say: hey, I live in Mogadishu; I didn't have anything to do with that man hitting the other one. I am not paying for his troubles.

'We need a government based on laws not this clan business,' I said but nobody wanted to hear about it, they could not see how it would work. Mohammed insisted that the old ways were dead and gone. 'Elders are no longer respected and the so-called military leaders can't control their own troops.' My brothers went on talking so I went to sit with the women and watch the moon rise between the clouds and light up my desert home.

I saw my mother walk over to the neighbors with a cup of goat milk. She had four goats to her name in this world and here she was bringing some milk to share with the woman next door. I watched her go between the row of little huts surrounded by thorn fences carefully carrying her little tin cup with the blue rim. She had on the same dress she always wore with a little torn scarf that she wrapped around her head. She had her broken pair of mis-matched flip-flops on her feet. She stooped down and went into the neighbor's house for a few little minutes. She came out quietly and stood back up. She rested her hands on her back for a moment and looked up at the sunset colors streaking the big sky from end to end. She walked back and dangled her empty cup on her finger and hung it on the nail outside her door. That was my Mama. That is the kindness I used to know; that's a neighbor.

'Mama, sit down for a minute. I want to show you the things I brought for you,' I begged her. The woman never sat down, she was moving from morning till night. What I really wanted to give to my mother was everything that she never had in life.

She gave me one of her half smiles and a funny sigh. 'I can only imagine what you brought,' she joked. Of course she wondered what I could possibly bring her from New York City that would be of any use. Mama looked around and said, 'Not out here Waris. If anybody sees you giving things away everybody in the whole town is going to come and sit there until you give them something too.' She was right. My relatives would never ask for anything, but they would sit there and look at you until you finally broke down and offered them a present. Nhur and Mama came with me into her little house and we lit a *feynuss*.

Nhur immediately started to rummage through my bag like a vulture, asking, 'What's this? What is this for?'

'Hold on, hold on,' I said, 'I know what's what and I'm going to tell you if you just wait a minute.' I took out a jar of cocoa butter. 'That is *subaq*,' I said and opened it so she could try it. Before I could stop them, both she and my mother stuck their fingers into it and licked it.

'Ug! This is horrible, no wonder you're so skinny – if that's what they have to eat in New York.'

'Hey,' I said, 'you don't eat cocoa butter. It's for your hands and skin.'

'You can't cook with it?' my mother said.

'No, it's lotion for your face, for your dry feet – for your skin.'

'Well, it smelled so lovely why can't I eat it?'

'It's only for your skin. Don't eat it.'

'OK, OK, I won't eat it but *subaq ghee* is a lot better than that stuff. You can cook with it and use it on your skin. What else do you have?' Mama asked, handing it back to me with a shrug.

I gave her a bottle of Johnson's baby oil. 'Now what is this?' she said turning it over in her hand.

'This is oil. You can put it on your face and everywhere you want, even in your hair. It's just like the cocoa butter.'

'OK,' she said but instead of taking a drop she squeezed the bottle too hard and it squirted out all over the dirt floor. That frightened my mother and she jumped back and dropped the bottle on the sand. 'What is that stuff?' she demanded rubbing it between her fingers.

'Smell it, Mama,' I said. 'You put it on your skin or on the baby's skin.'

My mother sniffed her hand and sniffed it again. 'Oh!' she smacked her lips in approval. 'That is very beautiful. I do like that, Waris.' She rubbed it up and down her arms and they glowed in the lamplight. 'I'm going to have to hide it.'

I said, 'Mama, no. This is not a big deal. If somebody wants some of this just give it to them. I'll bring all the baby oil you want.'

'I don't know when I'm going to see you again and I'm not taking that chance,' she told me and she got up and began to search in her little pile of belongings. Deep in the bottom of a basket she found a key. She unlocked a battered wooden box and carefully tucked the baby oil inside. 'That is very precious, and it will be safe in here,' she said patting the box before she put it back in the corner.

I brought a bunch of little mirrors and a beautiful one for my mother because she never saw herself in a mirror. I wanted her to know how beautiful she is. I got my looks from my mother and they provided me with a way to support myself for a long time. Her beauty has been a great friend to me. People often tell me that I am beautiful, but if I had a drop of my mother's beauty then maybe I would believe it. I unwrapped the tissue paper from the special mirror I bought for her. It had a silver handle and leaves carved all around it that twined into beautiful flowers on the back. 'Mama,' I said, 'I brought you something very special.'

'*Hiiyea*,' she said. 'I don't need anything special, Waris.'

'Mama,' I said. 'Come and sit next to me and see what I brought for you.' When I handed it to her she looked at the wrong side in puzzlement and didn't know quite what it was. I turned it over and held it up for her. 'Look at yourself, see how beautiful you are.' When Mama finally caught her reflection she thought that someone was behind her and she jumped back in fright. I said, 'No, Mama there is nobody there. That is you.' I held the mirror up again for her. She looked at herself, she looked away, then she looked again and again. She started to touch her face and her hair with her fingers. She pulled her cheeks back, looked at her teeth and twisted her head this way and that. She studied her face for a long time and then she moaned, 'Oh, my God! Allah! I look so old. I look terrible. I didn't know I looked like this.'

'Mama!' I whispered. 'How can you say that?'

'Look at me!' she answered. Mama stared at me then she looked at Nhur; her eyes squinted in the dim light. 'What happened to my face?' she sighed. 'I used to be a beautiful woman and your father and you all sucked my life out of me.' She turned the mirror over and handed it back to me.

I didn't know what to say. I was surprised as much as hurt. My mother does not pretend about anything. She is straight out with exactly how she feels and she certainly did not pretend to like my gift. I quickly tucked it back in my bag out of sight, sorry that I had given it to her. I felt ashamed and wanted to get rid of it. She wouldn't take something that she didn't need because possessions are difficult to haul around on trek. The important things are your family, your stories, and your animals. They are the source of life and the wellspring of joy. My mother was beautiful to me because of the way she took care of her family and her friends and her animals. Real beauty is not something you see in a mirror or on the cover of a magazine; it's the way that you live your life.

10

fathers and men

The man may be the head of the house; the wife is its heart.

Somali Saying

The next day was so beautiful I felt personally blessed by Allah. There were some high thin clouds and the morning was a fine one. We saw some lightning at dawn, an omen of rain. The intense heat of the previous days evaporated, chased away by the rain. Most importantly, my family was altogether. What a miracle! A little voice inside my head whispered, 'Didn't I tell you everything was going to be fine?' It was my spirit guide, Old Man, talking to me.

My mother sent Rashid and Mohammed to catch one of the baby goats to make a feast for us. They slaughtered the little white male goat because he would not give milk. My mother cut the head off, put it in a basket and very carefully scraped all the skin off and removed the eyes. The head of an animal is believed to hold special powers to heal the eyes and the brain and my mother was praying the entire time she prepared this medicine for my father. She only has one cooking pot and needed that for the rest of the meal so she didn't have anything to cook the head in. She went to the garbage dump and came back with an old can. 'Mama!' I said. 'You can't use an old can from the garbage to cook something in. It's filthy and full of germs. What do you want to do, kill father?'

She looked at me with her hands on her hips. 'I don't really give a care if he dies, he's old and useless anyway, so never mind.'

'Mama, please let me go and borrow one from somebody,' I pleaded.

'No, you are not touching this,' she said shaking her finger in my face. 'I am going to do this, and I'm going to do it my way. Trust me, your father's not going to die from this – he's never going to die, he's too mean.' I could hear my father laughing from behind the house and of course as soon as she said it I realized that the boiling water would kill any germs. 'Child, step out of the way. This is how it's going to cook and he will drink this later,' she said. The can was rusty and she scoured it with clean sand and rinsed it out. She put the goat head inside and filled it with water and some of the special dried leaves she keeps in a small basket to boil on the fire. She tended that head all day long to prepare the special soup for my father.

My mother carefully took the skin off the rest of the goat and saved it to make rope and stools. She dug a hole big enough to hold the animal, and deep enough to hold a fire as well. Nhur and I built a fire with big pieces of wood and when all the wood burned down to white hot coals Mama raked them smooth so she could put the goat on them. She sliced the legs so they could be tucked up close to the body.

You can put whatever you want inside the body of the goat but she put bread, garlic, onions, tomatoes, rice and her special spices. She and Nhur tied it up and placed the meat on top of the glowing coals. Steam and a wonderful smell filled the air and mother knew just when to turn the animal over to the other side so both sides got seared in the fire which keeps the outside dry. Nhur buried it with more glowing coals and ashes from the fire. Mother squatted down next to the fire and fanned it to get the coals hot again, then she shooed everybody away. I was so hungry the smell just about drove me crazy. 'Leave it alone,' she snapped. 'I'll tell you when it's ready. You people are like vultures standing around here.'

When we dug it out the meat was falling apart and melted in my mouth it was so tender. It was absolutely delicious. My father's face was so swollen and painful that he couldn't chew and right before we gathered to eat the goat my mother said his medicine was ready. The goat head had cooked down to a thick gel. She put it into a cup and told me, 'Take this to your father, take it to him.'

I sat down next to him and said, 'OK, Papa, the soup is ready.'

'Is it the same thing that you were fighting over this morning?'

'Yes, Papa. It's good though, it's good for your eyes.'

He said, 'Ah, I don't feel like drinking it now.'

My mother heard that and shouted, 'Hey – what did he say?'

'Mama, he's not going to drink it right now,' I told her.

'What a stinking old man!' she muttered loud enough for the entire camp to hear. 'I made that special medicine and he doesn't want to drink it.' Then she called to me, 'Waris, you bring it right back over here then.' I started to get up but she changed her mind and stated, 'No, you leave it right there. He's not getting anything else until he drinks that.' My father made a pouty mouth like a little baby but sure enough he drank it – the whole thing.

My mother continued haranguing him on her side of the fire, 'Now you are in my land, you hear! You are blind and old and hopeless. You will do whatever I say, you hear me.' What could he do? He had to let her take care of him; he had to drink the special medicine she made for him.

'Who are these other wives? When we went back to Father's house there were three children he said were his,' I asked my mother.

'Well,' she said, 'he says he got rid of one just before you got here. I heard she left him.'

'Why?' I asked. 'What happened?'

'I have no idea why, he doesn't tell me anything,' she said. 'He usually lives with his second wife,' she said matter-of-factly. 'I bet she'll be along to find him and see if you brought her a present.' Mama went back to moving her cooking pots over the fire and it was clear that I wasn't going to hear any more about this from her.

'Burhaan,' I asked, 'Is Father still living with the wife we hung upside down?' I hoped not. I hadn't seen his second wife since my brothers and I hung the poor woman upside down. It had been a big shock when my father came walking back into our camp so many years ago with another wife following behind him. She was not much older than I was but she was not a shy little girl at all. She took over and started ordering my brothers and me around like she was some Somali queen and we were the servants. One day when my father was away, my brothers and I tied her up and hung her from a tree. She behaved much better after that. If my father was still married to her I didn't know what she was going to say if she showed up.

402

'I don't think she remembers,' said Burhaan.

'How does he manage with three wives?' I asked my brother.

'Once a man had three wives,' he replied. 'They were all jealous of each other so they went to the husband and demanded to know who he loved the best. He told them to close their eyes and he would touch his favorite. The three wives closed their eyes and he touched them all, one after the other.'

Everybody was coming by to meet these relatives from so far away, see what they could get and maybe even say hello. I didn't have any idea what people needed so I brought every kind of thing I could think of – hair creams, soaps, combs, shampoos, toothbrushes and toothpaste. I gave Rashid a blue toothbrush and Colgate toothpaste with fluoride.

'What is this?' he asked.

I said, 'It's called a toothbrush. You put just a little bit of this paste on the bristles and then you brush like this.' I demonstrated with my finger.

He grunted at me and asked, 'Is this the thing that takes all of your gums away and then your teeth fall out?'

'Yes,' I hissed at him, rolling my eyes at the question, 'that's exactly what this does.'

'Well,' he said handing it back to me, 'I already have a *caday* (tooth cleaner),' and he pulled a twig about half an inch thick and three inches long from the pocket of his shirt. 'If you have a toothache this will help. Does the toothbrush do that?'

'No.'

'The camels and goats like to eat this. Can they eat that blue thing?'

'No, this is just for your teeth.'

403

'Can you eat the stuff in the tube?'

'No, you have to spit it out. It's not good to swallow it.'

'Why do you put something that isn't good for you in your mouth?'

'You just rinse your mouth out with water. It won't hurt you unless you swallow it.'

'Well that is a waste of water. What if you don't have the water to rinse with?'

I didn't have an answer and he went on to explain that when you find a good toothbrush tree you can make tooth cleaners out of the soft new twigs and the older ones are good for spears. You can use the bigger branches for firewood or build a windbreak. The bark on the roots will give you a blister but Mother makes tea from the leaves for people who suffer muscle aches and she grinds them into an antiseptic paste to put on cuts and wounds.

'The seeds contain oil and are edible,' he lectured me. 'When there is nothing else to eat they will keep you alive. Will this toothpaste keep you alive in the dry season?' he asked looking at the little cap with its perfectly formed ridges.

'OK, OK,' I said putting it back in my bag. I gave him a razor but I could tell he was not pleased. I tried to give the toothbrush to Nhur but she also declined.

Burhaan said that the young twigs of the toothbrush tree have resins that kill bacteria in the teeth. 'If you have a stain on your teeth from *khat* or something, we use charcoal to get it off,' he explained and flashed his beautiful teeth at me. They were perfectly white like a light, and lined up in a neat row.

'I know, I know,' I said waving my arms because I was exasperated with all of them. 'I was born here, I know these things. You chew the charcoal, and then you chew a little bit

---

off the end of the Somali tooth stick. You take the tooth stick and rub your teeth with charcoal powder to have the best and whitest teeth.'

'The best teeth you have ever seen,' Rashid said defiantly.

I decided to give the toothbrushes away to some other people. Before I left New York I thought, maybe they need toothbrushes. They don't have dentists and they need to take care of their teeth. Maybe there are no trees and they can't find the tooth stick – I didn't know. I wished I had brought things like shoes and clothes. Food I couldn't bring because it would be spoiled by the time I got there, and that is what they needed most.

That afternoon I sat next to my father, and tried to help him up and fix his pillow and his blanket. I had to put the drops in his eye and I cried when I saw it. It was bruised and swollen with infection. I knew it would be a miracle if he ever opened it again. How could anyone let someone cut his eye open with a knife? It was too much to bear. I gave him some Tylenol for the pain and I was pleased that I had brought it. At least there was one little thing I could do for my father. When I gave him the sandals I brought from New York he felt the leather and ran his finger around the bottom of the thick rubber sole. 'I know who will be able to use these,' he said. 'I'm going to save them for your brother, Rashid,' he said.

When he needed to go to the bathroom someone had to help him because he was weak and unsteady and couldn't see anything. He called for my mother but I said, 'Papa, I'm right here. I'll take you.'

'Are there any shoes around here?' he said.

I found some white flip-flops and put them side by side in front of his feet. 'Let me help you,' I said. 'Give me your hands.'

'No, I'm not that blind. Put the shoes down and I will find them,' he said getting into a squat and feeling around with his toes for the shoes. When he had them on his feet he said, 'Get your mother for me.'

'She's not here, Papa. I don't know where she is.'

'I'll wait for her,' he said and wrapped his arms around his legs.

'I can help you, Papa. I am your child, and I have a child of my own. I can help you,' I told him, but he refused my help. He was not going to listen to me. He just stayed there like a sculpture next to the house waiting for my mother. He sat there for over an hour, proud and stubborn.

I decided to take a nap because I was still tired from all the traveling. I put some mats out and lay down. However, it was impossible to sleep because of everybody coming and going and all the noise. I heard a woman talking to my mother then she walked over to where I was lying down.

'Waris!' she said with a big greeting in her voice. 'How are you?'

Half dazed, I didn't get up. I thought it was somebody who just came by to meet me. I certainly didn't recognize her.

'Waris, you don't remember me do you?' she said, cocking her head to the side like I should know her.

'A lot has changed,' I said. My father was lying there laughing. I looked at her real hard. She looked like she was the same age as my mother.

'Ask your father who I am,' she said.

He said to her, 'How's my baby today?' I wondered what baby he was talking about.

'I'll get him,' she said.

My father lay there and chuckled under his breath until she came back with a little baby in her arms. 'Give me my son,' my father said and then I realized that this was his second wife. She looked like she was as old as my mother but when he first married her, she and I were almost the same age.

I hugged her and said, 'When I left you were having a baby, and now after all these years you are still with a baby.' Dear God I hope she can't remember the time we hung her upside down, I thought. She stayed with us for three nights and never mentioned what we did to her. She had walked for a long way with the baby on her back to get to us. The poor woman was in bad shape; she was hungry and tired. She did not have shoes and her feet were bleeding. That's how I met a brother I hadn't even known about. I have a brother nearly forty years old and I have a brother who is three weeks old.

My father said, 'There is no use living if you have no family and no children.'

I said, 'You know, Father, it's not how many children you have; it's how strong and healthy and how united you are that is more important.'

He said, 'Don't tell me.'

That night around the fire we had a big discussion about men. Burhaan told me that my sister-in-law was asking why I wasn't married.

I said, 'It's not that easy. It's not like one of your camels or goats. You can't buy it and then sell it when you don't want it anymore. Nhur just looked at me and I knew she couldn't understand. That is how they are brought up and that is the only thing that they know – obeying a man. Nhur and her mother asked me if I had a baby.

'Yes, I have a beautiful baby boy,' I told them.

My mother asked, 'Is he anything like you?'

'In every way,' I assured her. She looked at me and rolled her eyes up to Allah. She didn't say anything but 'Uh huh!'

but everybody laughed especially my father. Mama shook her head and said, 'If your child is anything like you, you are going to have some interesting times with him, and you deserve it!'

Nhur said, 'Well, where is his father?'

I said, 'I kicked him out of my life.'

'Why?' they all cried together.

I said, 'Because I had no use for him in my life or my son's life; not at this point anyway.' They all laughed at that, but they were shocked.

'How did you do that?' asked Asha. 'Didn't he kick you out? I thought the man kicked the woman out.'

I said, 'No.'

My sister-in-law stopped laughing and she got very serious. She said, 'We are weak here. The women in this country couldn't do that.'

I said, 'Sister, I was born here. I was raised right here just like you. I learned a lot of great things here, like confidence. I also learned to be self-reliant. I don't sit around and wait for somebody else to do something – I get up and do it. That's what I learned here.' My father was sitting right next to me and my mother came over and joined us. I suppose she wanted to hear what everybody was laughing at. Those women laughed at me saying I learned confidence in Somalia. I said, 'Ask my father and my brothers, they are sitting right here. My brothers know what I am like and what I was like as a child.' I told them, 'Ask my parents, they know exactly what I am and who I am.'

My father joined in and said, 'Oh yes, if she decided to say, "this woman is a rock," there is nothing you could do but let her go. I always thought she was the one with a head like a rock.' Everybody enjoyed that quip, especially my Uncle Ahmed.

'Did you come back to look for a husband?' Nhur said. She just could not believe that I was not married; yet I had money. I was not a beggar.

'No,' I told her. 'I didn't come here to find a husband. I am not married and I have a child but I am not especially looking for a man. When I find one that suits me, then I will think about getting married. That is who I am.' I crossed my arms; I didn't care what they thought.

My father said, 'You are what you are.'

I said to him, 'Do you remember the day you told me, "You aren't one of my children because I don't know where you came from?" You said you had to get rid of me. Do you remember that?'

'I think so,' he said. He looked over in my direction and I could hear the regret in his voice that he once talked to me that way. Every single person was silent and I knew it was because I am the only one of my family who is really standing on her own today. I am very proud of that.

I tried to explain to my father and mother what Guban did to me when I was a small girl. My father asked over and over, 'What did he do?' Neither of my parents remembered anything about that terrible day. I asked if they remembered the afternoon Guban went with me to get the lambs.

'When we were far enough away so nobody could hear he grabbed me and I tried to get away. When I finally broke loose I was covered with sticky smelly stuff.' The words seemed to stick in my mouth. My heart was pounding and I started to sweat. Talking about what Guban did was painful – everyone stared at me and I was too embarrassed to say any more.

My mother shook her head, 'I don't remember him bothering you Waris. What are you talking about?'

'I can't tell you but he was a bad man.'

Father said, 'Child, I don't really even know who you are talking about.' He couldn't remember anybody named Guban and I explained that a relative they took into our home, a person they trusted had attacked me.

My mother said, 'We don't know what happened to you. We haven't seen Guban for many, many years.'

'I hope he's dead and that he went to hell!'

My father and mother were upset that I was so angry with him. 'That's not very nice,' my mother said, stroking my leg to comfort me. 'What are you saying?'

I finally decided that there was no point in going back over it again. Words about such a taboo subject would not come out with my father and mother sitting right there. Maybe a *djinn* slides into your mouth and sits on your tongue. 'You don't know but he did something very bad,' I finally said and everyone became very quiet. I wanted desperately to tell them exactly what happened, but I couldn't. We don't talk about such things – ever. However, the long silence was strangely comforting. At least my parents understood that Guban did a terrible thing to their daughter. The worst emotional pain is to be sexually violated and have everyone ignore it. Nobody said anything for a long time and Mama patted my leg with a worried face. She kept looking into my eyes to read their secrets and what she saw troubled her, but she wouldn't ask – we don't talk about such things. If you aren't allowed to talk about sex, you better sew the girls shut because then, like me, they won't know what is happening to them.

Sometimes great pain is a great gift and I believe that Allah had given me a gift. I knew now where to start with my campaign to eliminate female genital mutilation. Women had to be educated about sex. Men needed to know about women's bodies as well as their own.

My little cousin Amina interruped my thoughts, 'Could you take a letter for me to America?'

'America is a big place. I have to have an address.'

Her eyes filled with anxiety and she twisted her dress between her fingers. 'I have the address and I will give it to you.'

'Who lives there?' I asked, curious about who she knew.

'My husband is there,' she said quietly, not even looking into my eyes.

'What is your husband doing there?' I asked her, shaking my head. She mumbled something and I thought she couldn't have any idea what he was doing there. 'How long have you been married?'

She said, 'Four years.' I couldn't believe it; she looked like she was only sixteen.

'Do you have children?'

'No. He chose me and left me. I hope he'll come back and take me to wherever he is.'

I told her 'Don't wait for him!' Several people gasped and my mother shook her head and clicked her tongue against the roof of her mouth in disapproval. I agreed to take the letter. I didn't want to make any more trouble.

My family found most of my ideas upsetting or funny. My cousin said, 'Waris, you talk like a man and you act like you are very strong.'

'You can be strong too. Look, I was raised here just like you.' They all laughed at me again. I felt like I was the local comedy act. Everywhere I went people followed me. Basically I decided it was for two reasons. First because they thought I was rich, and second because they thought I was crazy and different. Despite all that I felt proud and grateful to be in my village and I was so glad I made it. I thanked Allah again and again. It was a miracle to find not only my mother but my brothers and all these cousins, nephews and other relatives I never even knew I had.

One of the most important things to me was that I was face to face with my father and feeling equal. I couldn't agree with some of what he said and I carefully explained what I thought. He asked questions when he didn't understand what I said. I educated him and he was pleased. He kept joking, 'Are you sure this is my daughter?' 'Who are you?' he repeated over and over. 'I thought my daughter was dead and gone a long time ago.'

'Why?'

'When a little girl runs away from her father what good can happen? The only things that you knew were your camels and your goats. First I thought that you were killed and eaten by lions and the hyenas sucked out the marrow in your bones. Then I heard you were in Mogadishu and London so I assumed you must be a prostitute. What else could you do? You went so far it's like you traveled to another *hydigi*, another planet, all by yourself. Child, you are alive and you are able to make a living all by yourself! You are talking with power and dignity.'

My father was proud of me; he was proud of me! That made me feel strong, passionate about life, and proud of myself. Once I was the little girl my father used to beat. If he noticed me at all he would say, 'Hey you! Get that for me. Hurry up!' I was terrified of him. When he could see me with his eyes, he saw a girl of no consequence. Now my father could see with the eyes of his heart. *Allah Bah Wain,* God is Great.

11

desert life

A daughter is not a guest

African Proverb

Every afternoon for the next several days it rained with heavy drops gushing out of gray clouds. Everyone watched the clouds gather and fill the sky all afternoon, waiting for the rain. The *gu* or rainy season took over the village and changed everything, but nobody complained. The hot, hot weather was gone, cooled off by the blessing of water. The town had a river running down the middle of the street where dust blew a few days before. My mother's little hut was totally flooded. Everything was soaked, even the poor little goats. They didn't know what to do and hid in the house, shaking and wet right to the ends of their brown tails. My brother, Burhaan, dug a trench around his house to try and keep the water from going inside. Everybody was smiling and happy because we love the rain so much. The little babies sat and played in the muddy water and sad to say, kept drinking it too. I knew they would soon be sick from diarrhea and be shitting all over the place. Women gathered water in the streets and poured their little buckets into bigger containers so the dirt would settle to the bottom and the water could be used for cooking and bathing.

We got up each day around six o'clock with the roosters crowing and the birds starting to gossip and the chickens squabbling about this and that. There were no lights after the sun dropped below the distant horizon and closed its eyes so everybody went to bed early and got up with the sun. There was not much to do at night and sometimes the shops ran out of oil for the lamps. It seemed like supplies were erratic, I suppose due to the dangerous conditions around Mogadishu.

Mohammed was sleeping at my uncle's house, and it was crowded there. Of course in this little village, there were no hotels or extra places to stay. Everything was used all the time. When someone came for a visit, everybody moved over a little bit to make room.

'Did you sleep well?' I said.

Mohammed brushed his hand in the air like he was swatting a fly. 'The next time we come back I want to have the extra room on Burhaan's house finished so we can all sleep together,' he said. Mohammed went into Mama's house to fill her yellow plastic pot with water to wash, bumping his head on the low door. He sat on a low stool in the courtyard, took off his glasses, carefully placed them on a rock and washed his face and arms. He took a little water in his hand and rubbed it all over his face and up and down his bare arms then he faced the sun for a moment to dry. He took off his right shoe and sock and washed his foot, and then he put them back on so he could balance while he did the other.

I noticed that all the trees and bushes had a wisp of light green color and only a few days ago they had seemed defeated and dead. My skin believes that all of the shrubs in Somalia have thorns. They need every bit of life they have and in the *jilaal* or dry season, the sharp thorns say, 'Stay away, I have nothing for you.' When it rains the leaves grow very quickly, everything is full of joy.

I didn't especially enjoy using the local bathroom. My mother does not have her own, you have to share, and you could smell it before you saw it. It was a small square room less than four feet on each side with a latch-less wooden door and open to the sky. In the middle of the cement floor was a small square hole. You squat over the hole and do your business, which falls into a deep hole. It smelled serious; the floor was wet and dirty and I was in and out as quick as I could be. People walked barefoot over rocks and through thorn bushes but not to the bathroom. If you didn't have any shoes you waited until somebody walked by with a pair you could borrow.

On the way back I saw some little village boys watching me. One boy had skin as black as I ever saw gleaming in the sunshine. 'Oh Blackie, Blackie,' I called to him. 'Give me your beautiful skin!' I got my camera to take some pictures of them and I also wanted to film my family. The boys danced around and smiled when they weren't staring at me. They posed for the camera with beautiful white teeth framed by lovely black faces. Every single child wore a protective leather amulet around their neck. Allah was everywhere.

Taking pictures of my family was a different matter. As soon as Mohammed saw me come back to the house with my camera, he started shouting at everyone, 'Do not let her take pictures of you until you're dressed up. Don't let her photograph you looking like that, she is going to sell the pictures to the magazines!' He would not stop sticking out his tongue at the camera and waving his hands so I couldn't get a good shot. Burhaan got up and went inside his house and wouldn't come back out. He looked out through the metal bars over his windows and backed away whenever I raised the camera to take his picture.

I shouted at them, 'Don't be ridiculous. I'm not selling your picture to any fashion magazines! Come on, I am just taking a few snapshots for myself. I want to show them to my friends. Come back out here, you guys.' I gave up on the boys and turned to my mother, 'Mama, mama, let me take your picture. I just want to have a picture of you to take back with me.'

Mohammed said, 'No, no, she is going to sell it to some magazine for the cover, I guarantee you!' Everybody thought he was serious. He told them to put on their best clothes and wash so they wouldn't be dusty and dirty in the pictures. 'If she takes a picture of you all dusty, beat her up! Break the camera,' he told them.

I stood right in front of my pesky brother and shouted at him, 'Mohammed! You're crazy and you know it. Stop telling them that.'

'No, no,' he said, enjoying the game. He pointed at me and repeated like he was some big authority on the subject, 'She's going to the fashion magazines.'

Finally I told them, 'You people look like a bunch of refugees! You know that. The only place I'm going to sell your picture is The National Geographic! I'm serious.' I couldn't believe they were giving me so much trouble over a little family snapshot I would get developed at the drugstore. '*Hoyo*, Mother,' I pleaded, 'please let me take your picture.'

'I'm busy,' she said. She never stopped; she was always doing something from early in the morning before anyone else even got up, until late at night.

'*Hoyo*,' I begged, 'please sit still. I want some pictures of you to show my son. I want him to know his grandmother and family.'

'Well then, take the picture,' she snapped, standing like a stick.

Rashid stood in front to block my shot and said, 'Mama, you have to put on some other dress for a picture.'

'I already got dressed this morning,' Mama said.

He snatched at her ragged brown dress and insisted, 'Go put on the one I bought for you. You can't wear this old thing in a picture.'

Mama muttered at him to leave her alone but she went inside her house and came out wearing another dress over the top of the old brown one. It had deep purple stripes and yellow flowers. She is so thin that it didn't show that she was wearing everything she owned. Suddenly she was shy and put her *chalmut* over her face while I snapped the camera shutter. Mohammed sat on his three-legged stool and kept ordering everybody around, as usual. He told her you had to stick out your tongue in pictures and of course she listened to him.

'Burhaan,' I pleaded. 'Help me take some pictures of *Aba*.' Burhaan and Mohammed went to get him. They supported him between them and walked him carefully out into the sun so he would not trip.

'Oh, it's the beautiful Dirie family,' I said with the video camera rolling. I noticed that my father was not as tall as Mohammed anymore. When *Aba* realized that I was taking a picture of him supported by my brothers he pushed both of them away from him and stood alone, erect and dignified even with a bandage covering one eye and the other blind. He would not have his picture taken leaning on somebody. He looked like the powerful father I knew as a child. Nothing could take the strength in his spirit from him.

Nhur was eight months pregnant but every day she walked all the way into town to get clean drinking water from the only supply. It was a standpipe and you could fill your jug for ten shillings. She carried six gallons back by herself. She filled two jugs and carried one in each hand. I saw her coming over the hill with the two jugs of water. She went a little way then stopped to rest and catch her breath. I ran to help her as soon as I saw her. Meanwhile my brothers sat around the house talking and arguing about politics. I said to her, 'Where is that useless husband of yours? Doing nothing. Why do you allow this?' She just gave me a look.

When Nhur came back from the well she walked to the village market in the heat to see what food was available that day. She bought rice wrapped in cones made of old newspaper and goat meat if she could find it. She bought spices wrapped in squares of paper; just enough for the day's pot of food, not a whole bottle. She gathered wood and built a cooking fire. She cut the meat into pieces and carefully removed the fat and bad parts. She cooked the rice and meat with a little oil, an onion or two and some tomato. She kept fanning the fire to keep it hot. When it was done, she piled the rice in the center of a round tin tray and made an indentation in the middle where she put the goat meat in its spicy sauce. She served the men the platter of rice with tea made with a little ghee. She cleaned the cooking pots while the men were eating. When they were finished she brought whatever was left over into the cooking area and only then did she eat with the children.

The first day I arrived Nhur's mother walked into the village from the desert encampment where she lived. She came back every day after that. She was one of the most beautiful women I have ever seen. She had green eyes and stood even taller than me. Her eyes and nose were evenly spaced and the shape of her face was a perfect oval but the woman had a faded rag for a dress, and I never saw her wear anything else. It might have been orange or red at one time, but it was so old it looked mostly gray. It must have been the only thing she had to put on her body. She, like most Somalis, was a proud woman and she would never, ever ask for anything. We fed her every day without a question because that is the way things are in my country.

I decided I had seen enough of this and the next day I told my sister-in-law, 'Nhur, I'll cook today. You go and visit with your beautiful mother. Nhur flashed me a smile and said she would get some water. She wrapped her blue *chalmut* over her head and took the water jugs. I put a bunch of wood on the fire to build it up and stuck the biggest pot I could find on top of it. It would not balance so I pushed the pot down hard and made a place for it in the wood so it wouldn't fall over. I filled it up with rice and beans and added water to the top.

The fire started to smoke because the wood was all wet from the rain. We didn't have any dry wood – there wasn't any place to keep it dry. I tried to fan it to get it burning hot again but it kept smoking and smoking. I was coughing and the smoke was getting in my eyes and burning me every time the wind shifted. I figured I did something wrong with the fire but I hadn't cooked on a fire in twenty years. Forever, really, because I didn't do a lot of cooking before I left Somalia. We don't have open cooking fires in New York City or London. I called Burhaan, 'Hey, come on over and help me with this would you?' I asked. He's been around a lot more fires than I have.

'That's women's work,' he said, sitting on the mats in the shade.

'Hey,' I said, 'I need some help over here.'

'Get Nhur to help you,' he said. 'Cooking is women's work.' He just watched me struggle and was totally unwilling to lend a hand because cooking is so-called women's work. He had nothing to do but sit there but he was still not going to help. I wanted to take off my shoe and beat him.

'Mohammed, don't you be as ridiculous as Burhaan,' I said. 'Get up and fix this fire or we won't eat.'

'That is not my problem. We do the men stuff,' he said.

'Like, what is the men stuff?' I stood up and asked. 'If something needs to be done, what is this, you do this, I can only do that business?' I threw a stick at the two of them and Mohammed threw it back at me, laughing. 'I don't see it,' I said. 'Would you sit there and starve if you didn't have a woman to cook for you?'

'No,' Burhaan laughed. 'We would just get the children to cook.' Finally Nhur came back with more water, walking slowly with her big baby belly. She put the water down and lifted that heavy pot off the fire. She poked the sticks around and positioned them differently. She put bigger sticks on either side and balanced the pot on top. Then she squatted down in front of the fire and fanned it back to life.

'One of the things that has ruined this country is *khat*,' I said to my brothers.

'We don't have any *khat* today,' Rashid said.

'If you could get it you would be chewing it,' I said. I hated that he had started that horrid habit. 'Men don't have any motivation,' I told them. 'They are not using their minds and they are wasting their lives sitting around chewing a ridiculous weed.'

After we ate I went to be with my mother. We were sitting in her little hut talking because it was raining outside. My aunt got up to go outside to the bathroom and I said, 'Can I hold him?' so she left me with her little baby. He looked just like me and we connected. He wouldn't cry if I held him. When we talked he would look me right in the eyes.

Mama went to get a little bit of goat milk she was saving for him in a cup. In Somalia we don't have baby bottles or cups. You just take the child's cheeks and gently squeeze them together then hold the cup up and carefully adjust it so the baby can suck on the edge of the cup. My nephew had such an itty-bitty perfect little mouth. I was happy to feed him but I heard my mother muttering under her breath.

She was talking to herself as she got the milk, 'Oh my God, don't leave the baby with her,' she said. 'Is she going to feed the baby? Does she know what she is doing?' She wasn't saying it to anyone, just talking to herself out loud.

I looked at her and said, 'Mama, what do you think I am? Am I that hopeless? Don't you know I am a mother myself?'

'*Hiiyea*,' she acknowledged.

'Like I am thirty something years old.'

'*Hiiyea.*'

'Didn't you raise me here?'

My mother looked at me and she said, 'Oh yes, that's right,' but she said it like she had no confidence in me.

I said, 'Come over and sit next to me. I am offended by what you said.' She gave me the cup and I took the baby's face and gently placed my opened fingers around his mouth while I held him close. He drank it without spilling one precious drop.

She said, 'Ah child, I didn't mean it like that. I thought

---

you lived so differently that you forgot what to do with the children.'

I had to think why she said that before I answered her. I thought she probably thinks I forgot everything I learned and what she taught me. Maybe that is what she is thinking. I said, 'Mama, I raised my own child myself and I fed him the way you taught me. You taught me how to feed a baby. This is something that I will never forget because you showed me. Please don't think that I don't know how to take care of children properly.'

'I'm sorry, Waris,' she said looking at me sideways. I think my mother was pleased with me. Even though we had a little fight, she could see that I valued her ways, and the things she taught me. I didn't forget the important things because I lived in a different place.

I am a very self-reliant person because of where I grew up. I learned how to do a lot of things most people don't do, like cutting hair so I tried to cut my baby brother's hair. There were no barbers in town and Rashid complained that his was getting too long.

'Father keeps asking me why I am hanging around here. I have to get back to the animals,' he said. 'I can't sit around and wait for a barber to show up.'

But when I picked up the scissors everyone said, 'Ah, no, no!'

I asked, 'What do you mean?'

They said, 'You can't do that.'

I said, 'I know how to cut hair. You can trust me.'

'No, Waris, that's not the point,' my father said flatly and waved his finger in the air.

'Well, what's the point then?'

'You can't have a woman cut a man's hair.'

'What are you talking about?' I said, totally exasperated

with them again. 'What difference does it make who cuts his hair? Are the camels going to notice?'

They all cried, 'He would be laughed at.'

I said, 'Who is going to laugh at him? You? Are you that way?'

'Don't worry, he's going to be laughed at,' my father insisted.

I found it hard to accept and I argued, 'As long as I know how to cut hair, and I have the intelligence to do it, what's the problem?'

My father said, 'That is not the real reason, Waris. That is just the way things are here.'

I said, 'Papa, don't insult my intelligence, please. It's not like I don't know the system, like I don't know the culture.' This is the clash we always had. I asked him and all my brothers, 'So when are you going to change?' I told them, 'It's like this circumcision thing with women. The women are ready to change.' A silence fell over the room like a cloud covering the sun. I knew that they would not discuss this in mixed company, if at all. 'You let me take your pictures,' I said, changing the subject. 'Yet a lot of people here believe that will steal your spirit.'

'Only ignorant people still believe that,' Burhaan said.

'Why is a woman cutting a man's hair different than that?'

I tried and tried to reason with them but I got nowhere. I could provoke them all I wanted, they were not going to change the way they did things. Still I could not get angry. I was so happy to be sitting in front of a hut with my mother, my father, my brothers and people I have not seen in so very long. I said, 'This is a dream I've been dreaming for thirty years. At least I think I'm almost thirty years old, I don't know.'

My father raised his head up and said, 'I think you are nearly forty.' Mohammed and I cracked up.

My mother said, 'No she's not. Burhaan is around twenty-seven years old and he follows her by two years or so.' Her voice trailed off because she didn't know how old any of us were any more than my father did.

I didn't care that dates were not important to my parents. Here I was under the stars of a beautiful African night. I forgot how many stars there are in the sky or maybe they had star babies while I was gone for so many years. It was so clear I felt like I could reach up and milk the sky. It's true what they say; there is no feeling like it – there is no feeling like home. Oh how I missed that feeling of belonging to something much greater than myself. I regretted that I hadn't been there for so many years. I had not seen my people age and grow old. I had not been there when they needed me. My father said, 'Don't worry about me, it's only age Waris, I am still strong. Tomorrow I am going to find me another big wife and have a couple more children to take care of the goats.' I loved that he was still cracking jokes and I realized how much I had missed my father and how much I cared about him. I pretended to be tough at one point and said, 'You did this to me, you made me run away,' but I wouldn't change a thing, not one thing in my life. I have said that before and I will say it again. I wish I could bring the time back but there is no regret in my mind. We all stumble through life and even though I didn't have a pair of shoes to cushion my rocky path, I don't regret the path I walked. Some parts have been hard; some things have been wonderful, but it is all experience and everything has a time and a place. I used to dream and wish that my father and mother and my sister and my brothers were in one place because I never had that. Now I had this one amazing week with my family. It was a dream that I wished for my whole life and I thanked Allah it came true.

12

somali education

To bear a girl is to bear a problem

Somali Saying

My mother's little village was full of people who left Mogadishu to find somewhere safe to live. They were running away from stray bullets and the constant battles for control in the streets. The village had grown like a column of army ants. There was not enough water, no electricity, no doctors, no medical dispensary and the nearest hospital was over a hundred miles away. When I asked about schools for the children Ragge told me 'I teach.'

Curious, I asked him, 'Where? I didn't know there was a school in this little place.'

'Come on and I'll show you,' he told me. Last year Ragge and a clansman from Mogadishu decided to put together a school. They got enough money from the United Nations Children's Fund to build one square room with a tin roof and a dirt floor. They opened a school for the children in the village. Ragge was educated in Mogadishu where my uncle was once a businessman. He knew how to read in Somali, Arabic, Italian and English. He didn't have a job so he thought, well, at least I can teach the children. His English was excellent and I enjoyed talking to him.

He said, 'Tomorrow morning I'll stop by and pick you up on my way to the school. Be ready.'

'OK, I'll be ready,' I said, eager to support him and the school in whatever way I could.

The next morning the goats still had long shadows when he came and called to me in the house, 'Are you ready?'

'Of course,' I replied and came outside to go with him. Every day the sun beamed down so strong that I got up early, very early. By six o'clock I already had breakfast and was dressed and ready to go. Nobody knows or cares what time it is because the sun gets you up and gets you moving and the dark puts you to sleep at night.

When I ducked my head and came out of the little hut my mother was sitting there cleaning her teeth with her tooth stick. She took it out of her mouth and said, 'Where does she think she's going?' She snatched at my dress as if it was an old rag.

I said, 'What? Mama – what's the matter with what I'm wearing?' My dress was the one I wore around the house. It was a long Somali *dirah* with a white petticoat underneath. I held a scarf that I borrowed from Dhura in Amsterdam. She kept shaking her head and I took my dress out of her hands and said, 'Who am I dressing for? I'm just going over to the school.'

My mother rolled her eyes and put both hands up in the air as if I had on a mini-skirt. She waved her palms in my face. 'I don't know where you came from girl, but you are not stepping out of the house looking like that. No, you are not shaming me with this dress.'

What was so shameful in what I had on? I wailed, 'Mama, look, I am all covered up.' I put the scarf on my head and turned around to show her that I was properly covered from head to toe.

She said, 'Get back in the house and get dressed nicely to go to the school.'

I said, 'What is the problem? Would you mind telling me what is the problem with what I am wearing?' Nhur and my mother were both shouting at me and acting like I had offended the Prophet Mohammed himself. They told me the color was tacky, the scarf didn't match, and to put on my nice dress. They acted like I was going to meet the queen or the president. I couldn't believe all this fuss. 'You've got to be kidding me! Getting dressed up is one thing that I know. Do you know Gucci? Have you ever heard of Armani? One of those dresses could feed this village for a week.'

'Why would you eat a dress?' Nhur asked and I realized that there was no way they could understand. I have talked to hundreds of people all over the world and been on television. I know how to dress! My own family treated me like a stupid, ignorant child and it was hopeless for me to protest. I had to listen to people who were sharing two pairs of flip-flops and had never used a napkin or been in an elevator. Ragge just stood there looking the other way. He was not going to get into the middle of this, no matter how he felt.

My mother insisted, 'No, you have to change.' She took my hands and gently led me back inside her little hut. In Somalia even a woman suffering from malnutrition will dress in the best things she can and carry herself regally. How you dress and carry yourself is all they worry about. I was concerned with getting people clean water, proper medical care and good schools; what did my dress mean? However, when my mother is determined, you will listen and do what she tells you. I had to take off the cool cotton *dirah* and put on my best one with the embroidered petticoat and the slippery silk scarf that matched. Mother said, 'Yes, put that one on, wear that one, the other one looked like you were some kind of woman without a good family or something.'

It was already getting hot as the sun climbed up over the house and I was sweating. Worried that I would make Ragge late for school I ripped everything off and dug through my suitcase to find my good dress. Then I had to get dressed all over again being careful not to let anything fall on the dirt floor of the tiny little hut. I could barely stand up straight inside and the sun beat through the tin roof making it into an oven.

Mama was not satisfied until I put on the silk scarf that would not stay on my head no matter how I tried to drape it. It had to be tied tightly around my neck for fear it would slip off and get dirty in the mud. When I went back outside another chorus of 'No, no, that dress is see through!' greeted me. 'Are you crazy? Put something under the top. Do you have a T-shirt?'

Putting my foot down I said, 'No, I don't want to put one on because it's too hot. I'm already sweating and it's still early.'

My three brothers showed up out of nowhere. They came around the corner, three tall men, arm in arm. Whenever you need them they are never around, but suddenly they were all over the place like a pack of hyenas nipping at me from every direction. 'Hey, what is she doing!' they all said.

Mohammed got very official like he was the boss of everybody. 'No, no you can't go like that,' he told me shaking his head. Everybody was all over me, all over again. I gave up and put on everything they told me just to get out of there.

Ragge was laughing and laughing as we walked through the village to the school. I told him to cut it out or I wasn't even going to go to his darn school and that made him whoop he laughed so hard. My official visit dressed up in my very best outfit was to one brick room with two holes cut out for windows, a flimsy wooden door, a dirt floor and covered by a flat tin roof. I looked fabulous.

There must have been a hundred children of all ages running and chasing each other all around. Ragge and his friend, Ali, who said he was the headmaster, were in charge of the school. Ragge clapped his hands and shouted to the children, 'Get in line, it's time to go in for school.' They don't start at some pre-determined time that it says on a clock; school begins whenever the teachers get there. The children immediately started to line up and go inside. The girls looked like flowers with bright blue and yellow dresses and red scarves. Most of them had dresses made from the same pattern, it was probably the only cloth in town. One of the girls had a round face like a ball and ears that stuck out to the side. She looked at me shyly and gave me the biggest smile when she passed by like she admired me. She reminded me of myself as a child because she was bold enough to look me right in the eyes and I loved her for that. I was amazed that somebody thought I was somebody! Most of the boys wore what looked to me like old school uniforms; white shirts with blue piping at the collars and cuffs. Several boys had on long blue pants that were so big on their skinny bones they dragged in the dirt. It was a wonder they didn't trip over them like I did on my dress. There were so many children that they were packed like bees in a hive. I thought, let them all settle down and then

I will go in and say good morning. I stood in front of the door and watched them all sit down together right on the dusty floor. They didn't have one single chair or table or even a book in the whole place. The kids sat on the dirt. A few had a thin cloth, but most were right on the packed earth floor. All those pairs of shining eyes looked up, they were so eager to learn but they had no materials to help them. I was proud that my cousin was trying to teach them. I could not understand why my father and brothers didn't trust Ragge. He didn't sit around all day complaining about how things were, he was trying to do something, trying to make a difference.

Ragge talked to the students and used a big stick to point at words. They didn't have a proper chalkboard but he had painted some of the wooden boards black. Every one of those sweet little children was listening to every single thing he said. They didn't even notice me taking pictures; they were so eager to learn. They watched the teacher as if he were a baby goat and they were hungry lions. Some of the boys were so intent they chewed on their pencil but most of the babies had absolutely nothing! If a child had a pencil and a piece of paper, that child was very rich. It was very sad for me to look at that and to think about the kids in my neighborhood who would rather hang around the street than go to school and learn something. I always wanted to go to school, to learn to read books easily and write and spell perfectly but I never had the chance. I have been working my whole life to support myself. I never had the opportunity to sit in a classroom and listen to a teacher. Everything I know I taught myself. Standing there I forgot about being hot and uncomfortable; school is a magic place for me.

Ragge asked if I would like to say hello to the children. 'I am so happy to meet you,' I said. 'School is a wonderful place and you are so lucky to have a teacher.' The children all wanted to know where I lived and I tried to tell them something about New York City. 'There are buildings so high you almost can't see the top. The streets are full of cars and they are all covered up with cement so there is no grass.'

Hands shot up and one of the boys asked, 'What do the goats eat?'

'There are no goats in New York.'

'How do you get milk to drink?' they all wanted to know.

I asked if anyone would like to come and live in New York and sad to say, almost every hand went up. The children were eager to leave Somalia, to get to the West even though they knew nothing about it – they just assumed it would be better than Somalia.

I asked the headmaster who built the building. He told me that UNICEF gave the village elders enough money to buy the bricks and the tin. The fathers worked together to build the school for their children. Ali showed me a sign on the front of the building from UNICEF. Already it was too crowded and more children lined up every morning. I asked him how the teachers were paid and he told me that they were lucky to get thirty dollars a month but they had not been paid for a long time. 'Somebody comes around with money every so often but I don't know if there is a Somali Ministry of Education any more, or if the funding is from the United Nations or where it comes from,' he told me.

'How can you get by without getting paid?'

'Teachers live because everybody helps everybody. If you go to somebody's house and they have food you don't have to ask for it; they will share whatever they have with you. Food is not what I worry about. Without a salary I can't build a life. I can't have a home of my own or get married or have children. See if you can help us,' Ali asked me. 'We don't get paid and we don't have any books or other supplies. Anything would help us.'

After I came out of the school I noticed that an old rooster was strutting around the school yard and crowing like he was the one in charge. He pecked importantly at the ground looking for a seed in the dust. I don't think anybody else noticed him and I feel that way about my country. People in the West don't notice my poor little country.

Nhur kept saying, 'We have to do some henna to celebrate your visit. You can't go home without henna,' she said. I was looking forward to it. It's an ancient tradition that celebrates a woman's beauty. Henna is a symbol of joy and is applied for your wedding night, or after you have a baby, to welcome the child to life. If a woman is very sick and is healed by God we will use henna to celebrate her return to life. Women may also apply it when they are going out to a celebration.

'Could you do it for me?' I asked Nhur but she declined. She wanted to wait for her cousin or two particular neighbors to do it. I didn't know when or if they would show up so I said, 'Let's not wait for them. You do it.' I just assumed that she could do henna designs as well as anybody, she lived in the village her whole life. I did notice that she wasn't wearing any, and Mama wasn't wearing any. Henna designs only last for about ten days so the darker and the deeper the color the better. Nhur and I went to the market one afternoon and brought back some henna. She mixed the powder with warm water, added a little bit of oil and stirred it into a paste. You let it sit for about ten minutes, then it is ready. Nhur picked up a stick and started to draw a design on my calf, down to my foot. The more she drew the more the designs started to all run together into a big puddle. I said, 'Hey, what's going on?'

Nhur explained that she really didn't know how to do henna designs. I didn't want to make her feel bad so I reassured her that it was OK. She carefully drew another henna design on the other leg and we had a nice talk. I offered her some oranges from the market but Nhur said she didn't want to eat them. 'I was so hungry when I was pregnant with Aleeke that I ate all the time,' I told her.

Nhur gave me a sad look. 'I don't want to eat so the baby won't get too big. I had a very difficult time when my daughter was born. They had to cut me open so that she could come out and sew the incision back up again.'

What could I say? I shook my head and patted her hand. I know the birth of a child is a big worry when you are infibulated. How will the baby be born when the opening is so small. 'I will pray that everything goes well for you,' I told her.

Nhur sang a little *hoobeyo*, or woman's song while she drew the designs. We always sing about our problems.

> *Oh my daughter, men have wronged us*
> *In a dwelling where there are no women*
> *No camels are milked*
> *Nor are the saddled horses mounted.*

After Nhur finished the designs on my arms and hands I went outside to sit in the sun, and let it dry. I was hot and I didn't want my henna to get all messed up while I was frying in the sun, so I took off my scarf and slip. I didn't want to sit in the sun all covered with clothes; I wanted to get a little tan. I pulled up my dress and tucked it under me and rolled up the sides to my shoulders. I sat with my arms and legs stretched out to that wonderful Somali sun like a lizard. Sorry to say my foot looked like I had stepped into red paint – like a cow's foot, but I didn't care. It felt so wonderful to be cared for and to be cared about by Nhur. It was a blessing from a sister-in-law I had grown to love.

Just as I got comfortable my brother Mohammed walked by and said, 'What! Did they lock her out of the little hut?'

My mother and Nhur heard him and they both rushed out shouting, 'Oh my God! Look at that, she has her dress up to her waist. Cover her up, cover her! What is she doing now?'

I looked up at the three of them dancing around like chickens chased by a dog. I said, 'Nhur, why don't you come over here because I'm going to slap you! You have given me enough problems already today.'

'Waris, you can't sit outside like this,' Nhur said shaking her head.

'Leave me alone you crazy woman,' I told her. 'What are you all worried about? Who is coming by this little hut and who is going to see? See what?'

I was laughing and they were sighing and saying, 'Oh she never changed, only she's worse now. She's even crazier than she was. She won't even listen now.'

Later that afternoon two women came by to visit with Nhur. I noticed that they had the most beautiful henna designs on their hands and feet. 'Who did these for you?' I asked. 'They are wonderful flowers and symbols.'

'We did it ourselves,' they said.

'Where do you live?' I asked.

'Right next door.'

Nhur said, 'These are the neighbors I wanted to do your henna, but you wanted me to do it.'

13

ummi

Ummi — An Arabic word meaning illiterate – untouched by knowledge from any source other than God

My mother, bless her heart, she won't stop. The day before we had to leave she disappeared for a long time. I looked for her all over the village and asked Mohammed, Rashid and Burhaan where she was. When Nhur came back from the outdoor market she told me Mama left before the chickens were up and squawking. Nhur pointed west into blue hills near the border with Ethiopia. When the sun's bottom squatted on the village I saw a tiny figure in the distance balancing a big load on her back. She looked like a *djinn* or a fire-spirit because the heat danced in waves all around her. Mama had gathered sticks and a huge dead branch, wrapped the dusty things in her *chalmut,* and tied it with a big knot. No wonder her headscarf was a rag! She used it to carry everything from goats to firewood. She lifted that heavy load and carried it from the other side of the horizon on her back. She had a five-gallon plastic jug in each hand filled with water. The wood wasn't enough; she had to get water at the well and carry that back too in the hottest part of the day.

I ran out to meet her and help her with that heavy load. 'Mama,' I shouted to her, 'why didn't you tell me where you were going? I would have helped you.'

She just shrugged and laughed at me, 'You were sleeping.'

'Mama!' I shouted and made her give me the water jugs. She looked at me with her funny smile and kept on walking. My mother is tougher than any three people I know. She has looked for wood every day of her life. While I have been strutting on the fashion runways in Paris and Milan she has been gathering the wood that Allah provides and sending smoke back up to Him.

Mother lifted the firewood off her back and talked to Nhur about what she found in the *suq* that morning. Some days there is very little to buy, even if you have money, and there hadn't been any meat that morning. Usually the skinned carcass of a goat or a sheep will hang on a nail to prove that it was properly slaughtered. The seller brushes the flies off and cuts out the part of the meat you want to buy – rib, shoulder, or leg. Each cut has a different price. Today, nothing had been available. My mother had carried wood back for a big fire, but we didn't have anything to cook but rice and goat milk. *Hoyo* called my brother Rashid. When I asked him to do something he argued with me, but when my mother said his name, he came to her immediately. She told him to go and get the last one of her baby goats. 'Go and find *Ourgi Yeri*, Little Baby,' she said and gestured in the direction of the termite mounds.

'What are you going to do with the pretty baby goat?' I

asked, but she ignored me and started building up the fire. *Ourgi Yeri*'s knees were black and brown against his white body, like he knelt in the mud to say prayers. 'Mama,' I pleaded, 'you don't need to do that. I don't have to eat meat, believe me I don't. Don't kill your baby goat because I'm here. Keep it for yourself! Please, Mama, I really don't care about meat.'

'Sometimes that is how life is, Waris,' Mama replied, firmly. She has so much faith that it spills over and fills up those around her. She believes that God will provide for her and I stopped my chatter.

Rashid didn't question her and he took the long slaughtering knife with him. Goats don't need much care in the rainy season when there are plenty of green shoots nearby for them to nibble on. Rashid quickly caught *Ourgi Yeri* and carried him in his arms to the back of the hut. Burhaan helped get him on his knees with his neck outstretched. The poor little thing knew something was up and he bleated and struggled. I couldn't watch them kill it, he was such a pretty animal. They needed to slaughter it properly or my family would not eat the meat. It was critical to slit his throat so that he would die quickly and without pain. That is the Muslim way.

It was upsetting because my mother loved that goat. Every morning she snuggled up to him and scratched him under his chin where a little beard was beginning to sprout. Those goats were everything to her, and no wonder – they provided milk and that was often the only thing she had to eat or give her family. The animals provided white nourishment to my brother's family, to little Mohammed, and to my mother's neighbors as well. Now she slaughtered the last young goat to feed her family. Mama gave whatever little thing she had without a thought for tomorrow.

Suddenly everything was silent and you could hear doves cooing on the neighbor's house. Mama was, of course, stoic, only she looked up at the soft hills for a minute. For me, hunger has a human face and it is my mother's. She only had five goats in this world, and three were left because we ate the two babies while we were there.

Rashid brought the goat's carcass to my mother, its head in a tightly woven conical basket. Mama took the knife and sharpened it on a stone. She skinned and gutted the goat. She set aside the hide to make a three-legged stool by stretching the wet hide over the legs for a seat. As it dries it will shrink tight and firm. Mama carefully cut up every single piece of that animal including its eyes, nose and lips. She gave the two little horns to Mohammed *Inyer* to play with; the meat went into her cooking pot. Mohammed *Inyer* danced around with the horns. He blew into them to see if he could make a sound and gaily tooted in my mother's face. Then he started to dig with one of them and the dust blew into her meat. 'Get away from my cooking pot or I'll take those back and wear them myself,' she said flicking her knife at him. He scampered off to show the other boys; free to go wherever he wanted.

My brothers and I figured out how old my mother is. In Somalia, a person's age is calculated by how many *gus* or rainy seasons they have lived. It's hard to figure exactly but we think she is fifty-seven even though she looks like eighty or ninety. I think it is because of all the pain and hardship she has endured in her life. The hard work she does every single day to stay alive shows in her body and her face. She does not have an ounce of fat anywhere and her feet are thick with calluses. They look almost like an elephant's hide, thick with cracks. Her eyes are cloudy and they don't shine in the sunshine. I am grateful that she is still able to work and that she is still really strong. Watching her work and sing I could see in her that everything works with faith. You must believe in God and all the powers that you have inside you. That is really all either one of my parents have, faith in the magic power of nature. They have no social security, no health insurance and no pension plan. My father is almost blind and my mother might weigh all of eighty pounds, but they are stronger than I am. Half of her children passed into God's hands and she carries a bullet in her chest, yet despite all the obstacles my mother has faced in her life, she is full of courage and hope.

That afternoon my father called and wondered who was around.

'It's just me, *Aba*,' I answered, walking over to where he was resting.

'Where is Mohammed?' he asked. 'It's time for my eye drops.'

'I don't know, there isn't anybody else here right now.'

'I need Mohammed or Burhaan or your mother to put the drops in my eyes,' he insisted.

He remembered me as a little girl and I had to reassure him that I could do it as well as Mama. 'Father, I am almost as tall as the boys now,' I said. 'I know what I am doing.' I gently took the bandage off and washed his face with clean water. Some of the swelling had gone down and he could chew and talk a little easier, but the eye looked frightful. The socket was shrunken and a nasty shade of yellow. When I put the drops in his eyes my father said that he could see better. 'What can you see?' I asked him.

'Shadows. I think I can see some colors and things,' he said.

'All I can say is that is really a gift from Allah,' I told him. 'I thank the Lord Allah that you even survived that encounter with the bush doctor. I hope you will go to the hospital in Galkayo from now on. Father, you don't have to go to some madman with a knife.'

'*Hiiyea,*' he said quietly and I put the bandage back on to keep the dust and flies away. I mashed up two Tylenol in his tea because he couldn't swallow them whole but he didn't drink much of the tea. At least there was one thing I brought that was useful for my family.

After we ate I told him, 'Father, I am going to come back and when I do I will stay longer,' I promised him. 'These eight days have gone by so fast. It would be much better if I could be here for two months or more and another time I will do that.'

Mohammed nodded and Rashid teased, 'Maybe you could learn to build a fire without smoking everybody out.'

'I wasn't talking to you – you bunch of useless men.' I took my father's hand and told him that I wanted my son to know his family and his people. 'When I bring Aleeke with me I'll stay for a few months. There are so many things I wanted to see; so many people I didn't even get to greet because I had so little time.'

Rashid looked puzzled and asked, 'Waris, how long have you been away?'

'Over twenty years.'

'How long did you come for?'

'A week.' My brother looked at me like I was crazy; to him it was unreal for a person to travel so far and stay for such a short time.

'That you came, Waris, that is what matters,' my father said.

My last night with my family was very special for all of us; it was a magic evening. When it got dark we spread woven mats and cloths on the ground around the fire. It was a clear night and the mosquitoes weren't bad so we all sat outside. Mother's goats wandered over and lay down near my mother. The oldest one, Whitey, snored when she fell asleep and everyone laughed at the old goat except Mama.

'Don't make fun of her,' she insisted. 'Her milk will be sour in the morning.'

'She farts a lot too,' Rashid said and my mother hissed.

I told my father, my mother, and my brothers how glad I was to have all of us together in one spot. It was a miracle for my nomadic family to be sitting together in front of a little hut. My brothers and sisters and I haven't been together in one place our whole lives.

'When is the last time when we have been gathered all together in one place?' I asked my father and mother.

My father said, 'Not ever.'

'So this is truly a great evening tonight and I thank Allah for that,' I said. Mohammed was very quiet and he turned his face up towards the zillions of stars. He's thinking about leaving tomorrow, I thought. He is thinking that we may never ever be all together again.

My mother watched her oldest son sitting quietly. 'Once there was a rich and famous sultan,' she said.

'*Hiiyea,*' her children all said together. A story! Mother's eyes shone in the firelight and she punctuated each sentence with arms and fingers across the flickering light of the fire.

'He had embroidered shirts and soft carpets. He owned a palace in Mogadishu on the shores of the Indian Ocean to catch the cool breeze. It was filled with precious jewels and silks from Arabia. The most expensive incense burned in the rooms whether he was there or not. Despite all his great wealth he was not happy and he could not understand what was wrong. He had many wives who bickered constantly, sons who fought with each other and daughters who sulked. He could buy anything he could think of but he never felt happiness or contentment. One morning after a sleepless night, he called to his servants and told them, 'Go and search until you find a truly happy man. When you find such a person bring him to me, I want to talk to him.'

The servants scoured the land and one day they noticed a poor man singing as he pulled water from a tiny well for his one skinny camel. He hummed as he milked the beast and shared the tiny bit of milk with the sultan's servants. Even with an empty stomach he laughed and joked.

'Are you a happy man?' the servants asked.

'What is there to be unhappy about?' the man answered.

'Please sir, come with me to the sultan's palace,' the oldest servant said. 'My master would like to meet you.' The poor man agreed and journeyed from the Haud into the great city of Mogadishu. He had never seen anything like it. There were so many people, so many colors, so many things to smell and taste. The sultan entertained him richly with wonderful fruits and sweetmeats, gave a lavish banquet and presented him with an embroidered *goa*.

'What is the secret of happiness?' the sultan asked perched on soft pillows. The poor man didn't know what to say, his tongue tangled with his teeth and he couldn't talk. He didn't know what made him happy when he lived in the desert – it was just the way he felt. Disappointed the sultan sent him away and the man returned to his camel and his milk bowl carved out of wood. He never forgot all the wonders of the sultan's palace and he was never happy again.'

'*Hiiyea*,' I said, because I know that story is true. Mohammed turned his face away from the firelight and wrapped his *goa* over his head.

It seemed as though the stars had babies every night,

there were so many of them. There was no sound anywhere, lovely deep silence filled up my ears. Anywhere I have been in the West you can hear the noise of a car running along a road somewhere. It never gets totally silent like the desert where there is space between the sounds. After the stories and jokes quieted down, Mama and Nhur and I went inside to sleep with the children. We could hear hyenas howling like wicked women outside the village but they don't come and bother people.

My dreams were terrible and I didn't sleep that night. I dreamed I was walking with my mother. We had been lost for a couple of days and were near death from hunger and thirst. After climbing up a big hill I saw a house with a fire and a teapot down below so I ran back to tell my mother. 'Mama, Mama, I see a house, I see people. Come, come! We are going to be OK.' I ran down the hill to the house and as I got closer I shouted, 'Hello, hello, anybody there?' No one answered, no one came out of the little hut. I could see something strange boiling up out of the spout and I looked in the teapot to see what was cooking. When we don't have much water you can cook in a teapot to conserve the water. When I took the lid off the pot it was filled with boiling blood and somebody being cooked. I dropped the lid in horror and stepped back and looked around. On each side of my shoulders there were strange people – they didn't look like normal people – they looked like white devils with sunken cheeks and hollow cloudy eyes. There were two of them on each side of me. My mother was coming down the hill behind me and I cried, 'Mama, Mama get out of here. Don't come down here – run, run away.'

She looked at me and said, 'No, Waris, you run. I can't run fast anymore. You run.' I didn't want to leave her but the evil *djinn* were coming too close. I pleaded with her,

443

'Mama! You gotta run with me.' She was not running fast enough and I was running, running, running. I called to her, 'Mama, slap the devils, slap them out of here!'

She shouted, 'Run, run away, Waris.'

'No, Mama,' I cried, 'what about you?'

'You run away, Waris,' she called, 'I'll be all right.' I looked back and saw that the devils were slashing at her back with long butchering knives. She fell down but when I tried to go back to her another one was after me so I had to run and couldn't help her. I was falling and screaming and I woke up screaming.

We had to leave early in the morning to get to Bosasso in one day but I could hardly get moving because I was so unhappy. My mother got up before the moon had faded away and brought her prayer mat out of her tiny hut. She unrolled it on the ground and turned her face to the holy city of Mecca, the navel of the world. She began to pray, bowing and kneeling. 'There is no God but Allah, and Mohammed is His Prophet,' she chanted. Oh, how I love the echo of that song! For my mother it is the song of life. It is her appointment calendar. She would never miss her prayers because it is a busy day. She says, I belong to Allah, that's the most important thing in my life; it is the only thing of importance. She touches eternity five times each day.

Me, I got clocks all over the house, I have watches, calendars, and date-books like the time itself is the most important thing. It's 2:00 so I'm supposed to call my booker about a job. So what if the baby is crying or the doorbell rings – somehow the little clock hands rule everything! I'm a slave to that dictator – I go out in the cold soaking rain because the little arrows must be obeyed. My mother is a slave to God. She gets dignity and strength from her God; I'm getting stressed and cold and wet.

Several doves flew down from the east and settled on the top of her little house. We call them angel birds because they wear the *tuspah*, a black necklace of feathers like a holy amulet. They bring angels and good news and I thought Allah will take care of Mother.

My dear sister-in-law Nhur made *angella* for me. When the coals of the fire burned hot and low she crouched next to it and spread the batter she beat the night before into pancakes. I couldn't take the *angella* home with me but I wanted some pictures to remind me of that special taste and smell. When I tried to photograph Nhur she picked up the long knife and poked it at me with a big smile, sticking out her tongue and jabbing at the air. 'Leave me alone, I'm cooking here,' she said.

'I know you'll use that if I get too close,' I said, but what could she do? Nhur was very pregnant and wearing a long dress. I filmed her from every angle just to tease her. She wasn't going to run after me and let the *angella* burn.

The neighbors came over to see what they could get. They knew I was leaving and would not need to carry things back with me. 'Give me the cocoa butter; give me that scarf!' they cried. 'You don't need that anymore.' I didn't have much to give, but I gave them whatever I could. It's a Somali garage sale.

There are times when the sun races across the sky and that morning was one of them. That's another problem with clocks; time isn't always the same. My father was resting inside Burhaan's house and I went to say goodbye to him first. My body was heavy and hard to move; I felt like I weighed ten tons. There is a Somali word that means talking to a person for the last time before a journey. I started crying as soon as *Aba* said it. He was so helpless and weak. He heard me and asked, 'What are you crying about, child?'

'I wish you could see my face before I leave.'

'Baby, you know that I can't see you.'

A bandage covered one eye, the other was cloudy, and both were sightless. 'I want you to see me – my face, my eyes; to take a good look at me,' I told him. 'It has been more than twenty years since you last saw me. Do you remember what I look like? I am a grown woman now – I was a little girl when I left.' He reached up and I took his hand and placed it on my face so he could feel my skin, the shape of my nose. His touch was shy and tender. More tears welled up in my eyes and wet his fingers. I wanted to see the cocky strong father that I used to know. I longed for the powerful father who frightened me more than lions.

My father read my thoughts and said, 'Waris, we all age and change and nothing can ever be the same.'

'I guess there is a reason for everything but only Allah knows the reason for this,' I sobbed. Everybody was waiting for me and I heard Mohammed calling and beeping the horn outside. 'Daddy, I've got to go now,' I said.

My father said, 'I have something for my grandson; a *xudden-xir*,' and he handed me a long hair plucked from a female camel. It is a gift for a newborn child. It made me cry even harder. 'Do me a favor,' he whispered, 'don't let them see you cry, you are a grown woman. I'm not dead – cry when I'm dead. Now get out of here.' That was his way of saying I love you. He wanted to make me tough because that is what he knows about life and getting through it.

'You know, Papa,' I said, 'remember the other day when everybody was sitting around talking and somebody said, "Waris, you look like your father," and other people said, "No, you look like your mother, you're the spitting image of your mother." Papa, I know what I am. I got hardheaded strength from my father's side and wisdom and looks from my mother. Everybody laughed then – but you know that it's true.'

He said, 'Remember that, Waris – you got my strength – keep that strength, keep it always.'

I had learned what gift my family needed and I knew that they would never ask for it. '*Aba*, I will send the money for Nhur's bride price as soon as I get to a bank,' I told him. He took my hand and held it next to his heart. My father turned to the wall and I know he cried when I left – but he would not let me see it.

As soon as I came out crying – my mother said, 'Hey, wait a minute! How come I never get the crying? Why are you crying for him and not for me?'

'Mama, please come back with me!' I took her hands and pleaded with her.

'Waris, I can't come with you now,' she said. 'I've got your father and Mohammed *Inyer.*'

'Mama, I'll come back and get you and bring you to New York with me.'

She said, 'Waris, I'm too old for those countries. I hated Abu Dhabi when I was there with your sister. I saw the piles of gold jewelry and a big tree made of gold. You look in the streets and there are little children gnawing on a bone and starving to death, sick and nobody cares. I can't live there.'

'Mama, New York is not like that.'

'Who am I going to talk to? I don't speak anything but Somali. Who am I going to go visit? All my friends are here.' She took my hands and walked with me to the waiting car while she talked. 'Baby,' she said, 'I didn't like Abu Dhabi and over there is the most like here. It is hot like Africa – people pray five times a day, but they don't mean it. How can they walk right past those hungry children?'

I said, 'Mama please, I need you.'

She shook her head, 'I don't need over there. This is my home and this is what I know and this is where I'm going to die.' She was right. I could not imagine her being in New York City. My Mama, she wouldn't last a day, she would be miserable. She would miss her way of knowing. I knew she wouldn't be able to get up in the morning and just go – she would have nowhere to go. Nobody in New York would understand a joke about a goat farting. Who would she joke with? She winked at me. 'I can't leave my children – I have to stay here in case the biggest one, your father, can't find himself another wife.'

'Mama,' I said, 'you need somebody to take care of you for a change. Please come with me.' I desperately wanted to bring her home with me – but it was a selfish wish. I wanted to bring her peace to my house in New York – to my son, to my life.

She drew me close to her, kissed my forehead, and said, 'No. I am here where God put me.' My mother is the unmovable foundation of our family; she is the tree with roots all the way down to heaven.

'Oh, Mama!' I cried and hugged her for the last time. I hugged Burhaan and Rashid, Ragge, Uncle Ahmed, little Asha, and Nhur. Rashid smiled and pointed to his beautiful row of perfect white teeth. Then he handed me about ten *caday* tooth sticks he cut fresh that morning. I laughed and put them in my bag to take back to New York. Mohammed and I got into the car and I watched everybody that I love get smaller and smaller as we drove over the little hills and on to Borama road back towards Bosasso. I was sobbing and I couldn't stop. My Mama! I love that woman. She has a grace and a dignity I'm never going to have. She was born a Somali woman and she is going to stay a Somali woman. She accepts where Allah placed her on the earth and she is thanking him every day for that. She doesn't want to question God; she's already safe with him. Me – I couldn't accept it, I had to run off and get all confused. I wish I had that part of her, that acceptance, but I don't. I felt, deep in my bones, that this life was not right for me, so I ran off. Honestly it didn't shock me or sadden me when my mother refused to come back with me. I understood exactly what she was saying. It's not hard to be in a Somali village if you were born there and raised there and you don't know anything else. She has something that is greater than all the wealth in the West. She has acceptance and peace in her life.

14

journey back

Women are the devil's snares

Somali Proverb

The journey back to the little airport at Bosasso was completely different than the trip to my mother's village. This time the dirt track was full of thick red mud and potholes of brown water. In some places the road was more like a river. You have to keep the car moving in mud so again we bounced all over the place and you had to hang on or else you might hit your head or fall over. If you get stuck there is nothing to do but wait until another car or truck comes along to help you get out. However, everywhere I looked it was lush green and beautiful. The sky had big puffy clouds hanging there and the temperature was comfortable. I sat in the back seat and cried because it was so hard to leave my parents. I prayed to Allah that my father would be all right, that I would see him again. Mohammed and the driver we hired, Musa, talked about how hot it had been the day we arrived. Musa said that some people had been out in the sun and had died from the terrible heat.

We traveled hard all that day in order to get back to Bosasso by dark. Musa was Daarood, and a friend of Mohammed's. He didn't stop for hours. He had never been to Bosasso and I wondered how he knew where he was going with no maps and no signs. Often tracks went off into different directions and none of them seemed bigger than the others. *Djinn* hang out at the intersections of roads and I hoped one would not jump in the car and play tricks on us. Musa never hesitated though – he just kept driving on and on away from the sun in the morning and towards the sunset in the afternoon. *Dikdik* darted through the scrub – they look like tiny deer on spindly legs. We passed a long-necked gerenuk, a kind of antelope, on its hind legs, stripping an acacia bush. It was too intent on eating to be disturbed by a car passing by. Old man baboon and his troop barked defiance from a hilltop showing us his big teeth and long hairy arms.

Late that afternoon, I was so hungry I said, 'Hey, I can't take much more. I am starving back here and I really need to stop for a little while.'

'OK,' Musa agreed, 'I know a tea shop not too far from here. We can stop there and eat.'

'What do they have?' I thought about a big plate of something good like rice and spiced goat meat or a shish kebab. I hoped they would have camel milk. I had been looking for it the entire time I was home but there was none in my mother's village. It had been so dry that the camels were not giving milk. Camel milk is rich and so nutritious that people can live on it. I remembered the three-cornered *zambusi* that are made to break the fast during the month of

Ramadan and sweet tea with cardamom and milk. I was so hungry, I think my stomach was flat up against my backbone.

'I don't know what they will have left this late in the day, everything might be almost gone by now but they will have something and it's a good place to eat,' Musa said. 'I've eaten there before.'

He slowed down and stopped in front of a ramshackle restaurant set a little way back from the edge of the road. It wasn't much of a village; there was a gas station, the tea shop and a few huts in the back. The restaurant was basically a large open area covered with a red tin roof. The kitchen area was behind it and smoke from the fire drifted straight up because there wasn't any wind. The terrace had been built in the shade of some big trees so that a breeze would come in. I was surprised to see at least fifty to sixty men just sitting there at broken down old metal tables and wooden benches. It was such a tiny village I didn't know where they all came from, or why these men were just sitting around.

Musa and Mohammed with his long legs walked in front of me and through the restaurant. As soon as I set foot in the place I heard men muttering, 'Oh no! Oh no, no,' then, 'what is she doing?' I ignored them and kept right on walking inside. As I tried to pass through the tables to the kitchen in the back, a man came over and stepped right in front of me. He apparently was the waiter but he didn't have an apron on or look especially clean. He blocked my path when I tried to go around him and said, 'Excuse me, excuse me.' I ignored him and he must have decided that I didn't speak Somali. He started shouting and waving his hands in my face. 'Hey! Hey! Hey!' he bellowed but I just kept walking towards my brother. I didn't feel like explaining myself to a man with sweaty armpits and dirty fingernails.

Suddenly several men started shouting at him, 'Stop her! Get her out of here.' The waiter came and directly blocked my path.

I looked at him right in the eyes and said, 'Is there a problem? *Warrier, Maa'hah d'ih?*' – I said it in Somali so he knew that I understood everything that had been said.

He refused to look in my face but hissed at me like I was a stray chicken he wanted to shoo back out the door, 'You can't come in here,' he said loudly. 'This is just for men, the women go elsewhere.'

'What? What are you talking about? Why can't I eat here if I want to?' I asked. Although Somali women won't eat in restaurants with men it was news to me that women weren't allowed to eat with men when they wanted to.

He repeated, 'This restaurant is for men only, no women are allowed in here.'

'That's ridiculous. I am not going to bother anybody.'

'I told you to get out,' he said spitting the words at me and puffing himself up with self-importance. I was so shocked that I didn't know what to do. Mohammed was only thinking about food and Musa was in a hurry to get back on the road. The nasty man would not even let me pass to tell them what was going on – he stood his ground between me and the kitchen. I was furious, but I was starving because we hadn't eaten all day. Standing as tall as I could I snarled at the skinny little man, 'Well, where do the women go?'

He said, 'Over there, back over there,' and pointed his long bony finger back out the door as if somehow I had violated the filthy dump with a dirt floor and beat-up tables held together with wire.

Meanwhile Mohammed looked back to see what happened to me. He needed money from me to pay for the food he had ordered and must have wondered where I was.

453

He came over and asked the greasy waiter, 'What's the problem?'

The waiter suddenly became polite and told him, 'I'm sorry, but no women are allowed in here. The women go back over there, they eat in another room.'

My brother looked up and down at this man with narrow eyes and a filthy shirt. He noticed that the place was quiet and every single man there was waiting to see what would happen. He shook his head at me and asked him, 'Well, where is the other room? Show us the room for women.'

The waiter led us outside, everything was quiet except for his cheap Chinese flip-flops slapping on the dirt. We walked all the way around the terrace and the trees to a little area set apart from the rest of the restaurant. He pointed to a tattered hut that was literally in the back of the bathroom, turned on his rubber heel, and slapped back into the restaurant.

The bathroom was not a nice room with tiled walls and a white porcelain toilet to sit on and flush, I didn't expect that. It was a Somali long drop; a deep hole dug into the ground. It was dirty and full of flies and big toast-colored cockroaches. They are fearless and will crawl right out of that stinky hole while you are hanging over it or into your food. It smelled so my eyes stung and flies came out of the dark corners and swarmed all over us. One wall of the bathroom was part of the women's eating room. It was nothing but three ramshackle walls and a dusty floor. There wasn't even a table or chairs in the place, just an old bench with a broken leg. I thought I was going to cry. My mother wouldn't keep her goats in such a terrible place. All the men were sitting like kings enjoying the shade in the restaurant while women were supposed to eat in a place full of shit.

I looked at my brother and he looked at me. Even though

he was acting like a big Somali man this was too much for him too. He shook his head and said, 'Fuck this.' We turned around and walked back around to the car. Mohammed said, 'Well what do you want to do?'

'Are there any other places we can get something to eat around here?' I asked Musa. 'I am starving.'

Mohammed agreed, 'I'm hungry too.'

Musa shook his head, 'Sorry, but there are no other places to eat anywhere near by.'

'Waris, did you say something to the waiter?' Mohammed asked like I had somehow insulted him.

'A woman walking into the place was an insult to that baboon,' I said.

'Let's try and talk to the cook. He seemed like a reasonable enough person,' Mohammed said and he went around the back to the kitchen area to talk to the cook. 'Excuse me, but I won't put my sister in that place – it's filthy back there,' he told him. 'All we want to do, we are just passing through, is to eat something and we will continue on our way.'

The cook listened to what he had to say but he was just as insistent as the waiter. 'I'm sorry but no women are allowed.'

My brother said, 'What exactly do you mean when you say no women allowed? We are hungry. Do you have some food?'

The cook said, 'Yes.'

'Are you selling it?'

'Yes.'

'Serving it?'

'Yes.'

'Well,' Mohammed said calmly, 'she is a human being isn't she? What is the big problem? All we want to do is have something to eat.' The cook just stood there and Mohammed decided not to push it any further. He said,

'OK, I understand that women cannot eat in here. Can you let my sister just sit outside for a minute and we will take some food with us.'

But the cook said, 'No.' He shook his head and became very surly. 'I told you that no women are allowed in here. Ever.' He stood there in a ragged shirt and worn out *maa-a-weiss* and crossed his arms over his chest like he was some royal lord or something.

My brother stood his ground and then he said, 'You know what? Fuck you and your food, *Aba'ha Wuss.*' He looked at me and he said, 'Come on Waris, let's get out of here.' I said not a word and I proudly followed my brother out of that place.

We got back in the car and drove off, kicking up a cloud of dust. Musa looked over at Mohammed and said, 'The food in there is rubbish anyway.'

I was so pleased at my brother actually taking my part that I wanted to hug him and cheer. He was fuming at the whole thing. 'This country is going nowhere if these people can't change some of the old, stupid traditions. It's crazy!'

I was glad my brother had started to see things differently. 'That is the ignorant bush mentality that is keeping this country down,' I said. 'Women and men don't eat together. A woman can't cut a man's hair, women are sewn shut. Women are not looked at as equal to men in any aspect of life.' I told Mohammed, 'I respect that people feel that way, I don't try to change the way they see things, but all the same I don't understand why they need to push their views down my throat.'

'It's got to change, Waris,' he said. 'When you treat women like dirt, it's easy to treat people from other tribes just as badly. It's got to change.'

Mohammed, you are one who has changed, I thought to myself, and tears of pride ran down my cheeks.

15

desert dawn

So give to the kinsman his due,
And to the needy, and to the wayfarer.
That is best for those
Who seek Allah's countenance.

Koran, Sura 30: 38–9,
The Romans

Musa crawled furiously across the belly of Somalia, from the Ethiopian border to the Indian Ocean. We passed the villages of Garowe, Nugal and Qardho. They were larger than my mother's settlement but still had no electricity, latrines, schools, or hospitals. There were puddles as big as lakes and ruts in the road up to my knees. We slipped and skidded over and into some pretty deep mud holes but Musa always managed to get the tires to catch on to something. We slid out the other side and on to dry ground more times than I care to remember.

Late in the afternoon we stopped by a river to wash our faces and cool off. Water in the desert is always rushing somewhere else. Starlings, with brilliant coats of blue and gold, flashed in the sun as they flew away. Two peacocks calmly waddled away. They are good luck – especially if you see two of them, however it's bad luck if you only see feathers. Mohammed took off his shoes and waded in the water. 'If only we had rivers like this all over the country Somalia would certainly be the most beautiful place on earth,' I said. Like a thirsty lion I wanted to stick my mouth in the clear water. I washed my face and arms but I wanted to take my clothes off and go for a swim. I hiked up my dress but Mohammed kept telling me to put my dress down. A camel with its front legs tied together hopped slowly down to the river for a drink. The hobble keeps it from wandering too far. 'That's how I feel about these dresses and headscarves,' I told Mohammed. 'You can't move because they trip you.'

'When are you going to stop running around anyway?' he asked.

I gave up on Mohammed ever really understanding my point of view and went back to dipping my scarf in the water and washing my face with it. Musa noticed a land tortoise next to the road. It looked at us with tiny black eyes but pulled into its shell as soon as I went over for a closer look. 'Maybe it's a spirit guide come to tell me something,' I said. 'This tortoise means my home is safe.'

By the time I could catch the smell of the Indian Ocean and see the lights of Bosasso it was long after the town had gone to bed. It was so quiet I could hear the waves lapping at the shore on the edge of town. Musa took us to a hotel and Mohammed went inside to get rooms and see if he could find anything to eat. I wanted a cool shower and a bed almost more than food. I really didn't think anything would be still open. People eat their main meal in the middle of the day and restaurants are not open after dark because the electricity is not very reliable. Mohammed tried several hotels but they didn't have any rooms. Musa took us down a side street to another hotel. It was not very nice, but I didn't really care, I was so tired. I went inside with Mohammed.

'No, nothing tonight,' the short attendant in the lobby informed us. He stood up and rubbed his eyes. His beard was dyed red from henna and his face was framed with the white hair on his head.

'Why don't you have any rooms?' Mohammed asked. 'The other hotels were full too.'

'Lots of people are waiting for the plane to Abu Dhabi,' he said, pointing to all the people hanging out in the lobby. 'There are people here working on many different projects for the United Nations and many other agencies. The place is full of construction these days! Everybody is coming and going all the time, except for last week.' Three of his bottom teeth were missing and the rest were black from chewing *khat.* 'The plane didn't land because there were some goats on the runway. Oh, that pilot was so mad, he turned around and went back to Abu Dhabi!' he said laughing.

I didn't think it was funny. I needed to get back to New York and I certainly didn't want to hang around Bosasso for a week because they couldn't keep animals off the runway. We didn't have boarding passes or confirmed seats – you go to the airport and wait in line. I looked at Mohammed and said, 'I hope we get on the flight! Do you think it will be a problem?'

'I'll go to the airport now and find out how to get on the plane.' He turned back to the clerk and asked, 'Is there another hotel in town?'

'I don't think you will find anything available tonight – it's late and there are only a few hotels in Bosasso. This town is so busy everything is full all the time.'

As we stood there trying to think of what to do a man I didn't know came up and asked Mohammed, 'Are you Mohammed Dirie?'

'My father is Dahee Dirie,' Mohammed replied. They talked about my father, but I was so tired I couldn't really think straight. The man had a round belly and wore the embroidered hat that means he has made the *Hajj* to Mecca. 'Waris, this is Hajji Suliman,' Mohammed told me. 'He is related on both the Majeerteen and Hawiye side of our family.'

Hajji glanced at me and told Mohammed, 'Your sister can have my hotel room tonight.'

I couldn't believe his generosity. He offered his bed to a stranger just because we are from the same family. For a moment I couldn't think what to say. In the West when such a gift is offered you must say, 'Oh no, I couldn't put you out.' You refuse the offer and if the person still insists, you can accept. However, that's the way a guest is treated in my country, it was the way everyone had been most of the trip. If I refused, Hajji would be insulted. 'Thank you, thank you,' I told him.

Mohammed and I followed Hajji to his room. He took his belongings and gave me the key. He warned me to lock myself in and to lock the door whenever I went out. 'Where are you going to sleep?' I asked Mohammed.

'I'll sleep outside, don't worry about it,' he said and left to see what he could find out at the airport.

My heart sank when I went into the room, and I didn't know what to do. It was unbearable. Even though it was over 100 degrees I had to close the door and lock it. When I opened the little window there was no breeze at all. Nothing was moving. Worst of all it was filthy and stank of sweat and urine. I wanted a cool shower and clean sheets. Hajji

Suliman's tiny room had a concrete floor and a cot thing – there was no bathroom. There was a ceiling fan but it didn't work. Mohammed would put his *goa* on the ground and settle down to sleep in the fresh clean air, washed by the sea.

The bed was a sort of a battered mat stretched over a wooden frame with no comfort to it at all. What could I say? I didn't complain – because I don't want to be an ungrateful bitch – but it was full of holes and it stank. I would rather have slept outside with the men, but I couldn't.

For the first time I was thankful for a long dress; I tucked it around my legs and pulled my scarf over my head to keep bugs out. Sleep would not come because of the heat and I was afraid of rats. In the darkness I heard something scratching around and spent most of the night trying to see what was making noise and praying that I didn't see a rat.

Even before the first glimmer of light I heard the call to prayers. It must have been around four in the morning. The muezzin climbs to the top of the minaret in the mosque and chants, 'There is no God but God and Mohammed is his Prophet.' When they pray it echoes in every direction. It was amazing to hear the prayer drift through the entire town. Every prayer, five times a day is the same thing. Everything stops and everything echoes with prayer. It is the only clock worth paying attention to.

Mohammed came to get me in the morning and we had tea and waited for Musa but he never showed up. Mohammed decided that he had collapsed from exhaustion. The man drove constantly to make a living. Mohammed had not been able to talk to anyone the night before and so we hired another car to take us out to the airport to make sure that we could get on the next flight. Several men wanted to go to the airport and two more waved and asked for a ride as we rode out of town. The car was packed, but we were happy to be able to help. The early morning is the hottest time of the day because there is no breeze off the water. The blue sea shimmering in the distance caught my eye as we approached the airport. 'Which road takes you to the ocean?' I asked, longing for a cool swim.

'What does she want to know that for?' a tall man with a long tribal scar on his cheek asked Mohammed.

'Hello,' I said. 'You don't need to talk to my brother. I am sitting right here.'

'What is she going to do in the ocean?' he continued to ignore me and talked to Mohammed.

'Look at my clothes, they are dripping I am so hot,' I said. 'I intend to cool off in the water and have a swim.'

'You better tell her that we don't swim here,' he announced to Mohammed. 'We are desert people.'

When we got to the airport Mohammed went into the brick building and I waited for him in the car. He returned with bad news. Damal Airlines would not arrive for two days and we would just have to sit in Bosasso.

'What!' I cried. 'First it took us a day to come to Bosasso from Galkayo. Then it will be two more days before the flight! Mohammed, I could have stayed with Mama another day. Why did we have to come back here so early? We didn't need to get here until tomorrow!'

'You have to stay in Bosasso to make sure you get on the flight because this is the only airplane,' Mohammed said. 'They don't have boarding passes – you just have to be there to make sure you get on the plane.'

'That is a ridiculous way to run an airline,' I said. 'We are wasting two days – two days I could have been with my family.'

'Well, that's the way things are around here. Don't worry – we will get on the plane when it comes.'

'*Enshallah*, if Allah wills,' I said, finding my mother's words on my lips. Allah has a plan for you, she told me and I decided to use the time to talk to people about United Nations projects. I wanted to see first-hand what their needs were – to find out the best ways to help.

Mohammed introduced me to another relative, another man who knew our father. Abdillahi Aden was the airport director and he arranged for us to get on the plane without personally waiting in line. Abdillahi came back into town with us and talked about the many projects in Bosasso.

'When people are full of hope they want to work and be a part of building something,' he said. 'The government in Somaliland has provided a degree of stability and is one that the people can respect,' he told us. 'There are a lot of people who come to live here in Bosasso. The town is growing and getting bigger every day.'

Mohammed explained, 'My sister is from New York and this is her first trip back to Somalia for over twenty years.'

'*Hiiyea*! New York! I heard that is a very dangerous place,' said Abdillahi.

'It can be,' I told him.

'I heard they eat dogs.'

'No,' I said, 'they don't eat dogs.'

'He means hot dogs,' Mohammed interrupted. 'Europeans and Americans eat something called hot dogs. But they aren't dog, it's pig.'

'What a terrible place,' Abdillahi said with grave sympathy and I finally realized he was teasing me. 'When are you two coming back to Somalia to live? It's safe here now, you should come back and stop eating dogs and pigs.' Abdillahi urged Mohammed to return and work to build the country but Mohammed looked away.

After lunch Abdillahi showed us another hotel. They had

only one room available with two narrow wooden cots but the room was clean and had a bathroom. It was humble but Mohammed and I were happy to have it. I took a shower in salt water piped in from the ocean and was grateful to God for the blessing of water.

There was a United Nations sign on a cinder block building not too far from our hotel and Mohammed and I walked over in the late afternoon. Everything closed in the hottest part of the day and opened back up after the afternoon meal and rest. Several men sat inside and the person in charge said he was from Sierra Leone. He didn't have the evenly spaced Somali features – his nose was too big and his skin was pock-marked.

'What kind of project is this?' I asked. He gave me a funny look when I started to talk. 'My name is Waris Dirie and I will be back at the United Nations in New York in a day or two. I have a big meeting there and I want to bring back some information about the projects in Bosasso. Can I ask you some questions about what is going on here?'

He pulled at his bottom lip and stared at the table without answering. Finally he turned to Mohammed and said suspiciously, 'Who do you work for? What do you want here?'

'My name is Waris Dirie and I work with the United Nations,' I repeated.

He totally ignored me like I was deaf or blind and kept asking Mohammed, 'Who are you? What do you want?'

I came over to stand right in front of him so that he would have to look at me. 'Excuse me,' I said, 'I am talking to you.'

'What are you doing here? What is this all about?' he started to scream at the top of his lungs. All the time he looked at my brother.

There were two other guys in chairs in the back of the room and one of them looked intelligent so I said to him, 'Hey, brother, could you please help me out here?'

He looked at me and at the old man who was screaming, then he turned to his friend and said, 'Let's get out of here.'

That seemed suspicious and made me more determined to find out about the project. I turned back to the man from Sierra Leone and said, 'Sir, excuse me, with all due respect, look me in the face. I am talking to you – this guy is not talking to you, he is not asking you questions – please look at me.' That angry man raised up his hand like he was going to push me but he stopped when Mohammed stood up. Mohammed did not say anything – he towered above both of us. Then my brother calmly explained that we were only gathering information – that we were not looking to report any wrongdoing.

'You have to be specific. What exactly do you want?' the man said pulling on his lip again.

'I do apologize if you felt I was spying on you. I would like to have information about women and children, especially about women's health and the United Nations projects to help them.'

'Ah,' he said, 'I cannot help you with that. There are people who talk about that kind of thing in another building – over there.' He pointed to a cement brick building around the corner.

We found the building and the sign above the door identified it as a United Nations project. About six or seven men were sitting inside the single room playing the game of *shax*. In *shax* there are two players. One man draws three squares in the dirt, one inside the other. Each player puts down twelve small stones at the intersections of the squares. If you can get three in a row you win one of your opponent's pieces. They hardly even looked up when we walked in. When the game was over they greeted us with suspicion. It was the same reaction as the first place. Everybody thought I was trying to get money from them even though I explained that I was a peaceful volunteer. 'I am not here to look for work or to interfere with you,' I told them. 'I came simply because I am concerned. I love my country and I thought I could help. I am going back to New York and I have a meeting with the big boys at the United Nations next week. I want to bring back some information. I'd like to know what you need and how we can help.' These men stood there shifting from one foot to another and choosing every word carefully no matter what I said. 'The most important thing that I can take back is information about what you need,' I repeated. 'I don't want anything from you, I am here to help.' They stood there uneasily and offered nothing. I was disgusted and confronted them. 'Why don't you help me to help you? What's the matter?' But no one would talk to me – they wouldn't trust me no matter what I said. They didn't want to talk to a woman.

When we left Mohammed told me, 'Women just can't do that, Waris. You can't go into a place and ask men questions. Women don't do that here.'

'I don't believe you people,' I told him. 'How are you going to change with this kind of attitude and way of doing things?' On the way back to the hotel I saw another low building with a UN sign. I looked in through the window and saw some women inside. They greeted me warmly and directed me to the woman who was in charge of health and education for children and women. Mohammed and I found her office in a group of low prefabricated buildings just at the edge of town. Assia Adan was a dignified woman with a direct manner. She was a great source of information.

Assia told me that her mission is to try and educate the women about health. She is a midwife and offers medical care as well as teaching about the dangers of FGM.

'We have lessons on the dangers of infection and we talk about the girls who have died.'

I remembered my beautiful sister who died after her infibulation.

'Of course we would like to eradicate this practice completely, but it is very hard to get people to even talk about it. The mothers don't even question that it is the right thing to do for their daughters. It is unimaginable for them not to have their daughters done.'

I agreed and said, 'My mother didn't think she was hurting me. She believed I would be pure and clean.'

Assia and I both knew that in my country they practice the most severe form, pharonic infibulation, where the entire inner lips of the labia and the clitoris are removed and the opening is sewn shut.

'My mother was very careful that I slept on my back after it was done, so that the wound would close smooth and flat. It was very important to her that my body was perfectly flat and smooth. What do you do to change that?' I said.

Assia explained that they were trying to teach mothers about Sunni circumcision, which involves no actual cutting and sewing, and is instead just a ritual. Apparently, some modern women in Saudi Arabia have taken this up as an alternative.

'I wasn't able to get a single person in my village to talk about this with me. Not one person! They all looked at me like I was crazy.'

'Yes,' Assia sympathized. 'We are only beginning – I have been at work here for six years and we haven't made any progress – but we are still here. That's the good news. We have not been forced to leave or stop. Frankly, I consider even a toe-hold here an important step. There is hope.'

I smiled. 'I can feel the hope. I was afraid to come back to my own country for fear that someone would attack me because I publicly speak out against FGM. People warned me that I might be detained at the border, kidnapped or worse. Assia, I'll be back and we are going to work together,' I promised her. 'I am going to help you in every way I can.' I told her about the plans for my Foundation, Desert Dawn, and the money we are going to raise to help women and children. We plan to build a community health center in Bosasso, provide educational seminars for women and fund mobile units to provide healthcare and education for nomad families in remote areas. I gave her a hug and a kiss. As long as there are people like Assia there is a way.

Mohammed was so tall that I took two steps for every one of his. It was hard to keep up with him when we walked through town back to our hotel, especially with a long dress dragging in the mud and wrapping around my ankles. I scurried after him and held my dress high so I could walk better. Two women were sitting on a stoop when I passed. 'Look at that! Her dress is up over her waist.'

'Well, she can't be Somali – walking like that.'

When we went out to eat that evening I took my camera with me so I could get some shots of the town and the different UN projects. After we ate, I saw a beautiful poster with wonderful colors and a map. I picked up the camera and took a shot of it with the flash. Suddenly a big rock hit my thigh. I jumped in pain and saw an entire cart of soda bottles tumble over and break all over the street. The boy who threw the rock at me must have slammed into the bottles with his arm and sent them flying. God took care of them, I thought. I didn't wait around to see what would happen next and ran to get in the car with Mohammed.

'Someone hit me with a rock!' I cried to my brother.

He was calmly cleaning his teeth with a tooth stick and looked over at me and shook his head. Always the comic Mohammed replied, 'They should have shot you too.'

'You bastard! I could have been hurt.'

'Waris, I have told you again and again, don't take pictures – they will kill you. You know that some people here truly believe that a picture will take your spirit. That is the way they feel, little sister. To you it's nothing but here it is disrespectful. I'd do the same if some strange woman stuck a camera in my face.'

That night several ladies sat in the hotel lobby sipping tea. We started to talk and an elegant lady said they were Somali too. She said, 'You know, you look like this lady I saw on TV.'

I wondered where she had a television and asked, 'Where are you from?'

'Sweden. I live in Sweden.'

'You saw a Somali woman on Swedish television?'

'Yes! But I can't remember her name. She is on TV in Germany.'

'Oh,' I said. 'What does this woman do?'

'She speaks out against female circumcision.'

'Well what do you think about that?' I asked her quietly.

'I think it's about time somebody spoke out about it! I am so proud of this Somali woman,' she said with flashing eyes. 'We definitely don't talk about that! She is so brave, I love her. She gives us all courage and hope that things will change.'

I asked, 'Do you know her name?'

'I think it's Waris,' she said. 'Are you sure you're not her?'

'No, I'm not very brave,' I replied, my head down.

469

How foolish I had been. I was ashamed. Why had I been so scared to come back to Somalia? Why did I think that they were going to kill me? My own people knew about me and they still loved me! When everybody in New York said, 'Don't go. Don't go to Somalia, it's too dangerous,' I hardly questioned them. I never thought, hey, I know my people, why would they harm me? When the news reported that Somalia was a war zone I didn't question it. When I got to Somalia I was just like anyone, anywhere. Not for one minute did I feel any fear. I felt angry at the way some men treated me because I am a woman, but from most people all I heard was welcome, welcome. 'Do you want me to show you this? Let me show you around. Have you been here? Have you seen this? You can't go back without seeing this,' people said. Maybe there is a crazy clan somewhere, but *khat*-crazed soldiers with guns never threatened me. I saw a beautiful country and my beautiful people.

It's easy to stand up and speak out about something far away – it's easy to talk about FGM to a room of strangers. It takes courage to risk disapproval among your own family, to question the beliefs of someone who stands in front of you. Talking about FGM in the West was easy – the real battle is in Somalia. Allah led me back to my country so that I would know what has to be done. I pray that he will give me the strength to speak to my own people in a way that they can hear and understand. My visit showed me how difficult it will be for people to change – but I am filled with hope. I love my country. If you ask me right this minute where I want to be – I'll sing about Africa. 'Hello Africa! How are you doing? I'm feeling good and I hope you are too.'